THE
WORLD
UNTIL
YESTERDAY

ALSO BY JARED DIAMOND

Collapse

Guns, Germs, and Steel

Why Is Sex Fun?

The Third Chimpanzee

JARED DIAMOND

THE
WORLD
UNTIL
YESTERDAY

WHAT CAN WE LEARN
FROM TRADITIONAL SOCIETIES?

VIKING

VIKING
Published by the Penguin Group
Penguin Group (USA) Inc., 375 Hudson Street, New York, New York 10014, U.S.A.
Penguin Group (Canada), 90 Eglinton Avenue East, Suite 700, Toronto, Ontario M4P 2Y3, Canada
(a division of Pearson Penguin Canada Inc.)
Penguin Books Ltd, 80 Strand, London WC2R 0RL, England
Penguin Ireland, 25 St. Stephen's Green, Dublin 2, Ireland (a division of Penguin Books Ltd)
Penguin Group (Australia), 707 Collins Street, Melbourne, Victoria 3008, Australia
(a division of Pearson Australia Group Pty Ltd)
Penguin Books India Pvt Ltd, 11 Community Centre, Panchsheel Park, New Delhi – 110 017, India
Penguin Group (NZ), 67 Apollo Drive, Rosedale, Auckland 0632, New Zealand
(a division of Pearson New Zealand Ltd)
Penguin Books, Rosebank Office Park, 181 Jan Smuts Avenue, Parktown North 2193, South Africa
Penguin China, B7 Jaiming Center, 27 East Third Ring Road North, Chaoyang District,
Beijing 100020, China

Penguin Books Ltd, Registered Offices: 80 Strand, London WC2R 0RL, England

First published in 2012 by Viking Penguin, a member of Penguin Group (USA) Inc.

1   3   5   7   9   10   8   6   4   2

Copyright © Jared Diamond, 2012

Photograph credits appear on page 499.

LIBRARY OF CONGRESS CATALOGING IN PUBLICATION DATA
Diamond, Jared M.
The world until yesterday : what can we learn from traditional societies? / Jared Diamond.
p. cm.
Includes bibliographical references and index.
ISBN 978-0-670-02481-0
ISBN 978-0-670-78589-6 (export edition)
1. Dani (New Guinean people)—History.   2. Dani (New Guinean people)—Social life and customs.
3. Dani (New Guinean people)—Cultural assimilation.   4. Social evolution—Papua New Guinea.
5. Social change—Papua New Guinea.   6. Papua New Guinea—Social life and customs.   I. Title.
DU744.35.D32D53 2013
305.89'912—dc23
2012018386

Printed in the United States of America
Designed by Nancy Resnick
Maps by Matt Zebrowski

PEARSON

To
Meg Taylor,
in appreciation for decades
of your friendship,
and of sharing your insights into our two worlds

Contents

List of Tables and Figures

At the Airport

An airport scene ▪ Why study traditional societies? ▪ States ▪ Types
of traditional societies ▪ Approaches, causes, and sources ▪ A small
book about a big subject ▪ Plan of the book

An airport scene

April 30, 2006, 7:00 A.M. I'm in an airport's check-in hall, gripping my
baggage cart while being jostled by a crowd of other people also checking
in for that morning's first flights. The scene is familiar: hundreds of travelers carrying suitcases, boxes, backpacks, and babies, forming parallel lines
approaching a long counter, behind which stand uniformed airline employees at their computers. Other uniformed people are scattered among
the crowd: pilots and stewardesses, baggage screeners, and two policemen
swamped by the crowd and standing with nothing to do except to be visible. The screeners are X-raying luggage, airline employees tag the bags,
and baggage handlers put the bags onto a conveyor belt carrying them off,
hopefully to end up in the appropriate airplanes. Along the wall opposite
the check-in counter are shops selling newspapers and fast food. Still
other objects around me are the usual wall clocks, telephones, ATMs, escalators to the upper level, and of course airplanes on the runway visible
through the terminal windows.

The airline clerks are moving their fingers over computer keyboards
and looking at screens, punctuated by printing credit-card receipts at
credit-card terminals. The crowd exhibits the usual mixture of good hu-
mor, patience, exasperation, respectful waiting on line, and greeting
friends. When I reach the head of my line, I show a piece of paper (my

flight itinerary) to someone I've never seen before and will probably never see again (a check-in clerk). She in turn hands me a piece of paper giving me permission to fly hundreds of miles to a place that I've never visited before, and whose inhabitants don't know me but will nevertheless tolerate my arrival.

To travelers from the U.S., Europe, or Asia, the first feature that would strike them as distinctive about this otherwise familiar scene is that all the people in the hall except myself and a few other tourists are New Guineans. Other differences that would be noted by overseas travelers are that the national flag over the counter is the black, red, and gold flag of the nation of Papua New Guinea, displaying a bird of paradise and the constellation of the Southern Cross; the counter airline signs don't say American Airlines or British Airways but Air Niugini; and the names of the flight destinations on the screens have an exotic ring: Wapenamanda, Goroka, Kikori, Kundiawa, and Wewak.

The airport at which I was checking in that morning was that of Port Moresby, capital of Papua New Guinea. To anyone with a sense of New Guinea's history—including me, who first came to Papua New Guinea in 1964 when it was still administered by Australia—the scene was at once familiar, astonishing, and moving. I found myself mentally comparing the scene with the photographs taken by the first Australians to enter and "discover" New Guinea's Highlands in 1931, teeming with a million New Guinea villagers still then using stone tools. In those photographs the Highlanders, who had been living for millennia in relative isolation with limited knowledge of an outside world, stare in horror at their first sight of Europeans (Plates 30, 31). I looked at the faces of those New Guinea passengers, counter clerks, and pilots at Port Moresby airport in 2006, and I saw in them the faces of the New Guineans photographed in 1931. The people standing around me in the airport were of course not the same individuals of the 1931 photographs, but their faces were similar, and some of them may have been their children and grandchildren.

The most obvious difference between that 2006 check-in scene etched in my memory, and the 1931 photographs of "first contact," is that New Guinea Highlanders in 1931 were scantily clothed in grass skirts, net bags over their shoulders, and headdresses of bird feathers, but in 2006 they wore the standard international garb of shirts, trousers, skirts, shorts, and baseball caps. Within a generation or two, and within the individual lives of many people in that airport hall, New Guinea Highlanders learned to write, use computers, and fly airplanes. Some of the people in the hall might actually have been the first people in their tribe to have learned reading and writing. That generation gap was symbolized for me by the image of two New Guinea men in the airport crowd, the younger leading the older: the younger in a pilot's uniform, explaining to me that he was taking the older one, his grandfather, for the old man's first flight in an airplane; and the gray-haired grandfather looking almost as bewildered and overwhelmed as the people in the 1931 photos.

But an observer familiar with New Guinea history would have recognized bigger differences between the 1931 and 2006 scenes, beyond the fact that people wore grass skirts in 1931 and Western garb in 2006. New Guinea Highland societies in 1931 lacked not just manufactured clothing but also all modern technologies, from clocks, phones, and credit cards to computers, escalators, and airplanes. More fundamentally, the New Guinea Highlands of 1931 lacked writing, metal, money, schools, and centralized government. If we hadn't actually had recent history to tell us the result, we might have wondered: could a society without writing really master it within a single generation?

An attentive observer familiar with New Guinea history would have noted still other features of the 2006 scene shared with other modern airport scenes but different from the 1931 Highland scenes captured in the photographs made by the first contact patrols. The 2006 scene contained a higher proportion of gray-haired old people, relatively fewer of whom survived in traditional Highland society. The airport crowd, while initially striking a Westerner without previous experience of New Guineans as "homogeneous"—all of them similar in their dark skins and coiled hair (Plates 1, 13, 26, 30, 31, 32)—was heterogeneous in other respects of their appearance: tall lowlanders from the south coast, with sparse beards and narrower faces; shorter, bearded, wide-faced Highlanders; and islanders and north coast lowlanders with somewhat Asian-like facial features. In 1931 it would have been utterly impossible to encounter Highlanders, south coast lowlanders, and north coast lowlanders together; any gathering of people in New Guinea would have been far more homogeneous than that 2006 airport crowd. A linguist listening to the crowd would have distinguished dozens of languages, falling into very different groups: tonal languages with words distinguished by pitch as in Chinese, Austronesian languages with relatively simple syllables and consonants, and non-tonal Papuan languages. In 1931 one could have encountered individual speakers of several different languages together, but never a gathering of speakers of dozens of languages. Two widespread languages, English and Tok Pisin (also known as Neo-Melanesian or Pidgin English), were the languages being used in 2006 at the check-in counter and also for many of the conversations among passengers, but in 1931 all conversations throughout the New Guinea Highlands were in local languages, each of them confined to a small area.

Another subtle difference between the 1931 and 2006 scenes was that the 2006 crowd included some New Guineans with an unfortunately common American body type: overweight people with "beer bellies" hanging over their belts. The photos of 75 years ago show not even a single overweight New Guinean: everybody was lean and muscular (Plate 30). If I could have interviewed the physicians of those airport passengers, then (to judge from modern New Guinea public health statistics) I would have been told of a growing number of cases of diabetes linked to being overweight, plus cases of hypertension, heart disease, stroke, and cancers unknown a generation ago.

Still another distinction of the 2006 crowd compared to the 1931 crowds was a feature that we take for granted in the modern world: most of the people crammed into that airport hall were strangers who had never seen each other before, but there was no fighting going on among them. That would have been unimaginable in 1931, when encounters with strangers were rare, dangerous, and likely to turn violent. Yes, there were those two policemen in the airport hall, supposedly to maintain order, but in fact the crowd maintained order by itself, merely because the passengers knew that none of those other strangers was about to attack them, and that they lived in a society with more policemen and soldiers on call in case a quarrel should get out of hand. In 1931 police and government authority didn't exist. The passengers in the airport hall enjoyed the right to fly or travel by other means to Wapenamanda or elsewhere in Papua New Guinea without requiring permission. In the modern Western world we have come to take the freedom to travel for granted, but previously it was exceptional. In 1931 no New Guinean born in Goroka had ever visited Wapenamanda a mere 107 miles to the west; the idea of traveling from Goroka to Wapenamanda, without being killed as an unknown stranger within the first 10 miles from Goroka, would have been unthinkable. Yet I had just traveled 7,000 miles from Los Angeles to Port Moresby, a distance hundreds of times greater than the cumulative distance that any traditional New Guinea Highlander would have gone in the course of his or her lifetime from his or her birthplace.

All of those differences between the 2006 and 1931 crowds can be summed up by saying that, in the last 75 years, the New Guinea Highland population has raced through changes that took thousands of years to unfold in much of the rest of the world. For individual Highlanders, the changes have been even quicker: some of my New Guinea friends have told me of making the last stone axes and participating in the last traditional tribal battles a mere decade before I met them. Today, citizens of industrial states take for granted the features of the 2006 scene that I mentioned: metal, writing, machines, airplanes, police and government, overweight people, meeting strangers without fear, heterogeneous populations, and so on. But all those features of modern human societies are relatively new in human history. For most of the 6,000,000 years since the proto-human and proto-chimpanzee evolutionary lines diverged from each other, all human societies lacked metal and all those other things. Those modern features began to appear only within the last 11,000 years, in just certain areas of the world.

Thus, New Guinea* is in some respects a window onto the human world as it was until a mere yesterday, measured against a time scale of the 6,000,000 years of human evolution. (I emphasize "in some respects"—of

* The terminology that has been applied to New Guinea is confusing. Throughout this book, I use the term "New Guinea" to refer to the island of New Guinea, the world's second-largest island after Greenland, lying near the equator just north of Australia (page 26). I refer to the island's diverse indigenous peoples as "New Guineans." As a result of accidents of 19th-century colonial history, the island is now divided politically between two nations. The island's eastern half, along with many adjacent smaller islands, forms the independent nation of Papua New Guinea, which arose from a former German colony in the northeast and a former British colony in the southeast and became administered by Australia until independence in 1975. Australians referred to the former German and British parts as New Guinea and Papua, respectively. The island's western half, formerly part of the Dutch East Indies, has been since 1969 a province (renamed Papua, formerly Irian Jaya) of Indonesia. My own fieldwork in New Guinea has been divided almost equally between the two political halves of the island.

course the New Guinea Highlands of 1931 were not an unchanged world of yesterday.) All those changes that came to the Highlands in the last 75 years have also come to other societies throughout the world, but in much of the rest of the world those changes appeared earlier and much more gradually than in New Guinea. "Gradual," however, is relative: even in those societies where the changes appeared first, their time depth of less than 11,000 years is still minuscule in comparison with 6,000,000 years. Basically, our human societies have undergone profound changes recently and rapidly.

Why study traditional societies?

Why do we find "traditional" societies so fascinating?* Partly, it's because of their human interest: the fascination of getting to know people who are so similar to us and understandable in some ways, and so unlike us and hard to understand in other ways. When I arrived in New Guinea for the first time, in 1964 at the age of 26, I was struck by the exoticness of New Guineans: they look different from Americans, speak different languages, dress differently, and behave differently. But over the subsequent decades, in the course of my making dozens of visits of one to five months each to many parts of New Guinea and neighboring islands, that predominant sense of exoticness yielded to a sense of common ground as I came to know individual New Guineans: we hold long conversations, laugh at the same jokes, share interests in children and sex and food and sports, and find ourselves angry, frightened, grief-stricken, relieved, and exultant to-

---

* By the terms "traditional" and "small-scale" societies, which I shall use throughout this book, I mean past and present societies living at low population densities in small groups ranging from a few dozen to a few thousand people, subsisting by hunting-gathering or by farming or herding, and transformed to a limited degree by contact with large, Westernized, industrial societies. In reality, all such traditional societies still existing today have been at least partly modified by contact, and could alternatively be described as "transitional" rather than "traditional" societies, but they often still retain many features and social processes of the small societies of the past. I contrast traditional small-scale societies with "Westernized" societies, by which I mean the large modern industrial societies run by state governments, familiar to readers of this book as the societies in which most of my readers now live. They are termed "Westernized" because important features of those societies (such as the Industrial Revolution and public health) arose first in Western Europe in the 1700s and 1800s, and spread from there overseas to many other countries.

gether. Even their languages are variations on familiar worldwide linguistic themes: although the first New Guinea language that I learned (Fore) is unrelated to Indo-European languages and hence has a vocabulary that was completely unfamiliar to me, Fore still conjugates verbs elaborately like German, and it has dual pronouns like Slovenian, postpositions like Finnish, and three demonstrative adverbs ("here," "there nearby," and "there faraway") like Latin.

All those similarities misled me, after my initial sense of New Guinea's exoticness, into thinking, "People are basically all the same everywhere." No, I eventually came to realize, in many basic ways we are not all the same: many of my New Guinea friends count differently (by visual mapping rather than by abstract numbers), select their wives or husbands differently, treat their parents and their children differently, view danger differently, and have a different concept of friendship. This confusing mixture of similarities and differences is part of what makes traditional societies fascinating to an outsider.

Another reason for the interest and importance of traditional societies is that they retain features of how all of our ancestors lived for tens of thousands of years, until virtually yesterday. Traditional lifestyles are what shaped us and caused us to be what we are now. The shift from hunting-gathering to farming began only about 11,000 years ago; the first metal tools were produced only about 7,000 years ago; and the first state government and the first writing arose only around 5,400 years ago. "Modern" conditions have prevailed, even just locally, for only a tiny fraction of human history; all human societies have been traditional for far longer than any society has been modern. Today, readers of this book take for granted farm-grown and store-bought food rather than wild food hunted and gathered daily, tools of metal rather than of stone and wood and bone, state government and its associated law courts and police and armies, and reading and writing. But all of those seeming necessities are relatively new, and billions of people around the world today still live in partly traditional ways.

Embedded even within modern industrial societies are realms where many traditional mechanisms still operate. In many rural areas of the First World, such as the Montana valley where my wife and children and

I spend our annual summer vacations, many disputes are still resolved by traditional informal mechanisms rather than by going to court. Urban gangs in large cities don't call the police to settle their disagreements but rely on traditional methods of negotiation, compensation, intimidation, and war. European friends of mine who grew up in small European villages in the 1950s described childhoods like those in a traditional New Guinea village: everybody knew everybody else in the village, everyone knew what everyone else was doing and expressed their opinions about it, people married spouses born only a mile or two distant, people spent their entire lives in or near the village except for young men away during the world war years, and disputes within the village had to be settled in a way that restored relationships or made them tolerable, because you were going to be living near that person for the rest of your life. That is, the world of yesterday wasn't erased and replaced by a new world of today: much of yesterday is still with us. That's another reason for wanting to understand yesterday's world.

As we shall see in this book's chapters, traditional societies are far more diverse in many of their cultural practices than are modern industrial societies. Within that range of diversity, many cultural norms for modern state societies are far displaced from traditional norms and lie towards the extremes of that traditional range of diversity. For example, compared to any modern industrial society, some traditional societies treat elderly people much more cruelly, while others offer elderly people much more satisfying lives; modern industrial societies are closer to the former extreme than to the latter. Yet psychologists base most of their generalizations about human nature on studies of our own narrow and atypical slice of human diversity. Among the human subjects studied in a sample of papers from the top psychology journals surveyed in the year 2008, 96% were from Westernized industrial countries (North America, Europe, Australia, New Zealand, and Israel), 68% were from the U.S. in particular, and up to 80% were college undergraduates enrolled in psychology courses, i.e., not even typical of their own national societies. That is, as social scientists Joseph Henrich, Steven Heine, and Ara Norenzayan express it, most of our understanding of human psychology is based on subjects who may be described by the acronym WEIRD: from Western, educated, industrialized, rich, and democratic societies. Most subjects also appear to be literally weird by the standards of world cultural variation, because they prove to be outliers in many studies of cultural phenomena that have sampled world variation more broadly. Those sampled phenomena include visual perception, fairness, cooperation, punishment, biological reasoning, spatial orientation, analytic versus holistic reasoning, moral reasoning, motivation to conform, making choices, and concept of self. Hence if we wish to generalize about human nature, we need to broaden greatly our study sample from the usual WEIRD subjects (mainly American psychology undergraduates) to the whole range of traditional societies.

While social scientists can thus surely draw conclusions of academic interest from studies of traditional societies, all the rest of us may also be able to learn things of practical interest. Traditional societies in effect represent thousands of natural experiments in how to construct a human society. They have come up with thousands of solutions to human problems, solutions different from those adopted by our own WEIRD modern societies. We shall see that some of those solutions—for instance, some of the ways in which traditional societies raise their children, treat their elderly, remain healthy, talk, spend their leisure time, and settle disputes—may strike you, as they do me, as superior to normal practices in the First World. Perhaps we could benefit by selectively adopting some of those traditional practices. Some of us already do so, with demonstrated benefits to our health and happiness. In some respects we moderns are misfits; our bodies and our practices now face conditions different from those under which they evolved, and to which they became adapted.

But we should also not go to the opposite extreme of romanticizing the past and longing for simpler times. Many traditional practices are ones that we can consider ourselves blessed to have discarded—such as infanticide, abandoning or killing elderly people, facing periodic risk of starvation, being at heightened risk from environmental dangers and infectious diseases, often seeing one's children die, and living in constant fear of being attacked. Traditional societies may not only suggest to us some better living practices, but may also help us appreciate some advantages of our own society that we take for granted.

States

Traditional societies are more varied in their organization than are societies with state government.* As a starting point to help us understand
unfamiliar features of traditional societies, let's remind ourselves of the
familiar features of the nation-states in which we now live.

Most modern nations have populations of hundreds of thousands or
millions of people, ranging up to over a billion people each for India and
China, the two most populous modern nations. Even the smallest separate
modern nations, the Pacific island countries of Nauru and Tuvalu, contain
over 10,000 people each. (The Vatican, with a population of only 1,000
people, is also classified as a nation, but it's exceptional as a tiny enclave
within the city of Rome, from which the Vatican imports all of its necessities.) In the past as well, states had populations ranging from tens of
thousands up to millions. Those large populations already suffice to tell us
how states have to feed themselves, how they have to be organized, and
why they exist at all. All states feed their citizens primarily by means of
food production (agriculture and herding) rather than by hunting and
gathering. One can obtain far more food by growing crops or livestock on
an acre of garden, field, or pasture that we have filled with the plant and
animal species most useful to us, than by hunting and gathering whatever
wild animal and plant species (most of them inedible) happen to live in an
acre of forest. For that reason alone, no hunter-gatherer society has ever
been able to feed a sufficiently dense population to support a state government. In any state, only a portion of the population—as low as 2% in modern societies with highly mechanized farms—grows the food. The rest of
the population is busy doing other things (such as governing or manufacturing or trading), doesn't grow its own food, and instead subsists off the
food surpluses produced by the farmers.

The state's large population also guarantees that most people within a
state are strangers to each other. It's impossible even for citizens of tiny

---

* Throughout this book, I'll use the word "state" not only with its usual meaning of "condition"
(e.g., "he was reduced to a state of poverty"), but also with its technical political meaning of a large
society with centralized bureaucratic government, as described below.

Tuvalu to know all 10,000 of their fellow citizens, and China's 1.4 billion citizens would find the challenge even more impossible. Hence states need police, laws, and codes of morality to ensure that the inevitable constant encounters between strangers don't routinely explode into fights. That need for police and laws and moral commandments to be nice to strangers doesn't arise in tiny societies, in which everyone knows everyone else.

Finally, once a society tops 10,000 people, it's impossible to reach, execute, and administer decisions by having all citizens sit down for a face-to-face discussion in which everyone speaks his or her mind. Large populations can't function without leaders who make the decisions, executives who carry out the decisions, and bureaucrats who administer the decisions and laws. Alas for all of you readers who are anarchists and dream of living without any state government, those are the reasons why your dream is unrealistic: you'll have to find some tiny band or tribe willing to accept you, where no one is a stranger, and where kings, presidents, and bureaucrats are unnecessary.

We'll see in a moment that some traditional societies were populous enough to need general-purpose bureaucrats. However, states are even more populous and need specialized bureaucrats differentiated vertically and horizontally. We state citizens find all those bureaucrats exasperating: alas again, they're necessary. A state has so many laws and citizens that one type of bureaucrat can't administer all of the king's laws: there have to be separate tax collectors, motor vehicle inspectors, policemen, judges, restaurant cleanliness inspectors, and so on. Within a state agency containing just one such type of bureaucrat, we're also accustomed to the fact that there are many officials of that one type, arranged hierarchically on different levels: a tax agency has the tax agent who actually audits your tax return, serving under a supervisor to whom you might complain if you disagree with the agent's report, serving in turn under an office manager, serving under a district or state manager, serving under a commissioner of internal revenue for the whole United States. (It's even more complicated in reality: I omitted several other levels for the sake of brevity.) Franz Kafka's novel *The Castle* describes an imaginary such bureaucracy inspired by the actual bureaucracy of the Habsburg Empire of which Kafka was a citizen. Bedtime reading of Kafka's account of the frustrations faced by his protagonist in dealing with the imaginary castle bureaucracy guarantees me a sleep filled with nightmares, but all of you readers will have had your own nightmares and frustrations from dealing with actual bureaucracies. It's the price we pay for living under state governments: no utopian has ever figured out how to run a nation without at least some bureaucrats.

A remaining all-too-familiar feature of states is that, even in the most egalitarian Scandinavian democracies, citizens are politically, economically, and socially unequal. Inevitably, any state has to have a few political leaders giving orders and making laws, and lots of commoners obeying those orders and laws. State citizens have different economic roles (as farmers, janitors, lawyers, politicians, shop clerks, etc.), and some of those roles carry higher salaries than do other roles. Some citizens enjoy higher social status than do other citizens. All idealistic efforts to minimize inequality within states—e.g., Karl Marx's formulation of the communist ideal "From each according to his abilities, to each according to his needs"—have failed.

There could be no states until there was food production (beginning only around 9000 BC), and still no states until food production had been operating for enough millennia to build up the large, dense populations requiring state government. The first state arose in the Fertile Crescent around 3400 BC, and others then arose in China, Mexico, the Andes, Madagascar, and other areas over the following millennia, until today a world map shows the entire planet's land area except for Antarctica divided into states. Even Antarctica is subject to partly overlapping territorial claims by seven nations.

Types of traditional societies

Thus, before 3400 BC there were no states anywhere, and in recent times there have still been large areas beyond state control, operating under traditional simpler political systems. The differences between those traditional societies and the state societies familiar to us are the subject of this book. How should we classify and talk about the diversity of traditional societies themselves?

While every human society is unique, there are also cross-cultural patterns that permit some generalizations. In particular, there are correlated trends in at least four aspects of societies: population size, subsistence, political centralization, and social stratification. With increasing population size and population density, the acquisition of food and other necessities tends to become intensified. That is, more food is obtained per acre by subsistence farmers living in villages than by small nomadic groups of hunter-gatherers, and still more is obtained per acre on the intensive irrigated plots cultivated by higher-density peoples and on the mechanized farms of modern states. Political decision-making becomes increasingly centralized, from the face-to-face group discussions of small hunter-gatherer groups to the political hierarchies and decisions by leaders in modern states. Social stratification increases, from the relative egalitarianism of small hunter-gatherer groups to the inequality between people in large centralized societies.

These correlations between different aspects of a society aren't rigid: some societies of a given size have more intensified subsistence, or more political centralization, or more social stratification, than do others. But we need some shorthand for referring to the different types of societies emerging from these broad trends, while acknowledging the diversity within these trends. Our practical problem is similar to the problem faced by developmental psychologists discussing differences among individual people. While every human being is unique, there are still broad age-related trends, such that 3-year-olds are on the average different in many correlated respects from 24-year-olds. Yet age forms a continuum with no abrupt cut-offs: there is no sudden transition from being "like a 3-year-old" to being "like a 6-year-old." And there are differences among people of the same age. Faced with these complications, developmental psychologists still find it useful to adopt shorthand categories such as "infant," "toddler," "child," "adolescent," "young adult," etc., while recognizing the imperfections of these categories.

Social scientists similarly find it useful to adopt shorthand categories whose imperfections they understand. They face the added complication that changes among societies can be reversed, whereas changes in age classes can't. Farming villages may revert to small hunter-gatherer bands under drought conditions, whereas a 4-year-old will never revert to being a 3-year-old. While most developmental psychologists agree on recognizing and naming the broadest categories of infant/child/adolescent/adult, social scientists use numerous alternative sets of shorthand categories for describing variation among traditional societies, and some scientists become indignant at the use of any categories at all. In this book I shall occasionally use Elman Service's division of human societies into four categories of increasing population size, political centralization, and social stratification: band, tribe, chiefdom, and state. While these terms are now 50 years old and other terms have been proposed since then, Service's terms have the advantage of simplicity: four terms to remember instead of seven terms, and single words instead of multi-word phrases. But please remember that these terms are just shorthand useful for discussing the great diversity of human societies, without pausing to reiterate the imperfections in the shorthand terms and the important variations within each category each time that the terms are used in the text.

The smallest and simplest type of society (termed by Service a band) consists of just a few dozen individuals, many of them belonging to one or several extended families (i.e., an adult husband and wife, their children, and some of their parents, siblings, and cousins). Most nomadic hunter-gatherers, and some garden farmers, traditionally lived at low population densities in such small groups. The band members are sufficiently few in number that everyone knows everyone else well, group decisions can be reached by face-to-face discussion, and there is no formal political leadership or strong economic specialization. A social scientist would describe a band as relatively egalitarian and democratic: members differ little in "wealth" (there are few personal possessions anyway) and in political power, except as a result of individual differences in ability or personality, and as tempered by extensive sharing of resources among band members.

Insofar as we can judge from archaeological evidence about the organization of past societies, probably all humans lived in such bands until at least a few tens of thousands of years ago, and most still did as recently as 11,000 years ago. When Europeans began, especially after Columbus's first voyage of AD 1492, to expand around the world and to encounter non-European peoples living in non-state societies, bands still occupied all or most of Australia and the Arctic, plus low-productivity desert and forest environments of the Americas and sub-Saharan Africa. Band societies that will frequently be discussed in this book include the !Kung of Africa's Kalahari Desert, the Ache and Siriono Indians of South America, the Andaman Islanders of the Bay of Bengal, the Pygmies of African equatorial forests, and Machiguenga Indian gardeners of Peru. All of the examples mentioned in the preceding sentence except the Machiguenga are or were hunter-gatherers.

Bands grade into the next larger and more complex type of society (termed by Service a tribe), consisting of a local group of hundreds of individuals. That's still just within the group size limit where everyone can know everyone else personally and there are no strangers. For instance, in my high school of about 200 students all students and teachers knew each other by name, but that was impossible in my wife's high school with thousands of students. A society of hundreds means dozens of families, often divided into kinship groups termed clans, which may exchange marriage partners with other clans. The higher populations of tribes than of bands require more food to support more people in a small area, and so tribes usually are farmers or herders or both, but a few are hunter-gatherers living in especially productive environments (such as Japan's Ainu people and North America's Pacific Northwest Indians). Tribes tend to be sedentary, and to live for much or all of the year in villages located near their gardens, pastures, or fisheries. However, Central Asian herders and some other tribal peoples practise transhumance—i.e., moving livestock seasonally between different altitudes in order to follow the growth of grass at higher elevations as the season advances.

In other respects tribes still resemble large bands—for instance, in their relative egalitarianism, weak economic specialization, weak political leadership, lack of bureaucrats, and face-to-face decision-making. I've watched meetings in New Guinea villages where hundreds of people sit on the ground, manage to have their say, and reach a conclusion. Some tribes have a "big man" who functions as a weak leader, but he leads only by his powers of persuasion and personality rather than by recognized authority. As an example of the limits of a "big man's" powers, we shall see in Chapter 3 how the ostensible followers of a leader named Gutelu of the New Guinea Dani tribe succeeded in thwarting Gutelu's will and launching a genocidal attack that split Gutelu's political alliance. Archaeological evidence of tribal organization, such as remains of substantial residential structures and settlements, suggests that tribes were emerging in some areas by at least 13,000 years ago. In recent times tribes have still been widespread in parts of New Guinea and Amazonia. Tribal societies that I'll discuss in this book include Alaska's Iñupiat, South America's Yanomamo Indians, Afghanistan's Kirghiz, New Britain's Kaulong, and New Guinea's Dani, Daribi, and Fore.

Tribes then grade into the next stage of organizational complexity, called a chiefdom and containing thousands of subjects. Such a large population, and the incipient economic specialization of chiefdoms, require high food productivity and the ability to generate and store food surpluses for feeding non-food-producing specialists, like the chiefs and their relatives and bureaucrats. Hence chiefdoms have built sedentary villages and hamlets with storage facilities and have mostly been food-producing (farming and herding) societies, except in the most productive areas available to hunter-gatherers, such as Florida's Calusa chiefdom and coastal Southern California's Chumash chiefdoms.

In a society of thousands of people it's impossible for everyone to know everyone else or to hold face-to-face discussions that include everybody. As a result, chiefdoms confront two new problems that bands or tribes did not. First, strangers in a chiefdom must be able to meet each other, to recognize each other as fellow but individually unfamiliar members of the same chiefdom, and to avoid bristling at territorial trespass and getting into a fight. Hence chiefdoms develop shared ideologies and political and religious identities often derived from the supposedly divine status of the chief. Second, there is now a recognized leader, the chief, who makes decisions, possesses recognized authority, claims a monopoly on the right to use force against his society's members if necessary, and thereby ensures that strangers within the same chiefdom don't fight each other. The chief is assisted by non-specialized all-purpose officials (proto-bureaucrats) who collect tribute and settle disputes and carry out other administrative tasks, instead of there being separate tax collectors, judges, and restaurant inspectors as in a state. (A source of confusion here is that some traditional societies that have chiefs and are correctly described as chiefdoms in the scientific literature and in this book are nevertheless referred to as "tribes" in most popular writing: for instance, Indian "tribes" of eastern North America, which really consisted of chiefdoms.)

An economic innovation of chiefdoms is termed a redistributive economy: instead of just direct exchanges between individuals, the chief collects tribute of food and labor, much of which is redistributed to warriors, priests, and craftsmen who serve the chief. Redistribution is thus the earliest form of a system of taxation to support new institutions. Some of the food tribute is returned to the commoners, whom the chief has a moral responsibility to support in times of famine, and who work for the chief at activities like constructing monuments and irrigation systems. In addition to these political and economic innovations beyond the practices of bands and tribes, chiefdoms pioneered the social innovation of institutionalized inequality. While some tribes already have separate lineages, a chiefdom's lineages are ranked hereditarily, with the chief and his family being at the top, commoners or slaves at the bottom, and (in the case of Polynesian Hawaii) as many as eight ranked castes in between. For members of higher-ranked lineages or castes, the tribute collected by the chief funds a better lifestyle in terms of food, housing, and special clothing and adornments.

Hence past chiefdoms can be recognized archaeologically by (sometimes) monumental construction, and by signs such as unequal distribution of grave goods in cemeteries: some bodies (those of chiefs and their relatives and bureaucrats) were buried in large tombs filled with luxury goods such as turquoise and sacrificed horses, contrasting with small unadorned graves of commoners. Based on such evidence, archaeologists infer that chiefdoms began to arise locally by around 5500 BC. In modern times, just before the recent nearly universal imposition of state government control around the world, chiefdoms were still widespread in Polynesia, much of sub-Saharan Africa, and the more productive areas of eastern and southwestern North America, Central America, and South America outside the areas controlled by the Mexican and Andean states. Chiefdoms that will be discussed in this book include the Mailu Islanders and Trobriand Islanders of the New Guinea region, and the Calusa and Chumash Indians of North America. From chiefdoms, states emerged (from about 3400 BC onwards) by conquest or amalgamation under pressure, resulting in larger populations, often ethnically diverse populations, specialized spheres and layers of bureaucrats, standing armies, much greater economic specialization, urbanization, and other changes, to produce the types of societies that blanket the modern world.

Thus, if social scientists equipped with a time machine could have surveyed the world at any time before about 9000 BC, they would have found everybody everywhere subsisting as hunter-gatherers, living in bands and possibly already in some tribes, without metal tools, writing, centralized government, or economic specialization. If those social scientists could have returned in the 1400s, at the time when the expansion of Europeans to other continents was just beginning, they now would have found Australia to be the sole continent still occupied entirely by hunter-gatherers, still living mostly in bands and possibly in some tribes. But, by then, states occupied most of Eurasia, northern Africa, the largest islands of western Indonesia, most of the Andes, and parts of Mexico and West Africa. There were still many bands, tribes, and chiefdoms surviving in South America outside the Andes, in all of North America, New Guinea, and the Arctic, and on Pacific islands. Today, the whole world except Antarctica is divided at least nominally into states, although state government remains ineffective in some parts of the world. The world regions that preserved the largest numbers of societies beyond effective state control into the 20th century were New Guinea and the Amazon.

The continuum of increase in population size, political organization, and intensity of food production that stretches from bands to states is paralleled by other trends, such as increases in dependence on metal tools, sophistication of technology, economic specialization and inequality of individuals, and writing, plus changes in warfare and religion that I'll discuss in Chapters 3 and 4 and in Chapter 9 respectively. (Remember again: the developments from bands to states were neither ubiquitous, nor irreversible, nor linear.) Those trends, especially the large populations and political centralization and improved technology and weapons of states with respect to simpler societies, are what have enabled states to conquer those traditional types of societies and to subjugate, enslave, incorporate, drive out, or exterminate their inhabitants on lands coveted by states. That has left bands and tribes in modern times confined to areas unattractive or poorly accessible to state settlers (such as the Kalahari Desert inhabited by the !Kung, the African equatorial forests of the Pygmies, the remote areas of the Amazon Basin left to Native Americans, and New Guinea left to New Guineans).

Why, as of the year of Columbus's first trans-Atlantic voyage of 1492, did people live in different types of societies in different parts of the world? At that time, some peoples (especially Eurasians) were already living under state governments with writing, metal tools, intensive agriculture, and standing armies. Many other peoples then lacked those hallmarks of civilization, and Aboriginal Australian and !Kung and African Pygmies then still preserved many ways of life that had characterized all of the world until 9000 BC. How can we account for such striking geographic differences?

A formerly prevalent belief, still held by many individuals today, is that those regionally different outcomes reflect innate differences in human intelligence, biological modernity, and work ethic. Supposedly, according to that belief, Europeans are more intelligent, biologically advanced, and hard-working, while Aboriginal Australians and New Guineans and other modern band and tribal peoples are less intelligent, more primitive, and less ambitious. However, there is no evidence of those postulated biological differences, except for the circular reasoning that modern band and tribal peoples did continue to use more primitive technologies, political organizations, and subsistence modes and were therefore assumed to be biologically more primitive.

Instead, the explanation for the differences in types of societies coexisting in the modern world depends on environmental differences. Increases in political centralization and social stratification were driven by increases in human population densities, driven in turn by the rise and intensification of food production (agriculture and herding). But surprisingly few wild plant and animal species are suitable for domestication to become crops and livestock. Those few wild species were concentrated in only about a dozen small areas of the world, whose human societies consequently enjoyed a decisive head start in developing food production, food surpluses, expanding populations, advanced technology, and state government. As I discussed in detail in my earlier book *Guns, Germs, and Steel,* those differences explain why Europeans, living near the world region (the Fertile Crescent) with the most valuable domesticable wild plant and animal species, ended up expanding over the world, while the !Kung and Aboriginal Australians did not. For the purposes of this book, that means that peoples still living or recently living in traditional societies are biologically modern peoples who merely happened to inhabit areas with few domesticable wild plant and animal species, and whose lifestyles are otherwise relevant to this book's readers.

Approaches, causes, and sources

In the preceding section we discussed differences among traditional societies that we can relate systematically to differences in population size and
population density, means of obtaining food, and the environment. While
the general trends that we discussed do exist, it would be folly to imagine
that everything about a society can be predicted from material conditions.
Just think, for example, about the cultural and political differences between French and German people, not obviously related to the differences
between France's and Germany's environments, which are in any case
modest by the standards of worldwide environmental variation.

Scholars take various approaches towards understanding differences
among societies. Each approach is useful for understanding some differences among some societies, but not appropriate for understanding other
phenomena. One approach is the evolutionary one discussed and illustrated in the preceding section: to recognize broad features differing between societies of different population sizes and population densities, but
shared among societies of similar population sizes and densities; and to
infer, and sometimes to observe directly, changes in a society as it becomes larger or smaller. Related to that evolutionary approach is what may
be termed an adaptationist approach: the idea that some features of a society are adaptive, and that they enable the society to function more effectively under its particular material conditions, physical and social
environment, and size and density. Examples include the need for all societies consisting of more than a few thousand people to have leaders, and
the potential of those large societies to generate the food surpluses required to support leaders. This approach encourages one to formulate generalizations, and to interpret changes of a society with time in terms of the
conditions and environment under which the society lives.

A second approach, lying at the opposite pole from that first approach,
views each society as unique because of its particular history, and considers cultural beliefs and practices as largely independent variables not dictated by environmental conditions. Among the virtually infinite number
of examples, let me mention one extreme case from one of the peoples to

be discussed in this book, because it is so dramatic and so convincingly unrelated to material conditions. The Kaulong people, one of dozens of small populations living along the southern watershed of the island of New Britain just east of New Guinea, formerly practised the ritualized strangling of widows. When a man died, his widow called upon her brothers to strangle her. She was not murderously strangled against her will, nor was she pressured into this ritualized form of suicide by other members of her society. Instead, she had grown up observing it as the custom, followed the custom when she became widowed herself, strongly urged her brothers (or else her son if she had no brothers) to fulfill their solemn obligation to strangle her despite their natural reluctance, and sat cooperatively as they did strangle her.

No scholar has claimed that Kaulong widow strangling was in any way beneficial to Kaulong society or to the long-term (posthumous) genetic interests of the strangled widow or her relatives. No environmental scientist has recognized any feature of the Kaulong environment tending to make widow strangling more beneficial or understandable there than on New Britain's northern watershed, or further east or west along New Britain's southern watershed. I don't know of other societies practising ritualized widow strangling on New Britain or New Guinea, except for the related Sengseng people neighboring the Kaulong. Instead, it seems necessary to view Kaulong widow strangling as an independent historical cultural trait that arose for some unknown reason in that particular area of New Britain, and that might eventually have been eliminated by natural selection among societies (i.e., through other New Britain societies not practising widow strangling thereby gaining advantages over the Kaulong), but that persisted for some considerable time until outside pressure and contact caused it to be abandoned after about 1957. Anyone familiar with any other society will be able to think of less extreme traits that characterize that society, that may lack obvious benefits or may even appear harmful to that society, and that aren't clearly an outcome of local conditions.

Yet another approach towards understanding differences among societies is to recognize cultural beliefs and practices that have a wide regional distribution, and that spread historically over that region without being clearly related to the local conditions. Familiar examples are the near-ubiquity of monotheistic religions and non-tonal languages in

Europe, contrasting with the frequency of non-monotheistic religions and tonal languages in China and adjacent parts of Southeast Asia. We know a lot about the origins and historical spreads of each type of religion and language in each region. However, I am not aware of convincing reasons why tonal languages would work less well in European environments, nor why monotheistic religions would be intrinsically unsuitable in Chinese and Southeast Asian environments. Religions, languages, and other beliefs and practices may spread in either of two ways. One way is by people expanding and taking their culture with them, as illustrated by European emigrants to the Americas and Australia establishing European languages and European-like societies there. The other way is as the result of people adopting beliefs and practices of other cultures: for example, modern Japanese people adopting Western clothing styles, and modern Americans adopting the habit of eating sushi, without Western emigrants having overrun Japan or Japanese emigrants having overrun the U.S.

A different issue about explanations that will recur frequently throughout this book is the distinction between the search for proximate explanations and the search for ultimate explanations. To understand this distinction, consider a couple consulting a psychotherapist after 20 years of marriage, and now intending to get divorced. To the therapist's question, "What suddenly brings you to see me and seek divorce after 20 years of marriage?," the husband replies: "It's because she hit me hard in the face with a heavy glass bottle: I can't live with a woman who did that." The wife acknowledges that she did indeed hit him with a glass bottle, and that that's the "cause" (i.e., the proximate cause) of their break-up. But the therapist knows that bottle attacks are rare in happy marriages and invite an inquiry about their own cause. The wife responds, "I couldn't stand anymore all his affairs with other women, that's why I hit him—his affairs are the real [i.e., the ultimate] cause of our break-up." The husband acknowledges his affairs, but again the therapist wonders why this husband, unlike husbands in happy marriages, has been having affairs. The husband responds, "My wife is a cold, selfish person, and I found that I wanted a loving relationship like any normal person—that's what I've been seeking in my affairs, and that's the fundamental cause of our break-up."

In long-term therapy the therapist would explore further the wife's childhood upbringing that caused the wife to become cold and selfish (if that really is true). However, even this brief version of the story suffices to show that most causes and effects really consist of chains of causes, some more proximate and others more ultimate. In this book we shall encounter many such chains. For example, the proximate cause of a tribal war (Chapter 4) may be that person A in one tribe stole a pig from person B in another tribe; A justifies that theft in terms of a deeper cause (B's cousin had contracted to buy a pig from A's father but hadn't paid the agreed-on price for the pig); and the ultimate cause of the war is drought and resource scarcity and population pressure, resulting in not enough pigs to feed the people of either tribe.

Those, then, are broad approaches that scholars take towards trying to make sense of differences among human societies. As for how scholars have acquired our knowledge about traditional societies, our sources of information can be divided somewhat arbitrarily into four categories, each with its own advantages and disadvantages, and blurring into each other. The most obvious method, and the source of most of the information in this book, is to send trained social or biological scientists to visit or live among a traditional people, and to carry out a study focusing on some specific topic. A major limitation in this approach is that scientists are usually not able to settle among a traditional people until the people have already been "pacified," reduced by introduced diseases, conquered and subjected to control by a state government, and thus considerably modified from the people's previous condition.

A second method is to attempt to peel back those recent changes in modern traditional societies, by interviewing living non-literate people about their orally transmitted histories, and by reconstructing in that way their society as it was several generations in the past. A third method shares the goals of oral reconstruction, insofar as it seeks to view traditional societies before they were visited by modern scientists. The approach, however, is to utilize the accounts of explorers, traders, government patrol officers, and missionary linguists who usually precede scientists in contacting traditional peoples. While the resulting accounts tend to be less systematic, less quantitative, and less scientifically rigorous than accounts by scientifically trained field workers, they offer the compensating advantage of describing a tribal society less modified than when studied later by visiting scientists. Finally, the sole source of information about societies in the remote past, without writing, and not in contact with literate observers is archaeological excavations. These offer the advantage of reconstructing a culture long before it was contacted and changed by the modern world—at the cost of losing fine detail (such as people's names and motives), and facing more uncertainty and effort in extracting social conclusions from the physical manifestations preserved in archaeological deposits.

For readers (especially for scholars) interested in learning more about these various sources of information on traditional societies, I provide an extended discussion on pages 476–481 of the Further Readings section at the back of this book.

A small book about a big subject

This book's subject is, potentially, all aspects of human culture, of all peoples around the world, for the last 11,000 years. However, that scope would require a volume 2,397 pages long that no one would read. Instead, for practical reasons I have selected among topics and societies for coverage, in order to produce a book of readable length. I hope thereby to stimulate my readers to learn about topics and societies that I do not cover, by consulting the many other excellent books available (many of them cited in my Further Readings section).

As for the choice of topics, I picked nine fields for discussion in 11 chapters, in order to illustrate a spectrum of the ways in which we can use our understanding of traditional societies. Two topics—dangers and child-rearing—involve areas in which we as individuals can consider incorporating some practices of traditional societies into our own personal lives. These are the two areas in which the practices of some traditional societies among which I have lived have most strongly influenced my own lifestyle and decisions. Three topics—treatment of the elderly, languages and multilingualism, and health-promoting lifestyles—involve areas in which some traditional practices may offer us models for our individual decisions, but may also offer models for policies that our society as a whole could adopt. One topic—peaceful dispute resolution—may be more useful for suggesting policies for our society as a whole than for guiding our individual lives. With respect to all of these topics, we must be clear that it is not a simple matter to borrow or adapt practices from one society into another society. For instance, even if you admire certain child-rearing practices of some traditional society, it may prove difficult for you to adopt that practice in rearing your own children if all other parents around you are rearing their children in the ways of most modern parents.

As regards the topic of religion, I don't expect any individual reader or society to espouse some particular tribal religion as a result of my discussion of religions in Chapter 9. However, most of us in the course of our lives go through a phase or phases in which we are groping for resolution of our own questions about religion. In such a phase of life, readers may find it useful to reflect on the wide range of meaning that religion has held for different societies throughout human history. Finally, the pair of chapters on warfare illustrates an area in which, I believe, understanding of traditional practices may help us appreciate some benefits that state government has brought us, compared to traditional societies. (Don't react instantly in outrage by thinking of Hiroshima or trench warfare and closing your mind to a discussion of the "benefits" of state warfare; the subject is more complicated than it may at first seem.)

Of course, this selection of topics omits many of the most central subjects of human social studies—such as art, cognition, cooperative behavior, cuisine, dance, gender relations, kinship systems, language's debated influence on perceptions and thought (the Sapir-Whorf hypothesis), literature, marriage, music, sexual practices, and others. In defense, I reiterate that this book does not aim to be a comprehensive account of human societies, that it instead selects a few topics for the reasons given above, and that excellent books discuss these other topics from the perspective of other frameworks.

As for my choice of societies, it isn't feasible in a short book to draw examples from all small-scale traditional human societies around the world. I decided to concentrate on bands and tribes of small-scale farmers and hunter-gatherers, with less on chiefdoms and still less on emerging states—because the former societies are more different from, and can teach us more by contrast with, our own modern societies. I repeatedly cite examples from a few dozen such traditional societies around the world (Plates 1–12). In that way, I hope that readers will build up a more

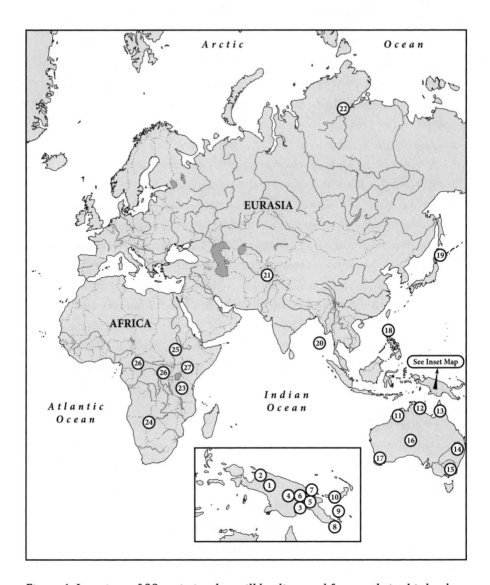

Figure 1. Locations of 39 societies that will be discussed frequently in this book.

New Guinea and neighboring islands. 1 = Dani. 2 = Fayu. 3 = Daribi. 4 = Enga. 5 = Fore. 6 = Tsembaga Maring. 7 = Hinihon. 8 = Mailu Islanders. 9 = Trobriand Islanders. 10 = Kaulong.

Australia. 11 = Ngarinyin. 12 = Yolngu. 13 = Sandbeach. 14 = Yuwaaliyaay. 15 = Kunai. 16 = Pitjantjatjara. 17 = Wiil and Minong.

Eurasia. 18 = Agta. 19 = Ainu. 20 = Andaman Islanders. 21 = Kirghiz. 22 = Nganasan.

Africa. 23 = Hadza. 24 = !Kung. 25 = Nuer. 26 = African Pygmies (Mbuti, Aka). 27 = Turkana.

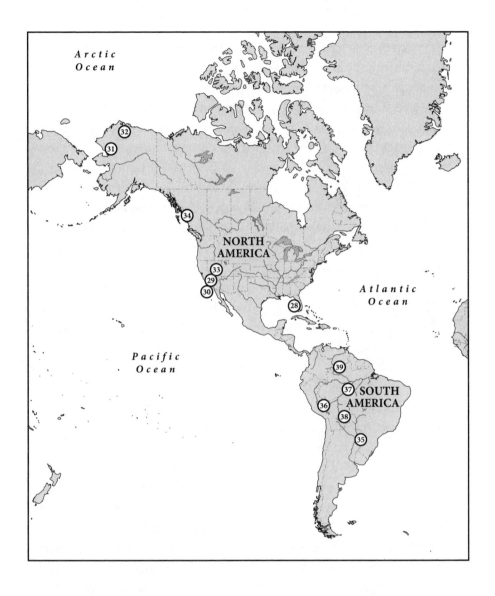

North America. 28 = Calusa. 29 = Mainland Chumash. 30 = Island Chumash. 31 = Iñupiat. 32 = Alaska North Slope Inuit. 33 = Great Basin Shoshone. 34 = Northwest Coast Indians.

South America. 35 = Ache. 36 = Machiguenga. 37 = Piraha. 38 = Siriono. 39 = Yanomamo.

complete and nuanced picture of these few dozen societies, and will see how different aspects of societies fit together: e.g., how child-rearing, old age, dangers, and dispute resolution play out in the same society.

Some readers may feel that disproportionate numbers of my examples are drawn from the island of New Guinea and adjacent Pacific islands. Partly, that's because it's the area that I know best, and where I have spent the most time. But it's also because New Guinea really does contribute a disproportionate fraction of human cultural diversity. It's the exclusive home of 1,000 of the world's approximately 7,000 languages. It holds the largest number of societies that even in modern times still lay beyond the control of state government or were only recently influenced by state government. Its populations span a range of traditional lifestyles, from nomadic hunter-gatherers, seafarers, and lowland sago specialists to settled Highland farmers, composing groups ranging from a few dozen to 200,000 people. Nevertheless, I discuss extensively the observations of other scholars about societies from all of the inhabited continents.

So as not to deter potential readers from reading this book at all by its length and price, I have omitted footnotes and references for individual statements inserted into the text. Instead, I gather references in a Further Readings section organized by chapters. The portions of that section providing references applicable to the whole book, and references for this Prologue, are printed at the end of the text. The portions providing references for Chapters 1–11 and the Epilogue are not printed but are instead posted on a freely accessible Web site, http://www.jareddiamondbooks .com. Although the Further Readings section is much longer than most readers will want, it still does not pretend to be a complete bibliography for each chapter. Instead, I select recent works that will offer readers with specialized interests bibliographies of that chapter's material, plus some classic studies that readers will enjoy.

Plan of the book

This book contains 11 chapters grouped into five parts, plus an epilogue. Part 1, consisting of the single Chapter 1, sets the stage on which the topics of the remaining chapters play out, by explaining how traditional societies divide space—whether by clear boundaries separating mutually exclusive territories like those of modern states, or by more fluid arrangements in which neighboring groups enjoy reciprocal rights to use each other's homelands for specified purposes. But there is never complete freedom for anyone to travel anywhere, so traditional peoples tend to view other people as split into three types: known individuals who are friends, other known individuals who are enemies, and unknown strangers who must be considered as likely enemies. As a result, traditional people could not know of the outside world distant from their homeland.

Part 2 then comprises three chapters on dispute resolution. In the absence of centralized state governments and their judiciaries, traditional small-scale societies resolve disputes in either of two ways, one of which is more conciliatory, the other more violent, than dispute resolution in state societies. I illustrate peaceful dispute resolution (Chapter 2) by an incident in which a New Guinea child was killed accidentally, and the child's parents and the killer's associates reached agreement on compensation and emotional reconciliation within a few days. The goal of such traditional compensation processes is not to determine right or wrong, but instead to restore a relationship or non-relationship between members of a small society who will encounter each other repeatedly for the rest of their lives. I contrast this peaceful form of traditional dispute resolution with the operation of the law in state societies, where the process is slow and adversarial, the parties are often strangers who will never encounter each other again, the focus is on determining right or wrong rather than on restoring a relationship, and the state has its own separate interests which may not coincide with those of the victim. For a state, a governmental justice system is a necessity. However, there may be some features of traditional peaceful dispute resolution that we could usefully incorporate into state justice systems.

If a dispute in a small-scale society is not resolved peacefully between the participants, the alternative is violence or war, because there is no state justice to intervene. In the absence of strong political leadership and of the state's assertion of a monopoly on the use of force, violence tends to lead to cycles of revenge killings. My brief Chapter 3 illustrates traditional warfare by describing an apparently tiny war among the Dani people of the western New Guinea Highlands. My lengthier Chapter 4 then reviews traditional warfare around the world, in order to understand whether it really deserves to be defined as war, why its proportionate death toll is often so high, how it differs from state warfare, and why wars are more prevalent among some peoples than among others.

This book's third part consists of two chapters about opposite ends of the human life cycle: childhood (Chapter 5) and old age (Chapter 6). The range of traditional child-rearing practices is broad, from societies with more repressive practices to societies with more laissez-faire practices than are tolerated in most state societies. Nevertheless, some frequent themes emerge from a survey of traditional child-rearing. Readers of this chapter are likely to find themselves admiring some but being horrified at other traditional child-rearing practices, and asking whether some of the admirable practices could be incorporated into our own child-rearing repertoire.

As for treatment of the elderly (Chapter 6), some traditional societies, especially nomadic ones or those in harsh environments, are forced to neglect, abandon, or kill their elderly. Others afford their elderly far more satisfying and productive lives than do most Westernized societies. Factors behind this variation include environmental conditions, the utility and power of the elderly, and society's values and rules. The greatly increased lifespans and apparently decreased utilities of the elderly in modern societies have created for us a tragedy, towards whose amelioration those traditional societies providing their elderly with satisfying useful lives may offer examples.

Part 4 consists of two chapters on dangers and our responses to them. I begin (Chapter 7) by describing three actually or apparently dangerous experiences that I survived in New Guinea, and what I learned from them about a widespread attitude of traditional peoples that I admire and term "constructive paranoia." By that paradoxical expression, I mean routinely reflecting on the significance of small events or signs that on each occasion carry low risks but that are likely to recur thousands of times in one's lifetime, and hence are ultimately likely to prove crippling or fatal if ignored. "Accidents" don't just happen at random or through bad luck: everything is traditionally viewed as happening for a reason, so one must remain alert to the possible reasons and be cautious. The following Chapter 8 describes the types of dangers inherent in traditional life, and the diverse ways in which people respond to them. It turns out that our perceptions of dangers, and our reactions to them, are systematically irrational in several ways.

The concluding Part 5 comprises three chapters on three topics central to human life and changing rapidly in modern times: religion, language diversity, and health. Chapter 9, about the uniquely human phenomenon of religion, follows straight on from Chapters 7 and 8 about dangers, because our traditional constant search for causes of danger may have contributed to religion's origins. Religion's near-ubiquity among human societies suggests that it fulfills important functions, regardless of whether its claims are true. But religion has fulfilled different functions whose relative importance has changed as human societies have evolved. It is interesting to speculate about which functions of religion are likely to be strongest over the coming decades.

Language (Chapter 10), like religion, is unique to humans: in fact, it's often considered the most important attribute distinguishing humans from (other) animals. While the median number of speakers of a language is only a few hundred to a few thousand individuals for most small-scale hunter-gatherer societies, members of many such societies are routinely multilingual. Modern Americans often assume that multilingualism should be discouraged, because it is supposed to hinder child language acquisition and immigrant assimilation. However, recent work suggests that multilingual people gain important life-long cognitive benefits. Nevertheless, languages are now disappearing so rapidly that 95% of the world's languages will be extinct or moribund within a century if current trends continue. The consequences of this undoubted fact are as controversial as are the consequences of multilingualism: many people would welcome a world reduced to just a few widespread languages, while other people point to advantages that language diversity brings to societies as well as to individuals.

The last chapter (Chapter 11) is also the one of most direct practical relevance to us today. Most of us citizens of modern states will die of non-communicable diseases—diabetes, hypertension, stroke, heart attacks, various cancers, and others—that are rare or unknown among traditional peoples, who nevertheless often proceed to acquire these diseases within a decade or two of adopting a Westernized lifestyle. Evidently, something about the Westernized lifestyle brings on these diseases, and we could minimize our risk of dying of these commonest causes of our deaths if we could minimize those lifestyle risk factors. I illustrate these grim realities by the two examples of hypertension and Type-2 diabetes. Both of these diseases involve genes that must have been advantageous to us under conditions of traditional lifestyles, but that have become lethal under conditions of the Westernized lifestyle. Many modern individuals have reflected on these facts, modified their lifestyles accordingly, and thereby extended their lifespans and improved their quality of life. Thus, if these diseases kill us, it is with our own permission.

Finally, the Epilogue comes full cycle from the Port Moresby airport scene with which my Prologue began. It's not until my arrival at Los Angeles airport that I begin my emotional reimmersion in the American society that is my home, after months in New Guinea. Despite the drastic differences between Los Angeles and New Guinea's jungles, much of the world until yesterday lives on in our bodies and in our societies. The recent big changes began only 11,000 years ago even in the world region where they first appeared, began just a few decades ago in the most populous areas of New Guinea, and have barely begun in the few remaining still-uncontacted areas of New Guinea and the Amazon. But for those of us who have grown up in modern state societies, modern conditions of life are so pervasive, and so taken for granted, that it's hard for us to notice the fundamental differences of traditional societies during short visits to them. Hence the Epilogue begins by recounting some of those differences as they strike me upon arriving at Los Angeles airport, and as they strike American children, or New Guinea and African villagers, who grew up in traditional societies and then moved to the West as teen-agers or adults. I have dedicated this book to one such friend, Meg Taylor (Dame Meg Taylor), who grew up in the Highlands of Papua New Guinea and spent many years in the United States as her country's Ambassador and as Vice President of the World Bank Group. Page 468 briefly summarizes Meg's experiences.

Traditional societies represent thousands of millennia-long natural experiments in organizing human lives. We can't repeat those experiments by redesigning thousands of societies today in order to wait decades and observe the outcomes; we have to learn from the societies that already ran the experiments. When we learn about features of traditional life, some of them are ones that we feel relieved to be rid of, and that make us appreciate our own societies better. Other features are ones that we are likely to envy, or to view their loss wistfully, or to ask whether we could selectively adopt or adapt them for ourselves. For instance, we certainly envy the traditional lack of the non-communicable diseases associated with the Westernized lifestyle. When we learn about traditional dispute resolution, child-rearing, treatment of the elderly, alertness to dangers, and routine multilingualism, we may also decide that some of those traditional features would be desirable and feasible for us to incorporate.

At minimum, I hope that you will come to share my fascination with the different ways in which other peoples have organized their lives. Beyond that fascination, you may decide that some of what works so well for them could also work well for you as an individual, and for us as a society.

PART ONE

SETTING THE STAGE BY DIVIDING SPACE

CHAPTER 1

Friends, Enemies, Strangers, and Traders

A boundary ▪ Mutually exclusive territories ▪ Non-exclusive land use ▪ Friends, enemies, and strangers ▪ First contacts ▪ Trade and traders ▪ Market economies ▪ Traditional forms of trade ▪ Traditional trade items ▪ Who trades what? ▪ Tiny nations

A boundary

Over much of the world today, citizens of many countries can travel freely. We face no restrictions on travel within our own country. To cross the border into another country, either we arrive unannounced and just show our passport (Plate 34), or else we have to obtain a visa in advance but can then travel without restrictions in that other country. We don't have to ask permission to travel along roads or on public land. The laws of some countries even guarantee access to some private lands. For instance, in Sweden a land-owner can exclude the public from his fields and gardens but not from his woods. We encounter thousands of strangers every day and think nothing of it. All of these rights we take for granted, without reflecting on how unthinkable they were almost everywhere in the world throughout human history and still are in parts of the world today. I'll illustrate traditional conditions of land access by my experiences while visiting a mountain village in New Guinea. Those traditional conditions set the stage for understanding war and peace, childhood and old age, dangers, and all the other features of traditional societies that we shall explore in the remainder of this book.

I had come to the village in order to survey birds on the ridge rising immediately to the south. On the second day after my arrival, a few villagers offered to guide me along an established trail up to the ridge crest, where I would pick a campsite for my surveys. The trail climbed through gardens above the village, then entered tall primary forest. After an hour and a half of steep climbing, we passed an abandoned hut in the middle of a small overgrown garden just below the ridge-line, at which the trail of our ascent ended in a T-junction. To the right from the junction, a good trail continued along the ridge-line.

Several hundred yards along that trail, I picked out a campsite just north of the ridge-line, i.e., on the side towards my new friends' mountain village. In the opposite direction, to the south of the trail and ridge-line, the ridge sloped gently downhill through tall forests traversed by a gully in which I could hear from below the sound of a stream. I was delighted to have found such a beautiful and convenient site, at the highest local elevation and thus with the best chance of locating high-altitude bird species, offering easy access to gentle terrain good for bird-watching, as well as a nearby source of water for drinking, cooking, washing, and bathing. And so I proposed to my companions that, on the following day, I move up to the campsite and spend a few nights there along with two men to point out birds and to maintain the camp.

My friends nodded in agreement until I came to the mention of just two men staying in camp with me. At that point they shook their heads and insisted that this was a dangerous area, and that my camp had to be protected by many armed men. What a dreadful prospect for a bird-watcher! If there were many people, they would inevitably make noise, talk constantly, and scare birds away. Why, I asked, did I need such a large entourage, and what was so dangerous about this beautiful and innocent-looking forest?

The prompt answer: at the base of the ridge's far side (its south side) were villages of bad people referred to as river people, enemies of my mountain friends. River people killed mountain people mainly by poison and sorcery, not by fighting openly with weapons. But the great-grandfather of one young mountain person had been shot and killed with arrows as he was sleeping in his garden hut some distance from the mountain village. The oldest man present during our conversation recalled seeing, as a child, the great-grandfather's body with the arrows still in him after he had been brought back to the village, and recalled people crying over the body, and his own fear.

Would we have the "right," I wondered, to camp on the ridge? The mountain people replied that the ridge-line itself formed the boundary between their own territory on the ridge's north slope and the territory of the bad river people on the south slope. But the river people claimed some of the mountain people's land beyond the ridge-line on the north side. Did I remember that abandoned hut and the overgrown garden just below the ridge-line? my friends asked. That hut and garden had been made by the evil river people, as a way of asserting their claim to land on the north side as well as on the south side of the ridge-line.

From my previous unpleasant experiences over perceived territorial trespassing in New Guinea, I realized that I had better take this situation seriously. Anyway, regardless of how I might assess the danger myself, the mountain people weren't going to let me camp on that ridge without a strong escort. They demanded that I be accompanied by 12 men, and I responded with a proposal of 7 men. We ended up "compromising" between 12 and 7: by the time that our camp was established, I counted about 20 men staying in camp, all armed with bows and arrows, and joined by women to do cooking and to fetch water and firewood. Furthermore, I was warned not to step off the ridge-line trail into that nice-looking forest on the gentle south slope. That forest unequivocally belonged to the river people, and it would cause big trouble, really big trouble, if I were caught trespassing there, even if just to watch birds. Also, the mountain women in our camp couldn't fetch water from the nearby gully on the south slope, because that would constitute not only trespass but also removal of valuable resources, for which a compensation payment would be due if the matter could be settled amicably at all. Instead, the women walked every day all the way back down to the village and carried 20-liter water containers 1,500 vertical feet uphill to our campsite.

On my second morning in camp there was some heart-pounding excitement that taught me how territorial relations between mountain people and river people were more complicated than just black-and-white claims of complete mutual exclusion from each other's land. With one of the mountain men I went back to the trail T-junction and continued left along the ridge-line to clean up an old trail that had become overgrown. My mountain companion didn't seem worried about our being there, and I figured that, even if river people found us there, they shouldn't object to our standing on the ridge-line as long as we didn't stray over to their side. But then we heard voices coming uphill from the south side. Uh-oh! River people!! If they carried on uphill as far as the ridge-line and T-junction, they would see the signs of fresh trail clearance and track us down, we'd be trapped there, they might consider us as violating their territory, and who knew what action they would take.

I listened anxiously and tried to follow the movements of the voices and estimate their location. Yes, they were indeed ascending towards the ridge-line from their side. Now, they must be at the T-junction, where they couldn't fail to notice the signs of our fresh trail. Were they coming after us? I kept following the voices as they seemed to get louder, over the noise of my heart-beats throbbing in my ears. But then the voices didn't come closer; they were definitely growing fainter. Were they returning towards the south side and the river people's village? No! They were descending the north side *towards* our mountain village! Incredible! Was this a war raid? But there seemed to be only two or three voices, and they were talking loudly: hardly what one would expect from a stealthy raiding party.

There was nothing to worry about, explained my mountain companion; everything was really OK. We mountain people (he said) acknowledge the right of river people to descend our trail peacefully to our village, and then to walk from there to the coast in order to trade. River people aren't permitted to get off the trail in order to gather food or cut wood, but just walking on the trail is OK. What's more, two river men had actually married mountain women and resettled in the mountain village. That is, there wasn't pure enmity between the two groups, but instead a tense truce. Some things were permitted and other things were forbidden by common consent, while still other things (such as land ownership at the abandoned hut and garden) were still in contention.

Two days later, I hadn't heard voices of river people again nearby. I still hadn't seen a river person and had no idea what they looked like and how they dressed. But their village was close enough that I once heard the sound of drums in their village coming up from the south watershed at the same time as I could hear faintly the sounds of shouting far below from the mountain village on the north watershed. As my mountain guide and I were walking back towards our campsite, we were making silly jokes with each other about what we would do to a river person if we caught one there. Suddenly, just as we turned a corner in the trail and were about to enter our camp, my guide stopped joking, raised his hand to his mouth, and warned me in a hushed voice, "Sh-h-h! River people!"

There, in our camp, was a group of our familiar mountain companions, talking with six people whom I had never seen before: three men, two women, and one child. There, at last, I saw the dreaded river people! They were not the dangerous monsters that I had been unconsciously imagining, but instead normal-looking New Guineans, no different from the mountain people who were my hosts. The river child and the two women were completely unintimidating. The three men carried bows and arrows (as did all the mountain men as well) but were wearing T-shirts and not looking as if they were dressed for war. The conversation between the river people and the mountain people seemed friendly and free of tension. It turned out that this group of river people was traveling down to the coast and had made a point of visiting our camp, perhaps just to make sure that their peaceful intent didn't get misinterpreted and that we didn't attack them.

To the mountain people and the river people, this visit was evidently a normal part of their complex relationship incorporating a broad range of behaviors: rarely, killings by stealth; more often, reputed killings by poison and sorcery; acknowledged reciprocal rights to do some things (such as passing in transit to the coast and making social visits) but not other things (such as gathering food and wood and water while in transit); disagreement about other things (such as that hut and garden) that sometimes flared into violence; and occasional intermarriage at about the same frequency as stealth murders (every couple of generations). All this between two groups of people who looked the same to me, spoke distinct but related languages, understood each other's language, described each other in terms otherwise reserved for evil subhumans, and viewed each other as their worst enemies.

Mutually exclusive territories

In theory, the spatial relations between neighboring traditional societies could encompass a whole spectrum of outcomes, ranging at the one extreme from non-overlapping exclusive territories with definite patrolled boundaries and no shared use, to free access of everybody to all land and no recognized territories at the other extreme. Probably no society strictly conforms to either extreme, but some come close to the first extreme. For instance, my mountain friends whom I just described are not far from it: they do have territories with defined boundaries that they patrol, they do assert exclusive claim to resources within their territory, and they permit access by outsiders just for transit and rare intermarriage.

Other societies which approach that extreme of exclusive territories include the Dani (Plate 1) of the Baliem Valley of western New Guinea's Highlands, the Iñupiat (an Inuit group)* of northwest Alaska, northern Japan's Ainu, the Yolngu (an Aboriginal group of Arnhem Land in Northwest Australia), Shoshone Indians of Owens Valley in California, and Yanomamo Indians of Brazil and Venezuela. For instance, the Dani irrigate and till gardens separated by a garden-less no-man's land from the gardens of the adjacent Dani group. Each group builds a line of wooden watch-towers up to 30 feet high on its own side of the no-man's land, with a platform at the top big enough for one man to sit there (Plate 13). For much of each day, men take turns keeping watch from each tower, while companions sit at a tower's base to protect it and the watchman, who scans the area to look out for stealthily approaching enemies and to give the alert in case of a surprise attack.

As another example, Alaska's Iñupiat (Plate 9) consist of 10 groups with mutually exclusive territories. People from one territory caught trespassing on another territory were routinely killed, unless they proved to be related to the territory-owners who caught them trespassing. The two commonest causes of trespass were hunters crossing a boundary in hot pursuit of reindeer, and seal hunters hunting on an ice shelf that broke off and drifted away from land. In the latter case, if the ice subsequently drifted back to shore and the hunters found themselves landing in another territory, they were killed. To us non-Iñupiat, that seems cruelly unfair: those poor hunters were already taking a big risk to have gone out onto a floating ice shelf, they had the bad luck that their shelf broke off, they were then at risk of

---

* People of Arctic North America refer to themselves as Inuit, and that is the term to be used in this book. The more familiar lay term is Eskimo.

death from drowning or being carried out to sea, now they had the great good fortune to drift back to shore after all, they had no intentions of trespassing but were just carried innocently and passively by an ocean current—yet they were still killed just at the moment of their salvation from drowning or drifting to sea. But those were the rules of Iñupiaq life. Nevertheless, Iñupiaq territorial exclusivity wasn't complete: outsiders occasionally were given permission to visit one's territory for a specific purpose such as a summer trade fair, or to transit one's territory for another specific purpose such as visiting or raiding a distant group living beyond the farther side of the transited territory.

When we collect the examples of societies (like my mountain friends, the Dani, and the Iñupiat) lying towards that extreme of mutually exclusive defended territories, we discover that that outcome arises under a combination of four conditions. First, defended territories require a population sufficiently large and dense that some people can be spared to devote time specifically to patrolling boundaries, so that the population doesn't have to rely just on everyone casually keeping out an eye for trespassers while in the course of normal foraging. Second, exclusive territories require a productive, stable, predictable environment within which the territory-owners can count on usually finding most or all of their necessary resources, such that they rarely or never need to go outside their territory. Third, the territory must contain some valuable fixed resources or capital improvements worth defending and dying for, such as productive gardens, groves of fruit trees, or fishing weirs or irrigation ditches requiring much effort to build and maintain. Finally, group membership must be rather constant, and neighboring groups must be largely distinct, with little migration between groups—the main exception being movements of unmarried young people (more often women than men) leaving their natal group in order to marry into another group.

We can observe how those four conditions are satisfied by the groups I've just mentioned as approaching the extreme of exclusive territories and defended boundaries. My New Guinea mountain friends have a significant investment in their year-round gardens, pigs, and forests, which traditionally gave them everything that they needed. Clearing forests and developing gardens are laborious for them, and are even more so for western New

Guinea's Dani, who dig and maintain elaborate systems of ditches to irrigate and drain their gardens. The Iñupiat and Ainu occupy rich year-round territories with abundant marine resources of salt-water fish, seals, whales, and seabirds, fresh-water fisheries and waterfowl, and inland areas with terrestrial mammals to hunt. Arnhem Land's Yolngu similarly lived in dense populations made possible by the combination of productive coastal and inland resources. Owens Valley's Shoshone Indians were hunter-gatherers living at relatively high densities in an area with ample water that let them irrigate land to increase its yields of edible wild grass seeds, and that provided storable harvests of pine nuts. Those food stores, pine groves, and irrigation systems were worth defending, and there were enough Owens Valley Shoshones to defend them. Finally, Yanomamo Indians maintain plantations of peach palm and plantain trees that produce their staple foods for many years and are also worth defending.

In areas with especially large and dense populations, such as those of the Dani and the Sudan's Nuer, not only are there separate groups each with its own territory, but those territorial groups are further organized into hierarchies of three or more levels. Those hierarchies remind us of the hierarchical organization of land, people, and political control familiar to us in our modern state societies, starting with individual house plots, and ranging up through cities, counties, and states to the national government. For instance, the Nuer (Plate 7), numbering 200,000 people in an area of 30,000 square miles, are divided into tribes of 7,000 to 42,000 people each, each tribe divided and subdivided into primary and secondary and tertiary subtribes, down to villages of 50 to 700 people and separated by 5 to 20 miles. The smaller and hierarchically lower the unit, the fewer are the disputes about boundaries and other matters, the stronger are the pressures that relatives and friends bring to bear on disputants to settle disputes quickly and without violence, and the more limited is any fighting that does occur. For instance, the Nuer observe few restrictions in their treatment of neighboring Dinka tribes: they regularly raid the Dinka, steal Dinka livestock, kill Dinka men, and take home some Dinka women and children as captives while killing the others. But Nuer hostilities against other Nuer tribes consist only of sporadic cattle raids, killing of just a few men, and no killing or kidnapping of women and children.

Non-exclusive land use

The opposite extreme of less or no exclusivity is approached under conditions that are the mirror image of the conditions selected for exclusivity. One such condition is sparse and small populations that make patrolling (other than casually looking for trespassers while out doing other things) impossible. For instance, a society consisting of just a single family can't afford dedicated patrols, because it can't have its single adult man spending all day seated at the top of a watch-tower. A second condition involves unproductive, marginal, variable environments with sparse and unpredictable resources, such that any territory one might feasibly claim would often (at some seasons or in a bad year) not contain essential resources, and one would then periodically have to seek resources in another group's territory and vice versa. Third, it doesn't pay to risk one's life defending a territory containing nothing worth dying for: if one's territory is attacked, it would then be preferable just to move to another area. Finally, territories are likely to be non-exclusive if group membership is fluid, and if group members often visit or transfer to other groups. It makes no sense to keep out another group if half of its members are visitors or transferees from your own group anyway.

However, the usual form of land division under these conditions selecting for non-exclusivity isn't the extreme of a free-for-all in which anybody can do anything anywhere. Instead, it still is the case that each group is identified with a specific core area. Non-exclusive societies differ from exclusive societies in that, instead of the Dani no-man's land clearly delineated by watch-towers, recognized borders don't exist, and land ownership just becomes increasingly vague as one moves increasing distances from one's core area. Another distinction of non-exclusive from exclusive societies is that neighboring groups receive permission to visit your territory more often and for more different purposes—especially to obtain food and water at certain seasons or in certain years. Correspondingly, you can readily obtain permission to visit your neighbor's territory when you are the one in need, so the arrangement becomes an exchange based on reciprocity and mutual benefit.

An example of non-exclusive land ownership that has been described in detail is the !Kung hunter-gatherers (Plate 6) of the Nyae Nyae area of the Kalahari Desert. When studied in the 1950s, they consisted of 19 bands, containing between 8 and 42 people per band, each band with its own "territory" (termed a *n!ore*) of between about 100 and 250 square miles in area. But boundaries between n!ores were vague: as anthropologists and !Kung informants walked together from the informants' camp towards the next n!ore, the informants became increasingly uncertain, or disagreed increasingly with each other, about which n!ore they were now in, the further they got from the center of their n!ore. There were no watch-towers or ridge-line trails to mark n!ore boundaries.

!Kung n!ores are occupied non-exclusively because it is both necessary and possible to share n!ores' resources. Resource sharing is necessary because water in the Kalahari Desert is scarce, and each band needs to spend much of its time near a waterhole. But there is unpredictable variation in rainfall between years. Many waterholes in the area go dry in the dry season. Only 2 waterholes in the area never failed during the period studied; 3 more were usually available throughout the year but failed in some years; 5 more lasted only occasionally through the dry season; and 50 were seasonal and always went dry for part of the year. Hence in the dry season, up to 200 people from various bands gather at a permanent waterhole with the permission of its owners, who in turn are permitted to visit and use resources of other n!ores when those are abundant. Thus, water considerations *require* the !Kung to have non-exclusive territories: it would be pointless to claim exclusive use of an area if that area might run out of water and thus become useless. Conversely, the seasonal superabundance of some resources *permits* non-exclusivity: it is pointless to offend potentially useful allies by keeping them out of your territory at a time when it is producing far more food than you yourself can eat. That's especially true of the food staple of mongongo nuts seasonally available in enormous crops, and it's also true of seasonal crops of wild beans and melons.

Supposedly, anyone from any band in the Nyae Nyae area can hunt anywhere, including outside of his own band's n!ore. However, if you kill an animal outside your n!ore, you should give a present of its meat if you then encounter a member of the band owning that n!ore. But that freedom of access for hunting doesn't apply to !Kung hunters from more distant areas. More generally, neighboring !Kung bands can readily obtain permission to use each other's n!ore for other purposes as well, such as obtaining water, nuts, beans, and melons—but they must first ask for permission, and they incur an obligation to reciprocate later by permitting the hosts to visit the visitors' n!ore. Fighting is likely to break out if they don't ask for permission. More distant bands have to be especially careful in requesting permission, and should limit the length of their visit and the number of people visiting. Outsiders who have no recognized connection by blood or marriage to the n!ore's owners cannot visit at all. Thus, non-exclusive territories certainly don't mean a free-for-all.

Rights to use land and resources, whether exclusively or non-exclusively, imply the concept of ownership. Who owns the n!ore of a !Kung band? The answer is: the band's *k'ausi,* meaning a core group of older people or else one older person descended from the people who have lived in that area for the longest time. But band composition is fluid and changes from day to day, because people often go visit relatives in other n!ores, people make seasonal visits to other n!ores for waterholes or for superabundant food, some people shift bands permanently for various reasons, and a new bridegroom plus his dependents (his old parents, and his first wife and children if he is now taking a second wife) may live with his new wife's band for about a decade until he and his new wife have given birth to several children. As a result, many !Kung spend more time outside than inside their n!ore. In an average year 13% of the population shifts residence permanently from one camp to another, and 35% of the population is dividing its residential time equally between two or three camps. Under those circumstances the band in the neighboring n!ore consists partly of your own people; they're not evil subhumans with whom the only inter-group transfers are just two intermarriages over the course of several generations, as in the case of my New Guinea mountain friends. You're not going to take a hard-line exclusive approach to your resources when many of the "intruders" are actually your siblings and cousins, your adult children, and your aged parents.

Another interesting illustration of non-exclusive territories involves North America's Great Basin Shoshone, Native Americans belonging to the same language group as the Owens Valley Shoshone whom I already mentioned as illustrating exclusive territories. Their Great Basin cousins differed in land use because of differences between the environments. Whereas Owens Valley land was well watered, suitable for irrigation, and worth defending, the Great Basin is a harsh dry desert, very cold in the winter, with sparse and unpredictable resources and little opportunity for food storage. Human population densities in the Great Basin were only about one person every 16 square miles. The Great Basin Shoshone lived in separate families for much of the year, aggregating in the winter into camps of 5 or 10 families near springs and pine nut groves, and infrequently aggregating into larger groups of up to 15 families for communal hunts of antelopes and rabbits. They did not maintain well-marked territories. Instead, individual families owned specific sites such as pine groves, which could be shared with other families but only by agreement: trespassers who attempted to harvest pine nuts without an agreement were driven off by a barrage of stones. Other plant and animal resources were shared under flexible non-exclusive rights.

Finally, a minimum in recognizing and patrolling territories was achieved by Peru's Machiguenga Indians and Bolivia's Siriono Indians in tropical forested areas. At the times that those groups were studied by anthropologists, the Machiguenga were gardeners living at only modest population densities, possibly because a previously denser population had crashed from effects of European-introduced diseases or else killings during the rubber boom, and also because agriculture in their area offered only low yields. The Machiguenga undertook seasonal movements for wild foods and cleared slash-and-burn gardens that produced food for just a few years and weren't worth fighting over. There were no territories: in theory all resources of all forests and rivers were open to all Machiguengas. In practice, multi-family groups maintained some distance from each other's home ranges. Similarly, the Siriono Indians studied by Allan Holmberg lived by hunting-gathering and some casual agriculture in bands of 60 to 80 people possessing no defined territories. But if one band came across hunting tracks made by another band, it chose not to hunt in that other band's area. That is, there was informal mutual avoidance.

Thus, traditional land use ranged over a spectrum, from well-marked territories that were patrolled and defended and from which outsiders were excluded on pain of death, through fuzzy home ranges without clear boundaries and which outsiders could use by mutual agreement, to home

areas kept separate just by informal mutual avoidance. No traditional society tolerated the relatively open access enjoyed by modern Americans or
European Union citizens, most of whom can travel anywhere within the
U.S. or European Union and can travel in many other countries as well
merely by presenting a valid passport and visa to a border passport control
officer. (Of course the September 11, 2001, World Trade Center attack has
pushed Americans back towards a traditional suspicion of strangers and
has resulted in restrictions on free travel, such as no-fly lists and airport
security checks.) But one could also argue that our modern system of relatively open access is an upscale extension of traditional access rights and
restrictions. Traditional peoples, living in societies of a few hundred individuals, obtain access to others' lands by being known individually, by
having individual relationships there, and by asking permission individually. In our societies of hundreds of millions, our definition of "relationship" is extended to any citizen of our state or of a friendly state, and the
asking of permission is formalized and granted en masse by means of pass-
ports and visas.

Friends, enemies, and strangers

All those restrictions on free movement cause members of small-scale
societies to divide people into three categories: friends, enemies, and
strangers. "Friends" are the members of your own band or village, and of
those neighboring bands and villages with which your band happens to
be on peaceful terms at the moment. "Enemies" are members of neighboring bands and villages with which your band happens to be on hostile
terms at the moment. Nevertheless, you probably know at least the names
and relationships, and possibly the appearances, of many or most individuals in those hostile bands, because you'll have heard of them or actually met them in the course of negotiations for compensation, periods of
peace resulting from shifting alliances, and exchanges of brides (or occasionally grooms) during those truces. An example is those two river men
who had married into the village of my mountain friends.

The remaining category is "strangers": unknown individuals belonging
to distant bands with which your band has little or no contact. Rarely or

never do members of small-scale societies encounter strangers, because it's suicidal to travel into an unfamiliar area to whose inhabitants you are unknown and completely unrelated. If you do happen to encounter a stranger in your territory, you have to presume that the person is dangerous, because (given the dangers of traveling to unfamiliar areas) the stranger is really likely to be scouting in order to raid or kill your group, or else trespassing in order to hunt or steal resources or kidnap a marriageable woman.

In a small-scale local population numbering several hundred people, you'll certainly know all members by name and face, the details of all their relationships by blood and marriage and adoption, and how they are related to you. When you add to your own band the several neighboring friendly bands, your potential universe of "friends" may number over a thousand people, including many whom you've heard of but never actually seen. Hence suppose that, while out alone away from your core area or near the boundary of your territory, you meet a person or people whom you don't recognize. If there are several of them and just one of you, you'll run away, and vice versa. If there is one of you and one of them, and if the two of you see each other at a distance, both of you may run away if a glance suggests a balance of strength (e.g., two adult men, rather than a man confronting a woman or a child). But if you come around a corner and suddenly confront another person unexpectedly, and it's too late to run away, that's a recipe for a tense situation. It can be resolved by the two of you sitting down, each of you naming yourself and your relatives and exactly how you are related to them, and continuing in an effort to identify a relative in common, such that the two of you would have some relationship to each other and wouldn't have grounds to attack each other. But if after several hours of such a conversation the two of you still can't identify any relative in common, then you can't just turn around and say, "It was nice to meet you, goodbye." Instead, you or he or both of you must consider the other a trespasser without a relationship justifying a visit, and a chasing-off or a fight becomes likely.

Speakers of the Central !Kung dialect within the Nyae Nyae area refer to other such speakers as *jū/wāsi*, where *jū* means "person," *si* is the plural suffix, and *wā* approximately means "true, good, honest, clean, not harmful." Back-and-forth visits between kin within the Nyae Nyae area create personal familiarities that unite all 19 bands and all thousand or so members of the area and make them all jũ/wāsi to each other. The opposite term *jũ/dole* (where *dole* has the sense of "bad, strange, harmful") is applied to all whites, all black Bantu people, and even !Kung people speaking the same dialect but belonging to a distant group among which you have no relatives or acquaintances. Like members of other small-scale societies, the !Kung are apprehensive of strangers. In practice, they succeed in finding some kin term to apply to almost every !Kung whom they meet. But if you meet a strange !Kung and can't discover any relationship to him after you've traced out your relationships and he has traced out his, then he is a trespasser whom you should drive off or kill.

For example, a !Kung man named Gao, at the request of the anthropologist Lorna Marshall, went on an errand for her to a place called Khadum, lying outside but not far north of the Nyae Nyae area. Gao had never visited Khadum, and very few other Nyae Nyae !Kung had ever been there either. The !Kung at Khadum at first called Gao a jũ/dole, which meant at minimum a frosty reception and possibly trouble. But Gao quickly said that he had heard that the father of someone living at Khadum had the same name as Gao's own father, and that someone else at Khadum had a brother named Gao, like Gao himself. The !Kung at Khadum then said to Gao, "So, you are Gao's [i.e., our Gao's] *!gun!a.*" (*!gun!a* is a relationship term.) They then accepted Gao at their campfire and gave him a present of food.

A similar categorization of people operated among Paraguay's Ache Indians (Plate 10). At the time of peaceful European contact the Ache numbered around 700 people, living in bands of 15 to 70 people each, and with several bands closely affiliated into a group of bands. There were four such groups, ranging in total number at the time of contact from 30 to 550 people. Ache referred to other members of their own group as *irondy* (meaning those who are customarily our people or brothers), and referred to Ache in the other three groups as *irolla* (meaning Ache who are not our people).

In modern large-scale societies whose citizens travel widely around their own country and around the world, we accumulate many friendships based on individual "chemistry" rather than on group affiliation. Some of our life-long friends are people with whom we grew up or went to school, but others are ones whom we met on our travels. What counts in friendship is whether people like each other and share interests, not whether one's group is politically allied with the other person's group. We take this concept of personal friendship so much for granted that it was only after years of working in New Guinea that an incident made clear to me the different concept of friendship prevailing in traditional small-scale New Guinea societies.

The incident involved a New Guinean named Yabu, whose village in the Central Highlands had practised a traditional lifestyle until the local establishment of government control and the end of intertribal warfare about a decade previously. In the course of my bird studies I brought Yabu as one of my field assistants to a campsite in the Southeast Highlands, where we were visited for several days by a British schoolteacher named Jim. Yabu and Jim spent much time talking and joking with each other, recounted long stories to each other, and evidently enjoyed each other's company. The Central Highlands town in which Jim taught school was located only a few dozen miles from Yabu's village. When Yabu completed his fieldwork with me, he would return to his village by taking a plane flight to the airport of Jim's town and then go on to his village by walking. Hence as Jim was leaving our camp and saying goodbye to Yabu and me, Jim did what seemed perfectly natural to me: he invited Yabu to stop and visit him while Yabu was traveling through Jim's town.

Some days after Jim had gone, I asked Yabu whether he did plan to visit Jim on his way home. Yabu's reaction was one of surprise and mild indignation at my suggestion of such a waste of time: "Visit him? What for? If he had work or a paid job to offer me, then I would. But he doesn't have a job for me. Of course I'm not going to stop in his town and look him up just for the sake of 'friendship'!" (This conversation took place in Papua New Guinea's lingua franca of Tok Pisin; the Tok Pisin expression that I have translated here as "just for the sake of 'friendship'" was "*bilong pren nating*".) I was astonished to realize that I had been making an incorrect assumption of supposed human universals that it hadn't even occurred to me to question.

Naturally, my realization shouldn't be exaggerated. Of course, members of small-scale societies enjoy some individuals more than others within their own society. As small-scale societies become larger or gain exposure to non-traditional outside influences, traditional outlooks change, including views of friendship. Nevertheless, I think that the difference between concepts of friendship in large-scale and small-scale societies, expressed in Jim's invitation and Yabu's reaction respectively, is on the average real. It's not just an artifact of Yabu's responding to a European differently from how he would have responded to a New Guinean. As one New Guinea friend familiar with both Western ways and traditional New Guinea ways explained it to me, "In New Guinea we don't just go and visit someone without a purpose. If you've just met and spent a week with someone, it doesn't mean that you've thereby acquired a relationship or friendship with that person." In contrast, the vast array of choices in large-scale Westernized societies, and our frequent geographic moves, give us more scope—and more need—for relationships based on personal bonds of friendship rather than on kinship, marriage, and the geographic accident of proximity during childhood.

In large hierarchical societies in which thousands or millions of people live together under the umbrella of a chiefdom or state, it's normal to meet strangers, and doing so is safe and non-threatening. For example, every time that I walk across my University of California campus or along the streets of Los Angeles, I encounter without fear or danger hundreds of people whom I have never seen before, and may never see again, and with whom I have no traceable relationship by either blood or marriage. An early stage in this changed attitude towards strangers is illustrated by the Sudan's Nuer people, whom I already mentioned as numbering about 200,000 and organized in a hierarchy of several levels from villages up to tribes. Obviously, no Nuer knows or has heard of all 199,999 other Nuer. Political organization is weak: each village has a figurehead chief with little real power, to be described in Chapter 2. Nevertheless (in the words of anthropologist E. E. Evans-Pritchard), "Between Nuer, wherever they hail from, and though they be strangers to one another, friendly relations are at once established when they meet outside their country, for a Nuer is never a foreigner to another as he is to a Dinka or a Shilluk. Their feeling of superiority and the contempt they show for all foreigners and their readiness to fight them are a common bond of communion, and their common tongue and values permit ready intercommunication."

Thus, compared to smaller-scale societies, the Nuer regard strangers no longer as threatening but instead as neutral or even as potentially friendly—provided that they are Nuer. Strangers who are not Nuer are either attacked (if they are Dinka) or merely despised (if they belong to any other type of people). In still larger societies with market economies, strangers have a potential positive value as prospective business partners, customers, suppliers, and employers.

First contacts

For traditional small-scale societies, the division of the world into friends of one's own and neighboring groups, neighboring enemies, and more distant strangers resulted in knowledge of the world being very local. People knew their own core area or territory, and they knew much about the first surrounding tier of neighboring territories as a result of visits under reciprocal rights of use or during intermittent truces. But people were unlikely to know the next (the second) surrounding tier of nearby territories: intermittent hostilities with people of the first tier meant that you couldn't cross that first tier during times of war to reach the second tier; and at times when you were at peace with a people of the first tier, they might in turn be at war with their neighbors in the second tier, again preventing you from visiting those neighbors.

Even travel into the territories of your immediate neighbors (the first tier) at presumed times of peace posed dangers. You might not realize that those neighbors had just started a war with some other allies of your people and therefore considered you now to be an enemy. Your hosts and relatives in that neighboring society might then be unwilling or unable to protect you. For instance, Karl Heider, Jan Broekhuijse, and Peter Matthiessen described an incident that happened on August 25, 1961, among the Baliem Valley's Dugum Dani people. The Dani were divided into several dozen confederations, of which two, called the Gutelu Alliance and the Widaia Alliance, fought over the Dugum neighborhood. Nearby was the separate Asuk-Balek confederation, founded by a Gutelu split-off group that had abandoned its original land and taken refuge along the Baliem River after battles. Four Asuk-Balek men allied to the Widaia Alliance visited a Gutelu hamlet called Abulopak, where two of the Asuk-Balek men had relatives. But the visitors did not realize that the Widaia had recently

killed two Gutelus, that the Gutelus had been unsuccessful in recent attempts to even the score by killing a Widaia, and that tension among the
Gutelus was high.

The arrival of the unsuspecting Asuk-Baleks, allied to the Widaia, provided the Abulopak Gutelus with the next-best opportunity for revenge,
second only to killing a Widaia. The two Asuk-Baleks with Abulopak
relatives were spared, but the two without relatives were attacked. One
managed to escape. The other took refuge in a hut's sleeping loft, but was
dragged down and speared. That attack triggered an explosion of general
rejoicing among the Abulopaks, who dragged the not-yet-dead Asuk-Balek's
body along a muddy path to their dance ground. The Abulopaks then
danced with joy that night around the corpse and finally threw it into an
irrigation ditch, pushed it under water, and covered it with grass. On the
following morning the two Asuk-Baleks with Abulopak relatives were
permitted to retrieve the corpse. The incident illustrates the need for pru-
dence verging on paranoia while traveling. Chapter 7 will say more about
this need for what I term "constructive paranoia."

Traditional distances of travel and of local knowledge were low in areas
of high human population density and environmental constancy, and
high in areas with sparse human population and variable environments.
Geographic knowledge was very local in Highland New Guinea, with its
dense populations and relatively stable environment. Travel and knowledge were wider in areas with stable environments but lower populations
(such as the New Guinea lowlands and the African rainforests inhabited
by African Pygmies), and were still wider in areas with variable environments and low populations (such as deserts and inland Arctic areas).
For example, Andaman Islanders knew nothing about Andaman tribes
living more than 20 miles distant. The known world of the Dugum Dani
was largely confined to the Baliem Valley, most of which they could see
from hilltops, but they could visit only a fraction of the valley because
it was divided up by war frontiers that it was suicidal to cross. Aka Pygmies, given a list of up to 70 places and asked which of them they had
visited, knew only half of the places lying within 21 miles and only
one-quarter of the places within 42 miles. To place these numbers in
perspective, when I lived in England in the 1950s and 1960s, it was still
true that many rural English people had spent their lives in or near their

villages, except possibly for traveling overseas as soldiers during World War I or II.

Thus, knowledge of the world beyond one's first or second neighbors was non-existent or only second-hand among traditional small-scale societies. For instance, no one in the densely populated mountain valleys of the main body of New Guinea had seen or even heard of the ocean, lying at distances of only 50 to 120 miles. New Guinea Highlanders did receive in trade marine shells and (after European arrival on the coast) a few steel axes, which were prized. But those shells and axes were traded from one group to another and passed through many successive hands in covering that distance from the coast to the Highlands. Just as in the children's game of telephone, in which children sit in a row or circle, one child whispers something to the next child, and what the last child hears bears no relation to what the first child said, all knowledge of the environment and people that supplied the shells and axes was lost by the time that they reached the Highlands.

For many small-scale societies, those traditional limitations on knowledge of the world were ended abruptly by so-called first contacts, when the arrival of European colonialists, explorers, traders, and missionaries proved the existence of a previously unknown outside world. The last peoples remaining "uncontacted" today are a few remote groups in New Guinea and tropical South America, but by now those remaining groups at least know of the outside world's existence, because they have seen airplanes flying overhead and have heard of outsiders from neighboring "contacted" New Guinea groups. (By "contacted," I mean contacted by distant outsiders such as Europeans and Indonesians; of course the "uncontacted" groups have been in contact with other New Guineans or South American Indians for thousands of years.) For example, when I was in western New Guinea's mountains in the 1990s, my hosts, who had first been contacted by the Dutch a few decades previously, told me of a group to the north of them that had not yet been contacted, in the sense that they hadn't yet been visited by missionaries or other outsiders. (Missionaries usually adopt the precaution of sending an emissary from a contacted neighboring group to ask whether a missionary would be welcomed, rather than expose themselves to the danger of walking in unannounced.) But those "uncontacted" mountaineers must have known of Europeans and

Indonesians from "contacted" neighboring groups with which the uncontacted group did have contact. In addition, the uncontacted group had for
many years seen airplanes flying over, such as the plane in which I arrived
at the village of their contacted neighbors. Hence the world's last remaining uncontacted groups do know that there is an outside world.

Conditions were different when Europeans began expanding over the
globe from AD 1492 onwards and "discovered" people long before there
were any airplane overflights to alert them to an outside world. The last
large-scale first contacts in world history will prove to be those that took
place in the New Guinea Highlands, where from the 1930s to the 1950s
patrols by Australian and Dutch government and army reconnaissance
expeditions, miners on prospecting trips, and biological expeditions "discovered" a million Highlanders of whose existence the outside world hadn't
known and vice versa—even though Europeans had by then been visiting
and settling the coasts of New Guinea for 400 years. Until the 1930s, first
contacts in New Guinea were made by Europeans exploring overland or by
river, and the first evidence of Europeans' existence to Highlanders was the
Europeans' physical arrival. Increasingly from the 1930s onwards, airplane
overflights preceded the overland parties and warned Highlanders that
there was something new out there. For example, the densest Highland
population in western New Guinea, the approximately 100,000 people in
the Baliem Valley, was "discovered" on June 23, 1938, when an airplane
belonging to a joint expedition of New York's American Museum of Natural History and the Dutch colonial government, financed by oil heir
Richard Archbold and exploring New Guinea for animals and plants, flew
over mountain terrain previously assumed to be rugged, forest-covered,
and uninhabited. Archbold and his team instead were astonished to find
themselves looking down on a broad, flat, deforested valley criss-crossed
by a dense network of irrigation ditches and resembling thickly populated
areas of Holland.

Those final sites of large-scale first contacts of Highlanders with Europeans are described in three remarkable books. One, entitled *First Contact*
by Bob Connolly and Robin Anderson, recounts the patrols by the miners
Michael Leahy, Michael Dwyer, and Daniel Leahy, who were the first Europeans to enter some densely populated Highland valleys of eastern New
Guinea between 1930 and 1935. (Lutheran missionaries had already

reached the eastern fringe of the Highlands in the 1920s.) A second is Michael Leahy's own account, *Explorations into Highland New Guinea, 1930–1935*. The remaining book is *The Sky Travelers* by Bill Gammage, describing the Australian government patrol led by Jim Taylor and John Black that trekked through the western portion of the Papua New Guinea Highlands in 1938 and 1939. Both expeditions took many photos, and Michael Leahy made motion pictures as well. The horrified expressions on the faces of New Guineans photographed at the moment of first contact convey the shock of first contact better than any words could (Plates 30, 31).

A virtue of the first and third of these books is that they relate the impressions made by first contact both on the New Guineans and on the Europeans involved. Both authors interviewed involved New Guineans 50 years after the events described. Just as older Americans will remember for the rest of their lives what they were doing at the moment of the three most traumatic events of modern American history—Japan's attack against Pearl Harbor on December 7, 1941, the assassination of President Kennedy on November 22, 1963, and the World Trade Center attack of September 11, 2001—so, too, New Guineans over 60 years old in the 1980s recalled clearly how they as children first saw whites of the Leahy-Dwyer patrol in 1930. Here is an account by one such New Guinean: "At that time, these bigger men [pointing to two old men]—they're old now—were just young men, and unmarried. They hadn't shaved yet. That's when the white men came. . . . I was so terrified, I couldn't think properly, and I cried uncontrollably. My father pulled me along by the hand and we hid behind some tall kunai grass. Then he stood up and peeped out at the white men. . . . Once they had gone, the people [we New Guineans] sat down and developed stories. They knew nothing of white-skinned men. We had not seen far places. We knew only this side of the mountains, and we thought we were the only living people. We believed that when a person died, his skin changed to white and he went over the boundary to 'that place'—the place of the dead. So when the strangers came we said: 'Ah, these men do not belong to the earth. Let's not kill them—they are our own relatives. Those who have died before have turned white and come back.' "

On first seeing Europeans, New Guinea Highlanders sought to fit these strange-looking creatures into known categories of their own world view.

Questions that they asked themselves included: Are these creatures human? Why have they come here? What do they want? Often, New Guineans took whites to be "sky people": people like New Guineans themselves, who were supposed to inhabit the sky, who traded and made love and war like New Guineans but were immortal, who were either spirits or ancestral ghosts, and who occasionally took human form and were then either red or white and descended to earth. At times of first contact, New Guineans carefully scrutinized Europeans, their behavior, and the debris that they left at their camps, for evidence about what they were. Two discoveries that went a long way towards convincing New Guineans that Europeans really were human were that the feces scavenged from their campsite latrines looked like typical human feces (i.e., like the feces of New Guineans); and that young New Guinea girls offered to Europeans as sex partners reported that Europeans had sex organs and practiced sex much as did New Guinea men.

Trade and traders

A remaining relationship between neighboring societies, besides defending boundaries and sharing resources and making war, is trade. I came to appreciate the sophistication of trading among traditional societies in the course of bird surveys that I was carrying out on 16 islands of Vitiaz Strait off northeastern New Guinea. Most of the islands were largely forest-covered, with only a few villages, each consisting of houses spaced dozens of feet apart and fronting on large open public spaces. Hence when I landed on an island called Malai, I was astonished by the contrast. I felt as if I had suddenly parachuted into a small-scale version of Manhattan. Crowded close to each other, almost side-by-side like a row of New York townhouses, were tall two-story wooden houses, veritable skyscrapers compared to the one-story huts prevailing elsewhere then on the Vitiaz Strait islands. Large wooden dugout canoes pulled up on the beach gave the sense of a First World marina all of whose berths had been rented out. In front of the houses were more people than I had seen gathered in a small area anywhere else in Vitiaz Strait. A 1963 census counted Malai's population as 448 people, which when divided by Malai's area of 0.32

square miles yields a population density of 1,400 people per square mile, higher than that of any European country. For comparison, even the Netherlands, Europe's most densely populated nation, supports only 1,010 people per square mile.

That remarkable settlement belonged to the famous long-distance Siassi traders, who ranged in their sailing canoes up to 300 miles through rough seas, carrying pigs, dogs, pots, beads, obsidian, and other goods. They rendered a service to the communities they visited, by supplying them with those necessities and luxuries. While doing good for others, they did well themselves, acquiring some of their own food and becoming immensely rich by New Guinea standards, which measured wealth in pigs. One voyage could yield a 900% profit, by loading pigs at Malai, converting each pig at the first stop of Umboi Island into 10 packets of sago, converting those 10 packets at the second stop at Sio Village on the New Guinea mainland into 100 pots, and converting those 100 pots at the next stop on New Britain into 10 pigs, to be brought back to Malai and consumed in ceremonial feasting. Traditionally, no cash was exchanged, because all those societies lacked cash. Siassi twin-masted canoes, up to 60 feet long and 5 feet deep, with a cargo pay load of about two tons, were technological masterpieces of wooden sailing ships (Plate 32).

The archaeological record demonstrates that our Ice Age ancestors were already trading tens of thousands of years ago. Cro-Magnon sites in the interior of Pleistocene Europe contain Baltic marine amber and Mediterranean seashells transported a thousand miles inland, plus obsidian, flint, jasper, and other hard stones especially suitable for stone-tool-making and transported hundreds of miles from the sites where they had been quarried. Only a few modern traditional societies have been reported as largely self-sufficient and carrying out little or no trade, including Siberia's Nganasan reindeer-herders and Bolivia's Siriono Indians as studied by Allan Holmberg. Most traditional societies, like all developed societies, did import some goods. As we shall see, even traditional societies that could have been self-sufficient usually chose not to be so and instead preferred to acquire by trade some objects that they could have obtained or produced for themselves.

Most trade in traditional small-scale societies was short-range trade between neighboring groups, because intermittent warfare made it dangerous for people to make trading trips that passed through several different populations. Even Siassi long-distance canoe traders were careful to land only at villages where they had established trading relationships. If they got blown off course or dismasted and made a forced landing on a coast where they lacked such relationships, they were likely to be killed as trespassers, and to have their goods seized, by villagers who didn't care about being nice and encouraging future visits.

Traditional trade differed in several respects from our modern equivalent method for acquiring goods from others, namely, by cash purchases at stores. For example, it would be unthinkable today for a customer buying a car at a new-car lot to drive off without paying anything or signing a contract, leaving the car salesman just to trust that at some time in the future the customer would decide to give him a gift of equal value. But that surprising modus operandi is common in traditional societies. However, a few features of traditional trade would be familiar to modern shoppers, especially the high proportion of our purchases devoted to functionally useless or unnecessarily expensive status symbols, such as jewelry and designer clothes. Hence let's begin by picturing what traditional outsiders soon after first contact found strange in our market cash economy. Some just-contacted New Guinea Highlanders were flown out to New Guinea coastal towns for an experience in culture shock. What must those Highlanders have thought as they learned how our market economy operates?

Market economies

The first surprise for the Highlanders would have been to discover that our overwhelmingly prevalent method of acquiring an item is not by barter, but by paying for it with money (Plate 33). Unlike most items exchanged in traditional trade, money has no intrinsic value, nor is it considered a beautiful luxury item like our jewelry or a Siassi trade bowl, serving either to be exchanged or to be kept and admired and conferring status. Money's sole use is to be spent and converted into other things. Also unlike a Siassi trade bowl, which any resident of certain villages possessing the necessary skill is permitted to carve, money is issued only by a government: if a First World citizen possessing the necessary skill plus a printing press attempts to exercise that skill by issuing money himself, he will be imprisoned as a counterfeiter.

The former traditional method of barter, in which two people exchange one desired object for another object face-to-face without the intermediary step of paying cash to a third party, now operates less frequently in modern societies. Conversely, some traditional societies used objects of arbitrary value in a way that sometimes approached our use of money. Examples included the use of gold-lipped pearl shells by New Britain's Kaulong people, and of large stone disks by the inhabitants of Yap Island in Micronesia. New Guinea Highlanders used cowrie shells, and people in Vitiaz Strait used carved wooden bowls, as exchange items, including to pay part of a bride-price at a fixed rate: so-and-so-many shells or bowls, plus other goods, for one bride. But those objects still differed from money in that they were used to pay only for certain things (not to be wasted on sweet potatoes for lunch), and that they were also attractive luxury items to be kept and shown off. Unlike New Guinea Highlanders, Americans with $100 bills keep them hidden in a wallet until they are to be spent, and don't strut around with a line of banknotes strung on a necklace around their neck for all to see.

A second feature of our market economy that would surprise many traditional peoples is that our process of buying something is conceived explicitly as an exchange, in which the buyer's handing-over of something else (usually money) is considered a payment, not a reciprocal gift. Almost always, the buyer either pays at the time of acquisition, or at least agrees on a price if the payment will be made later or in installments. If the seller does agree to wait until later for part or all of the payment, as in the case of many new-car purchases, the payment is still a specified obligation, not a subsequent reciprocal gift at the buyer's discretion. Contrast this procedure with the imaginary case of a car salesman "giving" a customer a car and expecting an unspecified future gift: we'd consider such a transaction absurd. But we'll see that that's exactly how trade does proceed in many traditional societies.

A third feature is that most of our market transactions take place between the buyer and a specialist professional middleman ("salesman") in a specialist professional facility ("store"), rather than between the buyer and the ultimate supplier near the house of either one. A simpler model operating at the lowest level of our economic hierarchy consists of one-off direct transactions whereby a seller advertises his wares (by a sign in front of his house, a newspaper ad, or an eBay notice) and sells his house or car directly to a buyer who has scanned ads. Conversely, a complex model at the highest level of our economic hierarchy consists of sales from governments to governments, such as contracts between governments for oil deliveries, or weapon sales by First World countries to other countries.

While our market transactions do assume these varied forms, in all forms the buyer and the seller usually have little or no on-going personal relationship beyond the transaction. They may never have seen or dealt with each other before, they may never deal with each other again, and they care mainly about the items that change hands (the purchased goods and the money), not about their relationship. Even in cases where the buyer and the seller repeatedly carry out transactions with each other, as in the case of a shopper who visits the farmers' market stall of some particular farmer every week, the transaction is primary, and the relationship is secondary. We shall see that this basic fact of market economies, which readers of this book take for granted, often does not apply to traditional small-scale societies, where the parties aren't professional sellers or buyers, the relationship between the two parties is on-going, and they may consider the exchanged items to be of negligible significance compared to the personal relationship that the exchange serves to strengthen.

A fourth feature of market economies is related to that third feature: most professional markets operate either constantly or else regularly and often. Typically, a store is open daily except Sundays, while a farmers' market operates weekly (e.g., on Wednesday mornings). In contrast, much traditional small-scale trade brings parties together infrequently, often just once a year or even once every several years.

The next-to-last feature of markets constitutes a similarity to rather than a difference from trading by traditional small-scale societies. In both cases the objects traded cover a spectrum from materially essential ("necessities") to materially useless ("luxuries"). At one extreme are objects that facilitate or are indispensable for surviving, such as food, warm clothing, and tools and machines. At the opposite extreme are objects irrelevant to survival but prized as luxuries, as decorations, for entertainment, or for conferring status, such as jewelry and television sets. In the gray middle ground lie objects that are materially useful, but that are available either as minimum-cost low-prestige functional items or as expensive high-prestige items with the same function. For instance, a $10 synthetic tote bag and a $2,000 leather Gucci tote bag are equally suitable for toting, but the latter confers status and the former doesn't. This example already hints that we shouldn't dismiss materially "useless" luxury items as useless: the status that they confer may bring huge material benefits, such as business opportunities or the wooing of prospective trophy wives and husbands. This same spectrum of "usefulness" already existed in the earliest trade that can be documented archaeologically: Cro-Magnons tens of thousands of years ago traded obsidian spear points necessary for hunting meat, shells and amber useful purely for decoration, and beautiful finely finished spear points of translucent quartz. The Cro-Magnons presumably no more dreamed of using their quartz spear points in hunting and thereby risking breaking them than we would use our best Gucci tote bag to carry home our fish purchase dripping with redolent fish oil from the seafood market.

The remaining feature of modern markets is one that is often duplicated by traditional trade, but that traditional societies in other cases replace with a behavior that has little precedent among us moderns. We buy something mainly just because we want the thing purchased (rather than to cement a personal relationship with the seller), and we buy it from someone who complements us economically and can sell us something to which we don't have access or that we don't know how to make. For instance, ordinary non-farming consumers don't have access to apples of their own: they have to buy apples from apple farmers or from grocery stores. Apple farmers in turn buy medical and legal services from physicians and lawyers who possess medical and legal knowledge lacking to apple farmers. No apple farmer would sell apples to and buy apples from other apple farmers merely to maintain the goodwill of other apple farmers. We shall see that traditional small-scale societies, like modern consumers and suppliers, often do trade objects to which one party has access and the other doesn't (e.g., a type of stone available only locally), and they trade objects that one party knows how to make but the other doesn't (e.g., sophisticated ocean-going wooden dugout canoes). But they also do much trading of objects equally available to either party, and they do that trading to maintain relationships for political and social reasons.

Traditional forms of trade

So far, we have considered trade from the perspective of members of traditional societies, and of what they would find different and surprising, or else familiar, in our market economies. Let's examine the corresponding mechanisms in traditional trade. I already mentioned the replacement of our cash purchases by their exchanges of objects, and occasionally by their use of valued objects such as cowrie shells in a manner somewhat similar to money. Now, let's consider the traditional equivalents of the other features of market economies that we just discussed.

While in some cases traditional societies negotiate explicit exchanges, and both items pass hands at the same time, in other cases one party presents a gift, and the recipient thereby incurs the obligation to provide a gift of comparable value at some unspecified time in the future. The simplest form of such reciprocal gifting occurs among Andaman Islanders (Plate 4), for whom there is little delay between the two halves of the transaction. A local group invites one or more other local groups to a feast that lasts a few days, and to which the visitors bring objects such as bows, arrows, adzes, baskets, and clay. A visitor gives an object to a host, who cannot refuse the gift but is then expected to give something of equal value. If the second gift does not meet the guest's expectations, the guest may become angry. Occasionally a giver, on making a present, names the gift that he would like in return, but that's exceptional. Among South America's Yanomamo Indians (Plate 12), reciprocal gift-giving is also associated with feasts to which one group invites a neighboring group. Yanomamo reciprocal gifting differs from the Andaman custom in that the second gift, which must be a different type of item from the first gift, is presented at a subsequent feast. Each Yanomamo gift is remembered long afterwards. The delay between the first and second gifts means that the accumulated obligations serve as an on-going excuse for neighboring villages to visit each other for feasts, because some members of one village always owe gifts to some members of another village from their last meeting.

Among the northwest Alaska Inuit, the Agta of the Philippines (Plate 3), Trobriand Islanders, and the !Kung, each person has recognized trading partners with whom gifts are exchanged. Each Inuit has between one and six such partners. Agta and African Pygmy hunter-gatherers have relationships with Philippine and Bantu farmer families respectively, and those relationships are passed on from generation to generation. Each Trobriand Islander traveling on a canoe trading voyage has on each visited island a trade partner to whom he gives a gift, and from whom he then expects an equivalent gift on his next visit a year later. The so-called *hxaro* long-distance trade system of the !Kung is distinctive in that each individual has dozens of trade partners, and it's also distinctive in the long interval between the giving of one gift and the receipt of an equivalent gift when the two parties next meet, typically months or years later.

Who are the traders, and under what circumstances and how often do they meet? In small-scale societies everybody trades. However, in large chiefdoms and early states with specialization of economic roles, professional traders like our modern ones emerge, as documented already by records from the dawn of writing 4,000 or 5,000 years ago in the Near East. Another modern phenomenon with precedents in simpler societies consists of entire societies specialized in trading. The Malai Islanders whose "skyscrapers" surprised me lived on an island too small to provide all their food needs, became middlemen and manufacturers and overseas traders, and thereby obtained the remainder of their food requirements. Malai Island thus serves as a model for modern Singapore.

The formats and frequencies of traditional trade encompass a spectrum. At the simplest level are the occasional trips made by individual !Kung and Dani to visit their individual trading partners in other bands or hamlets. Suggestive of our open-air markets and flea markets were the occasional markets at which Sio villagers living on the coast of northeast New Guinea met New Guineans from inland villages. Up to a few dozen people from each side sat down in rows facing each other. An inlander pushed forward a net bag containing between 10 and 35 pounds of taro and sweet potatoes, and the Sio villager sitting opposite responded by offering a number of pots and coconuts judged equivalent in value to the bag of food. Trobriand Island canoe traders conducted similar markets on the islands that they visited, exchanging utilitarian goods (food, pots, bowls, and stone) by barter, at the same time as they and their individual trade partners gave each other reciprocated gifts of luxury items (shell necklaces and armbands).

Andaman Island bands and Yanomamo Indian villages arranged to meet at irregular intervals for multi-day feasts that served as occasions for gifts. Northwest Alaska Inuit held summer trade fairs and winter messenger feasts at which groups that were passionate enemies for the rest of the year managed to sit down peacefully together for a week or two of trade and feasting. Specialized societies of canoe traders, such as the Siassi Islanders, Trobriand Islanders, southeast New Guinea's Mailu Islanders, and Indonesians (Macassans) who visited northern Australia to obtain trepang (dried sea cucumbers) for the Chinese soup market, sent groups of merchants hundreds or even thousands of miles over the ocean on annual trading trips.

Traditional trade items

As for the objects exchanged in trading, one is tempted to begin by dividing them into two categories: utilitarian items (like food and tools) versus luxury items (like cowrie shells and diamond rings). But this dichotomy becomes gray as soon as one tries to apply it. As the economist Frank Knight wrote, "Of all the fallacious and absurd misconceptions which so largely vitiate economic and social discussion, perhaps the very worst is the notion . . . that an interpretation of utility, or usefulness, in biological or physical survival terms has any considerable significance at the human level." For example, a BMW car is undoubtedly a luxury and a status symbol, but it can still be used to drive to the grocery store, and the image that it projects may be essential to its bearer in earning money by closing business deals and in wooing mates. The same is true for a beautiful Siassi wooden carved bowl, which is used to hold vegetables at feasts but is also a status symbol indispensable for buying a wife in the Vitiaz Strait region. As for pigs, they are by far the most valuable status symbol in New Guinea. That gave rise to Thomas Harding's remark, "It can be said of pigs, too, that the least important thing one can do is simply to eat them."

Table 1.1. Objects traded by some traditional societies

	"NECESSITIES"		"GRAY"	"LUXURIES"
	raw materials	manufactured products		
Cro-Magnon (Ice Age Europe)	stone			shells, ocher, amber
Daribi (New Guinea)	salt	polished stone axes		bird plumes
Dani (New Guinea)	salt, stone, wood	axe and adze blades, bark fiber	colored nets, decorated arrows	shells
Enga (New Guinea)	salt, stone, wood, bamboo	bark string	pigs	shells, bird plumes, cane, tree oil, ocher, drums
Trobriand Islands (New Guinea)	stone, fish, yams	sago	pots, carved bowls	shell necklaces, shell armbands
Siassi Islands (New Guinea)	obsidian, taro	sago, net bags, bows and arrows, canoes	pots, bowls, pigs, dogs, mats	pigs' and dogs' teeth, paint, ocher, beads, betelnut, tobacco
Calusa (North America)			pots, seal and whale meat	shells, shark teeth
Kamchatkans (Siberia)	meat, mushrooms, furs, sinews, animal hides			
African Pygmies	meat, mushrooms, iron, honey, garden crops	nets, bows, metal spear points	pots	tobacco, alcohol
!Kung (Africa)	meat, iron, honey, furs, animal hides	metal pots, clay pots	arrows, clothing	tobacco, necklaces, pipes, beads
Andaman Islands (Asia)	iron, wood, honey, clay for pots	adzes, rope, bows and arrows, baskets		shells, paint, betelnut

Table 1.1. *(continued)*

	"NECESSITIES"		"GRAY"	"LUXURIES"
	raw materials	manufactured products		
Yolngu (Australia)		metal axes, knives, fish-hooks, nails, spears, canoes, cloth, cycad-nut bread	trepang	shells, turtle shell, tobacco, alcohol
North Slope Inuit (Alaska)	stone, furs, driftwood, seal oil, whale skin and fat, pitch	wooden vessels, boat frames, pemmican	wood products, stone products, bags	ivory

Despite all those strictures, if one is presented with a list of 59 trade items, it is still useful to categorize them rather than to lump them all into an undivided laundry list. Hence **Table 1.1** gives examples of trade items in 13 small-scale societies, partitioned into four categories: objects immediately useful for survival, obtaining subsistence, and daily life, further divided into raw materials versus manufactured objects; luxuries or decorative objects not immediately useful for survival; and an intermediate category of objects that are used but that also convey status raising their value far above the material value of an object with the same utility but not conveying status (e.g., a cashmere jacket compared to a cheap synthetic jacket of similar size and warmth).

Table 1.1 shows that certain types of useful raw materials have been traded by many societies around the world: especially stone, and more recently metal, for making tools and weapons; plus salt, food, wood, animal hides and furs, pitch for caulking, and clay for making pots. Commonly traded useful manufactured objects include finished tools and weapons, baskets and other containers, fiber for weaving, bags and nets and ropes, cloth and clothing, and processed foods such as bread, sago, and pemmican. The long list of luxury and decorative items, sometimes traded as raw materials, more often worked into manufactured objects, includes bird feathers; shells of mollusks and turtles, raw or worked into necklaces and armbands; amber; dog, pig, and shark teeth; elephant and walrus ivory; beads; paints and paint bases, such as red ocher and black manganese oxide; tree oil; and stimulants such as tobacco, alcohol, and betelnut. For example, by 2,000 years ago long-distance specialist traders from Asia were bringing bird-of-paradise plumes from New Guinea to China, and the plumes were thence traded as far as Persia and Turkey. Finally, trade objects that are simultaneously useful and luxurious include pigs, trepang, spices, and other prestige foods (the traditional equivalents of our caviar); and beautiful but useful manufactured goods such as pottery, carved bows and arrows, and decorated bags, clothing, and mats.

Table 1.1 and the preceding discussion omit two other important categories of things that one people may offer to another people but that we don't normally count among trade goods: labor and spouses. African rainforest Pygmies and Agta forest Negritos of the Philippines, and more recently some !Kung, intermittently work for neighboring Bantu farmers, Philippine farmers, and Bantu herders respectively. That's a big part of the quid pro quo arrangement under which those groups of foragers receive iron plus garden crops or milk from those neighboring food-producers, in return for hunted and gathered products plus labor. Most neighboring peoples exchange spouses, occasionally as direct simultaneous exchanges (you give me your sister and I'll give you my sister), more often as separate acts (you give me your sister now, and I'll give you my little sister when she reaches the age of menarche). Between African rainforest Pygmies (Plate 8) and neighboring Bantu farmers such movements of spouses are virtually one way, with Pygmy women becoming wives of Bantu men but not vice versa.

Those are the main categories of objects exchanged. As for who trades what to whom, New Guinea's Daribi people, living at low population densities in a still heavily forested area at the edge of the densely populated and deforested Highland valleys, exported to Highlanders the plumes of birds of paradise, abundant in Daribi forests, in exchange for salt and polished stone axes imported from the Highlands. Pygmy groups of African rainforests export forest products such as honey, game meat, and mushrooms to neighboring Bantu farmers, from whom they import garden-grown foods, pots, iron, tobacco, and alcohol. In the Vitiaz Strait region the islanders export pig tusks, dogs, sago, betelnut, mats, beads, obsidian, and red ocher to mainlanders, from whom they import pigs, dog teeth, taro, tobacco, pots, net bags, bows and arrows, and black paint. In trade between coastal and inland Inuit of Alaska's north slope, coastal people could offer marine mammal products such as seal oil for fuel and food, seal and walrus skins, whale blubber, and walrus ivory, plus beach driftwood and wooden vessels, plus pottery and bags that they made. In-landers could in turn supply caribou hides and legs and antlers, furs of wolves and other terrestrial mammals, pitch for caulking, and pemmican and berries.

Who trades what?

These examples of objects exchanged illustrate a pattern that we moderns take for granted, because it describes almost all trade today: each partner supplies objects that it has or can readily make, and that the other partner lacks. Raw materials, and the skills required to manufacture finished products, are both unevenly distributed around the world. For example, the United States is the world's leading exporter of raw foods and manu-factured aircraft, because we can grow food and build airplanes in excess of our own needs. However, we are an importer of oil, because we don't produce enough of it for our needs, while some other countries (such as Saudi Arabia) produce oil in excess of their needs. Such imbalances of raw materials and of skills also characterize much, but not all, traditional trade.

As for unevenly distributed raw materials, a common pattern is for neighboring peoples occupying different habitats each to supply the other with raw materials confined to or more abundant in the exporter's habitat. Many examples include trade between coastal and inland peoples. In each such case, as I detailed two paragraphs above for Alaska's Inuit, the coastal partner has preferential or sole access to marine or coastal resources such as marine mammals and fish and shells, while the inland partner has preferential or sole access to terrestrial resources such as game, gardens, and forests.

Another common pattern consists of trade in very local raw materials not tied to specific habitat types, notably salt and stone. The Dugum Dani obtained all of their salt from the Iluekaima brine pool, and all of their stone for axes and adzes from a single quarry in the Nogolo Basin, while for much of the Southwest Pacific the main source of obsidian (the volcanic glass used to make the sharpest stone artifacts) was quarries near Talasea on the island of New Britain. Talasea obsidian became traded over an expanse of more than 4,000 miles, from Borneo 2,000 miles west of Talasea to Fiji 2,000 miles east of Talasea.

The remaining common pattern of trade in different types of raw materials involves neighboring groups with different subsistence strategies, giving them access to different materials. In many places around the world, hunter-gatherers trade meat, honey, resins, and other forest products that they hunt and gather to nearby village farmers in return for crops that the villagers grow. Examples include plains bison hunters and Pueblo farmers of the U.S. Southwest, Semang hunters and Malay farmers of peninsular Malaysia, and numerous hunter-farmer associations of India, as well as the African Pygmy hunters and Bantu farmers, and the Agta hunters and Philippine farmers whom I've already described. There are similar trade relations between herders and farmers in many parts of Asia and Africa, and between herders and hunter-gatherers in Africa.

Traditional trade, like modern trade, often also involves unevenly distributed skills. An example is the virtual local monopolies of pottery and ocean-going canoes enjoyed by the inhabitants of Mailu Island off the coast of southeast New Guinea, studied by the ethnographer Bronislaw Malinowski. While pottery was initially also produced by nearby New Guinea mainlanders, the Mailu achieved an export monopoly by figuring out how to mass-produce finer, thinner, stylistically standardized pots. Such pots were advantageous both to Mailu pot-makers and to their pot-using customers. Thin pots enabled the pot-makers to produce more pots from a given quantity of clay, to dry the pots faster, and to reduce the risk of damage while the pots were being fired. As for pot-using consumers, they preferred thin Mailu pots because less fuel was required for cooking in them, and the contents boiled faster. Mailu Islanders similarly acquired a monopoly on making and operating long-distance ocean-going canoes, which were more complicated and required more skill to construct than did the simpler canoes with which mainlanders were confined to making short trips in more sheltered coastal waters. Comparable manufacturing monopolies were enjoyed a thousand years ago by Chinese porcelain- and paper-makers, until their manufacturing secrets leaked out or were duplicated. In our modern times of industrial espionage and diffusion of knowledge, it has become difficult to maintain monopolies for long. However, the United States briefly (for four years) enjoyed a monopoly of making atomic bombs (which we didn't export), and the United States and Europe today dominate the world market in very large commercial jet aircraft (which we do export).

The remaining type of traditional trade, which scarcely has a parallel today, has been called "conventional monopolies." This term refers to trade in an item which either of the two trade partners could obtain or manufacture, but which one side chooses to rely on the other partner to supply, as an excuse for maintaining trade relations. For example, among the items that the Dugum Dani receive from the Jalemo area are wooden arrows with elaborate barbs and decorations, plus net bags with bright orchid fibers woven around the strings. The Dani make simple undecorated arrows and bags themselves. With a Jalemo arrow or bag in front of them, the Dani could perfectly well duplicate it, because the level of carving or weaving skill required is not high. But the Dani instead continue to depend on the Jalemo area for imported arrows and bags, as well as for forest materials that the Jalemo area has in more abundance than does the Dani homeland. Dani recognition of the Jalemo "conventional monopoly" of decorated arrows and bags is advantageous to both parties by helping to even out effects of fluctuations in supply and demand. The Jalemo people can continue to obtain salt from the Dani even if Jalemo harvests of forest products should temporarily decline, and the Dani can continue to sell salt to the Jalemo people even if Dani demand for forest products is temporarily glutted.

More elaborate conventional monopolies prevail among Brazil's and Venezuela's Yanomamo Indians, and among Brazil's Xingu Indians. Each Yanomamo village could be self-sufficient, but it isn't. Instead, each village specializes in some product that it provides to its allies, including arrow points, arrow shafts, baskets, bows, clay pots, cotton yarn, dogs, hallucinogenic drugs, or hammocks. Similarly, each Xingu village specializes in producing and exporting bows, pottery, salt, shell belts, or spears. Lest you think that most Yanomamo villagers really couldn't make the crude and undecorated Yanomamo pottery, consider recent changes in how the Yanomamo village of Mömariböwei-teri obtained pots. Initially, Mömariböwei-teri imported pots from another politically allied village, Möwaraöba-teri. In explanation, Mömariböwei-teri villagers vigorously insisted then that they didn't know how to make pots, that they formerly did make pots but had long ago forgotten how to do so, that the clay in their area was no good for making pots anyway, and that they got all the pots that they needed from Möwaraöba-teri. But then a war interrupted the alliance between Mömariböwei-teri and Möwaraöba-teri, so that Mömariböwei-teri could no longer import pots from Möwaraöba-teri. Miraculously, Mömariböwei-teri villagers suddenly "remembered" how they had long ago made pots, suddenly "discovered" that the hitherto scorned clay in their area was perfectly good for making pots, and resumed making their own pots. Thus, it's clear that the Mömariböwei-teri villagers had previously been importing pots from Möwaraöba-teri out of choice (to cement a political alliance), not out of necessity.

It's even clearer that !Kung engage in extensive trade of arrows out of choice, because all !Kung make similar arrows, which they nevertheless trade back and forth between each other. Anthropologist Richard Lee asked four !Kung men to tell him who owned each of the 13 to 19 arrows in each of their quivers. Of the four men, only one (Kopela Maswe) had no arrows from other men. One man (/N!au) had 11 arrows from a total of four other men, and only two arrows of his own. The other two men (/Gaske and N!eishi) had no arrows of their own: instead, each was carrying the arrows of six other men.

What is the point of these conventional monopolies and of arrow-for-arrow trading, seemingly senseless to us Westerners accustomed to trading only for objects that we can't readily provide for ourselves? Evidently, traditional trade has social and political as well as economic functions: not merely to obtain items for their own sake, but also to "create" trade for advancing social and political goals. Perhaps the foremost such goal is to strengthen an alliance or bond on which one can call if the need arises. Trade partners among the northwest Alaska Inuit had the obligation of supporting each other if necessary: should a famine arise in your district, you have the right to go to live with your trade partner in another district. Agta hunters "trading" among themselves or with Philippine farmers regard their exchanges as based on need rather than on supply and demand: it's assumed that different partners are likely to have surpluses or needs at different times, and that it will balance out in the long run, so a strict accounting is not kept. Each side in an Agta exchange makes major sacrifices at a time of crisis for the partner, such as at the time of a wedding or funeral ceremony, a typhoon, or a crop or hunting failure. For the Yanomamo, embroiled in constant warfare, the alliances developed through trade's regularly bringing neighbors together under friendly circumstances are far more important to survival than are the traded pots and hammocks—even though no Yanomamo would openly say that trade's real function is to maintain alliances.

Some trade networks and ceremonies—such as the Kula ring of the Trobriand Islanders, the Tee ceremonial exchange cycle of Highland New Guinea's Enga people, and the Siassi trade network upon which I stumbled at Malai Island—became the major means to gain and display status in their respective societies. It may seem silly to us that the Siassi Islanders spend months carrying cargos by canoe through treacherous seas just in order to feast publicly at the year's end on as many pigs as possible—until we reflect on what Siassi Islanders would say about modern Americans who toil in order to flaunt jewels and sports cars.

Tiny nations

Thus, traditional societies of the past, and those that survived into modern times, behaved like tiny nations. They maintained their own territories or core areas, visited and received visitors from some but not other nations, and in some cases delineated, defended, and patrolled boundaries as rigorously as do modern nations. They were far more restricted in their knowledge of the outside world than are citizens of modern nations, who increasingly use television, cell phones, and the Internet to learn about the rest of the world even if they never leave their own homeland. They divided other peoples more sharply into friends, enemies, and strangers than does even North Korea today. They intermarried with people of some other nations, sometimes. They traded with each other as do modern nations, and political and social motives played an even larger role in their trade relationships than they do in ours. In the next three chapters we shall discover how these tiny traditional nations maintained peace, and how they made war.

PART TWO

PEACE AND WAR

CHAPTER 2

Compensation for the Death of a Child

An accident ▪ A ceremony ▪ What if . . . ? ▪ What the state did ▪ New Guinea compensation ▪ Life-long relationships ▪ Other non-state societies ▪ State authority ▪ State civil justice ▪ Defects in state civil justice ▪ State criminal justice ▪ Restorative justice ▪ Advantages and their price

An accident

Late one afternoon towards the end of the dry season, a car driven by a man named Malo accidentally struck and killed a young schoolboy, Billy, on a road in Papua New Guinea. Billy was riding home from school in a public mini-bus (not a marked school bus), and his uncle Genjimp was waiting to meet him on the other side of the road. Malo, the driver for a local small business, was bringing office staff home at the end of the day and was driving in the opposite direction from the mini-bus carrying Billy. When Billy jumped down from the mini-bus, he saw his uncle Genjimp and started running across the road to join him. However, in crossing the road, Billy didn't walk in front of the mini-bus, which would have left him visible to Malo's car and other on-coming traffic. Instead, Billy ran out of sight behind the mini-bus and became visible to Malo only at the instant when he darted out into the middle of the road. Malo couldn't stop in time, and his car's hood struck Billy in the head and tossed him into the air. Uncle Genjimp took Billy straight to the hospital emergency room, but Billy died there several hours later from massive head injuries.

In the United States a driver involved in a serious accident is expected to remain at the scene until police arrive: if he leaves and doesn't report to the police, he is viewed as fleeing, and that itself is considered a crime. In Papua New Guinea, though, as in some other countries, the law permits, and police and common sense urge, the driver not to stay at the scene but to drive straight to the nearest police station. That's because angry bystanders are likely to drag the offending driver from his car and beat him to death on the spot, even if the accident was the pedestrian's fault. Adding to the risk to Malo and his passengers, Malo and Billy belonged to different ethnic groups, which in Papua New Guinea is often a recipe for tension. Malo was a local resident from a nearby village, but Billy belonged to a group of lowlanders originating many miles away. Many lowlanders who had migrated to the area for work lived near the accident's site. If Malo had stopped and gotten out to help the boy, he might well have been killed by lowlander bystanders, and possibly his passengers would have been dragged out and killed as well. But Malo had the presence of mind to drive to the local police station and surrender himself. The police locked up the passengers temporarily at the station for their own safety, and escorted Malo for his own safety back to his village, where he remained for the next several months.

The ensuing events illustrate how New Guineans, like many other traditional peoples living largely outside the effective control of systems of justice established by state governments, nevertheless achieve justice and peacefully resolve disputes by traditional mechanisms of their own. Such mechanisms of dispute resolution probably operated throughout human prehistory, until the rise of states with their codified laws, courts, judges, and police beginning 5,400 years ago. The case of Billy and Malo contrasts with a case that I shall relate in the next chapter, a case also resolved by traditional means, but ones opposite to those used in the case of Billy and Malo: by revenge killings and war. Depending on the circumstances and the parties involved, disputes in traditional societies may be resolved either peacefully, or else by war if the peaceful process breaks down or isn't attempted.

The peaceful process involves what is termed "compensation." (As we shall see, that usual English translation of a New Guinea term is misleading; it would be impossible to compensate for the death of a child, and that isn't the goal. The term in the New Guinea lingua franca of Tok Pisin is *sori money,* meaning "sorry money," and that translation is more appropriate, because it correctly describes the money as being paid out of shared sorrow or apology for what has happened.) The case of traditional compensation following Billy's death was related to me by a man named Gideon, at that time the local office manager of the business employing Malo as driver, and a participant in the ensuing process. It turns out that traditional New Guinea's mechanisms of justice have goals fundamentally different from those of state justice systems. While I agree that state justice offers big advantages and is absolutely essential for resolving many disputes between citizens of states, especially disputes between strangers, I now feel that traditional justice mechanisms may have much to teach us when the disputants are not strangers but will remain locked in on-going relationships after the dispute's settlement: e.g., neighbors, people connected by a business relationship, divorcing parents of children, and siblings disputing an inheritance.

A ceremony

Because of the risk that Billy's clansmen might seek to retaliate against Malo and Gideon and other employees of their company, Gideon told the staff not to come to work on the day after the accident. Gideon himself remained alone in his office, within a gated patrolled compound, only a hundred yards from the house where Gideon and his family lived. He instructed the security guards to remain alert, not to let strangers in, and especially to be on the look-out for any lowlanders and to keep them out. Nevertheless, in the course of the morning Gideon glanced up from his desk and to his horror saw three large men, recognizable as lowlanders from their appearance, standing outside the back window of his office.

Gideon's first thought was: either I smile at them, or I run. But then he reflected that his wife and his young children were nearby, and that running might save only his own life. He managed a smile, and the three men managed to smile back. Gideon went to the back window of the office and opened it, recognizing that that could immediately prove fatal but that he had no choice because the alternative was worse. One of the three men, who turned out to be Peti, father of the dead boy, asked Gideon, "Can I come into your office and talk with you?" (This and most of the other conversations that I shall relate took place not in the English language but in Tok Pisin. Peti's actual words to Gideon were "Inap mi kam insait long opis bilong yu na yumi tok-tok?")

Gideon nodded, went to the front of his office, opened the door, and invited Peti to come in alone and sit down. For a man whose son had just been killed, and who was now confronting the killer's employer, Peti's behavior was impressive: clearly still in a state of shock, he was nevertheless calm, respectful, and direct. Peti sat quietly for some time, and finally said to Gideon, "We understand that this was an accident, and that you didn't do it intentionally. We don't want to make any problems. We just want your help with the funeral. We ask of you a little money and food, in order to feed our relatives at the ceremony." Gideon responded by offering his sympathies on behalf of his company and its staff, and by making some vague commitment. Immediately that afternoon, he went to the local supermarket to start buying the standard food items of rice, tinned meat, sugar, and coffee. While in the store, he happened to encounter Peti again, and once again there was no trouble.

Already on that second day, the day after the accident, Gideon talked to the senior member of his staff, an older New Guinean named Yaghean, who was a native of a different district but was experienced in New Guinea compensation negotiations. Yaghean offered to handle the negotiations. On the following day (day 3) Gideon convened a staff meeting of his company to discuss how to proceed. Everybody's main fear was that the extended family of the dead boy (his more distant relatives and clanspeople) might prove violent, even though the father had given assurance that the immediate family would cause no trouble. Encouraged by Peti's calm behavior during their two encounters, Gideon's first inclination was to go straight to the lowlander settlement himself, to seek out Billy's family, to "say sorry" (formally apologize), and to attempt to defuse the threat from the extended family. But Yaghean insisted that Gideon should not do this: "If you yourself, Gideon, go there too soon, I'm concerned that the extended family and the whole lowlander community may still have hot tempers. We should instead go through the proper compensation process. We'll send an emissary, and that will be me. I'll talk to the councilor for the ward that includes the lowlander settlement, and he in turn will talk to the lowlander community. Both he and I know how the compensation process should proceed. Only after the process has been completed can you and your staff have a say-sorry [*tok-sori* in Tok Pisin] ceremony with the family."

Yaghean went to speak to the councilor, who arranged for the next day (day 4) a meeting involving Yaghean, the councilor, Billy's family, and the extended clan. Gideon has little knowledge of what went on at that meeting, other than Yaghean's report that they talked at length about how to handle the issue, that the family itself had no intention to resort to violence, but that some men in the settlement felt strongly for Billy and were still stirred up. Yaghean told Gideon that he should buy more food for the compensation ceremony and funeral, and that agreement had been reached on a compensation payment of 1,000 kina (equivalent to about $300) from Gideon's company to the family. (The kina is the national currency of Papua New Guinea.)

The compensation ceremony itself took place on the following day, day 5, with formal and structured arrangements. It began with Gideon, Yaghean, and the rest of the office staff except for Malo driving in the company car into the lowlander settlement. They parked the car, walked through the settlement, and entered the yard behind Billy's family's house. Traditional New Guinea ceremonies of mourning take place under some kind of shelter, to cover the mourners' heads; in this case the shelter that the family set up was a tarpaulin, under which everyone—the family and the visitors—was to gather. When the visitors came in, one of the dead boy's uncles pointed out to them their place to sit and motioned the family to other seats.

The ceremony began with an uncle speaking, to thank the visitors for coming, and to say how sad it was that Billy had died. Then Gideon, Yaghean, and other office staff talked. In describing the event to me, Gideon explained, "It felt awful, just awful, to have to give that talk. I was crying. At that time, I, too, had young children. I told the family that I was trying to imagine their level of grief. I said that I was trying to grasp it by supposing the accident to have happened instead to my own son. Their grief must have been unimaginable. I told them that the food and the money that I was giving them were nothing, mere rubbish, compared to the life of their child."

Gideon went on to tell me, "Next came the talk of Billy's father, Peti. His words were very simple. He was in tears. He acknowledged that Billy's death was an accident, and not due to negligence on our part. He thanked us for being there, and said that his people wouldn't make any problems for us. Then he talked about Billy, held up a photograph of his son, and said, 'We miss him.' Billy's mother sat quietly behind the father as he spoke. A few others of Billy's uncles stood up and reiterated, 'You people won't have any problems with us, we are satisfied with your response and with the compensation.' Everybody—my colleagues and I, and Billy's whole family—was crying."

The transfer of food consisted of Gideon and his colleagues handing the food over in order to "say sorry," with the words "This food is to help you in this hard time." After the talks, the family and the visitors ate to-gether a simple meal of sweet potato (the traditional New Guinea staple food) and other vegetables. There was much shaking of hands at the end of the ceremony. I asked Gideon whether there had also been any hugging, and whether for instance he and the father had hugged each other while they were crying. But Gideon's answer was "No, the ceremony was struc-tured, and it was very formal." Still, I have difficulty imagining in the U.S. or any other Western society a similar meeting of reconciliation, in which a dead child's family and the child's accidental killers, previously strang-ers to each other, sit down and cry together and share a meal a few days after the death. Instead, the child's family would be planning a civil law-suit, and the accidental killer's family would be consulting lawyers and their insurance broker in order to prepare to defend themselves against the lawsuit plus possible criminal charges.

What if . . . ?

As Billy's father and relatives agreed, Malo hadn't intended to kill Billy. I asked Malo and Gideon what would have happened if Malo really had murdered Billy intentionally, or if Malo had at least been unequivocally negligent.

Malo and Gideon replied that, in that case, the matter could still have been settled by the same compensation process. The result would just have been more uncertain, the situation more dangerous, and the required compensation payment larger. There would have been a greater risk that

Billy's relatives would not have awaited the outcome of compensation negotiations, or else would have refused payment and instead would have
carried out a so-called payback killing: preferably by killing Malo himself,
or else someone of his close family if they didn't succeed in killing Malo,
or else a more distantly related fellow clansman of Malo's if they couldn't
kill a member of his immediate family. If, however, Billy's relatives could
have been prevailed on to await the outcome of the compensation process,
they would have demanded much higher compensation. Malo estimated
for me the required compensation (if he had been clearly responsible for
Billy's death) as approximately five pigs, plus 10,000 kina (equal to about
$3,000), plus a quantity of local food including a bunch of bananas, taro,
sweet potatoes, sago, garden vegetables, and dried fish.

I also wondered what would have happened if Malo hadn't been a
driver for a company but just a private New Guinean, and thus if the company hadn't been involved. Malo answered that the compensation negotiations from his side would then not have been handled by his office
colleague Yaghean, but instead by some of his uncles and by elders from
his village. The compensation itself would not have been paid by the company, but rather by Malo's whole village, including his family, his fellow
clanspeople, and villagers belonging to other clans whom Malo might
have had to call upon for help in raising the payment. Malo would thereby
have incurred obligations to all those who had contributed. At some later
time in his life, Malo would have had to make payments to those people
for their contributions, and to his uncles for their hard work in handling
the negotiations. Had Malo died before making such payments, the con-
tributors and his uncles would have claimed payment from Malo's family
and clan. However, apart from those differences in who handled the negotiation and who made the payments, the compensation process if the company hadn't been involved would have unfolded much as it actually did.

What the state did

The chain of events that I recounted is an example of how traditional New
Guinea mechanisms can deal peacefully with a loss suffered by people at
the hands of others. It contrasts with how Western state systems of justice

deal with such losses. In the case of Billy and Malo, the response of the Papua New Guinea state was that the police did not concern themselves with the grieving or vengeful feelings of Billy's relatives but did charge Malo with dangerous driving. Although Billy's family, including his uncle Genjimp, who had actually been present at the accident scene, didn't blame Malo's driving, the police nevertheless claimed that Malo had been driving too fast. For many months Malo remained in his village, except for when he came into town to talk to the police. That's because Malo was still afraid of possible retaliation by hot-headed young lowlanders. Malo's fellow villagers remained alert and ready to protect him in case of such an attack.

After the initial police hearing, several months passed until the second hearing, at which Malo was ordered to come into town twice a week to report to the traffic officer while waiting for his case to come up for trial. Each such reporting visit ended with Malo waiting in the traffic office for between half a day and a full day. Malo's driving license was taken away from him at the second hearing. Because Malo's job with the company was as a driver, the loss of his license also cost Malo his job.

The dangerous-driving case against Malo finally came up for trial a year and a half later. During that time, Malo continued to live in limbo in his village, unemployed. When Malo did appear at court on the appointed date for trial, it turned out that the responsible judge was busy with a conflicting obligation, and the trial date had to be rescheduled for three months later. Again on that rescheduled second date, the judge was unable to be present, and another trial date was set three months later. That third date and still another trial date had to be postponed because of further problems involving the judge. Finally, on the fifth date set for trial, now two and a half years after the accident, the judge did appear, and the case was heard. But the police called by the prosecutor did not appear, and so the judge had to dismiss the case. That ended the state's involvement with the matter of Billy and Malo. Lest you think that such no-shows and postponements mark the Papua New Guinea judicial system as uniquely inefficient, a close friend of mine recently on trial in Chicago experienced a similar course and outcome of his criminal proceedings.

New Guinea compensation

The traditional compensation process, illustrated by the story of Billy and Malo, has as its aims the dispute's speedy peaceful resolution, emotional reconciliation between the two sides, and restoration of their previous relationship. This sounds simple, natural, and appealing to us, until we reflect how fundamentally it differs from the aims of our state systems of justice. Traditional New Guinea didn't possess a state system of justice, a state government, a centralized political system, or professional leaders and bureaucrats and judges exercising decision-making powers and claiming a monopoly on the right to use force. States have their own separate interests in settling disputes and administering justice among their citizens. Those state interests don't necessarily coincide with the interests of either participant in a dispute. Traditional New Guinea justice is, instead, of the do-it-yourself sort, arranged by the disputants themselves and by their respective supporters. The compensation process is one prong, the peaceful one, of the two-pronged system of traditional dispute resolution. The other prong (Chapters 3 and 4) is to seek personal retribution by violence, tending to escalate into cycles of counter-retribution and ultimately war.

An essential fact shaping the traditional New Guinea compensation process, and distinguishing it from Western disputes, is that the participants in almost any traditional New Guinea dispute were previously known to each other, either from already having been involved in some sort of personal relationship, or at least from knowing of each other by name or father's name or group affiliation. For instance, even if you as a New Guinean don't personally know the man in the village a few miles away who killed your pig while it was wandering in the forest, you surely have heard of him by name, you know of the clan to which he belongs, and you personally know some members of that clan. That's because traditional New Guinea consisted of small-scale localized societies of a few dozen to a few hundred individuals. People traditionally maintained their area of residence for life or else moved short distances just for specific reasons, such as for marriage or to join relatives. Traditional New Guineans rarely or never encountered complete "strangers," as do we citizens of modern state societies. But we citizens of Westernized states, unlike New Guineans, live in societies of millions, so of course we daily encounter and have to deal with previously unknown members of our own society. Even in sparsely inhabited rural areas where all the residents know each other, such as Montana's Big Hole Basin, where I spent summers as a teen-ager, strangers routinely appear—e.g., someone driving through town and stopping to fill his car with gas. Furthermore, we move long distances for work, vacation, or just personal preference and thereby undergo almost complete turnovers of our circle of contacts repeatedly throughout our lives.

As a result, whereas in state societies most of our disputes arising from car accidents or business transactions are with strangers whom we didn't know previously and with whom we shall never have dealings again, in traditional New Guinea any dispute is with someone with whom you will continue to have an actual or potential relationship in the future. At the maximum, your dispute will be with someone, such as a fellow villager, whom you encounter repeatedly and with whom you can't avoid having continued daily dealings. At minimum, the other party in the dispute will be someone whom you won't have to encounter repeatedly in the future (e.g., that villager a few miles distant who killed your pig), but that person still lives within traveling distance of you, and you at least want to be able to count on having no more trouble with him. That's why the main aim of traditional New Guinea compensation is to restore the previous relationship, even if it was merely a "non-relationship" that consisted only of giving each other no trouble despite the potential for doing so. But that aim, and the essential facts underlying it, represent a huge difference from Western state systems of dispute resolution, in which restoring a relationship is usually irrelevant because there wasn't any relationship before and there won't be any again in the future. For instance, in my lifetime I have become involved in three civil disputes—with a cabinet-maker, with a swimming-pool contractor, and with a real estate agent—in which I didn't know the other party involved before the disputed transaction involving cabinets or a pool or real estate, and I haven't had any further contact with them or even heard of them after our dispute was resolved or dropped.

For New Guineans, the key element in restoring a damaged relationship is an acknowledgment of and respect for each other's feelings, so that the two parties can clear the air of anger as well as possible under the circumstances and get on with their former involvement or non-involvement. Although the payment cementing the restored relationship is now universally referred to in Papua New Guinea by the English word "compensation," that term is misleading. The payment is actually a symbolic means to reestablish the previous relationship: side A "says sorry" to side B and acknowledges B's feelings by incurring its own loss, consisting of the compensation paid. For instance, in the case of Billy and Malo, what Billy's father really wanted was for Malo and his employers to acknowledge the great loss and grief that he had suffered. As Gideon said explicitly to Billy's father in turning over to him the compensation, the money was worthless rubbish compared to the value of Billy's life; it was just a way of saying sorry and sharing in Billy's family's loss.

Reestablishing relationships counts for everything in traditional New Guinea, and establishing guilt or negligence or punishment according to Western concepts is not the main issue. That perspective helps explain the resolution, astonishing to me when I learned of it, of a long-running dispute between some New Guinea mountain clans, one of the clans being my friends at Goti Village. My Goti friends had become embroiled with four other clans in a long series of raids and reciprocal killings, in the course of which the father and an older brother of my Goti friend Pius were killed. The situation became so dangerous that most of my Goti friends fled from their ancestral lands and took refuge among allies at a neighboring village in order to escape from further attacks. Not until 33 years later did the Gotis feel safe enough to move back to their ancestral lands. Three years after that, to put a definitive end to living under fear of raids, they hosted at Goti a ceremony of reconciliation, in which the Gotis paid compensation of pigs and other goods to their former attackers.

When Pius told me this story, I at first couldn't believe my ears and was sure that I had misunderstood him. "*You* paid *them* compensation?" I asked him. "But *they* killed *your* father and other relatives; why aren't *they* paying *you*?" No, explained Pius, that's not how it works; the goal wasn't to extract payment for its own sake, nor to pretend to equalize accounts by A receiving X pigs from B after B has inflicted Y deaths on A. The goal was instead to reestablish peaceful relations between recent enemies, and to make it possible to live safely again at Goti Village. The enemy clans had their own complaints over claimed encroachment on their land, and over the killing of some of their own members by Goti people. After negotiations, both parties declared themselves satisfied and willing to set aside their hard feelings; on the basis of that agreement under which the enemy clans received pigs and other goods, the Goti people reclaimed their former lands, and both sides could live in freedom from further attacks.

Life-long relationships

In traditional New Guinea society, because networks of social relationships tend to be more important and lasting than in Western state societies, the consequences of disputes are prone to radiate beyond the immediate participants to a degree difficult for Westerners to understand. To us Westerners, it seems absurd that the damaging of the garden of a member of one clan by a pig belonging to a member of another clan could trigger a war between the two clans; to New Guinea Highlanders, that outcome is unsurprising. New Guineans tend to retain for life the important relationships into which they are born. Those relationships give each New Guinean support from many other people, but also bring obligations towards many other people. Of course we modern Westerners also have long-lasting social relationships, but we acquire and shed relationships throughout our lives much more than do New Guineans, and we live in a society rewarding individuals who seek to get ahead. Hence in New Guinea disputes the parties who receive or pay compensation are not just the immediate participants concerned, such as Malo and Billy's parents, but also more distantly related people on both sides: Billy's clansmen, from whom payback killings were feared; Malo's fellow workers, who were the potential targets of retaliation, and whose employer actually paid the compensation; and any member of Malo's extended family or clan, who would have been both a target of retaliation and a source of compensation payments if Malo had not been employed by a business. Similarly, if in New Guinea a married couple is considering a divorce, then other people are affected and get involved in the arguments about divorce far more than in the West. Those others include the husband's relatives, who paid the bride-price and will now demand its repayment; the wife's relatives, who received the bride-price and will now face demands for its repayment;

and both clans, for whom the marriage may have represented a significant political alliance, and for whom the divorce would thus constitute a threat to that alliance.

The flip side of that overriding emphasis on social networks in traditional societies is our greater emphasis on the individual in modern state societies, especially in the United States. We not only permit, we actually encourage, individuals to advance themselves, to win, and to gain advantages at the expense of others. In many of our business transactions we aim to maximize our own profit, and never mind the feelings of the person on the other side of the table on whom we have succeeded in inflicting a loss. Even children's games in the U.S. commonly are contests of winning and losing. That isn't so in traditional New Guinea society, where children's play involves cooperation rather than winning and losing.

For instance, the anthropologist Jane Goodale watched a group of children (the Kaulong people of New Britain) who had been given a bunch of bananas sufficient to provide one banana for each child. The children proceeded to play a game. Instead of a contest in which each child sought to win the biggest banana, each child cut his/her banana into two equal halves, ate one half, offered the other half to another child, and in turn received half of that child's banana. Then each child proceeded to cut that uneaten half of the banana into two equal quarters, ate one of the quarters, offered the other quarter to another child, and received another child's uneaten quarter banana in return. The game went on for five cycles, as the residual piece of banana was broken into equal eighths, then into equal sixteenths, until finally each child ate the stub representing one-thirty-second of the original banana, gave the other thirty-second to another child to eat, and received and ate the last thirty-second of another banana from still another child. That whole play ritual was part of the practising by which New Guinea children learn to share, and not to seek an advantage for themselves.

As another example of traditional New Guinea society's deemphasis of individual advantage, a hard-working and ambitious teen-ager called Mafuk worked for me for a couple of months. When I paid him his salary and asked him what he intended to do with the money, he answered that he was going to buy a sewing machine with which he would mend other people's torn clothes. He would charge them for the repairs, thereby recoup and multiply his initial investment, and start accumulating money to improve his lot in life. But Mafuk's relatives were outraged at what they considered his selfishness. Naturally, in that sedentary society the people whose clothes Mafuk would be mending would be people whom he already knew, most of them his close or distant relatives. It violated New Guinea societal norms for Mafuk to advance himself by taking money from them. Instead, he was expected to mend their clothes for free, and in turn they would support him in other ways throughout his life, such as by contributing to his bride-price obligation when he married. Similarly, gold miners in Gabon who don't share their gold and money with jealous friends and relatives become targets of sorcerers believed responsible for causing their victims to contract the usually fatal disease Ebola hemorrhagic fever.

When Western missionaries who have lived in New Guinea with their young children return to Australia or the United States, or when they send their children back to Australia or the U.S. to attend boarding school, the children tell me that their biggest adjustment problem is to deal with and adopt the West's selfish individualistic ways, and to shed the emphasis on cooperation and sharing that they have learned among New Guinea children. They describe feeling ashamed of themselves if they play competitive games in order to win, or if they try to excel in school, or if they seek an advantage or opportunity that their comrades don't achieve.

Other non-state societies

What about differences in dispute resolution among non-state societies? While resort to mediation, as in the case of Billy and Malo, may work well in traditional New Guinea villages, it may be either unnecessary or ineffective in other types of societies. It turns out that there is a virtual continuum, from small societies with no centralized authority or justice system, through chiefdoms in which the chief resolves many disputes, on to weak states in which individuals often still take justice into their own hands, and concluding with strong states exercising effective authority. Let us consider peaceful dispute resolution in five different non-state societies, ranging from ones smaller than New Guinea villages to a large society with the beginnings of political centralization (Plate 15).

We begin with disputes in the smallest societies, consisting of local groups with just a few dozen members. The !Kung (Plate 6) impressed a visiting anthropologist as a society in which people talked constantly, disputes were in the open, and everybody in the band became involved in disputes between any two band members. The anthropologist happened to visit for a month when a husband and wife were unhappy with each other, and when other band members (all of them somehow related to the husband or wife or both) were constantly joining in the couple's arguments. A year later, the anthropologist returned for another visit, to find the couple still together, still unhappy with each other, and other band members still involved in the resulting arguments.

The Siriono of Bolivia, who also lived in small groups, were also described as quarreling constantly, especially between husband and wife, between co-wives of the same husband, between in-laws, and between children within the same extended family. Of 75 Siriono disputes witnessed, 44 were over food (failing to share it, hoarding it, stealing it, eating it secretly at night in camp, or stealing off into the forest to eat it secretly there); 19 were over sex, especially over adultery; and only 12 disputes were over something other than food or sex. Without an arbiter, most Siriono disputes were settled between the disputants, occasionally with the involvement of a relative joining to support one side. If enmity between two families in the same camp became intense, one family might move out of camp to live separately in the forest until hostile feelings subsided. If enmity still persisted, one family split off to join another band or to form a new band. That illustrates an important generalization: among nomadic hunter-gatherers and other mobile groups, disputes within a group can be settled just by the group dividing so that disputants move apart. That option is difficult for settled village farmers with a big investment in their gardens, and even more difficult for us Western citizens tied to our jobs and houses.

Among still another small group, Brazil's Piraha Indians (Plate 11), social pressure to behave by the society's norms and to settle disputes is applied by graded ostracism. That begins with excluding someone from food-sharing for a day, then for several days, then making the person live some distance away in the forest, deprived of normal trade and social exchanges. The most severe Piraha sanction is complete ostracism. For instance, a Piraha teen-ager named Tukaaga killed an Apurina Indian named Joaquim living nearby, and thereby exposed the Piraha to the risk of a retaliatory attack. Tukaaga was then forced to live apart from all other Piraha villages, and within a month he died under mysterious circumstances, supposedly of catching a cold, but possibly instead murdered by other Piraha who felt endangered by Tukaaga's deed.

My next-to-last example involves the Fore, a New Guinea Highland group among whom I worked in the 1960s, and who live at a considerably higher population density, and hence appear to be more aggressive, than the !Kung, Siriono, or Piraha. The Fore were studied between 1951 and 1953 by a husband-and-wife anthropologist couple, Ronald and Catherine Berndt, at a time when fighting was still going on in the area. Without a central authority or formal mechanism to deal with offenses, Fore dispute resolution within a clan or lineage was of the do-it-yourself variety. For instance, the responsibility for defending one's property against theft rested on the owner. While theft was condemned by community standards, it was up to the owner to seek compensation in pigs or another form. The magnitude of compensation was not standardized to the value of the object stolen but depended on the relative strength of the offender and the offended, on past grudges, and on how the thief's kin regarded the thief and whether they were likely to support him.

A Fore dispute was likely to drag in people other than the two initially concerned. In the case of dissension between a husband and wife, the kin of both would become involved but could themselves experience conflicting interests. While a man belonging to the same clan as the husband might support his fellow clansman (the husband) against his clansman's wife, he might instead support the wife against the husband because of having contributed to the bride payment to acquire the wife for the clan. Hence disputes within a lineage were usually under pressure to be settled quickly, by payment of compensation, exchanging gifts, or holding a feast to signal the reestablishment of friendly relations. Disputes between two lineages of the same district could also be settled by payment of compensation, but (as we shall see in the next two chapters) the risk of resort to violence was higher than if the dispute were within a lineage, because of less pressure for settlement being applied by other people.

The last of the non-state societies that I compare here is the Nuer of the Sudan (Plate 7), who numbered about 200,000 people (divided into many tribes) when studied by the anthropologist E. E. Evans-Pritchard in the 1930s. Among the five societies, they are the largest, the one with apparently the highest prevalence of formalized violence, and the only one with a formally recognized political leader, termed a "leopard-skin chief." The Nuer are quick to feel insulted, and the admired way for men to settle disputes within a village is by fighting with clubs until either one man is badly injured, or (usually) until other villagers intervene and pull the fighters apart.

The most serious offense among the Nuer is a killing, which triggers a blood-feud: if X kills Y, Y's relatives are obliged to seek vengeance by killing X and/or one of X's close relatives. Hence a killing marks a dispute not only between the killer and the slain but also among all the close relatives of both, and among their whole communities. Immediately after a killing, the killer, knowing that he is now a target for revenge, takes asylum in the chief's house, where he is immune from attack—but his enemies keep watch to spear him if he should make the mistake of leaving the chief's house. The chief waits a few weeks for tempers to cool (similar to the briefer delay in the case of Billy's death in New Guinea that I related), then opens negotiations for compensation between the killer's relatives and the victim's relatives. The usual compensation for a death is 40 or 50 cows.

However, it is crucial to understand that a Nuer chief has no authority to rule, to decide the merits of a dispute, or to impose a settlement. Instead, the chief is just a mediator who is used if and only if both parties want to reach a settlement and to return to the pre-existing state of affairs. The chief elicits from one side a proposal, which the other side usually refuses. Eventually, the chief urges one side to accept the other side's offer, and the former side does so with a show of reluctance, insisting that it is doing so only to honor the chief. That is, the chief provides a face-saving way to accept a compromise necessary for the good of the community. A feud cannot be tolerated within a village and is difficult to sustain for long between nearby villages. But the greater the distance between the two lineages involved, the more difficult it becomes to settle the feud (because there is less desire to restore normal relations), and the more likely is the initial killing to escalate to further violence.

The Nuer leopard-skin chief may also be used to mediate lesser disputes, such as ones over stealing cattle, clubbing someone, or a bride's family failing after a divorce to return the bride-price cows that they received at the time of marriage. However, Nuer disputes do not pose clear issues of deciding between right and wrong. If for instance the dispute is about stealing cattle, the thief does not deny the theft but instead boldly justifies it by invoking some score to be settled: a previous theft of cattle by the present owner or the owner's relatives, or some debt (e.g., as compensation for adultery, for an injury, for having sex with an unmarried girl, for divorce, for claimed underpayment or non-return of bride-price, or for a wife's death in childbirth which is considered the husband's responsibility). Just as Nuer compensation does not involve right or wrong, the offended party will not succeed in extracting his compensation unless he is prepared to use force, and unless it is feared that he and his kin will resort to violence if not compensated. As with the Fore, self-help or do-it-yourself is the basis of Nuer dispute resolution.

Compared to the other four non-state societies discussed here, the role of Nuer chiefs suggests a first step towards dispute adjudication. But it is worth re-emphasizing the features of state dispute adjudication still absent among the Nuer, as among most other non-state societies except for strong chiefdoms. The Nuer chief has no authority to settle the dispute, and is just a mediator, a means to save face and promote a cool-off period if both parties so desire, as was also true of Yaghean's role in the dispute between Billy's family and Malo's employer. The Nuer chief has no monopoly on force, nor indeed any means to apply force at all; the disputing parties are still the ones able to use force. The aim of Nuer dispute resolution is not to decide right or wrong, but to re-establish normal relations in a society where everyone knows or at least knows of everyone else, and where persistence of ill will between any two members of the society endangers the society's stability. All these limitations of Nuer tribal chiefs change when one encounters more populous chiefdoms (such as those of large Polynesian islands and large Native American polities), whose chiefs hold real political and judicial power, assert a monopoly on the use of force, and represent potential intermediate stages towards the origins of state government.

State authority

Let's now compare those non-state systems of dispute resolution with the systems of states. Just as the various non-state systems that we discussed share features in common while differing among themselves in other respects, state systems also share other common themes amidst their diversity. My comments about state dispute resolution will mostly be based on the system most familiar to me, that of the United States, but I shall mention some differences in other state systems.

Both state dispute resolution and non-state dispute resolution have two alternative procedures: mechanisms for reaching mutual agreement between the disputing parties, and then (if those mechanisms are attempted but fail) mechanisms for reaching a contested solution. In non-state societies the flip side of the compensation process for reaching mutual agreement is escalating violence (Chapters 3, 4). Non-state societies lack formal central state mechanisms for preventing dissatisfied individuals from pursuing their aims by violent means. Because one act of violence tends to provoke another, violence escalates and becomes an endemic threat to peace in non-state societies. Hence a prime concern of effective state government is to guarantee or at least improve public safety by preventing the state's citizens from using force against each other. In order to maintain internal peace and safety, the central political authority of the state claims a near-monopoly on the right to use retaliatory force: only the state and its police are permitted (with sufficient cause) to employ violent retaliatory measures against the state's own citizens. However, states do permit citizens to use force to defend themselves: e.g., if citizens are attacked first, or if they reasonably believe that they or their property are in imminent serious danger.

Citizens are dissuaded in two ways from resorting to private violence: by fear of the state's superior power; and by becoming convinced that private violence is unnecessary, because the state has established a system of justice perceived to be impartial (at least in theory), guaranteeing to citizens the safety of their person and their property, and labeling as wrong-doers and punishing those who damage the safety of others. If the state does those things effectively, then injured citizens may feel less or no need to resort to do-it-yourself justice, New Guinea–style and Nuer-style. (But in weaker states whose citizens lack confidence that the state will respond effectively, such as Papua New Guinea today, citizens are likely to continue traditional tribal practices of private violence.) Maintenance of peace within a society is one of the most important services that a state can provide. That service goes a long way towards explaining the apparent paradox that, since the rise of the first state governments in the Fertile Crescent about 5,400 years ago, people have more or less willingly (not just under duress) surrendered some of their individual freedoms, accepted the authority of state governments, paid taxes, and supported a comfortable individual lifestyle for the state's leaders and officials.

An example of the behavior that state governments aim to prevent at all costs was the Ellie Nesler case in the small town of Jamestown, California, a hundred miles east of San Francisco. Ellie (Plate 35) was the mother of a six-year-old son, William, whom a camp counselor named Daniel Driver was suspected of sexually molesting at a Christian summer camp. At a preliminary courtroom hearing on April 2, 1993, at which Daniel was being charged with abusing William and three other boys, Ellie fired five shots at close range into Daniel's head, killing him instantly. That constituted retaliatory force: Ellie was not defending her son against an attack in progress, nor against the imminent prospect of an attack, but she was retaliating *after* a suspected event. In her defense, Ellie declared that her son had been so distraught over being abused that he was vomiting and incapable of testifying against Daniel. She feared that Daniel would go free, and she lacked faith in an inept justice system that had allowed a sexual predator with a history of such behavior to remain at large and continue his crimes.

Ellie's case provoked a national debate on vigilantism, with her defenders hailing her for exacting her own justice, and her critics condemning her for doing so. Every parent will understand Ellie's outrage and feel some sympathy for her, and probably most parents of an abused child have fantasies of doing exactly what Ellie did. But the view of the state of California was that only the state had the authority to judge and punish the abuser, and that (however understandable Ellie's rage) state government would collapse if citizens took justice into their own hands, as Ellie did. She was tried and convicted of manslaughter and served 3 years of a 10-year sentence before being released on appeal based on jury misconduct.

Thus, the overriding goal of state justice is to maintain society's stability by providing a mandatory alternative to do-it-yourself justice. All other goals of state justice are secondary to that main one. In particular, the state has less or no interest in the overriding goal of justice in small-scale non-state societies: to restore a pre-existing relationship or non-relationship (e.g., by promoting an exchange of feelings) between disputing parties who already knew or knew of each other and must continue to deal with each other. Hence non-state dispute resolution is not primarily a system of justice in the state sense: that is, a system to decide right and wrong, according to a state's laws. Bearing in mind those different overriding goals, how similar are state and non-state systems of dispute resolution in their operation?

State civil justice

A starting point is to realize that state justice is divided into two systems, which often employ different courts, judges, lawyers, and bodies of the law: criminal justice and civil justice. Criminal justice is concerned with crimes against the state's laws, punishable by the state. Civil justice is concerned with non-criminal injuries inflicted by one individual (or group) on another, and further subdivided into two types of actions: contract cases, resulting from breach of a contract, and often or usually involving money; and tort cases, resulting from injury done to a person herself or to her property through the action of another person. The state's distinction between criminal and civil actions is gray in a non-state society, which has societal norms of behavior between individuals but does not have codified laws defining crimes against a formally defined institution, the state. Compounding the grayness is that an injury to an individual is likely to affect other individuals as well, and small societies are much more concerned than are state societies with those effects on others—as exemplified by the case I related of everyone in a !Kung band being affected by and joining the arguments between an unhappy husband and wife. (Imagine if a judge in a California divorce court were to take testimony about how the divorce would affect everybody in town.) In New Guinea, essentially the same system for negotiating compensation is used to deal with the intentional killing of one person by another, the repayment of a bride-price after a divorce, and one man's pig damaging another man's garden (respectively a crime, a contract, and a tort in Western courts).

Let's begin by comparing state and non-state systems for civil disputes. One similarity is that both use third parties to mediate, to separate the disputing parties, and thereby to promote cooling-off. Those intermediaries are experienced negotiators like Yaghean in New Guinea, leopard-skin chiefs among the Nuer, and lawyers in state courts. In fact, states have other types of intermediaries besides lawyers: many disputes are handled outside the court system by third parties such as arbitrators, mediators, and insurance adjusters. Despite Americans' reputation for being litigious, the great majority of civil disputes in the U.S. are settled outside the courts or before going to trial. Some professions consisting of a small number of members monopolizing a resource—such as Maine lobster fishermen, cattle ranchers, and diamond traders—commonly settle member disputes by themselves without state involvement. Only if third-party negotiation fails to produce a settlement mutually agreeable to the parties do they resort to their society's method of dealing with a dispute without a mutual agreement: violence or war in a non-state society, and a trial or formal adjudication in a state society.

A further similarity is that both state and non-state societies often spread the cost owed by the offending party over many other payers. In state societies we purchase automobile and homeowner insurance policies that pay the costs if our car injures a person or another car, or if someone is injured by falling on our house's steps that we negligently left slippery. We and many others pay insurance premiums that permit the insurance company to pay those costs, so that in effect other policy-holders share our liability and vice versa. Similarly, in non-state societies the relatives and fellow clan members share in payments owed by an individual: for instance, Malo told me that his fellow villagers would have contributed to the compensation payment for Billy's death if Malo hadn't been working for a company able to make the payment.

In state societies the civil cases whose courses are most similar to that of a New Guinea compensation negotiation are business disputes between parties involved in a long-term business relationship. When an issue arises that such business parties cannot work out by themselves, one party may become angry and consult an attorney. (That's much more likely in the U.S. than in Japan and other countries.) Especially in a long-term relationship in which there has been a build-up of trust, the aggrieved party feels taken advantage of, betrayed, and even more angry than if it were just a "one-off" relationship (i.e., the first business encounter for the parties). As in a New Guinea compensation negotiation, channeling business-dispute discussions through lawyers cools off the dispute by substituting (one hopes) calm reasoned statements of lawyers for angry personal recriminations of the parties, and reduces the risk that opposing positions will harden. When the parties have the prospect of continuing a profitable business relationship in the future, they are motivated to accept a face-saving solution—just as New Guineans in the same village or neighboring villages, expecting to continue to encounter each other for the rest of their lives, are motivated to find a solution. Nevertheless, lawyer friends tell me that a New Guinea–style genuine apology and emotional closure are rare even in business disputes, and that usually the most that can be expected is a scripted apology produced as a settlement tactic at a late stage. If, however, business parties are involved in a one-off relationship and never expect to deal with each other again, then their motivation for amicable settlement is lower (just as is true of New Guinea or Nuer disputes between members of distant tribes), and the risk increases that the dispute will proceed to the state's equivalent of war: a trial. Nevertheless, trials and adjudications are expensive, their outcomes are unpredictable, and even one-off business disputants experience pressures to settle.

Yet another parallel between state and non-state dispute resolution involves international disputes between states (as opposed to disputes between fellow citizens within the same state). While some international disputes are now settled by the International Court of Justice by agreement of the governments involved, others are dealt with by essentially the traditional approach operating on a large scale: direct negotiations or mediated negotiations between the parties, aware that failure of the negotiations may trigger the flip-side mechanism of war. Prime examples are the 1938 dispute between Hitler's Germany and Czechoslovakia over the Czech border region of Sudetenland with an ethnic German majority, resolved by mediation by Britain and France (which pressured their Czech ally to settle); and the series of European crises in the years before World War I, each temporarily settled by negotiation until the 1914 crisis provoked by the assassination of Archduke Franz Ferdinand did end in war.

Those are some of the parallels between non-state dispute resolution and state civil justice. As for the differences, the most basic is that, if a civil case does pass from the negotiating stage to trial, then the state's concern at the trial is not primarily with emotional clearance, restoring good relations, or promoting a mutual understanding of feelings between the disputing parties—even when the parties are siblings, estranged spouses, parents and children, or neighbors who share a huge emotional investment in each other and may have to deal with each other for the rest of their lives. Of course, in many or most cases in populous state societies, consisting of millions of citizens who are strangers to each other, the people involved had no prior relationship, don't anticipate any future relationship, and were brought together just on a one-shot basis by the event underlying the case: a customer and a merchant, two drivers involved in a traffic accident, a criminal and a victim, and so on. Yet the underlying event and the subsequent judicial proceedings still create a legacy of feelings in both of those strangers, and the state does little or nothing to assuage the feelings.

Instead, at a trial the state is first concerned with determining right or wrong (Plate 16). If the case involves a contract, did or did not the defendant breach the contract? If the case involves a tort, was or was not the defendant negligent, or did the defendant at least cause the injury? Note the contrast between that first question asked by the state and the case of Malo and Billy. Billy's relatives agreed that Malo had not been negligent, but they still requested compensation, and Malo's employer immediately agreed to pay compensation—because the goal of both parties was to reestablish a previous relationship (in this case, a previous non-relationship) rather than to debate right or wrong. That feature of New Guinea peace-making applies to many other traditional societies as well. For example, in the words of Chief Justice Robert Yazzie of the Navajo Nation, one of the two most populous Native American communities of North America, "Western adjudication is a search for what happened and who did it; Navajo peace-making is about the effect of what happened. Who got hurt? What do they feel about it? What can be done to repair the harm?"

Once the state has resolved that first step of determining whether the defendant is legally liable in a civil dispute, the state then proceeds to the second step of calculating the damages owed by the defendant if the defendant is found to have breached the contract or been negligent or liable. The purpose of the calculation is described as "making the plaintiff whole"—i.e., insofar as is possible, to restore the plaintiff to the condition that she would have been in if there had been no breach or negligence. For instance, suppose that the seller signed a contract to sell to the buyer 100 chickens at $7 per chicken, that the seller then breached the contract by failing to deliver the chickens, and that the buyer as a result had to buy 100 chickens at the higher price of $10 per chicken on the open market, thereby forcing the buyer to spend an extra $300 above the contractual amount. In a court case the seller would be ordered to pay to the buyer those damages of $300, plus costs incurred in securing the new contract, plus perhaps interest for the lost use of that $300, thereby restoring the buyer (at least nominally) to the position in which he would have been if the seller had not breached the contract. Similarly, in the case of a tort, the court will attempt to calculate the damages, although that is more difficult to calculate for physical or emotional injury to a person than for damage to property. (I recall a lawyer friend of mine who was defending a motorboat-owner whose motorboat propeller had severed the leg of an elderly swimmer, and who argued to the jury that the value of the severed leg was modest because of the victim's advanced age and short expected remaining lifespan even before the accident.)

Superficially, the state's calculation of damages seems similar to compensation negotiated in New Guinea or among the Nuer. But that is not necessarily true. Whereas the standardized compensation for some New Guinea and Nuer offenses (e.g., 40 to 50 Nuer cows for taking a person's life) could be construed as damages, in other cases non-state compensation is calculated as whatever amount the disputing parties agree on as the basis for putting behind them their injured feelings and resuming their relationship: e.g., the pigs and other goods that my Goti Village friends agreed to pay *to* the clans that had killed the father of my Goti friend Pius.

Defects in state civil justice

The defects in our state system of civil justice are widely discussed by lawyers, judges, plaintiffs, and defendants alike. The defects of the American system are variously more or less severe in other state societies. One problem is that court resolution of civil disputes tends to take a long time, often up to five years, because criminal cases take precedence over civil cases, and judges may get re-assigned from civil court to criminal court in order to try criminal cases. For instance, at the time that I drafted this paragraph, no civil cases were being tried in Riverside County just east of my home city of Los Angeles because of a backlog of criminal cases. That means five years of irresolution, living in limbo, and emotional torment, compared to the five days that it took to settle the case of Malo's accidental killing of Billy. (However, the clan warfare that might have resulted if Malo's and Billy's case hadn't been resolved by negotiation could have lasted much longer than five years.)

A second claimed defect of state civil justice in the U.S. is that, in most cases, it fails to require the losing party to pay the lawyers' fees of the successful party, unless that had been specified at the outset in the contract under dispute. That failure, it is often argued, creates an asymmetry favoring the wealthier party (whether that is the plaintiff or the defendant), and placing pressure on a less wealthy plaintiff to settle for less than the actual loss, and on a less wealthy defendant to settle by paying a frivolous claim. That's because wealthy parties threaten expensive litigation, adopt delaying tactics, and file endless discovery motions in order to wear down the other party financially. It is illogical that the goal of civil justice should be to make the aggrieved party whole, but that the loser should not be required to pay the winner's attorney fees in the U.S. In contrast, legal systems in Britain and some other countries require the loser to pay at least some of the winner's fees and costs.

The remaining defect of state civil justice is the most fundamental one:

that it is concerned with damages, and that emotional closure and reconciliation are secondary or irrelevant. For civil disputes pitting against each
other strangers who will never encounter each other again (e.g., two people whose cars collide), in some cases something could be done to promote
emotional closure and avoid a life-long legacy of non-resolution, even if it
merely involved offering both parties the opportunity (if they consent) to
air their feelings to each other, and to perceive each other as humans with
their own motives and sufferings. That can be possible even under such
extreme circumstances as when one of the parties has killed a close relative of the other party. Better than no emotional exchange at all was the
exchange that did take place between Gideon and Billy's father—or the
exchange between Senator Edward Kennedy and Mary Jo Kopechne's parents, when Kennedy on his own private initiative courageously visited and
looked into the faces of the parents whose daughter's death he had caused
through his own gross negligence.

Worst of all are the innumerable civil cases in which the parties in a
dispute do potentially have the prospect of an on-going relationship: notably, divorcing couples with children, siblings in inheritance disputes,
business partners, and neighbors. Far from helping to resolve feelings,
court proceedings often make feelings worse than they were before. All of
us know disputants whose relationship became poisoned for the rest of
their lives by their court experience. In merely the latest in a long list of
such stories among my own acquaintances, one close friend of mine and
her sister were subpoenaed in an inheritance court case between her
brother and her father, who were suing each other. The bitterness left by
those judicial proceedings was such that my friend and her sister are now
being sued by their own stepmother, and that both my friend and her
sister expect never again to speak to their brother as long as they live.

One suggestion often made about how to mitigate this fundamental
defect of our civil justice is to make increased use of mediation programs.
They do exist, and they are often helpful. But we don't have enough mediators and family-law judges, our mediators are undertrained, and our
family courts are understaffed and underfunded. As a result, divorcing
couples often end up talking to each other only through their lawyers.
Anyone who has repeatedly visited family-law courts knows that the scene
there can be horrible. Opposite parties in a divorce case, their lawyers, and

their children may have to wait in the same waiting room with each other, and with disputants in inheritance cases. To mediate effectively, one must make the parties feel comfortable first: that's impossible if they have been glaring at each other for hours in the same waiting room. Children get caught in the middle of arguments between divorcing parents.

A judge can and often does require parties to participate in an attempted settlement conference before letting the case proceed to trial. But it takes time and skill for a mediator to make a mediation or settlement conference work. Mediation commonly requires much more time than is allowed for a mandatory settlement conference. Even if the parties in the dispute are not going to have any future relationship, successful mediation would decrease future burdens on the court system: burdens arising from the parties going to the expense of a trial, or else being dissatisfied with the decision and coming back to court with future complaints, or settling only after a long expensive fight.

If our state societies would pay for more mediation and more family-law judges, perhaps many divorce and inheritance cases could be resolved more cheaply and with fewer hurt feelings and more quickly, because the extra money and emotional energy and time required for mediation are likely to be less than the extra money and energy and time required for bitter court proceedings in the absence of mediation. Divorcing couples who agree to it and can afford it are able to obtain those advantages by opting out of the family-law court system, through hiring retired judges to settle their dispute. The retired judge conducts a pseudo-trial and commands a high hourly fee, but that fee would otherwise be dwarfed by weeks of lawyers' fees. The judge is there to hammer out a deal for everyone and isn't rushed as are our judges in family courts. The hearing is predictably timed: the parties know that it will take place at a certain hour, and they don't have to appear several hours ahead merely because they can't predict whether the judge will be running late on previous cases on the docket, as commonly happens in divorce courts.

I don't want to overstate the value of mediation, or to imply that it is a panacea. Mediation presents many problems of its own. Its outcome can be kept secret and so may not establish a judicial precedent or serve a broader educational purpose. Litigating parties who accept mediation know that, if mediation fails, the case will be litigated according to the usual criteria of legal right, wrong, guilt, and responsibility, so mediators do not feel entirely free to adopt different criteria. Many disputing parties want to be heard in court, do not want mediation, and resent being pressured or forced to mediate.

For example, in a famous case based on an incident in New York City on December 22, 1984, a man named Bernhard Goetz was approached by four young men whom he took to be muggers. He pulled out a gun, shot all four of them in claimed self-defense, and was subsequently indicted by a grand jury for attempted murder. His case provoked vigorous and divergent public discussion, some people praising him for having the courage to fight back, others condemning him for over-reaction and vigilantism. Only later did the background become known: Goetz had actually been mugged four years earlier by three young men who chased him and beat him severely. When one of those assailants was caught, the wily assailant filed a complaint claiming that he had instead been attacked by Goetz. Hence the court invited Goetz to a mediation hearing with his mugger. Goetz declined the invitation and was never told that the mugger was eventually jailed after committing another mugging. Goetz decided to buy a gun, having lost faith in a legal system that appeared to offer only mediation between muggers and their victims. While Goetz's case is unusual, it remains sadly true that our courts are so overburdened that they not infrequently do propose or mandate mediation for parties who are adamantly opposed to their case being mediated. But these facts should not blind us to the potential value of mediation in many cases, and to our underinvestment in this pathway.

I'll conclude this discussion of mediation and emotional closure by quoting comments on pros and cons by a lawyer colleague of mine, Professor Mark Grady of UCLA Law School: "Many people object that the state has no business concerning itself with damaged personal relationships and feelings. They argue that only a 'nanny state' would take on that task, and that for a state even to try to repair personal relationships and damaged feelings is a threat to liberty. They also argue that it is an infringement of people's liberty to be forced to settle their differences with wrongdoers. Instead, victims should have the right to seek the state's judgment against their adversaries and, having received that judgment, simply to walk away from those who have wronged them.

"A response is that states maintain costly systems of justice that serve

highly evolved and distinctive purposes in mass, non-face-to-face societies. Nevertheless, we can learn something valuable from New Guineans
without compromising the distinctive purposes of our justice systems.
Once the state takes jurisdiction over a dispute, it has incurred a cost to
settle that dispute. Why not at least give the parties the option to settle the
dispute on a personal level as well as on a legal level? No one should require
disputing parties to avail themselves of mediation systems that the state
might offer them, and the systems would not necessarily replace the usual
formal systems of adjudication unless the parties agreed that they should
do so. Instead, mediation systems would be an adjunct and possible substitute for a more formal legal system, which would still remain available.
There would be no harm in offering people this opportunity, and a lot of
good could come from it. The danger, which is well illustrated by the New
Guinea system, is that people could be coerced into mediation under circumstances that compromise their dignity and liberty, and that might
even extend the injustice of the original wrong. The reformed system
would have to safeguard against these abuses, but the possibility of these
abuses is no reason wholly to neglect the possibility that human wrongs
can be resolved on the human level."

State criminal justice

Having thus compared state and non-state dispute resolution systems
with respect to civil justice, let's now turn to criminal justice. Here we
immediately encounter two basic differences between state and non-state
systems. First, state criminal justice is concerned with punishing crimes
against the state's laws. The purpose of state-administered punishment is
to foster obedience to the state's laws and to maintain peace within the
state. A prison sentence imposed upon the criminal by the state doesn't,
and isn't intended to, compensate the victim for his injuries. Second, as a
result, state civil justice and criminal justice are separate systems, whereas
those systems are not distinct in non-state societies, which are generally
concerned with compensating individuals or groups for injuries—
regardless of whether the injury would in a state society be considered a
crime, a tort, or a breach of contract.

Just as is true of a state civil case, a state criminal case proceeds in two stages. In the first stage the court assesses whether the accused criminal is or is not guilty of one or more of the charges. That sounds black and white and seems to call for a yes-or-no answer. In practice, the decision is not so absolute, because there can be alternative charges differing in severity: a killer may be judged guilty of premeditated murder, killing of a police officer in the course of duty, killing in the course of an attempted kidnapping, killing as a spontaneous act of passion, killing in the sincere but unreasonable belief that the victim was threatening imminent and grave bodily injury, or killing as an act of temporary insanity or under conditions of diminished responsibility—with differing punishments according to the charge. In reality, many criminal cases are settled by plea-bargaining before coming to trial. But, if the case does come to trial, the charge still requires a verdict of guilty or not guilty: Ellie Nesler was found guilty of killing Daniel Driver, even though her motive of avenging the abuse of her son won her the sympathy of much of the public. In contrast, in non-state societies an injury inflicted is routinely viewed as something gray: yes, I did kill him but—I was justified, because he practiced sorcery on my child, or his cross-cousin killed my paternal uncle, or his pig damaged my garden and he refused to pay for the damages, so I owe his relatives no compensation or else lower compensation. (But similar mitigating circumstances do play a wide role at the sentencing stage of a Western criminal trial.)

If the accused is found guilty of a crime, the state then proceeds to the second stage of imposing a punishment, such as a prison sentence. The punishment's aims include serving three purposes, on which the relative emphasis differs between different national systems of justice: deterrence, retribution, and rehabilitation. These three purposes differ from the main purpose of non-state dispute resolution, namely, to compensate the victim. Even if Daniel Driver had been sentenced to prison, that wouldn't have compensated Ellie Nesler and her son for the trauma of the son's sexual abuse.

One major purpose of punishment for crimes is deterrence: to deter other citizens from breaking the state's laws, and thereby creating new victims. The wishes of the current victim and her relatives, or of the criminal and his relatives, are largely irrelevant: the punishment aims instead to serve that purpose of the state, as representative of the state's other citizens. At most, the victim, the criminal, and their relatives and friends may be permitted to address the judge at the time of sentencing, and to express their own desires about sentencing, but the judge is free to ignore those desires.

These separate interests of the state and of the victim are illustrated by a widely publicized criminal case brought by the state of California. The film director Roman Polanski was accused of drugging, raping, and sodomizing a 13-year-old girl (Samantha Geimer) in 1977, pleaded guilty in 1978 to the felony of having sex with a minor, but then fled to Europe before he could be sentenced. Polanski's victim, now a woman in her 40s, has said that she has forgiven him and doesn't want him prosecuted or imprisoned. She has filed a statement in court asking for dismissal of the case. While it may at first strike us as paradoxical that the state of California should seek to imprison a criminal against the explicit wishes of the crime's victim, the reasons for nevertheless doing so were stated forcefully in an editorial in the *Los Angeles Times*: "The case against Polanski was not brought to satisfy her [the victim's] desire for justice or her need for closure. It was brought by the state of California on behalf of the people of California. Even if Geimer no longer holds a grudge against Polanski, that doesn't mean he doesn't pose a continuing danger to others. . . . Crimes are committed not just against individuals but against the community. . . . People accused of serious crimes must be apprehended and tried and, if convicted, must face their sentences."

A second purpose of punishment, besides deterrence, is retribution: to enable the state to proclaim, "We, the state, are punishing the criminal, so you the victim have no excuse for trying to inflict punishment yourself." For reasons that are much debated, imprisonment rates are higher, and punishments more severe, in the U.S. than in other Western countries. The U.S. is the only Western country still applying the death penalty. My country often imposes long-term imprisonment or even life imprisonment, which in Germany is reserved for only the most heinous crimes (e.g., postwar Germany's worst case of serial murder, in which a nurse was convicted of killing 28 patients in a German hospital by injecting them with lethal drug mixtures). While long-term imprisonment in the U.S. has traditionally been reserved for serious crimes, the "three-strikes-and-you're-out" policy now adopted by my state of California *requires* judges to impose long terms on criminals convicted of a third felony following two serious felony convictions—even when the third offense is a minor one such as stealing a pizza. Partly as a result, the amount of money that California spends on its prison system is now approaching its expenditures on higher education in its colleges and universities. Californians opposed to this budgetary allocation consider it not only a reversal of human priorities but also a bad economic policy. They argue that California's current widely advertised economic woes might best be reduced by spending less money on keeping criminals imprisoned for long terms for minor offenses, spending more money on rehabilitating criminals and quickly returning them to productive jobs, and spending more money on educating non-imprisoned Californians to become capable of filling high-paying jobs. It is unclear whether these severe punishments in the U.S. are effective in promoting deterrence.

The remaining purpose behind punishing convicted criminals is to rehabilitate them, so that they can reenter society, resume a normal life, and make an economic contribution to society instead of imposing a heavy economic cost on society as prisoners of our costly prison system. Rehabilitation rather than retribution is the focus of European approaches to criminal punishment. For instance, a German court case forbade the showing of a documentary film accurately depicting a criminal's role in a notorious crime—because the criminal's right to demonstrate his rehabilitation, and to have a fair chance of making a healthy return to society after serving his prison term, was considered even more sacred than freedom of the press or the public's right to know. Does this outlook reflect greater European concern with human dignity, nurturing, and mercy, and lower European concern with Old Testament retribution and with free speech, compared to the U.S.? And how effective, really, is rehabilitation? For instance, its effectiveness seems limited in cases of pedophiles.

Restorative justice

Missing so far from our discussion of purposes of state criminal punishment has been mention of the main purposes of state civil justice (to make the injured party whole) and of non-state dispute resolution (to restore relationships and achieve emotional closure). Both of those purposes, which address needs of a crime's victim, are not the major goals of our criminal justice system, although there is some provision for them. In addition to furnishing testimony helpful in convicting an accused criminal, the victim or the victim's relatives may at the time of sentencing be permitted to address the court in the criminal's presence, and to describe the crime's emotional impact. As for making the victim whole, some state compensation funds for victims exist, but they are generally small.

For example, the most publicized criminal case in recent American history was the trial of ex-football star O. J. Simpson for the murder of his wife Nicole and her friend Ron Goldman. After a criminal trial lasting eight months, Simpson was found not guilty. But the families of Nicole and Ron then prevailed in a civil suit against Simpson on behalf of Simpson's and Nicole's children and of the families, and won (but had little success in collecting) a verdict totaling about $43,000,000. Unfortunately, cases of compensation being obtainable from a civil suit are exceptional, because most criminals are not wealthy and do not have significant assets that could be attached. In traditional societies the victim's chances of obtaining compensation are increased by the traditional philosophy of collective responsibility: as in Malo's case, not only the perpetrator but also the perpetrator's relatives, fellow clansmen, and associates are obliged to pay compensation. American society instead emphasizes individual responsibility over collective responsibility. In New Guinea, if my male cousin is deserted by his wife, I would be angrily demanding from the wife's clan the refund of the portion of her bride-price that I paid to acquire her for my cousin; as an American, I am glad not to share responsibility for the success of my cousins' marriages.

A promising approach towards bringing emotional closure in some cases, to both a criminal not condemned to death and to the surviving victim or the dead victim's closest relative, is a program called restorative justice. It views a crime as an offense against the victim or community as well as against the state; it brings the criminal and victim together to talk directly (provided that both are willing to do so), rather than keeping them apart and having lawyers speak for them; and it encourages criminals to accept responsibility, and victims to say how they have been affected, rather than discouraging those expressions or providing little opportunity for them. The criminal and the victim (or the victim's relative) meet in the presence of a trained mediator, who lays down ground rules such as no interrupting and no abusive language. The victim and the criminal sit face-to-face, look each other in the eye, and take turns relating to each other their life stories, their feelings, their motives, and the crime's effect on their subsequent lives. The criminal gets a flesh-and-blood view of the harm that he has caused; the victim sees the criminal as a human with a history and motives, rather than as an incomprehensible monster; and the criminal may come to connect the dots in his own history, and to understand what set him on a criminal path.

For instance, one such encounter in California brought together a 41-year-old widow, Patty O'Reilly, and her sister Mary, with a 49-year-old prisoner, Mike Albertson. Mike was serving a 14-year prison term for killing Patty's husband Danny two and a half years previously, by striking Danny from behind with Mike's truck while Danny was bicycling. Over the course of four hours, Patty told Mike her initial feelings of hatred towards him, the details of her husband's last words to her, how she and her two young daughters were brought the news of Danny's death by a sheriff's deputy, and how she was still reminded every day of Danny by such seeming trivia as hearing a song on the radio or seeing a bicyclist. Mike told Patty his life story of sexual abuse by his father, drug addiction, a broken back, running out of painkiller pills on the night of the killing, phoning and being rejected by his girlfriend, setting off drunk in his truck to check himself in at a hospital, seeing a bicyclist—and confessing that he may have hit Danny on purpose, in rage against his father, who had repeatedly raped him, and against his mother, who hadn't stopped it. At the end of the four hours, Patty summed up the process by saying, "Forgiving is hard, but not forgiving is harder." Over the next week she felt unburdened, empowered, and strong from having watched across a table her husband's killer see the devastation that he had caused. Thereafter, Mike felt alternately drained, depressed, and uplifted by Patty's willingness to meet and forgive him. Mike kept on his bedside table a card that Patty had brought him from her daughter Siobhan: "Dear Mr. Albertson, Today is the 16th of August and I will be 10 years old on September first. I just want to make sure you know that I forgive you. I do still miss my Dad, I think that's a life-long thing. I hope you're feeling OK. Bye bye, Siobhan."

Such restorative justice programs have been operating for up to 20 years in Australia, Canada, New Zealand, the United Kingdom, and various American states. There is still much experimentation going on—e.g., as to whether the meeting should involve just the criminal and the victim or should also involve relatives, friends, and teachers; whether the meeting takes place at an early stage (soon after arrest) or at a late stage (in prison, as in the case of Patty and Mike); and whether there is an effort at restitution by the criminal to the victim. There are many anecdotal accounts of outcomes, and some control tests that randomly assign criminals to one of several alternative programs or else to a control group with no such programs, and that then evaluate outcomes statistically. Favorable results reported in cumulative statistical analyses of cases by some programs include lower rates of further offenses being committed by the criminal, less severe offenses if any are committed, a decrease in the victim's feelings of anger and fear, and an increase in the victim's feelings of safety and closure. Not surprisingly, better results are obtained in cases in which the criminal is willing to meet the victim, actively participates in the meeting, and realizes the harm that he has done, than in cases in which the criminal unwillingly participates in a court-mandated meeting.

Naturally, restorative justice is not a panacea for all criminals and victims. It requires a trained facilitator. Some criminals do not feel remorse, and some victims would feel traumatized rather than helped by re-living the crime in the criminal's presence. Restorative justice is at best an adjunct to, not a substitute for, our criminal justice system. But it holds promise.

Advantages and their price

What conclusions can we draw from these comparisons of dispute resolution in states and in small-scale societies? On the one hand, in this area of dispute resolution as in the other areas to be discussed in succeeding chapters of this book, we should not naively idealize small-scale societies, view them as uniformly admirable, overstate their advantages, and castigate state government as at best a necessary evil. On the other hand, many small-scale societies do possess some features that we could profitably incorporate into our state societies.

At the outset, let me prevent misunderstanding and reiterate that dispute resolution even within modern industrial states already contains areas that utilize tribal-like dispute resolution mechanisms. When we have a dispute with a merchant, most of us don't immediately hire a lawyer or sue; we begin by discussing and negotiating with the merchant, perhaps even asking a friend to contact the merchant on our behalf if we feel too angry or helpless ourselves. I already mentioned the many professions and groups within industrial societies that have their own routine procedures for dispute resolution. In rural areas and other small enclaves where everyone knows everyone else and expects relationships to be life-long, motivation and pressure to settle disputes informally are strong. Even when we do resort to lawyers, some disputants expecting an on-going relationship—such as some divorcing parents of children, or business partners or counterparts—end up using the lawyers to reestablish a non-hostile relationship. Many states besides Papua New Guinea are sufficiently new or weak that much of the society continues to function in its traditional ways.

With that as background, let's now recognize three inherent advantages of state justice when it functions effectively. First and foremost, a fundamental problem of virtually all small-scale societies is that, because they lack a central political authority exerting a monopoly of retaliatory force, they are unable to prevent recalcitrant members from injuring other members, and also unable to prevent aggrieved members from taking matters into their own hands and seeking to achieve their goals by violence. But violence invites counter-violence. As we shall see in the next two chapters, most small-scale societies thereby become trapped in cycles of violence and warfare. State governments and strong chiefdoms render a huge service by breaking those cycles and asserting a monopoly of force. Of course, I don't claim that any state is completely successful at curbing violence, and I acknowledge that states themselves to varying degrees employ violence against their citizens. Instead, I note that, the more effective the control exercised by the state, the more limited the non-state violence.

That's an inherent advantage of state government, and a major reason why large societies in which strangers regularly encounter each other have tended to evolve strong chiefs and then state government. Whenever we find ourselves inclined to admire dispute resolution in small-scale societies, we have to remind ourselves that it consists of two prongs, of which one prong is admirable peaceful negotiation and the other prong is regrettable violence and war. State dispute resolution also has its own two prongs of which one is peaceful negotiation, but the state's confrontational second prong is merely a trial. Even the most horrible trial is preferable to a civil war or a cycle of revenge murders. That fact may make members of small-scale societies more willing than members of state societies to settle their private disputes by negotiation, and to focus those negotiations on emotional balance and the restoration of relationships rather than on vindicating rights.

A second advantage or potential advantage of state-administered justice over do-it-yourself traditional justice involves power relationships. A disputant in a small-scale society needs to have allies if his bargaining position is to be credible, and if he really wants to collect those cattle that the Nuer leopard-skin chief has proposed as appropriate compensation. This reminds me of an influential article about Western state justice, entitled "Bargaining in the Shadow of the Law"—meaning that mediation in states takes place with both parties aware that, if mediation fails, the dispute will be settled in court by the application of laws. By the same token, compensation negotiations in small-scale societies take place "in the shadow of war"—meaning that both parties know that, if the negotiation is unsuccessful, the alternative is war or violence. That knowledge creates a non-level playing field in small-scale societies and gives a strong bargaining advantage to the party expected to be able to marshal more allies in the eventuality of war.

Theoretically, state justice aims to create a level playing field, to offer equal justice to all, and to prevent a powerful or rich party from abusing her power so as to obtain an unfair settlement. Of course, I and every reader will immediately protest: "Theoretically, but . . . !" In reality, a rich litigant enjoys an advantage in civil and criminal cases. She can afford to hire expensive lawyers and expert witnesses. She can pressure a less affluent adversary into settling, by filing extensive discovery motions in order to drive up the adversary's legal costs, and by filing suits that have little merit but that will be costly for the other party to contest. Some state justice systems are corrupt and favor wealthy or politically well-connected parties.

Yes, it's unfortunately true that the more powerful disputant enjoys an unfair advantage in state justice systems, as in small-scale societies. But states at least provide *some* protection to weak parties, whereas small-scale societies provide little or none. In well-governed states a weak victim can still report a crime to the police and will often or usually be heard; a poor person starting a business can seek the state's help in enforcing contracts; a poor defendant in a criminal case is assigned a court-paid lawyer; and a poor plaintiff with a strong case may be able to find a private lawyer willing to accept the case on contingency (i.e., a lawyer willing to be paid a fraction of the award if the case is successful).

Still a third advantage of state justice involves its goal of establishing right and wrong, and punishing or assessing civil penalties against wrong-doers, so as to deter other members of the society from committing crimes or wrongs. Deterrence is an explicit goal of our criminal justice system. In effect, it's also a goal of our tort system of civil justice, which scrutinizes causes of and responsibility for injuries, and which thereby seeks to discourage injury-provoking behavior by making everyone aware of the civil judgments that they may have to pay if they commit such behaviors. For example, if Malo had been sued for civil damages for killing Billy under an effective state justice system, Malo's lawyers would have argued (with good chances of success) that the responsibility for Billy's death did not lie with Malo, who was driving safely, but instead with the mini-bus driver who let Billy off in the face of on-coming traffic, and with Billy's uncle Genjimp, who was waiting to greet Billy on the opposite side of a busy road. An actual case in Los Angeles analogous to that of Billy and Malo was that of *Schwartz v. Helms Bakery.* A small boy was killed by a car while running across a busy street to buy a chocolate doughnut from a Helms Bakery truck; the boy had asked the driver to wait while the boy ran across the street to his house to fetch money; the driver agreed and remained parked awaiting the boy on that busy street; and the court held that a jury should decide whether Helms Bakery was partly responsible for the boy's death, through the driver's negligence.

Such tort cases put pressure on citizens of state societies to be constantly alert to the possibility that their negligence may contribute to causing an accident. In contrast, the private negotiated settlement between Billy's clan and Malo's colleagues provided no incentive to New Guinea adults and mini-bus drivers to reflect on risks to schoolchildren running across streets. Despite the millions of car trips daily on the streets of Los

Angeles, and despite the few police cars patrolling our streets, most Los Angelenos drive safely most of the time, and only a tiny percentage of those millions of daily trips end in accidents or injuries. One reason is the deterrent power of our civil and criminal justice system.

But let me again prevent misunderstanding: I'm not praising state justice as uniformly superior. States pay a price for those three advantages. State criminal justice systems exist primarily to promote goals of the state: to reduce private violence, to foster obedience to the state's laws, to protect the public as a whole, to rehabilitate criminals, and to punish and deter crimes. The state's focus on those goals tends to diminish the state's attention to goals of individual citizens involved in dispute resolution in small-scale societies: the restoration of relationships (or of non-relationships), and reaching emotional closure. It is not inevitable that states ignore these goals, but they often do neglect them because of their focus on the state's other goals. In addition, there are other defects of state justice systems that are not so inherent, but are nevertheless widespread: limited or no compensation through the criminal justice systems to victims of a crime (unless through a separate civil suit); and, in civil suits, the slowness of resolution, the difficulty of monetizing personal and emotional injuries, the lack of provision (in the U.S.) for recouping of attorney fees by a successful plaintiff, and the lack of reconciliation (or often, worse yet, increased bad feelings) between disputants.

We have seen that state societies could mitigate these problems by adopting practices inspired by procedures of small-scale societies. In our civil justice system we could invest more money in the training and hiring of mediators and the availability of judges. We could put more effort into mediation. We could award attorney fees to successful plaintiffs under some circumstances. In our criminal justice system we could experiment more with restorative justice. In the American criminal justice system we could re-assess whether European models emphasizing rehabilitation more and retribution less would make better sense for criminals, for society as a whole, and for the economy.

All of these proposals have been much discussed. They pose difficulties of their own. I hope that, with wider knowledge of how small-scale societies resolve disputes, legal scholars may figure out how better to incorporate those admired procedures of small-scale societies into our own systems.

CHAPTER 3

A Short Chapter, About a Tiny War

The Dani War ▪ The war's time-line ▪ The war's death toll

The Dani War

This chapter will serve to introduce traditional warfare by recounting a rather ordinary series of battles and raids among New Guinea's Dani people, unusual only in that they were actually observed and filmed by anthropologists. The Dani are one of New Guinea's most numerous and densest populations, centered on the Grand Valley of the Baliem River. Between 1909 and 1937, eight Western expeditions contacted and briefly visited outlying Dani groups or their neighbors without entering the valley itself. As mentioned in Chapter 1, the valley and its teeming population were "discovered"—i.e., first spotted by Europeans, about 46,000 years after the arrival of ancestral New Guineans—on June 23, 1938, from an airplane carrying out reconnaissance flights for the Archbold Expedition. First contact face-to-face followed on August 4, when an expedition patrol led by Captain Teerink walked into the valley. After the Archbold Expedition left the valley in December 1938, further contact of Baliem Dani with Europeans (apart from a brief U.S. Army rescue of a crashed airplane crew in 1945) was postponed until 1954 and subsequent years, when several mission stations and a Dutch government patrol post were established in the valley.

In 1961 an expedition from Harvard University's Peabody Museum arrived to carry out anthropological studies and filming. The campsite selected was in the Dugum Dani neighborhood, because that area had no government or mission station and relatively little outside contact. It turned out that traditional warfare was still going on. Accounts of fighting there between April and September 1961 have appeared in several forms: especially, the doctoral dissertation (in Dutch) of social scientist Jan Broekhuijse from the University of Utrecht; two books by anthropologist Karl Heider, based on Heider's doctoral dissertation at Harvard; a popular book, *Under the Mountain Wall,* by the writer Peter Matthiessen; and a documentary film, *Dead Birds,* produced by Robert Gardner and including remarkable footage of battles between spear-wielding tribesmen.

The following brief summary of Dugum Dani warfare during those months of 1961 is derived especially from Broekhuijse's thesis because it is the most detailed account, supplemented by information from Heider plus a few details from Matthiessen. Broekhuijse interviewed battle participants, who described to him their assessment of each battle, their resulting mood, and specifics of each person's wounds. There are some minor discrepancies among these three accounts, notably in the spelling of Dani names (Broekhuijse used Dutch orthography while Heider used American orthography), and in some details such as a one-day difference in the date of one battle. However, these three authors shared information with each other and with Gardner, and their accounts are largely in agreement.

As you read this combined account, I think that you'll be struck, as was I, by many features of Dani warfare that turn out to be shared with wars in many other traditional societies to be mentioned in Chapter 4. Those shared features include the following ones. Frequent concealed ambushes and open battles (Plate 36), each with few deaths, are punctuated by infrequent massacres that exterminate a whole population or kill a significant fraction of it. So-called tribal warfare is often or usually actually intra-tribal, between groups speaking the same language and sharing the same culture, rather than inter-tribal. Despite that cultural similarity or identity between the antagonists, one's enemies are sometimes demonized as subhuman. Boys are trained already in childhood to fight, and to expect to be attacked. It is important to enlist allies, but alliances shift frequently. Revenge plays a dominant role as a motive for cycles of violence. (Karl Heider instead described the motive as the need to placate the ghosts of one's recently killed comrades.) Warfare involves the whole population rather than just a small professional army of adult men: there is intentional killing of "civilian" women and children as well as of male "soldiers." Villages are burned and pillaged. Military efficiency is low by the standards of modern warfare, as a result of the availability of only short-range weapons, weak leadership, simple plans, lack of group military training, and lack of synchronized firing. However, because warfare is chronic, it has omnipresent consequences for people's behavior. Finally, absolute death tolls are inevitably low from the small size of the populations involved (compared to the populations of almost all modern nations), but relative death tolls as a proportion of the population involved are high.

The war's time-line

The Dani War to be described pitted two alliances against each other, each numbering up to 5,000 people. To help readers keep track of the unfamiliar Dani names that will recur in the following pages, I summarize alliance compositions in **Table 3.1.** One alliance, termed the Gutelu Alliance after its leader Gutelu, consisted of several confederations of about 1,000 people each, including the Wilihiman-Walalua Confederation encompassing the Dugum Dani neighborhood, plus their allies the Gosi-Alua, the Dloko-Mabel, and other confederations. The other alliance, living to the south of the Gutelu Alliance, included the Widaia and their allies such as the Siep-Eloktak, the Hubu-Gosi, and the Asuk-Balek Confederations. The Gutelu Alliance was also simultaneously fighting a war on its northern frontier, which is not discussed in the following account. A few decades before the events of 1961, the Wilihiman-Walalua and the Gosi-Alua had been allied with the Siep-Eloktak and had been enemies of the Dloko-Mabel, until thefts of pigs and disputes over women induced the Wilihiman-Walalua and the Gosi-Alua to ally with the Dloko-Mabel, form an alliance under Gutelu, and attack and drive out the Siep-Eloktak, who became allies of the Widaia. Subsequent to the events of 1961, the Dloko-Mabel again attacked and became enemies of the Wilihiman-Walalua and the Gosi-Alua.

All of these groups speak the Dani language and are similar in culture and subsistence. In the following paragraphs I shall label the opposing sides for short as the Wilihiman and the Widaia, but it should be

Table 3.1. Membership of two warring Dani alliances

GUTELU ALLIANCE	WIDAIA ALLIANCE
Wilihiman-Walalua Confederation	Widaia Confederation
Gosi-Alua Confederation	Siep-Eloktak Confederation
Dloko-Mabel Confederation	Hubu-Gosi Confederation
other confederations	Asuk-Balek Confederation
	other confederations

understood that each of those confederations was usually joined in battle by one or more allied confederations.

In February 1961, before the main accounts of Broekhuijse, Heider, and Matthiessen begin, four women and one man of the Gutelu Alliance were killed by the Widaia while visiting clan relatives in a nearby tribe for a pig feast, enraging the Gutelu. There had been other killings before that one. Thus, one should talk about chronic warfare, rather than a war with a specifiable beginning and cause.

On April 3 a Widaia man wounded in a previous battle died. For the Wilihiman, that avenged the death of a Wilihiman man in January and confirmed the benevolent attitude of their ancestors, but for the Widaia the new Widaia death demanded revenge in order to restore their relationship with their own ancestors. At dawn on April 10 the Widaia shouted out a challenge to an open battle, which the Wilihiman accepted and fought until rain ended the battle at 5:00 P.M.* Ten Wilihiman were lightly

---

* Here and in several of the following paragraphs, we encounter a feature of Dani warfare that initially puzzles us: battles by appointment. That is, one side challenges the other side to meet at an appointed place on an appointed day for a battle. The other side is free to accept or ignore the challenge. When a battle has started, either side may call it off if rain begins. These facts have misled some commentators into dismissing Dani warfare as ritualized, not seriously intending to kill, and just a form of sporting contest. Against this view stand the undoubted facts that Dani nevertheless do get wounded and killed in these battles, that other Dani are killed in raids and ambushes, and that large numbers are killed in rare massacres. Anthropologist Paul Roscoe has argued that the apparent ritualization of Dani battles was made inevitable by the swampy and waterlogged terrain, with only two narrow dry hills on which large groups of warriors could safely maneuver and fight. To fight in large groups elsewhere would have posed a suicidal risk of pursuing or retreating from the enemy through swamps with hidden underwater bridges familiar to the enemy. In support of Roscoe's interpretation, this apparent ritualization of Dani warfare is not paralleled among many other New Guinea Highland groups fighting on firm dry terrain. Rumors circulated, apparently originating with missionaries, that the Harvard Expedition itself, eager for dramatic film footage, somehow provoked the Dani to fight and kill each other. However, the Dani fought before the expedition arrived and after it left, and government investigation of the rumor found it baseless.

wounded, one of the Gosi-Alua allies (a man named Ekitamalek) was seriously wounded (an arrow point broke off in his left lung and he died 17 days later), and an unspecified number of Widaia were wounded. That outcome left both sides eager for another battle.

On April 15 a battle challenge was again issued and accepted, and about 400 warriors fought until the onset of darkness compelled everyone to go home. About 20 men were wounded on each side. Three Hubikiak allies of the Widaia had to be carried away, accompanied by derisive laughter and jeers from the Wilihiman, who shouted out remarks such as "Make those jerks walk themselves, they're not pigs! . . . Go home, your wives will cook potatoes for you." One of those wounded Hubikiak died six weeks later.

On April 27 Ekitamalek, the Gosi-Alua man wounded on April 10, died and was cremated. The Widaia noticed that no Gosi-Alua and few Wilihiman were out in their gardens, so 30 Widaia crossed a river into Wilihiman land and waited in ambush. When no one appeared, the Widaia knocked over a Wilihiman watch-tower and went home (Plate 13).

On May 4 the Wilihiman and their allies issued a battle challenge and waited at a preferred battlefield, but no Widaia appeared, so they went home.

On May 10 or May 11 the father of Ekitamalek led a raid of Gosi-Alua, Walalua, and many Wilihiman men into Widaia gardens while the remaining Wilihiman men and women worked in their gardens and behaved as if everything were normal, so that the Widaia wouldn't suspect an ambush. The raiders spotted two Widaia men working in a Widaia garden while a third stood guard on top of a watch-tower. For hours, the raiders crept closer until the Widaia man on watch spotted them at a distance of 50 meters. All three Widaia fled, but the attackers managed to catch one named Huwai, pierced him repeatedly with spears, and fled. A counter-ambush that the Widaia staged in Wilihiman territory was unsuccessful. The wounded Widaia man died later that day. Three Wilihiman were lightly wounded in the day's action. The Wilihiman now felt that they had avenged the death of their Gosi-Alua ally, and they celebrated by dancing into the night.

On May 25 Gutelu warriors on their alliance's northern front killed a man of the Asuk-Balek Confederation, allied with the Widaia and figuring in the August 25 death to be described below.

On May 26 both sides issued challenges, carried out raids, and fought until late in the afternoon, whereupon they went home. Twelve Wilihiman were wounded, none of them seriously.

On May 29 the Widaia reported that their warrior wounded on April 15 had just died, leading the Wilihiman to launch a celebratory dance that had to be interrupted because of a report of a Widaia raid on the northern frontier.

The Widaia were now feeling restless because they had suffered two deaths without being able to take revenge. On June 4 they sent out an ambush party that developed into a battle involving a total of about 800 men, broken off because of darkness. Three Wilihiman were lightly wounded.

A full-fledged battle developed on June 7, involving 400 or 500 warriors on each side. Amidst a hail of spears and arrows from opposing groups 20 meters apart, hotheads dashed to within 5 meters of the enemy, constantly darting to avoid being hit. About 20 men were wounded.

A Widaia raid on June 8 was inferred from footprints but not spotted.

On June 10 the Wilihiman devoted themselves to a ceremony, and no one was out in the gardens or manning the watch-towers. In the late afternoon of the hot day a Wilihiman man and three young boys went to drink cold water at the river, where they were surprised by 30 Widaia divided into two groups. When the first group popped out, the four Wilihiman fled, whereupon the second group of Widaia in hiding attempted to cut them off. The Wilihiman man and two of the boys managed to escape, but Wejakhe, the third boy, could not run fast because of an injured leg, was caught, was severely wounded with spears, and died that night.

On June 15 Wejakhe's Wilihiman relatives staged an unsuccessful raid.

On June 22 the Widaia shouted out a challenge, and a battle with about 300 men on each side developed along with an ambush. Four men were lightly wounded. A Dloko-Mabel man was seriously wounded by an arrow point that broke off in his shoulder and that his companions attempted to extract, first by gripping it with their teeth and pulling, then by operating (without anesthetic) with a bamboo knife.

On July 5, after two weeks without fighting, the Wilihiman raided a Widaia garden. A Wilihiman man named Jenokma, who was faster than his companions, impetuously sprinted ahead after a group of six fleeing Widaia, was cut off, and was speared. His companions fled, and the Widaia carried off his corpse but brought it back that evening and set it down in the no-man's land for the Wilihiman to retrieve. Three Gosi-Alua allies of the Wilihiman were lightly wounded. The Wilihiman were now depressed: they had hoped to make a kill, but instead it was they who had just suffered another death. An old Wilihiman woman lamented, "Why are you trying to kill the Widaia?" A Wilihiman man replied, "Those people are our enemies. Why shouldn't we kill them?—they're not human."

On July 12 the Wilihiman spent all day waiting in ambush until they issued an open challenge around 5:00 P.M. However, it was a rainy day, so the Widaia didn't accept the challenge or go out into their gardens.

On July 28 the Widaia staged a raid that was spotted by a group of eight Wilihiman men at a watch-tower. The Wilihiman hid themselves nearby. Not realizing that there were any Wilihiman around, the Widaia came to their tower, and one of them climbed it for a look. At that point the hidden Wilihiman jumped out, the Widaia on the ground fled, and the one man up on the tower attempted to jump down but wasn't fast enough and was caught and killed. That evening the Wilihiman returned his body to the Widaia.

On August 2 a small battle was provoked when a Widaia pig either was stolen by the Wilihiman or strayed from their territory.

On August 6 a large battle developed between the Wilihiman, the Widaia, and allies on both sides. A parallel battle took place between Widaia and Wilihiman boys as young as six years old, standing on opposite sides of a river, firing arrows at each other, and urged on by older men. Only five men were lightly wounded, because the battle degenerated into more name-calling than fighting. Some sample insults: "You are women, you are cowards." "Why do you have so many more women than your low status deserves?" "I have five wives, and I'm going to get five more, because I live on my own land. You are landless fugitives, that's why you have no wives."

On August 16 another large battle drawing in allies on both sides took place. At least 20 men were wounded, one possibly seriously by an arrow shot into his belly. The Wilihiman now felt tense, pressured by their inability to avenge their two recent dead, and under a collective obsession to kill an enemy quickly. The spirits of their ancestors wanted revenge, which they themselves had not delivered. They felt that ancestral spirits were no longer supporting them, and that they depended only on themselves; that fear lowered their desire to fight.

On August 24 a Widaia woman unhappy with her husband fled to Wilihiman land in order to seek refuge. A group of Wilihiman wanted to kill her to avenge Jenokma's death on July 5, but they were dissuaded from doing so.

On August 25, as I related in Chapter 2, four Asuk-Balek men from the other side of the Baliem River came to visit relatives of two of the men in the Dloko-Mabel area. They ran into a Wilihiman group, who immediately realized that these were allies of their enemies, and that the two who had no local relatives should be killed. One of the two succeeded in fleeing, but the other was overpowered and killed. As Wilihiman men dragged off the dying Asuk-Balek, young boys ran alongside him, piercing his body with tiny spears. The killing triggered wild rejoicing and singing everywhere among the Wilihiman, followed by a celebratory dance. The Wilihiman concluded that the Asuk-Balek had been steered to them by their ancestral spirits, or else by Jenokma's ghost. Even though the revenge was not tit-for-tat (the death of just one enemy for the earlier deaths of two Wilihiman), tension decreased. The killing of even one enemy was the surest sign that ancestral spirits were now again helping them.

In early September a Widaia raid killed a young boy named Digiliak, while a Gutelu raid killed two Widaia. On the next day, warfare was abruptly ended on the Gutelu southern frontier by the establishment of a Dutch patrol post there, but it continued on another Gutelu frontier.

Each of the actions described so far produced only limited tangible consequences, because few people died and no population was driven out of its homeland. Five years later, on June 4, 1966, a large-scale massacre took place. Its origins lay in tensions within the Gutelu Alliance, between the alliance's leader, Gutelu of the Dloko-Mabel Confederation, and jealous leaders of the allied Wilihiman-Walalua and Gosi-Alua Confederations. Several decades previously, the latter two confederations had been at war with the Dloko-Mabel Confederation until a switch of alliances. It is unclear whether Gutelu himself planned the attack on his former enemies, or whether he was unable to restrain hotheads among his own people. If the latter interpretation were true, it would illustrate a recurrent theme in tribal societies that lack the strong leadership and monopolization of force characterizing chiefdom and state societies. The attack was carefully scheduled for a day when the local missionary and Indonesian police (who had gained control of western New Guinea from the Dutch in 1962) happened to be away. Dloko-Mabel warriors and other northern members of the Gutelu Alliance snuck across the Elogeta River at dawn under cover of fog to attack the alliance's southern members. Within an hour, 125 southern adults and children of both sexes were dead or dying, dozens of settlements were burning, and other alliances alerted to the impending attack joined in to steal pigs. The southerners would have been exterminated except for help that they received from another alliance further to the south that had formerly been their allies. The result, besides all those deaths, was a flight of southerners further towards the south, and a split in the Gutelu Alliance between southerners and northerners. Such massacres are infrequent events with big consequences. Karl Heider was told of four other such massacres, burnings of villages, pig plundering, and population shifts between the 1930s and 1962.

The war's death toll

All of the fighting between April and early September 1961 resulted in only about 11 deaths on the southern frontier. Even the massacre of June 4, 1966, produced a death toll of only 125. To us survivors of the 20th century and two world wars, such numbers are so low as not even to be worth dignifying with the name of war. Think of some of the far higher death tolls of modern state history: 2,996 Americans killed within one hour in the World Trade Center attacks of September 11, 2001; 20,000 British soldiers killed on a single day, July 1, 1916, at the Battle of the Somme during World War I, mowed down as they charged across open ground against German positions heavily defended by machine guns; about 100,000 Japanese killed on or after August 6, 1945, by the American atomic bomb dropped on Hiroshima (Plate 37); and over 50,000,000 total deaths as a result of World War II. By these standards, the Dani fighting that I just summarized was a tiny war, if it is considered a war at all.

Yes, as measured by the absolute number of people killed, the Dani War was indeed tiny. But the nations involved in World War II were far more populous, and offered far more potential victims, than did the two alliances involved in the Wilihiman-Widaia war. Those alliances numbered perhaps 8,000 people in all, while the major participants in World War II had populations ranging from tens of millions to nearly a billion. The relative death toll of the Dani War—the number of Dani killed as a proportion of the total population involved—rivaled or eclipsed the casualty rates suffered by the U.S., European countries, Japan, or China in the world wars. For example, the 11 deaths suffered by the two Dani alliances on the Gutelu southern front alone, in the six months between April and September 1961, represented about 0.14% of the alliances' population. That's higher than the percentage death toll (0.10%) from the bloodiest battle on the Pacific front during World War II: the three-month struggle for Okinawa, employing bombers and kamikaze planes and artillery and flame-throwers, in which about 264,000 people (23,000 American soldiers, 91,000 Japanese soldiers, and 150,000 Okinawan civilians) died, out of a total American/Japanese/Okinawan population then of around 250,000,000. The 125 men, women, and children killed within an hour in the Dani massacre of June 4, 1966, represented about 5% of the targeted population (about 2,500), the southern confederations of the Gutelu Alliance. To match that percentage, the Hiroshima atomic bomb would have had to kill 4,000,000 rather than 100,000 Japanese, and the World Trade Center attack would have had to kill 15,000,000 rather than 2,996 Americans.

By world standards, the Dani War was tiny only because the Dani population at risk of being killed was tiny. By the standards of the local population involved, the Dani War was huge. In the next chapter we shall see that that conclusion also applies to traditional warfare in general.

CHAPTER 4

A Longer Chapter, About Many Wars

Definitions of war ▪ Sources of information ▪ Forms of traditional warfare ▪ Mortality rates ▪ Similarities and differences ▪ Ending warfare ▪ Effects of European contact ▪ Warlike animals, peaceful peoples ▪ Motives for traditional war ▪ Ultimate reasons ▪ Whom do people fight? ▪ Forgetting Pearl Harbor

Definitions of war

Traditional warfare, as illustrated by the Dani War described in the previous chapter, has been widespread but not universal among small-scale societies. It raises many questions that have been hotly debated. For example, how should war be defined, and do so-called tribal wars really constitute wars at all? How do the death tolls from warfare in small-scale societies compare to death tolls from state warfare? Does warfare increase or decrease when small-scale societies become contacted and influenced by Europeans and other more centralized societies? If fighting between groups of chimpanzees, lions, wolves, and other social animals furnishes precedents for human warfare, does that suggest a genetic basis of warfare? Among human societies, are there some especially peaceful ones? If so, why? And: what are the motives and causes of traditional warfare?

Let's begin with the question of how to define warfare. Human violence assumes many forms, only some of which are normally taken to constitute war. Anyone will agree that a battle between large armies of trained professional soldiers in the service of rival state governments that have issued formal declarations of war does constitute war. Most of us would also agree that there are forms of human violence that don't constitute war, such as individual homicides (the killing of one individual by another individual belonging to the same political unit), or family feuds within the same political unit (such as the feud between the Hatfield and McCoy families of the eastern United States beginning around 1880). Borderline cases include recurrent violence between rival groups within the same political unit, such as fighting between urban gangs (commonly referred to as "gang warfare"), between drug cartels, or between political factions whose fighting has not yet reached the stage of declared civil war (such as the fighting between armed militias of fascists and socialists in Italy and Germany leading up to Mussolini's and Hitler's assumptions of power). Where should we draw the line?

The answer to that question may depend on the purpose of one's study. To future soldiers in training at a state-sponsored military college, it may be appropriate to exclude from a definition of warfare Chapter 3's stories of violence between rival Dani alliances. However, for our purposes in this book, which is concerned with the whole spectrum of related phenomena observed from the smallest human bands of 20 people to the largest states of over a billion people, we must define warfare in a way that doesn't define traditional warfare between small bands out of existence. As Steven LeBlanc has argued, "Definitions of war must not be dependent on group size or methods of fighting if they are to be useful in studying past warfare. . . . Many scholars define *warfare* in such a way that it refers to something that only complex societies employing metal tools can have [i.e., pitched battles and professional soldiers]. Anything else—say, a raid or two now and then—is not 'real' warfare, they believe, but is something more akin to game playing and not a subject of much concern. Such an approach or attitude, however, confuses the methods of war with the results of war. . . . Does conflict between independent political units lead to significant deaths and loss of territory, while resulting in some territory being rendered useless because it's too dangerous to live in? Are people spending a great deal of time and energy defending themselves? . . . If fighting results in significant impacts on people, it is war regardless of how the fighting is conducted." From that perspective, war should be defined sufficiently broadly so as to include the Dani fighting described in Chapter 3.

Consider one fairly typical definition of war, that from the *Encyclopaedia Britannica*'s 15th edition: "A state of usually open and declared armed hostile conflict between political units, such as states or nations or between rival political factions of the same state or nation. War is characterized by intentional violence on the part of large bodies of individuals who are expressly organized and trained to participate in such violence. . . . War is generally understood to embrace only armed conflicts on a fairly large scale, usually excluding conflicts in which fewer than 50,000 combatants are involved." Like many other apparently common-sense definitions of war, this one is much too restrictive for our purposes, because it requires "large bodies of individuals who are expressly organized and trained," and it thereby refuses to admit the possibility of war in small band societies. Its arbitrary requirement of at least 50,000 combatants is more than six times the entire population (men warriors, women, and children) involved in Chapter 3's Dani War, and far larger than most of the small-scale societies discussed in this book.

Hence scholars studying small-scale societies have come up with various alternative broader definitions of war, similar to each other and usually requiring three elements. One element is violence carried out by groups of any size, but not by single individuals. (A killing carried out by one individual is considered a murder, not an act of war.) Another element is that the violence is between groups belonging to two different political units, not belonging to the same political unit. The remaining element is that the violence must be sanctioned by the whole political unit, even if only some members of the unit carry out the violence. Thus, the killings between the Hatfield and McCoy families didn't constitute war, because both families belonged to the same political unit (the U.S.), and the U.S. as a whole did not approve of that family feud. These elements may be combined into a short definition of war that I shall use in this book, and that is similar to definitions formulated by other scholars of small-scale as well as state societies: "War is recurrent violence between groups belonging to rival political units, and sanctioned by the units."

Sources of information

Chapter 3's account of Dani warfare might suggest that it's straightforward to study traditional war: send out graduate students and a film crew, observe and film battles, count the wounded and dead warriors being carried back, and interview participants for more details. That's the evidence available to us for Dani warfare. If we had hundreds of such studies, there would be no arguments about traditional war's reality.

In fact, for several obvious reasons, direct observations of traditional war by scholars carrying cameras are exceptional, and there is some controversy about its extent in the absence of European influence. As Europeans expanded over the globe from AD 1492 onwards and encountered and conquered non-European peoples, one of the first things that European governments did was to suppress traditional warfare: for the safety of Europeans themselves, and to administer the conquered areas, and as part of a perceived civilizing mission. By the time that the science of anthropology entered the era of abundant well-funded field studies and graduate students after World War II, warfare among traditional small-scale societies had become largely confined to the island of New Guinea and to parts of South America. It had ended much earlier in other Pacific islands, North America, Aboriginal Australia, Africa, and Eurasia, although modern forms of it have recently been resurfacing in some areas, especially in Africa and New Guinea.

Even in New Guinea and South America, recent opportunities for anthropologists to observe traditional warfare first-hand have been limited. Governments don't want the problems and publicity resulting from unarmed vulnerable outsiders being attacked by warring tribespeople. Governments also don't want anthropologists to be armed, to be the first representatives of state societies to enter an unpacified tribal area, and to try to end fighting by force themselves. Hence both in New Guinea and in South America there have been government restrictions on travel until an area is considered officially pacified and safe for anyone to visit. Nevertheless, some scholars and missionaries have succeeded in working in areas where fighting was still going on. Notable examples were the observers in 1961 in the Dani area, where there already was a Dutch patrol post established in the Baliem Valley, but where the Harvard Expedition was permitted to operate beyond the area of government control; the Kuegler family's work among the Fayu people of western New Guinea beginning in 1979; and Napoleon Chagnon's work among the Yanomamo Indians of Venezuela and Brazil. Even in those studies that did yield some first-hand observations of warfare, however, much or most of the detail was still not observed directly by the Westerner writing about it, but was instead acquired second-hand from local informants: e.g., Jan Broekhuijse's detailed accounts of who in each Dani battle was wounded under what circumstances in which part of the body.

Most of our information about traditional warfare is entirely second-hand and based on accounts given by participants to Western visitors, or else is based on first-hand observations by Europeans (such as government officers, explorers, and traders) who were not trained scientists gathering data for doctoral dissertations. For instance, many New Guineans have reported to me their own experiences in traditional warfare. However, in all my visits to Australian-administered eastern New Guinea (now independent Papua New Guinea) and Indonesian-administered western New Guinea, I have never personally witnessed New Guineans attacking other New Guineans. The Australian and Indonesian governments would never have permitted me to enter areas where fighting was still going on, even if I had wanted to do so, which I didn't.

Most of the Westerners who did observe and describe traditional warfare have not been professional scholars. For instance, Sabine Kuegler, daughter of missionaries Klaus and Doris Kuegler, described in her popular book *Child of the Jungle* how, when she was six years old, a fight with bows and arrows erupted between the Tigre clan of the Fayu (among whom her family was living) and visitors from the Sefoidi clan, and how she saw arrows flying around her and wounded men being carried away in canoes. Similarly, the Spanish priest Juan Crespí, a member of the Gaspar de Portolá Expedition, which was the first overland European expedition to reach the Chumash Indians on the coast of southern California, in 1769–1770, wrote in detail about groups of Chumash shooting arrows at each other.

A problem associated with all of these accounts of traditional warfare by outside (usually European) observers, whether anthropologists or laypeople, is reminiscent of the Heisenberg Uncertainty Principle of physics: the observation itself perturbs the phenomenon observed. In anthropology this means that the mere presence of outsiders inevitably has large effects on previously "untouched" peoples. State governments routinely adopt a conscious policy of ending traditional warfare: for example, the first goal of 20th-century Australian patrol officers in the Territory of Papua and New Guinea, on entering a new area, was to stop warfare and cannibalism. Non-government outsiders may achieve that same result in different ways. For instance, Klaus Kuegler eventually had to insist that his host Fayu clan stop fighting around his house and go somewhere else to shoot each other, otherwise he and his family would have to leave for their own safety and peace of mind. The Fayu agreed, and gradually stopped fighting altogether.

Those are examples of Europeans intentionally ending or decreasing tribal fighting, but there are also claims of Europeans intentionally provoking tribal fighting. There are also many ways in which outsiders, through their activities or mere presence, may unintentionally increase or decrease fighting. Thus, whenever an outside visitor reports observations of traditional warfare (or lack of warfare), there is inevitable uncertainty about how much fighting there would have been if no outside observer had been present. I shall return to this question later in this chapter.

An alternative approach has been to scrutinize evidence of tribal fighting preserved in the archaeological record laid down before the arrival of outsiders. This approach carries the advantage of removing the influence of contemporary outside observers entirely. However, in analogy with the Heisenberg Uncertainty Principle, we gain that advantage at the cost of a disadvantage: increased uncertainty about the facts, because fighting was not observed directly nor was it described on the basis of reports of local eyewitnesses, but it instead had to be inferred from archaeological evidence, which is subject to various uncertainties. One undeniable type of archaeological evidence for fighting is piles of skeletons, thrown together without the usual hallmarks of intentional proper burial, with cut marks or breaks on bones recognizably made by weapons or tools. Such marks include bones with imbedded arrow points, bones with cut marks made by a sharp weapon such as an ax, skulls with long straight cut marks indicative of scalping, or skulls with the first two vertebrae attached as normally results from decapitation (e.g., for head-hunting). For instance, at Talheim in southwestern Germany, Joachim Wahl and Hans König studied 34 skeletons of what turned out to be identifiable as 18 adults (nine men, seven women, and two of uncertain sex) and 16 children. They had been heaped haphazardly around 5000 BC in a pit without the usual grave goods associated with respectful burial by relatives. Unhealed cut marks on the right rear surfaces of 18 skulls showed that those people had died of blows administered from behind by at least six different axes, evidently wielded by right-handed assailants. The victims were of all ages from young children to a man of about 60. Evidently, an entire group consisting of half a dozen families had been massacred simultaneously by a much larger group of attackers.

Other types of archaeological evidence for warfare include finds of weapons, armor and shields, and fortifications. While some weapons aren't unequivocal signs of war, because spears and bows and arrows can be used to hunt animals as well as to kill people, battle axes and piles of large slingshot missiles do provide evidence of war, because they are used only or mainly against people, not against animals. Armor and shields are similarly employed only in war, not in hunting animals. Their use in war has been described ethnographically among many living traditional peoples, including New Guineans, Aboriginal Australians, and Inuit. Hence finds of similar armor and shields in archaeological sites are evidence of fighting in the past. Further archaeological signs of warfare are fortifications, such as walls, moats, defensible gates, and towers for launching missiles against enemy attempts to scale walls. For instance, when Europeans began to settle in New Zealand in the early 1800s, New Zealand's indigenous Maori population had hill forts, called *pa,* used initially to fight each other and then eventually also to fight Europeans. About a thousand Maori pa are known, many of them excavated archaeologically and dated to many centuries before European arrival, but similar to the ones that Europeans saw in use. Hence there is no doubt that Maori were fighting each other long before European arrival.

Finally, other archaeological settlement sites are on hilltop, cliff-top, or cliff-face locations that make no sense except for defense against enemy assault. Familiar examples include Anasazi Indian settlements at Mesa Verde and elsewhere in the U.S. Southwest, on cliff ledges and overhangs accessible only by ladders. Their positions high above the valley floor meant that water and other supplies had to be carried hundreds of feet up to them. When Europeans arrived in the Southwest, Indians used such sites as retreats to hide or protect themselves against European attackers. It's therefore assumed that cliff dwellings dated archaeologically to many centuries before European arrival were similarly used for defense against Indian attackers, especially as recourse to such sites increased with time as population density and evidence of violence were increasing. If all of this archaeological evidence weren't enough, rock paintings dating back to the Upper Pleistocene show fighting between opposing groups, depict people being speared, and depict groups of people fighting each other with bows, arrows, shields, spears, and clubs. Sophisticated later but still pre-European art works in this tradition are the famous Maya wall paintings at Bonampak, from a society around AD 800, depicting battles and torture of prisoners in realistic gory detail.

Thus, we have three extensive bodies of information—from modern observers, from archaeologists, and from art historians—about traditional warfare, in small-scale societies of all sizes, ranging from small bands to large chiefdoms and early states.

Forms of traditional warfare

Warfare has assumed multiple forms, both in the past and today. Traditional warfare utilized all basic tactics that are now used by modern states and that were technologically possible for tribal societies. (Naturally, the means for aerial warfare were not available to tribes, and naval warfare with specialized warships is not documented until the emergence of state governments after 3000 BC.) One familiar and still-practised tactic is the pitched battle, in which large numbers of opposing combatants face off against each other and fight openly. This is the first tactic that comes to mind for us when we think of modern state warfare—famous examples including the Battles of Stalingrad, Gettysburg, and Waterloo. Except for scale and weapons, such battles would have been familiar to the Dani, whose battles developing spontaneously on June 7, August 2, and August 6, 1961, I described in Chapter 3.

The next familiar tactic is the raid, in which a group of warriors small enough to conceal itself, advancing under cover or at night, makes a surprise attack on enemy territory with the limited goal of killing some enemies or destroying enemy property and then retreating, but without the expectation of destroying the whole opposing army or permanently occupying enemy territory. This is perhaps the most widespread form of traditional warfare, documented in most traditional societies, such as the Nuer raids against the Dinka, or the Yanomamo raids against each other. I described Dani raids that occurred on May 10, May 26, May 29, June 8, June 15, July 5, and July 28, 1961. Examples of raids, by infantry and now also by ships and airplanes, abound in state warfare as well.

Related to raids, and also widespread in traditional warfare, are ambushes, another form of surprise attack in which the aggressors, instead of moving by stealth, hide themselves and remain in wait at a site to which unsuspecting enemies are likely to come. I described Dani ambushes that took place on April 27, May 10, June 4, June 10, July 12, and July 28, 1961. Ambushes remain equally popular in modern warfare, abetted by radar and code-breaking methods that facilitate detecting movements of enemy who are less likely to detect the ambushing party.

A traditional tactic without parallel in modern state warfare is the treacherous feast documented among the Yanomamo and in New Guinea: inviting neighbors to a feast, then surprising and killing them after they have laid down their weapons and focused their attention on eating and drinking. We moderns have to wonder why any Yanomamo group would let itself fall into that trap, having heard stories of previous such treachery. The explanation may be that honorable feasts are common, that accepting an invitation usually brings big advantages in terms of alliance-building and food-sharing, and that the hosts go to much effort to make their intentions appear friendly. The only modern example I can think of involving state governments is the massacre of the Boer commander Piet Retief and his whole party of a hundred men by the Zulu king Dingane on February 6, 1838, while the Boers were Dingane's guests at a feast in his camp. This example may be considered the exception that proves the rule: the Zulus had been just one of hundreds of warring chiefdoms until unification and the foundation of the Zulu state a few decades previously.

Such blunt treachery has for the most part been abandoned under the rules of diplomacy which modern states now find it in their own self-interest to follow. Even Hitler and Japan issued formal declarations of war against the Soviet Union and the U.S., respectively, simultaneous with (but not before) their attacks on those countries. However, states do employ treachery against rebels whom they consider as not binding them to the usual rules of diplomacy between states. For instance, the French general Charles Leclerc had no qualms about inviting the Haitian independence leader Toussaint-Louverture to a parley on June 7, 1802, seizing him there, and shipping him to a French prison, where he died. Within modern states, treacherous killings are still carried out by urban gangs, drug cartels, and terrorist groups, which do not operate by the rules of state diplomacy.

Another form of traditional warfare without close modern parallels is the non-treacherous gathering that degenerates into fighting. Far commoner than a treacherous feast, this involves neighboring peoples meeting for a ceremony without any intention of fighting. But violence may nevertheless erupt because individuals who have unsettled grievances and who rarely encounter each other now find themselves face-to-face, can't restrain themselves, and begin fighting, and relatives then join in on both sides. For example, an American friend of mine who was present at a rare gathering of several dozen Fayu people told me of the tension prevailing as men periodically burst out in mutual insults and explosions of anger, pounded the ground with their axes, and in one case rushed at each other with axes. The risk of such unplanned fighting breaking out at gatherings intended to be peaceful is high for traditional societies in which neighboring peoples meet rarely, revenge for grievances is left to the individual, and there is no leader or "government" able to monopolize force and restrain hotheads.

Escalation of spontaneous individual fighting into organized warfare of armies is rare in centralized state societies but does sometimes happen. One example is the so-called Soccer War of June–July 1969 between El Salvador and Honduras. At a time when tensions between the two countries were already high over economic disparities and immigrant squatters, their soccer teams met for three games in a qualifying round for the 1970 World Cup. Rival fans began fighting at the first game on June 8 in the Honduran capital (won 1–0 by Honduras), and the fans became even more violent at the second game on June 15 in the El Salvador capital (won 3–0 by El Salvador). When El Salvador won the decisive third game 3–2 in overtime on June 26 in Mexico City, the two countries broke diplomatic relations, and on July 14 the El Salvador army and air force began bombing and invading Honduras.

Mortality rates

How high is the mortality from traditional tribal warfare? How does it compare with the mortality from warfare between state governments?

Military historians routinely compile national casualty totals for each modern war: e.g., for Germany during World War II. That permits one to calculate national war-related mortality rates averaged over a century of a country's history of alternating war and peace: e.g., for Germany over the whole of the 20th century. Such rates have also been calculated or estimated in dozens of studies of individual modern traditional societies. Four surveys—by Lawrence Keeley, by Samuel Bowles, by Steven Pinker, and by Richard Wrangham and Michael Wilson and Martin Muller—summarized such evaluations for between 23 and 32 traditional societies. Not surprisingly, there proves to be much variation between individual societies. The highest annual time-averaged war-related death tolls are 1% per year (i.e., 1 person killed per year per 100 members of the population) or higher for the Dani, Sudan's Dinka, and two North American Indian groups, ranging down to 0.02% per year or less for Andaman Islanders and Malaysia's Semang. Some of those differences are related to subsistence mode, with average rates for subsistence farmers being nearly 4 times those for hunter-gatherers in Wrangham, Wilson, and Muller's analysis. An alternative measure of war's impact is the percentage of total deaths that are related to warfare. That measure ranges from 56% for Ecuador's Waorani Indians down to only 3%–7% for six traditional populations scattered around the globe.

For comparison with those measures of war-related mortality in traditional small-scale societies, Keeley extracted 10 values for societies with state government: one of them for 20th-century Sweden, which experienced no wars and hence zero war-related deaths, the other nine for states and time periods selected for notoriously horrible suffering in war. The highest-percentage long-term death tolls averaged over a century in modern times have been for 20th-century Germany and Russia, which reached 0.16% and 0.15% per year respectively (i.e., 16 or 15 people killed per year per 10,000 members of the population) due to the combined horrors of

World Wars I and II. A lower value of 0.07% per year held for France in the century that included the Napoleonic Wars and the winter retreat of Napoleon's army from Russia. Despite the deaths inflicted by the two atomic bombs on Hiroshima and Nagasaki, the fire-bombing and conventional bombings of most other large Japanese cities, and the deaths by gunfire and starvation and suicide and drowning of hundreds of thousands of Japanese soldiers overseas during World War II, plus the casualties from Japan's invasion of China in the 1930s and the Russo-Japanese war of 1904–1905, Japan's percentage war-related death toll averaged over the 20th century was much lower than Germany's or Russia's, "only" 0.03% per year. The highest long-term estimate for any state is 0.25% per year for the famously bloody Aztec Empire in the century leading up to its destruction by Spain.

Let's now compare these war-related death rates (expressed again as percentages of the population dying per year of war-related causes, averaged over a long period of alternating war and peace) for traditional small-scale societies and for modern populous societies with state government. It turns out that the *highest* values for any modern states (20th-century Germany and Russia) are only one-third of the *average* values for traditional small-scale societies, and only one-sixth of Dani values. *Average* values for modern states are about one-tenth of average traditional values.

It may astonish you readers, as it initially astonished me, to learn that trench warfare, machine guns, napalm, atomic bombs, artillery, and submarine torpedoes produce time-averaged war-related death tolls so much lower than those from spears, arrows, and clubs. The reasons become clear when one reflects on the differences between traditional and modern state warfare that we shall discuss in more detail below. First, state warfare is an intermittent exceptional condition, while tribal warfare is virtually continuous. During the 20th century Germany was at war for only 10 years (1914–1918 and 1939–1945), and its war deaths during the remaining 90 years were negligible, while the Dani were traditionally at war every month of every year. Second, casualties of state war are borne mainly just by male soldiers age 18 to 40 years; even within that age range, most state wars use only small professional armies, with the mass conscription of the two world wars being exceptional; and civilians were not at direct risk in large numbers until saturation aerial bombing was adopted in World

War II. In contrast, in traditional societies everyone—men and women, prime-age adults and old adults, children and babies—is a target. Third, in state warfare soldiers who surrender or are captured are normally permitted to survive, whereas in traditional warfare all are routinely killed. Finally, traditional but not state wars are periodically punctuated by massacres in which much or all of the population on one side gets surrounded and exterminated, as in the Dani massacres of June 4, 1966, the late 1930s, 1952, June 1962, and September 1962. In contrast, victorious states nowadays routinely keep conquered populations alive in order to exploit them, rather than exterminating them.

Similarities and differences

In what respects is traditional warfare similar to state warfare, and in what respects is it different? Before answering this question, we should of course recognize that there isn't a polar opposition between these two types of warfare, with no middle ground, but that warfare instead changes along a continuum from the smallest to the largest society. The larger the society, the larger the armed force that it can muster, hence the lower the possibility of concealing the force, the lower the potential for raids and ambushes by small concealed groups of a few men, and the greater the emphasis on open battles between large forces. The leadership becomes stronger, more centralized, and more hierarchical in larger societies: national armies have officers of various ranks, a war council, and a commander-in-chief, while small bands just have equal-ranked men fighters, and medium-sized groups (like the Gutelu Alliance among the Dani) have weak leaders directing by persuasion rather than by authority to give orders. Warfare in large centralized chiefdoms may approximate warfare in small states. Despite this continuity of societal size, it's still useful to compare small and large societies in how they fight.

One similarity is in the importance of enlisting allies. Just as the Wilihiman-Walalua Confederation of Dani sought allies among other confederations in fighting against the Widaia and their allies, World War II pitted two alliances against each other, whose main members were Britain, the U.S., and Russia on one side, and Germany, Italy, and Japan on the other side. Alliances are even more essential for warring traditional societies than for warring nations. Modern nations differ greatly in military technology, so that a small nation may be able to rely on superior technology and leadership rather than on more allies to win a war. (Think of the successes of Israel's armies against far more numerous Arab alliances.) But traditional warfare tends to take place between opponents with similar technology and similar leadership, so that the side with the advantage of numbers from enlisting more allies is likely to win.

Another similarity involves the reliance of societies of all sizes on both hand-to-hand fighting and long-range weapons. Even the small Fayu bands fighting around the Kueglers' house had bows and arrows, while the Dani threw spears as well as killing Wejakhe and Jenokma at close quarters with spear thrusts. The range of weapons increases with a society's increasing size and level of technology. Although Roman soldiers continued to use swords and daggers for hand-to-hand fighting, their weapons-at-a-distance included arrows, javelins, slings, and catapults with a range of up to half a mile. By the time of World War I, the German army had developed a cannon (nicknamed Big Bertha) to bombard Paris from a distance of 68 miles, while modern intercontinental ballistic missiles have ranges of up to half of the world's circumference. But modern soldiers still have to be prepared to use a pistol or a bayonet to kill at close quarters.

A psychological consequence of this increasing range of modern long-range weapons is that most military killing today is by "push-button" technology (bombs, artillery, and missiles), permitting soldiers to kill unseen opponents and not to have to overcome their inhibitions about killing face-to-face (Plate 37). In all traditional fighting one selects one's target individually and sees his face, whether one is stabbing him at close quarters or shooting an arrow at him from a distance of tens of yards (Plate 36). Men in traditional societies grow up from childhood encouraged to kill, or at least knowing how to kill, but most modern state citizens grow up taught constantly that killing is bad, until after age 18 they suddenly enlist or are inducted into the army, given a gun, and ordered to aim at an enemy and shoot him. Not surprisingly, a significant fraction of soldiers in World Wars I and II—some estimates run as high as one-half—could not bring themselves to shoot an enemy whom they saw as another human being. Thus, while traditional societies lack both the moral inhibitions against killing an enemy face-to-face, and the technology necessary to bypass those inhibitions by killing unseen victims at a distance, modern state societies have tended to develop both the inhibitions and the technology necessary to bypass the inhibitions.

As for the numerous differences between traditional and state warfare, one difference follows straight on from that discussion of the psychology of killing. Even when modern soldiers see an enemy face-to-face, the enemy is almost always a nameless person, someone whom they never met before and against whom they hold no individual grudge. In contrast, in small-scale traditional societies one recognizes and knows by name not only every member of one's own society, but also many or most of the enemy warriors one is trying to kill—because shifting alliances and occasional intermarriages make one's neighbors familiar as individuals. The taunts that Dani warriors shouted at each other in the battles recounted in Chapter 3 included personal insults. Readers of the *Iliad* will recall how opposing Greek and Trojan leaders addressed each other by name before attempting to kill each other in battle—a famous example being the speeches of Hector and Achilles to each other just before Achilles fatally wounded Hector. Personal vengeance against an individual enemy known to have killed one of your own relatives or friends plays a major role in traditional warfare, but much less of a role or none in modern state war.

Another psychological difference involves self-sacrifice, praised in modern warfare and unknown in traditional warfare. Modern state soldiers have often been ordered, on behalf of their country, to do things highly likely to get them killed, such as charging across open ground towards barbed-wire defenses. Other soldiers decide themselves to sacrifice their lives (e.g., by throwing themselves onto a primed hand grenade) in order to save the lives of their comrades. During World War II thousands of Japanese soldiers, at first voluntarily and later under pressure, made attacks intended to be suicidal, by piloting kamikaze airplanes, rocket-powered *baka* gliding bombs, and *kaiten* human torpedoes into American warships. Such behavior requires that prospective soldiers be programmed from childhood onwards to admire dutiful obedience and sacrifice for one's country or religion. I have never heard of such behavior in New Guinea traditional warfare: every warrior's goal is to kill the enemy *and* to stay alive himself. For instance, when Wilihiman raiders caught and killed the Widaia man Huwai on May 11, 1961, Huwai's outnumbered two companions fled without trying to save him; and when Widaia raiders in ambush caught and killed the already-injured Wilihiman boy Wejakhe on June 10, the other three outnumbered Wilihiman man and boys with Wejakhe similarly fled.

Traditional societies and states differ as to who are their soldiers. All state armies have included full-time professional soldiers who can remain in the field for years at a time, supported by civilians who grow food for themselves and for the soldiers. Either the professionals make up the entire army (as is currently true in the U.S.), or else their ranks are augmented (mainly in time of war) by non-professional volunteers or conscripts. In contrast, all band and tribal warriors, like the Dani warriors described in Chapter 3, and all or most warriors of chiefdoms, are non-professionals. They are men normally occupied with hunting or farming or herding, who suspend those subsistence activities for periods ranging from a few hours up to a few weeks in order to fight, and then go home again because they are needed for hunting or planting or harvesting. Hence it's impossible for traditional "armies" to remain in the field for lengthy periods. That basic reality gave a decisive advantage to European colonial soldiers in their wars of conquest against tribes and chiefdoms around the world. Some of those non-European peoples, like New Zealand's Maori, Argentina's Araucanian Indians, and North America's Sioux and Apache Indians, were determined and skilled fighters who could muster large forces for short times and achieved some spectacular successes against European armies. But they were inevitably worn down and eventually defeated because they had to break off fighting in order to resume obtaining and producing food, while professional European soldiers could continue to fight.

Modern military historians regularly comment on what strikes them as the "inefficiency" of traditional warfare: that hundreds of people can fight for an entire day, at the end of which no one or only one or two people have been killed. Part of the reason, of course, is that traditional societies lack artillery, bombs, and other weapons capable of killing many people at once. But the other reasons are related to the tribes' non-professional army and lack of strong leadership. Traditional warriors don't undergo group training that might enable them to be more lethal by executing complex plans or even just by coordinating their shooting. Arrows would be more effective if fired in a synchronized volley rather than one at a time: a targeted enemy can dodge an individual arrow but can't dodge a whole flight of arrows. Nevertheless, the Dani, like most other traditional bowmen, had not practiced synchronizing their volleys. (Northwest Alaska Inuit were exceptional in that respect.) Discipline and organized formations are minimal: even if fighting units are well formed before a battle, the units quickly fall apart, and the battle degenerates into an uncoordinated melee. Traditional war leaders cannot issue orders for which the price of disobedience is court-martial. The 1966 massacre that broke apart the alliance of the Dani leader Gutelu may have resulted from Gutelu's inability to prevent his own hot-headed northern warriors from massacring his southern allies.

One of the two biggest differences between traditional and state warfare involves the distinction between total war and limited war. We Americans are accustomed to thinking of total war as a new concept introduced by the northern general William Tecumseh Sherman during the American Civil War (1861–1865). Warfare by states and large chiefdoms tends to have limited goals: to destroy the enemy's armed forces and capacity to fight, but to spare the enemy's land, resources, and civilian population because those are what a would-be conqueror hopes to take over. General Sherman, in his march to the sea (from the inland hub of Atlanta to the Atlantic Ocean) through the heart of the Confederacy and then north through South Carolina, became famous for his explicit policy of total war: destroying everything of possible military value, and breaking Southern morale, by taking food, burning crops, killing livestock, wrecking farm machinery, burning cotton and cotton gins, burning railroads and twisting their rails to preclude their being repaired, and burning or blowing up bridges, railroad stock, factories, mills, and buildings. Sherman's actions resulted from a calculated philosophy of war, which he described as follows: "War is cruelty and you cannot refine it. . . . We are not only fighting hostile armies, but a hostile people, and must make young and old, rich and poor, feel the hard hand of war. . . . We cannot change the hearts of those people of the South, but we can make war so terrible . . . make them so sick of war that generations would pass before they would again appeal to it." But Sherman did not exterminate Southern civilians or kill Confederate soldiers who surrendered or were captured.

While Sherman's behavior was indeed exceptional by standards of state warfare, he did not invent total warfare. Instead, he practiced a mild form of what has been practiced by bands and tribes for tens of thousands of years, as documented by the skeletal remains of the massacre at Talheim described on page 134. State armies spare and take prisoners because they are able to feed them, guard them, put them to work, and prevent them from running away. Traditional "armies" do not take enemy warriors as prisoners, because they cannot do any of those things to make use of prisoners. Surrounded or defeated traditional warriors do not surrender, because they know that they would be killed anyway. The earliest historical or archaeological evidence of states taking prisoners is not until the time of Mesopotamian states of about 5,000 years ago, which solved the practical problems of getting use out of prisoners by gouging out their eyes to blind them so that they could not run away, then putting them to work at tasks that could be carried out by the sense of touch alone, such as spinning and some gardening chores. A few large, sedentary, economically specialized tribes and chiefdoms of hunter-gatherers, such as coastal Pacific Northwest Indians and Florida's Calusa Indians, were also able routinely to enslave, maintain, and make use of captives.

However, for societies simpler than Mesopotamian states, Pacific Northwest Indians, and the Calusa, defeated enemies were of no value alive. War's goal among the Dani, Fore, Northwest Alaskan Inuit, Andaman Islanders, and many other tribes was to take over the enemy's land and to exterminate the enemy of both sexes and all ages, including the dozens of Dani women and children killed in the June 4, 1966, massacre. Other traditional societies, such as the Nuer raiding the Dinka, were more selective, in that they killed Dinka men and clubbed to death Dinka babies and older women but brought home Dinka women of marriageable age to force-marry to Nuer men, and also brought home Dinka weaned children to rear as Nuer. The Yanomamo similarly spared enemy women in order to use them as mates.

Total warfare among traditional societies also means mobilizing all men, including the Dani boys down to age six who fought in the battle of August 6, 1961. State war, however, is usually fought with proportionally tiny professional armies of adult men. Napoleon's Grande Armée with which he invaded Russia in 1812 numbered 600,000 men and thus rates as huge by the standards of 19th-century state warfare, but that number represented under 10% of the total population of France at that time (actually even less, because some of the soldiers were non-French allies). Even within modern state armies, combat troops are generally outnumbered by support troops: the ratio is now 1 to 11 for the U.S. Army. The Dani would have been scornful of Napoleon's and the U.S. armies' inability to field combat troops, measured as a proportion of the society's whole population. But the Dani would have found familiar Sherman's behavior on his march to the sea, reminiscent of Dani behavior during the dawn raid of June 4, 1966, when they burned dozens of settlements and stole pigs.

Ending warfare

The remaining big difference between tribal and state warfare, after that distinction between total and limited warfare, involves the differing ease of ending war and maintaining peace. As illustrated by the Dani War of Chapter 3, wars of small-scale societies often involve cycles of revenge killings. A death suffered by side A demands that side A take vengeance by killing someone from side B, whose members now in turn demand vengeance of their own against side A. Those cycles end only when one side has been exterminated or driven out, or else when both sides are exhausted, both have suffered many deaths, and neither side foresees the likelihood of being able to exterminate or drive out the other. While analogous considerations apply to ending state warfare, states and large chiefdoms go to war with much more limited goals than do bands and tribes: at most, just to conquer all of the enemy's territory.

But it's much harder for a tribe than for a state (and a large centralized chiefdom) to reach a decision to seek an end to fighting, and to negotiate a truce with the enemy—because a state has centralized decision-making and negotiators, while a tribe lacks centralized leadership and everyone has his say. It's even harder for a tribe than for a state to maintain peace, once a truce has been negotiated. In any society, whether a tribe or a state, there will be some individuals who are dissatisfied with any peace agreement, and who want to attack some enemy for their own private reasons and to provoke a new outbreak of fighting. A state government that asserts a centralized monopoly on the use of power and force can usually restrain those hotheads; a weak tribal leader can't. Hence tribal peaces are fragile and quickly deteriorate to yet another cycle of war.

That difference between states and small centralized societies is a major reason why states exist at all. There has been a long-standing debate among political scientists about how states arise, and why the governed masses tolerate kings and congressmen and their bureaucrats. Full-time political leaders don't grow their own food, but they live off of food raised by us peasants. How did our leaders convince or force us to feed them, and why do we let them remain in power? The French philosopher Jean-Jacques Rousseau speculated, without any evidence to back up his speculations, that governments arise as the result of rational decisions by the masses who recognize that their own interests will be better served under a leader and bureaucrats. In all the cases of state formation now known to historians, no such farsighted calculation has ever been observed. Instead, states arise from chiefdoms through competition, conquest, or external pressure: the chiefdom with the most effective decision-making is better able to resist conquest or to outcompete other chiefdoms. For example, between 1807 and 1817 the dozens of separate chiefdoms of southeastern Africa's Zulu people, traditionally warring with each other, became amalgamated into one state under one of the chiefs, named Dingiswayo, who conquered all the competing chiefs by proving more successful at figuring out how best to recruit an army, settle disputes, incorporate defeated chiefdoms, and administer his territory.

Despite the excitement and the prestige of tribal fighting, tribespeople understand better than anyone else the misery associated with warfare, the omnipresent danger, and the pain due to the killings of loved ones. When tribal warfare is finally ended by forceful intervention by colonial governments, tribespeople regularly comment on the resulting improved quality of life that they hadn't been able to create for themselves, because without centralized government they hadn't been able to interrupt the cycles of revenge killings. Anthropologist Sterling Robbins was told by Auyana men in the New Guinea Highlands, "Life was better since the government had come because a man could now eat without looking over his shoulder and could leave his house in the morning to urinate without fear of being shot. All men admitted that they were afraid when they

Plate 1. A Dani man, from the Baliem Valley of the New Guinea Highlands.

Plate 2. An Australian Aboriginal man.

Plate 3. An Agta woman, from the mountain forest of Luzon Island in the Philippines.

Plate 4. An Andaman Islander, from the Bay of Bengal.

Plate 5. A Hadza man, from Tanzania.

Plate 6. A !Kung hunter, from Africa's Kalahari Desert.

Plate 7. A Nuer woman, from the Sudan.

Plate 8. An Aka father and his child, from Africa's equatorial forest.

Plate 9. An Inuit woman (Iñupiaq), from Alaska.

Plate 10. An Ache Indian man, from the forests of Paraguay.

Plate 11. A Piraha Indian couple and their baby, from the Amazonian rainforest of Brazil.

Plate 12. A Yanomamo Indian girl, from the forests of Venezuela.

Plate 13. A traditional border between tribes, guarded by a Dani man on a watchtower, from the Baliem Valley of the New Guinea Highlands. (Pages 42 and 123)

Plate 14. A modern border between nations, guarded by remote-controlled cameras on a U.S. Customs and Border Patrol watchtower, at the border between the United States and Mexico.

Plate 15. Traditional dispute resolution, in a Ugandan village. Disputants who have already known one another personally gather to settle their dispute, in a way that will permit them to resolve their feelings and continue to encounter each other peacefully for the rest of their lives. (Chapter 2)

Plate 16. Modern dispute resolution, in an American courtroom. A defense attorney (left) and a criminal prosecutor (right) argue a point before a judge (middle). The alleged criminal, the victim, and the victim's family did not know each other before the alleged crime and will probably never encounter each other again. (Chapter 2)

Plate 17. Traditional toys: Mozambique boys with toy cars that they have made themselves, thereby learning how axles and other car components are designed. Traditional toys are few, simple, made by the child or its parents, and thus educational. (Pages 205 and 459)

Plate 18. Modern toys: an American girl surrounded by her dozens of manufactured toys bought in stores, thereby depriving her of the educational value that traditional children gain from designing and making their own toys. (Page 204)

Plate 19. Traditional child autonomy: Pume Indian baby playing with a large sharp knife. Children in many traditional societies are permitted to make their own decisions, including whether to do dangerous things that most modern parents would never permit a child to do. (Page 198)

Plate 20. Traditional toy: an Aka baby carrying a home-made toy basket on his head, similar to the head-held baskets that Aka adults carry. (Page 204)

Plate 21. A Hadza grandmother foraging while carrying her grandchild. One reason old people are considered valuable in traditional societies is that they serve as care-givers and food-producers to their grandchildren. (Pages 185, 188, and 218)

Plate 22. An older Pume Indian man making arrow points. Another reason older people are considered valuable in traditional societies is that they serve as the best makers of tools, weapons, baskets, pots, and textiles. (Page 218)

Plate 23. A Chinese advertisement for Coca-Cola. The American cult of youth and the low status of the elderly, now spreading to China, are reflected even in the choice of models for ads. Old as well as young people drink soft drinks, but who ever saw an ad depicting old people exuberantly drinking Coca-Cola? (Page 226)

"I want options that are right for *me*."

We help find, plan and implement the right senior living and care choices, tailored just for you.

Call for a needs assessment:
760-522-6478

Starfish Resources, LLC
www.StarfishResources.net

Plate 24. Advertisement for a consulting service specializing in senior living. Instead of older people appearing in ads to sell drinks, clothes, and new cars, they appear in ads for retirement homes, arthritis drugs, and adult diapers. (Page 226)

Plate 25. Ancient religion?: the famous rock wall paintings deep inside France's Lascaux cave still inspire awe in modern visitors. They suggest that human religion dates back at least to the Ice Age 15,000 years ago. (Page 340)

Plate 26. Traditional feasting among Dani people in the Baliem Valley of the New Guinea Highlands. Traditional feasting is very infrequent, the food consumed is not fattening (low-fat sweet potatoes in this case), and the feasters do not become obese or end up with diabetes. (Chapter 11)

Plate 27. Modern feasting. Americans and members of other affluent modern societies "feast" (i.e., consume in excess of their daily needs) three times every day, eat fattening foods (fried chicken in this case), become obese, and may end up with diabetes. (Chapter 11)

Plate 28. A victim of diabetes?: the composer Johann Sebastian Bach. His puffy face and hands in this sole authenticated portrait, and his deteriorating handwriting and vision in his later years, are consistent with a diagnosis of diabetes. (Page 449)

fought. In fact, they usually looked at me as though I were a mental defective for even asking. Men admitted having nightmares in which they became isolated from others in their group during a fight and could see no way back."

That reaction explains the surprising ease with which small numbers of Australian patrol officers and native policemen were able to end tribal warfare in the then-territory of Papua New Guinea. They arrived at a warring village, bought a pig, shot the pig to demonstrate the power of firearms, tore down village stockades and confiscated the war shields of all warring groups in order to make it lethally dangerous for anyone to initiate war, and occasionally shot New Guineans who dared to attack them. Of course, New Guineans are pragmatic and could recognize the power of guns. But one might not have predicted how easily they would give up warfare that they had been practicing for thousands of years, when achievement in war had been praised from childhood onwards and held up as the measure of a man.

The explanation for this surprising outcome is that New Guineans appreciated the benefits of the state-guaranteed peace that they had been unable to achieve for themselves without state government. For instance, in the 1960s I spent a month in a recently pacified area of the New Guinea Highlands, where 20,000 Highlanders who until a decade or so previously had been constantly making war against each other now lived along with one Australian patrol officer and a few New Guinea policemen. Yes, the patrol officer and the policemen had guns, and the New Guineans didn't. But if the New Guineans had really wanted to resume fighting each other, it would have been trivially easy for them to kill the patrol officer and his policemen at night, or to ambush them by day. They didn't even try to do so. That illustrates how they had come to appreciate the biggest advantage of state government: the bringing of peace.

Effects of European contact

Did traditional warfare increase, decrease, or remain unchanged upon European contact? This is not a straightforward question to decide, because if one believes that contact does affect the intensity of traditional warfare,

then one will automatically distrust any account of it by an outside observer as having been influenced by the observer and not representing the
pristine condition. Lawrence Keeley used the analogy of supposing that
watermelons are white inside and become red only as soon as they are cut
with a knife: how could one ever hope to demonstrate that watermelons
really are red even before they are cut open in order to examine their
color?

However, the mass of archaeological evidence and oral accounts of war
before European contact discussed above makes it far-fetched to maintain
that people were traditionally peaceful until those evil Europeans arrived
and messed things up. There can be no doubt that European contacts or
other forms of state government in the long run almost always end or reduce warfare, because all state governments don't want wars disrupting
the administration of their territory. Studies of ethnographically observed
cases make clear that, in the short run, the initiation of European contact
may either increase or decrease fighting, for reasons that include
European-introduced weaponry, diseases, trade opportunities, and increases or decreases in the food supply.

A well-understood example of a short-term increase in fighting as a
result of European contact is provided by New Zealand's original Polynesian inhabitants, the Maori, who had settled in New Zealand by around
AD 1200. Archaeological excavations of Maori forts attest to widespread
Maori warfare long before European arrival. Accounts of the first European explorers from 1642 onwards, and of the first European settlers from
the 1790s onwards, describe the Maori killing Europeans as well as each
other. From about 1818 to 1835 two products introduced by Europeans triggered a transient surge in the deadliness of Maori warfare, in an episode
known in New Zealand history as the Musket Wars. One factor was of
course the introduction of muskets, with which Maori could kill each
other far more efficiently than they had previously been able to do when
armed just with clubs. The other factor may initially surprise you: potatoes, which we don't normally imagine as a major promoter of war. But it
turns out that the duration and size of Maori expeditions to attack other
Maori groups had been limited by the amount of food that could be
brought along to feed the warriors. The original Maori staple food was
sweet potatoes. Potatoes introduced by Europeans (although originating

in South America) are more productive in New Zealand than are sweet potatoes, yield bigger food surpluses, and permitted sending out bigger raiding expeditions for longer times than had been possible for traditional Maori depending upon sweet potatoes. After potatoes' arrival, Maori canoe-borne expeditions to enslave or kill other Maori broke all previous Maori distance records by covering distances of as much as a thousand miles. At first only the few tribes living in areas with resident European traders could acquire muskets, which they used to destroy tribes without muskets. As muskets spread, the Musket Wars rose to a peak until all surviving tribes had muskets, whereupon there were no more musket-less tribes to offer defenseless targets, and the Musket Wars faded away.

In Fiji as well, the introduction of European muskets around 1808 made it possible for Fijians to kill each other in much larger numbers than they had traditionally been able to do with clubs, spears, and arrows. European guns, boats, and steel axes transiently facilitated inter-island head-hunting in the Solomon Islands in the 19th century: unlike stone axes, steel axes can behead many humans without losing their sharp edge. Similarly, European guns and horses, and European guns and slave-buyers, stimulated warfare in the North American Great Plains and in Central Africa, respectively. For each of these societies that I have just mentioned, warfare had been endemic long before European arrival, but effects of Europeans caused an exacerbation of warfare for a few decades (New Zealand, Fiji, Solomon Islands) or a few centuries (Great Plains, Central Africa) before it died out.

In other cases the arrival of Europeans or of other outsiders led instead to warfare's end without any hint of an initial flare-up. In many parts of the New Guinea Highlands the first Europeans were government patrols that immediately ended warfare before European traders, missionaries, or even indirectly transmitted European trade goods could appear. When first studied by anthropologists in the 1950s, Africa's !Kung bands were no longer raiding each other, although the frequency of individual murders within bands or between neighboring bands remained high until 1955. Four of the last five murders (in 1946, 1952, 1952, and 1955) resulted in the Tswana administration taking the killers off to jail, and that plus the availability of Tswana courts for settling disputes induced the !Kung to abandon murder as a means for resolving conflicts after 1955. However, !Kung oral histories report inter-band raids several generations earlier, until the time when increased Tswana contact introduced iron for arrowheads and other changes. Somehow, that contact resulted in an end to raiding long before the Tswana police intervened to arrest killers.

My remaining example comes from northwest Alaska, where formerly widespread fighting and exterminations among Yupik and Iñupiaq Inuit ended within a decade or a generation of European contact—not because of patrol officers, police, and courts forbidding war but because of other consequences of contact. The end of Yupik warfare is attributed to an 1838 smallpox epidemic that depleted the populations of several groups. The end of Iñupiaq warfare appears to have been due to the Iñupiaq chronic obsession with trade, and to their greatly increased new opportunities to trade furs to the Europeans with whom regular contact became intense after 1848: continued warfare would have been an obvious impediment to those opportunities.

Thus, the long-term effect of European, Tswana, or other outside contact with states or chiefdoms has almost always been to suppress tribal warfare. The short-term effect has variously been either an immediate suppression as well or else an initial flare-up and then suppression. It cannot be said that traditional warfare is an artifact of European contact.

Nevertheless, there has been a long history of denial of traditional warfare among Western scholars. Jean-Jacques Rousseau, already mentioned for his speculative theory of state formation not based on any empirical evidence, had an equally speculative and ungrounded theory of warfare: he claimed that humans were naturally compassionate in a state of nature, and that wars began only with the rise of states. Trained ethnographers studying traditional societies in the 20th century mostly found themselves dealing with tribes and bands that had already been pacified by colonial governments, until some anthropologists were able to witness the last examples of traditional wars in the 1950s and 1960s in the New Guinea Highlands and Amazonia. Archaeologists excavating fortifications associated with ancient wars have often overlooked, ignored, or explained them away, e.g., by dismissing defensive ditches and palisades surrounding a village as mere "enclosures" or "symbols of exclusion." But the evidence of traditional warfare, whether based on direct observation or oral histories or archaeological evidence, is so overwhelming that one has to wonder: why is there still any debate about its importance?

One reason is the real difficulties, which we have discussed, in evaluating traditional warfare under pre-contact or early-contact conditions. Warriors quickly discern that visiting anthropologists disapprove of war, and the warriors tend not to take anthropologists along on raids or allow them to photograph battles undisturbed: the filming opportunities available to the Harvard Peabody Expedition among the Dani were unique. Another reason is that the short-term effects of European contact on tribal war can work in either direction and have to be evaluated case by case with an open mind. But the widespread denial of traditional warfare seems to go beyond those and other uncertainties in the evidence itself, and instead to involve reluctance to accept evidence for its existence or extent. Why?

There may be several reasons at work. Scholars tend to like, to identify with, or to sympathize with the traditional people among whom they live for several years. The scholars consider war bad, know that most readers of their monographs will also consider war bad, and don't want "their" people to be viewed as bad. Another reason involves unfounded claims (to be discussed below) that human warfare has an inexorable genetic basis. That leads to the false assumption that war would be unstoppable, and hence to a reluctance to acknowledge the apparently depressing conclusion that war traditionally really has been widespread. Still another reason is that some state or colonial governments are eager to get indigenous people out of the way by conquering or dispossessing them or by turning a blind eye to their extermination. Branding them as warlike is used as an excuse to justify that mistreatment, so scholars seek to remove that excuse by trying to absolve the indigenous people of the charge of being warlike.

I sympathize with scholars outraged by the mistreatment of indigenous peoples. But denying the reality of traditional warfare because of political misuse of its reality is a bad strategy, for the same reason that denying any other reality for any other laudable political goal is a bad strategy. The reason not to mistreat indigenous people is not that they are falsely accused of being warlike, but that it's unjust to mistreat them. The facts about traditional warfare, just like the facts about any other controversial phenomenon that can be observed and studied, are likely eventually to come out. When they do come out, if scholars have been denying traditional warfare's reality for laudable political reasons, the discovery of the facts will undermine the laudable political goals. The rights of indigenous people should be asserted on moral grounds, not by making untrue claims susceptible to refutation.

Warlike animals, peaceful peoples

If one defines war as I defined it on p. 131—"recurrent violence between groups belonging to rival political units, and sanctioned by the units"— and if one takes a broadened view of "political units" and "sanctioned," then war characterizes not only humans but also some animal species. The species most often mentioned in discussions of human war is the common chimpanzee, because it is one of our two closest living animal relatives. War among chimpanzees resembles human band and tribal warfare in consisting of either chance encounters or else apparently intentional raids involving adult males. Calculated war-related death rates in chimpanzees, 0.36% per year (i.e., 36 chimpanzees per year in a population of 10,000), are similar to those for traditional human societies. Does this mean that warfare was transmitted to humans in a straight line from our chimpanzee ancestors, hence that it has a genetic basis, hence that we are helplessly pre-programmed to make war, hence that it's inevitable and can't be prevented?

The answer to all four of these questions is no. Chimpanzees are not the ancestors of humans; instead, chimpanzees and humans are both descended from a common ancestor that lived about 6,000,000 years ago, and from which modern chimpanzees may be more divergent than are modern humans. It is not the case that all descendants of that common ancestor make war: bonobos (formerly known as pygmy chimpanzees), which genetically are the same distance from us as are chimpanzees and hence are the other one of our two closest animal relatives, are also derived from that common ancestor but have not been observed to make war; and some traditional human societies don't make war. Among social animal species other than chimpanzees, some (e.g., lions, wolves, hyenas, and some ant species) are known to practise lethal fighting between groups, while others are not known to do so. Evidently, war does arise repeatedly and independently but is not inevitable among social animals in general, nor within the human-chimpanzee evolutionary line in particular, nor among modern human societies more particularly. Richard Wrangham argues that two features distinguish those social species that do practise war from those that don't: intense resource competition, and occurrence in groups of variable size such that large groups sometimes encounter small groups or individual animals which they can safely attack and overwhelm by numbers with little risk to the aggressors.

As for a genetic basis to human warfare, it of course has a genetic basis, in the same broad and distant sense in which cooperation and other multi-faceted human behaviors have a genetic basis. That is, the human brain and hormones and instincts are laid down ultimately by genes, such as the genes that control the synthesis of the hormone testosterone associated with aggressive behavior. However, the normal range of aggressive behavior, like the normal range of body height, is influenced by many different genes and by environmental and social factors (like effects of childhood nutrition on adult height). That's unlike single-gene traits such as sickle-cell hemoglobin, which a person carrying the gene for that trait synthesizes regardless of childhood nutrition, other genes, or environmental competition. Like warfare, warfare's converse of cooperation is widespread but variably expressed among human societies. We already saw in Chapter 1 that cooperation between neighboring human societies is favored by certain environmental conditions, such as resource fluctuations within or between years, and whether or not a territory contains all resources necessary for self-sufficient survival. It is not inevitable or genetically programmed that neighboring small-scale societies cooperate; there are reasons why some cooperate more and some cooperate less.

Similarly, there are external reasons why some human societies are peaceful, although most are not. Most modern state societies have been involved in recent wars, but a few haven't, for understandable reasons. The Central American nation of Costa Rica hasn't had a recent war, and even abolished its army in 1949, because its historical population and social conditions resulted in relatively egalitarian and democratic traditions, and its only neighbors (Nicaragua and Panama) are unthreatening and offer no targets of great value to conquer except the Panama Canal, which would be defended by the U.S. Army if Costa Rica were foolish enough to invest in an army to attack the canal. Sweden and Switzerland haven't had recent wars (although Sweden formerly did), because they now do have aggressive and far more powerful and populous neighbors (Germany, France, and Russia) which they could never hope to conquer themselves, and because they have successfully deterred those neighbors from attacking them by being armed to the teeth.

Like these modern states without recent involvement in wars, a small minority of traditional societies have also been peaceful for understandable reasons. Greenland's Polar Eskimos were so isolated that they had no neighbors, no outside contacts, and no possibility of war even if they had wanted it. Absence of war has been reported for quite a few small bands of nomadic hunter-gatherers living at very low population densities, in harsh unproductive environments, with large home ranges, with few or no possessions worth defending or acquiring, and relatively isolated from other such bands. These include the Shoshone Indians of the U.S. Great Basin, Bolivia's Siriono Indians, some Australian desert tribes, and the Nganasan of northern Siberia. Farmers without a history of war include Peru's Machiguenga Indians, living in a marginal forest environment not coveted by others, without pockets of good land sufficiently dense or dependable to warrant war or defense, and with currently low population density, possibly because of a recent population crash during the rubber boom.

Thus, it could not be claimed that some societies are inherently or genetically peaceful, while others are inherently warlike. Instead, it appears that societies do or don't resort to war, depending on whether it might be profitable for them to initiate war and/or necessary for them to defend themselves against wars initiated by others. Most societies have indeed participated in wars, but a few have not, for good reasons. While those societies that have not are sometimes claimed to be inherently gentle (e.g., the Semang, !Kung, and African Pygmies), those gentle people do have intra-group violence ("murder"); they merely have reasons for lacking organized inter-group violence that would fit a definition of war. When the normally gentle Semang were enlisted by the British army in the 1950s to scout and kill Communist rebels in Malaya, the Semang killed enthusiastically. It is equally fruitless to debate whether humans are intrinsically violent or else intrinsically cooperative. All human societies practise both violence and cooperation; which trait appears to predominate depends on the circumstances.

Motives for traditional war

Why do traditional societies go to war? We can try to answer this question in different ways. The most straightforward method is not to attempt to interpret people's claimed or underlying motives, but simply to observe what sorts of benefits victorious societies gain from war. A second method is to ask people about their motives ("proximate causes of war"). The remaining method is to try to figure out their real underlying motives ("ultimate causes of war").

Victorious traditional societies are observed to obtain many benefits. Listing some of the major benefits alphabetically without any pretense of ranking them in importance, they include children captured, cows, food, heads (for head-hunters), horses, human bodies to eat (for cannibals), land, land resources (such as fishing areas, fruit orchards, gardens, salt pools, and stone quarries), pigs, prestige, protein, slaves, trade rights, and wives.

But the motives that people give for going to war, just like the motives that they give for any other important decision, may not coincide with the observed payoffs. In this as in other areas of life, people may be unconscious of or not frank about what is driving them. What do people allege as their motives for war?

The commonest answer is "revenge" for killings of fellow tribespeople or band members, because most tribal battles are preceded by other battles rather than by a long period of peace. Examples from the Dani War of Chapter 3 are the craving for vengeance by the Wilihiman after the battles or deaths of January, April 10 and 27, June 10, July 5, and August 16, 1961, and by the Widaia after April 3 and 10 and May 29.

If revenge is the main motive cited for continuing a war, what motives initiate a war? In the New Guinea Highlands, common answers are "women" and "pigs." For men from New Guinea as from other parts of the world, women give rise to escalating disputes by being involved in or victims of adultery, desertion of husbands, kidnapping, rape, and bride-price disputes. The Yanomamo and many other peoples similarly report women as a or the major cause of war. When anthropologist Napoleon Chagnon had occasion to tell a Yanomamo headman about people of Chagnon's "group" (i.e., Americans and British) "raiding" their enemies (i.e., Germans), the headman guessed, "You probably raided because of women theft, didn't you?" That motive no longer applies to modern large-scale state societies. However, the origins of the Trojan War in the seduction of King Menelaus's wife Helen by King Priam's son Paris testify that women remained a casus belli at least until the times of small ancient states.

As for New Guineans ranking pigs on a par with women as causes of war, recall that pigs to a New Guinean are not mere food and the largest available source of protein: they are the main currency of wealth and prestige, and are convertible into women as essential components of bride-price. Like women, pigs are prone to wander and desert their "owners," are easily kidnapped or stolen, and thus provoke endless disputes.

For peoples other than New Guineans, other domestic animal species, especially cows and horses, replace pigs as prized measures of wealth and causes of disputes. The Nuer are as obsessed with cows as New Guineans are with pigs, and the main goal of the Nuer in raiding the Dinka and other Nuer tribes is to steal cows. Nuer cows also lend themselves to disputes over trade and compensation ("You didn't pay me the cows that you promised"). As one Nuer man (quoted by Evans-Pritchard) summarized it, "More people have died for the sake of a cow than for any other cause." Horses and horse theft played the role of cows and pigs in triggering wars among Indians of North America's Great Basin and among peoples of the Asian steppes. Many other types of material things besides women and animals have led to wars by being coveted, stolen, or subject to dispute among other peoples.

Small-scale societies go to war not only to acquire women as wives, but also to acquire other individuals for other purposes. The Nuer captured Dinka children to raise as Nuer and to incorporate into their own numbers. The long list of head-hunting peoples that went to war to capture and kill enemies for their heads included the Asmat and Marind in New Guinea, the Roviana people in the Solomon Islands, and various peoples of Asia, Indonesia, the Pacific islands, Ireland, Scotland, Africa, and South America. Cannibalistic peoples who ate captured or dead enemies included Caribs, some peoples of Africa and the Americas, some New Guineans, and many Pacific islanders. Capture of enemies to use them as slaves was practised by some complex chiefdoms and tribal societies such as northwest New Guineans, western Solomon Islanders, Native Americans of the Pacific Northwest and Florida, and West Africans. Slavery was practised on a large scale by many or perhaps most state societies, including ancient Greece, the Roman Empire, China, the Ottoman Empire, and European colonies in the New World.

There are at least two other frequently offered reasons that traditional people themselves mention as motives for war. One is sorcery: it's routine in New Guinea and many other small-scale societies to blame anything bad that happens (such as an illness or a death that we would consider natural) on an enemy sorcerer, who must be identified and killed. The other is the common view that one's neighbors are intrinsically bad, hostile, subhuman, and treacherous and thus deserve to be attacked whether or not they have committed some specific evil deed recently. I already quoted an example for New Guinea in Chapter 3: a Wilihiman Dani man's answer to a Dani woman about why he was trying to kill the Widaia Dani ("Those people are our enemies, why shouldn't we kill them?—they're not human").

In addition to all these conflicts over people and animals serving as motives for war, land conflicts are regularly mentioned as motives. A typical example is the land dispute that I described in Chapter 1, between my New Guinea mountain friends and the neighboring river people over the ridge-line between their villages.

Ultimate reasons

This enumeration of motives offered by members of small-scale societies for going to war—women, children, heads, and so on—doesn't exhaust the list. However, it already suffices to make clear why these named motives by themselves aren't a satisfying explanation for traditional warfare. Everybody's neighbors have women, children, heads, and edible bodies, and many or most traditional neighbors have domestic animals, practise sorcery, and can be viewed as bad. Coveting of these individuals and things, or disputes about them, don't inevitably trigger wars. Even in especially warlike societies, the usual response to a dispute arising is to try to settle it peacefully, e.g., by payment of compensation (Chapter 2). Only if efforts at peaceful resolution fail does the offended party resort to war. Why, then, are compensation negotiations more likely to fail among some peoples than among others? Why are there such differences, when women and the other claimed motives for war are ubiquitous?

The ultimate factors behind a war aren't necessarily the factors that the participants themselves understand or enunciate at the time. For instance, one theory of Yanomamo warfare debated by anthropologists postulates that its ultimate purpose is to acquire scarce protein by assuring abundant availability of game animals to be hunted. However, traditional Yanomamo don't know what protein is, and they persist in citing women rather than availability of game animals as their motive for making war. Hence even if the protein theory of Yanomamo warfare were correct (which it probably isn't), we would never learn about it from the Yanomamo themselves.

Unfortunately, understanding ultimate factors that you can't ask people about is much more difficult than understanding proximate motives that people can describe to you. Just reflect on our difficulties in establishing the ultimate cause(s) of World War I, despite the availability of enormous quantities of relevant documents to whose study hundreds of historians have devoted their lives. Everyone knows that the proximate cause of World War I was the assassination of Archduke Franz Ferdinand, heir to the throne of the Habsburg Empire, by the Serb nationalist Gavrilo Princip at Sarajevo on June 28, 1914. However, numerous other heads of state and heirs apparent have been assassinated without such dire consequences, so what were the ultimate reasons why this particular assassination did trigger World War I? The debated candidate theories of World War I's ultimate cause(s) include the pre-war system of alliances, nationalism, threats to the stability of two major multi-ethnic empires (the Habsburg and Ottoman empires), festering territorial disputes over Alsace-Lorraine and transit through the Dardanelles, and Germany's rising economic power. Because we still can't agree about the ultimate causes even of World War I, we can't expect it to be easy to understand the ultimate causes of traditional warfare either. But students of traditional warfare enjoy a big advantage over students of the two world wars, in that we have an almost infinite number of traditional wars to compare.

The ultimate factor most often proposed for traditional warfare is to acquire land or other scarce resources such as fisheries, salt sources, stone quarries, or human labor. Except in harsh fluctuating environments whose conditions keep human populations periodically or permanently low, human groups grow in size to utilize their land and its resources, and can then increase further only at the expense of other groups. Hence societies go to war to seize land or resources belonging to other groups, or to defend their own land and resources that other groups seek to seize. This motive is often proclaimed explicitly by state governments going to war to acquire land and labor. For instance, Hitler wrote and spoke of Germany's need for Lebensraum (living space to the east), but Russians and other Slavs lived to the east of Germany, so Hitler's goal of acquiring eastern living space for Germany led him to invade Poland and then Russia in order to conquer, enslave, or kill the Slavs who lived there.

The most extensive test of this theory that land and resource shortages lead to war was by Carol and Melvin Ember, using a cross-cultural sample of 186 societies. From ethnographic information about these societies summarized in the Human Relations Area Files (a large cross-cultural survey), Ember and Ember extracted measures of several causes of resource shortages: the frequencies of famines, of natural disasters such as droughts or frosts, and of food scarcity. It turned out that these measures were the strongest predictor of war's frequency. The authors took this finding to mean that people go to war to take resources (especially land) from their enemies, and thereby to protect themselves against unpredictable resource scarcity in the future.

Although this interpretation is plausible, it doesn't operate so straightforwardly that all scholars accept it. While some traditional wars are indeed followed by the losers fleeing and the victors occupying their land, there are also cases of the vacated land being left unoccupied for some time. It is not the case that traditional wars are consistently fiercer in more densely populated areas, because some habitats and subsistence modes can comfortably support much higher population densities than can other habitats and subsistence modes. For instance, hunter-gatherers living at a density of 5 people per square mile in a desert feel more resource-starved and pressed to expand than do farmers living at 100 people per square mile in fertile, warm, well-watered farmlands. That is, what counts is not population density itself, but population density in relation to resource density, resulting in actual or potential resource shortages. If one compares traditional peoples with similar subsistence modes and living in similar habitats with similar resources, the frequency of warfare does increase with population density.

Other ultimate factors proposed to explain traditional warfare are social factors. People may go to war to keep troublesome neighbors at a distance, to get rid of the neighbors altogether, or to acquire a bellicose reputation and thereby to deter the likelihood of attacks by neighbors who wouldn't hesitate to attack a group with a reputation for not defending itself. This social interpretation isn't incompatible with the previous theory in terms of land and resources: an ultimate reason for wanting to keep one's neighbors at a distance may be to maintain secure control of one's land and resources. But it's worth mentioning social considerations as a factor separate from resource considerations, because one's desire to maintain distance from neighbors may cause one to take actions far more extreme than what others would consider necessary just for securing resources.

For example, until around 500 years ago Finland's population was concentrated on the seacoast and Finland's forested interior was sparsely inhabited. When individual families and small groups began moving as colonists into the interior, they tried to live as far as possible from each other. Finnish friends told me a story to illustrate how those colonists hated feeling crowded. A man cleared for himself and his family a small farm by a river, pleased that there were no signs of any neighbors. But one day he was horrified to observe a cut log floating down the river. Someone else must be living somewhere upstream! Enraged, the man started walking upstream through unbroken forest to track down the trespasser. On his first day of walking he met no one; on the second day, again no one. At last, on the third day he came to a new clearing, where he found another colonist. He killed that colonist and marched three days back to his own clearing and family, relieved that he had once again secured his family's privacy. While that story may be apocryphal, it illustrates the social factors that cause small-scale societies to have concerns even about distant "neighbors" far out of sight.

Still other ultimate factors proposed involve benefits, to the individual rather than to the social group, of being warlike. A bellicose individual or war leader is likely to be feared and to gain prestige for his war exploits. That can translate into his being able to win more wives and to rear more children. For instance, the anthropologist Napoleon Chagnon calculated, from Yanomamo genealogies that he gathered, that if one compares Yanomamo men who have or haven't killed people, the killers have on the average over two and a half times more wives and over three times more children. Of course the killers are also more likely to die or to be killed at an earlier age than are non-killers, but during that shorter lifespan they win more prestige and social rewards and can thereby obtain more wives and rear extra children. Naturally, even if this correlation does apply to the Yanomamo, I'm not recommending it to all you readers, nor can it even be generalized to apply to all traditional societies. In some societies the shorter lifespan of warlike men is likely not to be compensated by an ability to attract more wives per decade of their shorter life. That is the case for Ecuador's Waorani Indians, who are even more warlike than the Yanomamo. Nevertheless, more zealous Waorani warriors don't have more wives than do milder men, and they have fewer rather than more children surviving to reproductive age.

Whom do people fight?

Having thus addressed the question why small-scale societies fight, let's now ask: whom do they fight? For instance, are tribes more likely to go to war against tribes speaking a different language than against speakers of their own language? Do they fight, or do they instead avoid fighting with, tribes with which they trade or intermarry?

We can place the answers in a more familiar context by first asking the same questions about modern nations going to war. A distinguished British meteorologist named Lewis Richardson, whose official career focused on mathematically analyzing complex patterns of atmospheric winds, spent two years during World War I attached to a motor ambulance convoy transporting sick and wounded soldiers. Two of his wife's three brothers were killed during that war. Possibly impelled by those experiences and by his own Quaker family background, Richardson developed a second career of mathematically studying the causes of wars, in the hope of drawing lessons about how to avoid wars. His method consisted of tabulating all wars that he could learn of between 1820 and 1949, recording their numbers of deaths, dividing his table into five sub-tables according to those numbers, and then testing questions about when and why different nations went to war.

During that period of 1820–1949 the number of wars in which a country was involved varied greatly among countries, from over 20 each for France and Britain down to 1 for Switzerland and 0 for Sweden. The main source of this variation was simply the number of nations with which a given country shared a common frontier: the more neighbors, the more wars averaged over the long run; the number of wars was approximately proportional to the number of adjoining states. Whether neighboring states spoke the same or different languages had little effect. The sole exceptions to this pattern were that there were fewer wars in which both sides spoke Chinese, and more wars in which both sides spoke Spanish, than expected statistically from the total world number of speakers of Chinese languages or Spanish. Richardson speculated about what cultural factors apparently make Spanish-speakers especially prone, and Chinese-speakers especially unlikely, to go to war. His speculations are intriguing, but I shall leave it to interested readers to read Richardson's analysis for themselves, on pages 223–230 and 240–242 of his 1960 book, *Statistics of Deadly Quarrels*.

Richardson did not test statistically the effect of trading between countries on the probability of war. However, because war is disproportionately between neighboring countries, which are also disproportionately likely to be trade partners, one would expect trade relations and war to tend to be associated with each other. It does appear, at least from anecdotal impressions, that modern nations that are trade partners fight more often than those that are not. Presumably that's partly because the apparent correlation of trade with fighting is really just because both trade and fighting are in turn correlated with propinquity; and partly, too, because trade often gives rise to disputes. Even for nations that aren't neighbors, the biggest modern wars have pitted trade partners against each other. For instance, in World War II Japan's two main targets of attack were its leading source of imported materials (the U.S.) and its leading export market for its goods (China). Similarly, Nazi Germany and Russia were trading right up until the eve of Germany's invasion of Russia on June 22, 1941.

With that discussion of nations as background, let's now consider the same questions for small-scale traditional societies. We don't have available for analysis a tabulation of all recent traditional wars, corresponding to Richardson's table of modern state wars. Instead, we'll have to content ourselves with anecdotes. These suggest that small-scale societies, even more than nations, fight their neighbors, because they lack the capacity for long-distance transport that enabled Britain to send troops halfway around the world in the mid-1800s to fight New Zealand's Maori. There is little evidence of small-scale societies differentiating between neighbors speaking the same or different languages in matters of war. Most traditional wars were between neighbors speaking the same language, because neighbors are more likely to speak the same rather than different languages. Everyone involved in the Dani War of Chapter 3 spoke the Dani language. The long list of other societies that fought societies speaking the same language include the Enga, Fayu, Fore, Hinihon, Inuit, Mailu, Nuer, and Yanomamo; the list could be extended indefinitely. One partial exception, however, is that, while Nuer tribes fought other Nuer tribes as well as the Dinka, they fought the Dinka more often, and they observed restrictions in fighting the Nuer that they didn't observe in fighting the Dinka. For instance, they didn't kill Nuer women and children, they didn't carry off Nuer as captives, and they didn't burn Nuer huts; they limited themselves to killing Nuer men and stealing Nuer cattle.

As for the effects of trade and intermarriage, anecdotal evidence again suggests that a traditional society's enemies are often the same people as their partners in trade and marriage. As Lawrence Keeley put it, "Many societies tend to fight the people they marry and to marry those they fight, to raid the people with whom they trade and to trade with their enemies." The reasons are the same as the reasons producing this result for nations: propinquity fosters trade and marriage, but also war; and trade and marriage give rise to disputes for members of small-scale societies, just as for modern states. Among so-called trade relations, neighboring societies may actually exchange goods at prices and exchange rates varying along a continuum from real trade (mutually voluntary exchanges between equally strong parties at fair prices), through "extortion" (unequal exchanges at unfair prices between a strong and a weak party, whereby the weak party gives up goods at low prices so as to buy peace), to raiding (one party "supplies" goods and the other party gives nothing in exchange, whenever one party's weakness enables the other to raid and thereby to obtain goods for no price at all). Famous "raiders," such as the Apache of the U.S. Southwest and the Tuareg of northern Africa's deserts, actually practised a sophisticated mixture of such fair trade, extortion, and raiding, depending on the capacity of their partners at the moment to defend themselves.

As for marriage between bands and tribes, it often precipitates war for reasons similar to the reasons for wars resulting from trade agreements gone sour. One tribe's baby girl is promised at birth as a bride to an older male of another tribe, and is paid for, but isn't delivered on reaching the age of puberty. A bride-price or dowry is owed and initially paid in installments, until an installment is missed. Disputes over quality of "goods" (e.g., adultery, spouse abandonment, divorce, or inability or refusal to cook or garden or fetch firewood) produce demands for refund of the bride-price, but the demand is refused because the alleged quality defect is disputed, or else the payment received has already been traded away or (if it was a pig) eaten. Any consumer, business owner, exporter, or importer reading this paragraph will recognize analogies with the problems facing traders in modern states.

Frequent results of fighting the people with whom you intermarry are divided loyalties in times of war. Some of the enemy are one's in-laws and blood relatives. When shooting an arrow or throwing a spear, a warrior must aim, insofar as possible, so as to avoid hitting a relative on the other side. When an Inuit woman moves upon marriage to her husband's group, if her blood relatives in her natal society then plan a raid against her husband's people, the blood relatives may warn her in advance to stay out of the way of the raid and not get killed herself. Conversely, if she learns from her husband's people that they are getting ready to raid her blood relatives, she may warn the latter—or she may not; she may side with either her in-laws or her blood relatives. Similarly, a Fore man who hears that his own clan is planning to attack the village to which his sister has moved in marriage may warn her and then expect a payment from her husband. Conversely, he may hear from his sister that the village into which she has married is going to attack his own village, whose members he warns and who give him presents in gratitude.

Forgetting Pearl Harbor

Finally, let's return to the theme of revenge, with which small-scale societies may seem to us inordinately pre-occupied, giving it as their commonest explanation for going to war. We citizens of modern states commonly ignore how strong can be the thirst for vengeance. Among human emotions, it ranks along with love, anger, grief, and fear, about which we talk incessantly. Modern state societies permit and encourage us to express our love, anger, grief, and fear, but not our thirst for vengeance. We grow up being taught that vengeful feelings are primitive, to be ashamed of, and something that we should transcend. Our society inculcates those beliefs in order to discourage us from seeking personal vengeance.

There is no doubt that it would be impossible for us to coexist peacefully as fellow citizens of the same state, if we did not forswear the right to personal vengeance, and if we did not leave punishment to the state. Otherwise, we, too, would be living under the conditions of constant warfare prevailing in most non-state societies. But even for us Westerners who are wronged and who do receive satisfaction from the state, torment remains because of the lack of personal satisfaction. One friend of mine whose sister was murdered by robbers is still angry, decades afterwards, although the state did capture, try, and imprison the robbers.

We state citizens are thereby left in a bind that we are unable to acknowledge. The state's insistence on its sole right to punish is essential to our living in peace and safety. But that gain for us comes at a severe personal cost. My conversations with New Guineans have made me understand what we have given up by leaving justice to the state. In order to induce us to do so, state societies and their associated religions and moral codes constantly hammer into us the message that seeking revenge is bad.

But, while acting on vengeful feelings has to be prevented, acknowledging those feelings should be not merely permitted but encouraged. To a close relative or friend of someone who has been killed or seriously wronged, and to the victims of harm themselves, those feelings are natural and powerful. Many state governments do attempt to grant the relatives of crime victims some personal satisfaction: by allowing them to be present at the trial of the accused; in some cases, to address the judge or jury (Chapter 2); to meet privately with the criminal, through the restoration justice system (Chapter 2); or even to watch the execution of their loved one's murderer.

Readers who haven't spent years talking with New Guinea Highlanders may still find themselves wondering: How did these societies come to be apparently so unlike us, and to revel in and reward killing? What sort of warped ogres are they, to talk so unabashedly of their pleasure in killing enemies?

Actually, ethnographic studies of traditional human societies lying largely outside the control of state government have shown that war, murder, and demonization of neighbors have been the norm, not the exception, and that members of those societies espousing those norms are often normal, happy, well-adjusted people, not ogres. What differs in many state-level societies is that we are taught to start embracing those traditional norms suddenly and only at a certain moment (upon a declaration of war), then to jettison them suddenly at a later moment (the conclusion of a peace treaty). The result is confusing: hatreds once acquired are not so easily jettisoned. Many of my European friends born like me in the 1930s—Germans, Poles, Russians, Serbs, Croats, British, Dutch, and Jews—were taught from birth to hate or fear certain other peoples, underwent experiences giving them good reason to do so, and are now still carrying those feelings more than 65 years later, even though my friends were subsequently taught that those feelings are no longer considered nice and are best not expressed unless you feel confident of your listeners' approval.

In Western state societies today, we grow up learning a universal code of morality that is promulgated every week in our houses of worship, and codified in our laws. The sixth commandment declares simply, "Thou shalt not kill"—with no distinction between how we should behave towards citizens of our own state and towards citizens of other states. Then, after at least 18 years of such moral training, we take young adults, train them to be soldiers, give them guns, and command that they should now forget all of that former upbringing forbidding them to kill.

It's no wonder that many modern soldiers can't bring themselves in battle to point their gun at an enemy and fire. Those who do kill often suffer long-lasting post-traumatic stress disorder (e.g., about one-third of American soldiers who have served in Iraq or Afghanistan). When they come home, far from boasting about killing, they have nightmares and don't talk about it at all, unless to other veterans. (Imagine how you, if you are not yourself a war veteran, would feel about an American soldier who described to you proudly the personal details of how he killed an Iraqi, or even how he killed a Nazi soldier in World War II.) In the course of my life I have had hundreds of conversations with American and European veterans, some of them close friends or close relatives, but not one has ever related to me how he killed, as have many of my New Guinea friends.

In contrast, traditional New Guineans from their earliest childhood onwards saw warriors going out and coming back from fighting, saw the dead bodies and the wounds of their relatives and clansmen killed by the enemy, heard stories of killing, heard fighting talked about as the highest ideal, and witnessed successful warriors talking proudly about their killings and being praised for it. Remember the Wilihiman Dani boys excitedly jabbing their small spears into the dying Asuk-Balek man, and the six-year-old Wilihiman Dani boys shooting arrows at six-year-old Widaia Dani boys under the tutelage of their fathers (Chapter 3). Of course New Guineans end up feeling unconflicted about killing the enemy: they have had no contrary message to unlearn.

On reflection, for Americans old enough to recall Japan's 1941 bombing of our naval base at Pearl Harbor (viewed by us as a treacherous outrage, because it was not preceded by a declaration of war), the intense hatred of enemy people, and the craving for revenge, that traditional people learn from their elders should not feel so remote after all. We Americans of the 1940s grew up in an atmosphere saturated with demonization of the Japanese, who did indeed do unspeakably cruel things to us and to other peoples (think of the Bataan Death March, the Sandakan Death March, the Rape of Nanking, and other such events). Intense hatred and fear of Japanese became widespread even among American civilians who never saw either a live Japanese soldier or the dead body of an American relative killed by the Japanese; my New Guinea friends did see the corpses of their relatives. Hundreds of thousands of American men volunteered to kill hundreds of thousands of Japanese, often in face-to-face combat, by brutal methods that included bayonets and flame-throwers. Soldiers who killed Japanese in particularly large numbers or with notable bravery were publicly decorated with medals, and those who died in combat were posthumously remembered as heroes who had died nobly.

Then, less than four years after Pearl Harbor, we Americans were told to stop hating and killing Japanese, and to forget the slogan that had dominated American life: "Remember Pearl Harbor!" Many Americans alive during those years have struggled for the rest of their lives with what they were taught and subsequently told to unlearn—especially if they were directly affected then, for instance through having survived the Bataan Death March, or through having had close friends and relatives who did not come back. Yet those legacies of American attitudes resulted from just four years of experience, for most of us second-hand. Having grown up during the anti-Japanese hysteria of World War II, I find it unsurprising that the Wilihiman Dani became so passionate about killing the Widaia Dani, when those attitudes were inculcated into them for decades by both teaching and extensive first-hand experience. The thirst for revenge isn't nice, but it can't be ignored. It has to be understood, acknowledged, and addressed—in ways other than actually taking revenge.

PART THREE

YOUNG AND OLD

CHAPTER 5

Bringing Up Children

Comparisons of child-rearing ▪ Childbirth ▪ Infanticide ▪ Weaning and birth interval ▪ On-demand nursing ▪ Infant-adult contact ▪ Fathers and allo-parents ▪ Responses to crying infants ▪ Physical punishment ▪ Child autonomy ▪ Multi-age playgroups ▪ Child play and education ▪ Their kids and our kids

Comparisons of child-rearing

On one of my visits to New Guinea I met a young man named Enu, whose life story struck me then as remarkable. Enu had grown up in an area where child-rearing was extremely repressive, and where children were heavily burdened by obligations and by feelings of guilt. By the time he was five years old, Enu decided that he had had enough of that lifestyle. He left his parents and most of his relatives and moved to another tribe and village, where he had relatives willing to take care of him. There, Enu found himself in an adoptive society with laissez-faire child-rearing practices at the opposite extreme from his natal society's practices. Young children were considered to have responsibility for their own actions, and were allowed to do pretty much as they pleased. For example, if a baby was playing next to a fire, adults did not intervene. As a result, many adults in that society had burn scars, which were legacies of their behavior as infants.

Both of those styles of child-rearing would be rejected with horror in Western industrial societies today. But the laissez-faire style of Enu's adoptive society is not unusual by the standards of the world's hunter-gatherer societies, many of which consider young children to be autonomous individuals whose desires should not be thwarted, and who are allowed to play with dangerous objects such as sharp knives, hot pots, and fires (Plate 19).

Why should we be interested in child-rearing practices of traditional hunter-gatherer, farmer, and herder societies? One answer is an academic one: children account for up to half of a society's population. A sociologist who ignored half of a society's members couldn't claim to understand that society. Another academic answer is that every feature of adult life has a developmental component. One can't understand a society's practices of dispute resolution and marriage without knowing how children become socialized into those practices.

Despite those good reasons for us to be interested in child-rearing in non-Western societies, it has received much less study than it deserves. Part of the problem is that many of the scholars who go out to study other cultures are young, don't have children of their own, aren't experienced in talking with or observing children, and mainly describe and interview adults. Anthropology, education, psychology, and other academic fields have their own ideologies, which at any given time focus on a certain range of research topics, and which impose blinders on what phenomena are considered worth studying.

Even studies of child development that claim to be broadly cross-cultural—e.g., comparing German, American, Japanese, and Chinese children—are actually sampling societies all drawn from the same narrow slice of human cultural diversity. All of those cultures just mentioned are similar in sharing centralized government, economic specialization, and socioeconomic inequality, and in being very atypical of the wide range of human cultural diversity. As a result, those and other state-level modern societies have converged on a small range of child-rearing practices that by historical standards are unusual. Those practices include systems of school education administered by a state (as opposed to learning as part of everyday life and play), protection of children by police and not just by parents, same-age playgroups (as opposed to children of all ages routinely playing together), children and parents sleeping in separate bedrooms (as opposed to sleeping together in the same bed), and mothers nursing infants (if the infants are nursed at all) on a schedule often set by the mother rather than by the infant.

A result is that generalizations about children by Jean Piaget, Erik

Erikson, Sigmund Freud, pediatricians, and child psychologists are based heavily on studies of WEIRD (Western, educated, industrial, rich, democratic) societies, especially on studies of their college undergraduates and children of college professors, and have been inappropriately generalized to the rest of the world. For example, Freud emphasized the sex drive and its frequent frustration. But that psychoanalytic view doesn't apply to the Siriono Indians of Bolivia, nor to many other traditional societies, where willing sex partners are almost constantly available, but where hunger for food, and preoccupation with the food drive and its frequent frustration, are ubiquitous. Formerly popular Western child-rearing theories that stressed the need of infants for love and emotional support viewed other societies' widespread practice of breast-feeding infants on demand as "overindulgence," and classified it in Freudian terms as "excessive gratification at the oral stage of psychosexual development." However, we shall see that breast-feeding on demand was formerly almost universal, that it has much to recommend it, and that the common modern practice of breast-feeding at infrequent intervals to suit the mother's convenience is, from a historical perspective, a rare exception.

Those are academic reasons for us to be interested in traditional child-rearing practices. But there are compelling practical reasons for all of us non-academics to be interested as well. Small-scale societies offer us a vast database on child-rearing. They reveal the outcomes of thousands of natural experiments on how to rear children. Western state societies would not permit us to carry out the experiments that Enu lived through, of either extreme repression or extreme laissez-faire as the norm. While few readers of this book would consider it admirable to let children roll into fires, we shall see that many other traditional child-rearing practices do recommend themselves for consideration. Thus, another reason for studying them is that they can inform our own choices. They may suggest practices different from those now routine in the West, but that we may find appealing when we learn about their consequences for children.

In recent decades, there has at last been increasing interest in comparative studies of child-rearing by small-scale societies. For instance, there have been half a dozen dedicated studies of children, not just incidental to other anthropological observations, among some of the world's last human groups still obtaining much of their subsistence by hunting and gathering: the Efe and Aka Pygmies of African rainforests, the !Kung of southern African deserts, the Hadza of East Africa, the Ache Indians of Paraguay, and the Agta of the Philippines. In this chapter I shall discuss what such studies of small-scale societies have shown us about childbirth and infanticide, nursing and weaning, infant/adult physical contact, the role of fathers and of care-givers other than the parents, responses to a child crying, punishment of children, a child's freedom to explore, and children's play and education.

Childbirth

Today, childbirth in Westernized societies usually takes place in a hospital, with the help of trained professionals: physicians, midwives, and nurses. Mortality of infants and mothers associated with childbirth is low. But traditional childbirth was different. Before or in the absence of modern medicine, death of the infant and/or the mother in childbirth was much more common than it is now.

The circumstances of childbirth vary among traditional societies. In the simplest case, very exceptionally, a cultural ideal is for the mother to give birth alone and unassisted. For instance, among the !Kung people of southern African deserts, a woman about to give birth is expected to walk a few hundred yards from the camp and give birth alone. In practice, especially for a first-time !Kung mother, she may be accompanied by other women to help, but with successive births the mother is more likely to achieve that ideal of giving birth alone. However, even if the mother does so, she remains close enough to camp that other women can hear the first cries of the baby and then go join the mother to help in cutting the umbilical cord, cleaning the baby, and carrying it back to the camp.

The Piraha Indians of Brazil (Plate 11) are another group in which women often give birth unassisted. The commitment of the Piraha to that ideal is illustrated by an experience of linguist Steve Sheldon, related by Daniel Everett: "Steve Sheldon recounted a story once of a woman giving birth alone on a beach. Something went wrong. A breech birth. The woman was in agony. 'Help me, please! The baby will not come,' she cried out. The Pirahas sat passively, some looking tense, some talking normally.

'I'm dying! This hurts. The baby will not come!' she screamed. No one answered. It was late afternoon. Steve started toward her. 'No! she doesn't want you. She wants her parents,' he was told, the implication clearly being that he was not to go to her. But her parents were not around and no one else was going to her aid. The evening came and her cries came regularly, but ever more weakly. Finally, they stopped. In the morning Steve learned that she and the baby had died on the beach, unassisted. . . . [This tragic incident] tells us that the Pirahas let a young woman die, alone and without help, because of their belief that people must be strong and get through difficulties on their own."

Much more commonly, traditional childbirth takes place with the assistance of other women. For example, among the Kaulong people of New Britain, whose men are obsessed with the polluting effects of women during menstruation and childbirth, a woman about to give birth goes to a shelter in the forest, accompanied by several older women. At the opposite extreme are societies in which birth is virtually a public event. Among the Agta people of the Philippines, a woman gives birth in a house in the camp, and everyone in camp may crowd into the house and shout out instructions to the mother and midwife ("push," "pull," "don't do that").

Infanticide

Infanticide—the intentional acknowledged killing of an infant—is illegal in most state societies today. In many traditional societies, however, infanticide is acceptable under certain circumstances. While this practice horrifies us, it is difficult to see what else the societies could do under some of the conditions associated with infanticide. One such condition is when an infant is born deformed or weak. Many traditional societies experience lean seasons of marginal food supply, when it becomes difficult for the small number of productive adults to provide food for the larger number of non-producing children and old people. An additional consuming but non-productive mouth is then a burden that the society can ill afford.

Another circumstance associated with infanticide is a short birth interval: i.e., an infant born within only two years of the birth of the mother's previous child that is still nursing and being carried. It is difficult or impossible for a woman to produce enough milk for a two-year-old and also for a newborn, and to carry not just one but two children while shifting camp. For the same reason, twin births by hunter-gatherer women may result in the killing or neglect of at least one of the twins. Here is an interview with an Ache Indian named Kuchingi reported by Kim Hill and A. Magdalena Hurtado: "The one [the sibling] who followed me [in birth order] was killed. It was a short birth spacing. My mother killed him because I was small. 'You won't have enough milk for the older one [i.e., Kuchingi],' she was told. 'You must feed the older one.' Then she killed my brother, the one who was born after me."

Still another factor predisposing towards infanticide at childbirth is if the father is absent or dead, and thus unable to help feed the mother and protect the child. For a single mother, life is hard even today. It was harder in the past, especially in societies in which lack of a father tended to result in a higher probability of a child dying, e.g., because fathers provided most of the calories or protected their children against violence by other men.

Finally, in some traditional societies the ratio of boys to girls increases from birth to adolescence, as a result of female infants dying through passive neglect, or (in exceptional cases) even being intentionally killed by strangling, exposure, or burying alive—because many societies value boys over girls. For example, among the Ache Indians, 14% of boys but 23% of girls have been killed by the age of 10. The absence of either the father or the mother increases by four-fold the chance that an Ache child will be killed by homicide, but the risk is higher for girls than for boys. In modern China and India that widespread valuing of boys over girls results in an excess of infant boys by a new mechanism: pre-natal sex determination permitting the selective abortion of female fetuses.

The !Kung consider it a mother's obligation to evaluate the case for or against infanticide at the time of childbirth. The sociologist Nancy Howell wrote, "The custom that women should or can give birth alone gives the mother the unquestioned right to control infanticide. At the scene of the birth, usually before the baby is named and certainly before bringing the baby back to the village, it is the mother's responsibility to examine the baby carefully for birth defects. If it is deformed, it is the mother's duty to smother it. Many !Kung informants told me that this examination and decision is a regular and necessary part of the process of giving birth. !Kung infanticide is not equivalent to murder in their eyes, since they do not consider birth to be the beginning of life of a zun/wa [a !Kung person]. Life begins with giving a name and the acceptance of the baby as a social person back in the village after the birth. Before that time, infanticide is part of the mother's prerogatives and responsibility, culturally prescribed for birth defects and for one of each set of twins born. There are no pairs of twins surviving in the population. . . ."

However, infanticide is certainly not universal in traditional societies and is less common than infant death due to "benign neglect." (That euphemism means that an infant is not actively killed but instead dies through neglect, e.g., due to the mother stopping nursing, or nursing the infant less often, or rarely cleaning or washing the infant.) For example, when Allan Holmberg lived among a group of Siriono Indians in Bolivia, he found that infanticide and abortion were unknown. Even though 15% of Siriono children were born with club feet, and only one out of five of those children survived to adulthood and raised a family, those children received normal love and feeding.

Weaning and birth interval

In the U.S. the proportion of infants who were nursed at all by their mothers, and the age at which those nursed infants were weaned, decreased through much of the 20th century. For example, by the 1970s only 5% of American children were being nursed at the age of six months. In contrast, among hunter-gatherers not in contact with farmers and without access to farmed foods, infants are nursed far beyond six months, because the only suitable infant food available to them is mother's milk: they have no access to cow's milk, baby formula, or soft food replacements. The age of weaning averaged over seven hunter-gatherer groups is about three years old, an age at which children finally become capable of fully nourishing themselves by chewing enough firm food. While some solid pre-chewed foods may be introduced around the age of six months, a hunter-gatherer child may not be fully weaned off its mother's milk until the mother is pregnant with the next child. Individual !Kung children continue to nurse beyond the age of four if a next sibling has not yet been born. Studies show that, the older the age of a !Kung child when it is weaned, the more likely is the child to survive to adulthood. But in settled agricultural populations and among hunter-gatherers trading with farmers, those weaning ages and birth intervals of two and a half to four years for nomadic hunter-gatherers decrease to an average age of two years, because farmers do have livestock milk and soft cereal gruels onto which to wean a small child. For instance, when the !Kung themselves settle down to become farmers, as has been happening increasingly in recent decades, their birth interval quickly drops from three and a half years to the two years typical of farmers.

The ultimate evolutionary causes and the proximate physiological mechanisms responsible for those long birth intervals of nomadic hunter-gatherers have been the subject of much discussion. It appears that the ultimate reasons are two-fold. First, a mother without access to cow's milk or cereal gruel, and hence likely to nurse a child until the age of three or more years, cannot produce enough milk to nurse both a newborn and a not-yet-weaned older child. If she tried, one of those children would be likely to starve for lack of milk.

The other reason is that only when a child is around four years old or more does it become capable of walking fast enough to keep up with its parents when they are shifting camp. Younger children have to be carried then. While walking, a 90-pound !Kung woman has to carry an under-four-year-old child of up to 28 pounds, a load of wild vegetables weighing from 15 to 40 pounds or more, and several pounds of water, plus utensils. That's already a large burden, and it would be even heavier if a younger infant were added to the load. We thus have a second ultimate evolutionary factor contributing to the rapid decrease in birth interval when nomadic hunter-gatherers settle down to become farmers: most farmers live in permanent villages and don't face the problem of having to carry all children less than four years old whenever they shift camp.

That late weaning age means that, for a hunter-gatherer mother, much physical and emotional energy goes into the rearing of one child. Western observers have the impression that a !Kung child's very close relationship with the mother, and the exclusive attention that it enjoys for several years without younger siblings, provide an emotional security in childhood that translates itself into the emotional security of !Kung adults. But when a hunter-gatherer child finally does become weaned, the result can be traumatic. Within a short time, the child receives much less maternal attention, becomes hungry without mother's milk, has to cede to the next infant its sleeping place at night next to the mother, and may be increasingly expected to enter the adult world. !Kung children being weaned are miserable and have tantrums. !Kung who survive to become old adults still look back on weaning 70 years earlier as a painful experience. In camps of Piraha Indians at night, one often hears children screaming, almost always because they are being weaned. Nevertheless, while traditional societies do wean at a later age than do modern Americans, the specific patterns vary among societies. For example, Bofi and Aka Pygmy children wean gradually rather than abruptly, tantrums are rare, and weaning is often initiated by the child rather than by the mother.

On-demand nursing

Those two ultimate causes responsible for the long birth intervals of hunter-gatherers leave open the question of the proximate physiological mechanism ensuring that there are not two children less than several years old to be cared for simultaneously. One mechanism is the resort to neglect or (less often) infanticide, as we have already mentioned: if a hunter-gatherer mother becomes pregnant when her previous child is still less than two and a half years old, then she may neglect or even kill the newborn, knowing that she cannot take care of it as well as of the older child. The other proximate factor is that physiological mechanisms operating in a mother nursing according to the on-demand schedule of frequent feedings characteristic of hunter-gatherer babies (as opposed to the infrequent nursing bouts set for the convenience of the mother in Western society) make it less likely that a nursing mother will become pregnant, even if she resumes sex while nursing.

In hunter-gatherer groups in which nursing has been specifically studied, it is often "on demand." That is, the infant has constant access to the mother's breast, is held in contact with the mother during the day, sleeps next to the mother at night, and can nurse at any time it wants, whether or not the mother is awake. For example, measurements among the !Kung have shown that an infant nurses on the average four times per hour during the day, 2 minutes per nursing bout, with an average interval of only 14 minutes between bouts. The mother wakes to nurse the infant at least twice a night, and the infant nurses without waking the mother several times per night. This constant opportunity for nursing on demand usually continues for at least three years of the !Kung child's life. In contrast, many or most mothers in modern societies schedule nursing at times when the mother's activities permit it. The organization of a mother's work, whether the work is a job outside the house or domestic work within the house, often involves mother-child separations of several hours. The result is many fewer daily nursing bouts than the dozens of bouts for a hunter-gatherer mother, longer individual bouts, and much longer intervals between bouts.

That high nursing frequency of hunter-gatherer mothers has physiological consequences. As mentioned above, nursing hunter-gatherer mothers usually do not conceive for several years after a child's birth, even if the mother resumes sexual activity. Evidently, something about traditional on-demand nursing acts as a contraceptive. One hypothesis is termed "lactational amenorrhea": suckling releases maternal hormones that not only stimulate the secretion of milk but that may also inhibit ovulation (a woman's release of eggs). But that inhibition of ovulation requires a constant regime of frequent nursing; a few bouts of nursing per day do not suffice. The other hypothesis is termed the "critical-fat hypothesis": ovulation requires that the mother's fat levels exceed a certain critical threshold. In a nursing woman from a traditional society without abundant food, the high energy costs of milk production keep the mother's fat level below that critical value. Thus, sexually active nursing mothers in modern Western industrial societies, unlike their hunter-gatherer counterparts, may still conceive (to their surprise) for either or both of two reasons: their nursing frequency is much too low for hormonally induced lactational amenorrhea; and they are sufficiently well nourished that their body fat levels remain above the critical threshold for ovulation, even despite the caloric expenditure of lactation. Many educated Western mothers have heard of lactational amenorrhea, but fewer have heard that it is effective only at high nursing frequencies. A friend of mine who recently, to her dismay, conceived again only a few months after the birth of her previous child thereby joined the long list of modern women exclaiming, "But I thought that I couldn't conceive while I was nursing!"

Nursing frequency differs among mammal species. Some mammals, including chimpanzees and most other primate species, bats, and kangaroos, nurse continuously. Other mammals, of which rabbits and antelopes are prime examples, nurse discontinuously: a mother rabbit or antelope leaves her infant hidden in the grass or in a den while she goes out to forage, then she returns after a long interval and suckles the infant only a few times per day. Human hunter-gatherers resemble chimpanzees and Old World monkeys in being continuous nursers. But that pattern, which we inherited from our primate ancestors and presumably maintained for the millions of years of human evolution separate from the evolution of chimpanzees, changed only in the thousands of years since the origins of farming, when we developed lifestyles involving mother-infant separations. Modern human mothers have acquired the suckling habits of rabbits, while retaining the lactational physiology of chimpanzees and monkeys.

Infant–adult contact

Associated with those mammalian species differences in nursing frequency are differences in the percentage of an infant's time spent in contact with an adult (especially with the mother). In the discontinuously nursing species the infant is in contact with the mother just for brief bouts of nursing and care. In the continuously nursing species the mother carries the infant while she forages: a mother kangaroo keeps the infant in her pouch, a mother bat holds the infant on her stomach even while she is flying, and chimpanzee and Old World monkey mothers carry the infant on their back.

In modern industrial societies today, we follow the rabbit-antelope pattern: the mother or someone else occasionally picks up and holds the infant in order to feed it or play with it, but does not carry the infant constantly; the infant spends much or most of the time during the day in a crib or playpen; and at night the infant sleeps by itself, usually in a separate room from the parents. However, we probably continued to follow our ancestral ape-monkey model throughout almost all of human history, until within the last few thousand years. Studies of modern hunter-gatherers show that an infant is held almost constantly throughout the day, either by the mother or by someone else. When the mother is walking, the infant is held in carrying devices, such as the slings of the !Kung, string bags in New Guinea, and cradle boards in the north temperate zones. Most hunter-gatherers, especially in mild climates, have constant skin-to-skin contact between the infant and its care-giver. In every known society of human hunter-gatherers and of higher primates, mother and infant sleep immediately nearby, usually in the same bed or on the same mat. A cross-cultural sample of 90 traditional human societies identified not a single one with mother and infant sleeping in separate rooms: that current Western practice is a recent invention responsible for the struggles at putting kids to bed that torment modern Western parents. American pediatricians now recommend not having an infant sleep in the same bed with its parents, because of occasional cases of the infant ending up crushed or else overheating; but virtually all infants in human history until the last few thousand years did sleep in the same bed with the mother and usually also with the father, without widespread reports of the dire consequences feared by pediatricians. That may be because hunter-gatherers sleep on the hard ground or on hard mats; a parent is more likely to roll over onto an infant in our modern soft beds.

For example, !Kung infants spend their first year of life in skin-to-skin contact with the mother or another care-giver for 90% of the time. !Kung infants are carried by the mother wherever she goes, interrupted only when the infant is passed from the mother to other care-givers. A !Kung child begins to separate more frequently from its mother after the age of one and a half, but those separations are initiated almost entirely by the child itself, in order to play with other children. The daily contact time between the !Kung child and care-givers other than the mother exceeds *all* contact time (including contact with the mother) for modern Western children.

One of the commonest Western devices for transporting a child is the stroller, which provides no physical contact between the baby and the care-giver (Plate 39). In many strollers, the infant is nearly horizontal, and sometimes facing backwards. Hence the infant does not see the world as its care-giver sees the world. In recent decades in the United States, devices for transporting children in a vertical (upright) position have been more common, such as baby carriers, backpacks, and chest pouches, but many of those devices have the child facing backwards. In contrast, traditional carrying devices, such as slings or holding a child on one's shoulders, usually place the child vertically upright, facing forwards, and seeing the same world that the care-giver sees (Plates 21, 38). The constant contact even when the caretaker is walking, the constant sharing of the care-giver's field of view, and transport in the vertical position may contribute to !Kung infants being advanced (compared to American infants) in some aspects of their neuromotor development.

In warm climates, it is practical to have constant skin-to-skin contact between a naked baby and a mostly naked mother. That is more difficult in cold climates. Hence about half of traditional societies, mostly those in the temperate zones, swaddle their infants, i.e., wrap the infant in warm fabric. The swaddled infant is often strapped to a board called a cradle board. That practice was formerly widespread around the world, mainly in societies at high latitudes. The basic idea of swaddling and of the cradle board is to wrap the baby as protection against the cold, and to restrict the baby's ability to move its body and limbs. Navajo Indian mothers who use cradle boards explain that the purpose is to induce the child to go to sleep, or to keep the child asleep if the child is put on the cradle board when it is already asleep. The Navajo mother usually adds that the cradle board prevents the infant from suddenly jerking while asleep and thereby waking itself up. A Navajo infant spends 60%–70% of its time on a cradle board for the first six months of life. Cradle boards were formerly also common practice in Europe but began to disappear there a few centuries ago.

To many of us moderns, the idea of a cradle board or swaddling is abhorrent—or was, until swaddling recently came back into vogue. The notion of personal freedom means a lot to us, and a cradle board or swaddling undoubtedly does restrict an infant's personal freedom. We are prone to assume that cradle boards or swaddling retard a child's development and inflict lasting psychological damage. In fact, there are no personality or motor differences, or differences in age of independent walking, between Navajo children who were or were not kept on a cradle board, or between cradle-boarded Navajo children and nearby

Anglo-American children. The probable explanation is that, by the age that an infant starts to crawl, the infant is spending half of its day off of the cradle board anyway, and most of the time that it spends on the cradle board is when the infant is asleep. Actually, immobilizing an infant on a cradle board lets the infant be kept near its mother, and taken with the mother when she goes anywhere. Hence it is argued that doing away with cradle boards brings no real advantages in freedom, stimulation, or neuromotor development. Typical Western children sleeping in separate rooms, transported in baby carriages, and left in cribs during the day are often socially more isolated than are cradle-boarded Navajo children.

Fathers and allo-parents

The investment of fathers in caring for their offspring varies greatly among animal species. At one extreme are some species, such as ostriches and sea horses, in which, after a male has fertilized a female and the female has produced eggs, the female goes off and leaves brooding of the eggs and care for the hatched offspring entirely to the father. At the opposite extreme are many species of mammals and some birds: after the male fertilizes the female, the male deserts her to pursue other females, and the entire burden of parenting falls upon the female. Most species of monkeys and apes fall between these two extremes but nearer the latter one: the father lives with the mother and her offspring, perhaps as part of a larger troop, but provides the offspring with little other than protection.

In humans, paternal care is low by the standards of ostriches, high by the standards of apes and most other primate species, but the father's involvement in the care of infants is less than that of the mother in all known human societies. Nevertheless, fathers play a significant role in food provisioning, protection, and education in most human societies, with the result that the death of a child's biological father decreases a child's probability of surviving in some societies. Fathers' involvement tends to be greater for older children (especially for sons) than for infants, and fathers in modern societies usually succeed in delegating many aspects of child care, such as changing diapers, wiping bottoms and noses, and bathing a child.

Among human societies, there is much variation in that involvement of fathers, partly related to a society's subsistence ecology. Paternal involvement is highest in societies in which women spend time obtaining most of the food. For instance, Aka Pygmy fathers furnish more direct care to their infants than do the fathers of any other studied human population (Plate 8), perhaps related to the fact that Aka Pygmy mothers not only gather plant foods but also participate in hunting with nets. On the average, child care by fathers, and also women's contribution to the food supply, are higher in societies of hunter-gatherers than in societies of herders. Fathers' direct care of their children tends to be low in societies, such as those of New Guinea Highlanders and African Bantu groups, in which the men devote much of their time and identity to being warriors, and to protecting their family against aggressive other men. In much of the New Guinea Highlands, men traditionally even lived in separate communal men's houses, together with their sons after the age of six, while each wife lived in a separate hut with her daughters and young sons. The men and boys ate by themselves, consuming food that a man's wife and a boy's mother brought to the men's house.

What about the child-rearing contribution of care-givers other than the mother and the father? In modern Western society, a child's parents are typically by far its dominant care-givers. The role of "allo-parents"—i.e., individuals who are not the biological parents but who do some care-giving—has even been decreasing in recent decades, as families move more often and over longer distances, and children no longer have the former constant availability of grandparents and aunts and uncles living nearby. This is of course not to deny that babysitters, schoolteachers, grandparents, and older siblings may also be significant care-givers and influences. But allo-parenting is much more important, and parents play a less dominant role, in traditional societies.

In hunter-gatherer bands the allo-parenting begins within the first hour after birth. Newborn Aka and Efe infants are passed from hand to hand around the campfire, from one adult or older child to another, to be kissed, bounced, and sung to and spoken to in words that they cannot possibly understand. Anthropologists have even measured the average frequency with which infants are passed around: it averages eight times per hour for Efe and Aka Pygmy infants. Hunter-gatherer mothers share care of infants with fathers and allo-parents, including grandparents, aunts, great-aunts, other adults, and older siblings. Again, this has been quantified by anthropologists, who have measured the average number of care-givers: 14 for a four-month-old Efe infant, 7 or 8 for an Aka infant, over the course of an observation period of several hours.

In many hunter-gatherer societies, older grandparents often stay in camp with children, enabling the parents to go off and forage unencumbered. Children may be left in the care of their grandparents for days or weeks at a time. Hadza children who have an involved grandmother gain weight faster than do children without involved grandmothers (Plate 21). Aunts and uncles also serve as important allo-parents in many traditional societies. For instance, among Bantu of Southern Africa's Okavango Delta, the strongest influence of an older male on a boy is not from the boy's father but from a maternal uncle, the mother's oldest brother. In many societies, brothers and sisters take care of each other's children. Older siblings, especially older girls and especially in farming and herding societies, often play a major role as care-givers of younger siblings (Plate 38).

Daniel Everett, who lived for many years among the Piraha Indians of Brazil, commented, "The biggest difference [of a Piraha child's life from an American child's life] is that Piraha children roam about the village and are considered to be related to and partially the responsibility of everyone in the village." Yora Indian children of Peru take nearly half of their meals with families other than their own parents. The son of American missionary friends of mine, after growing up in a small New Guinea village where he considered all adults as his "aunts" or "uncles," found the relative lack of allo-parenting a big shock when his parents brought him back to the United States for high school.

As children of small-scale societies grow older, they spend more time making longer visits to stay with other families. I experienced one such case while I was studying birds in New Guinea and hiring local people as porters to carry my supplies from one village to the next. When I arrived at one particular village, most of the porters from the previous village who had brought me there left, and I sought help from people of any age capable of carrying a pack and wanting to earn money. The youngest person who volunteered was a boy about 10 years old, named Talu. He joined me, expecting to be away from his village for a couple of days. But when we reached my destination after a delay of a week caused by the trail becoming blocked by a river in flood, I sought someone to stay and work with me, and Talu volunteered again. As it thus worked out, Talu remained with me for a month until I finished my study and he walked back to his home. At the time that he had set out with me, his parents had been away from the village, so Talu just came, knowing that other people in the village would tell his parents on their return that he had gone off for a few days. His village friends who also came along as porters and then returned to the village would have told his parents more than a week later that he was going to stay for an uncertain length of time longer. It was evidently considered normal that a 10-year-old boy would decide by himself to go away for an indeterminate length of time.

In some societies those lengthy trips of children without their parents become lengthened even further into recognized adoptions. For example, after the age of 9 or 10, Andaman Island children rarely continue to live with their own parents but are adopted by foster parents, often from a neighboring group, and thereby help to maintain friendly relations between the two groups. Among the Iñupiat of Alaska, adoption of children was common, especially within Iñupiaq groups. Adoption in the modern First World is primarily a link between the adopted child and the adoptive parents, who until recently were not even told the identity of the biological parents, so as to preclude an on-going relationship of the biological parents with the child or with the adoptive parents. However, for the Iñupiat the adoption served as a link between the two sets of parents and between their groups.

Thus, a major difference between small-scale societies and large state societies is that responsibility for children becomes widely diffused beyond the child's parents in the small-scale societies. The allo-parents are materially important as additional providers of food and protection. Hence studies around the world agree in showing that the presence of allo-parents improves a child's chances for survival. But allo-parents are also psychologically important, as additional social influences and models beyond the parents themselves. Anthropologists working with small-scale societies often comment on what strikes them as the precocious development of social skills among children in those societies, and they speculate that the richness of allo-parental relationships may provide part of the explanation.

Similar benefits of allo-parenting operate in industrial societies as well. Social workers in the United States note that children gain from living in extended, multi-generational families that provide allo-parenting. Babies of unmarried low-income American teenagers, who may be inexperienced or neglectful as mothers, develop faster and acquire more cognitive skills if a grandmother or older sibling is present, or even if a trained college student just makes regular visits to play with the baby. The multiple care-givers in an Israeli kibbutz or in a quality day-care center serve the same function. I have heard many anecdotal stories, among my own friends, of children who were raised by difficult parents but who nevertheless became socially and cognitively competent adults, and who told me that what had saved their sanity was regular contact with a supportive adult other than their parents, even if that adult was just a piano teacher whom they saw once a week for a piano lesson.

Responses to crying infants

There has been a long debate among pediatricians and child psychologists about how best to respond to a child's crying. Of course, the parent first checks whether the child is in pain or really needs some help. But if there seems to be nothing wrong, is it better to hold and comfort a crying child, or should one put down the child and let it cry until it stops, however long that takes? Does the child cry more if its parents put the child down and walk out of the room, or if they continue to hold it?

Philosophies about this question differ among Western countries, and differ from generation to generation within the same country. When I was living in Germany over 50 years ago, the prevailing view there was that children should be left to cry, and that it was harmful to attend to a child that cried "without reason." Studies showed that, when a German infant cried, its crying was ignored on the average one out of three times, or else the parent responded only after an interval of between 10 and 30 minutes. German infants were left alone in a crib for a long time, while the mother went out shopping or was working in another room. The magic words for German parents were that children should acquire *Selbständigkeit* (meaning approximately "self-reliance") and *Ordnungsliebe* (literally, "love of order," including self-control and complying with the wishes of others) as quickly as possible. German parents considered American children spoiled, because American parents attended too quickly to a child's crying. German parents were afraid that too much attention would make a child *verwöhnt*—an important and very, very bad word in German vocabulary regarding children, meaning "spoiled."

The attitudes of urban American and British parents in the decades from 1920 to 1950 were similar to contemporary German attitudes. American mothers were told by pediatricians and by other experts that regular schedules and cleanliness were all-important for infants, that rapid response would spoil the baby, and that it was essential for babies to learn to play by themselves and to control themselves as early as possible. The anthropologist Sarah Blaffer Hrdy described as follows the philosophy prevailing in the United States in the mid-20th century about how to respond to a baby's crying: "Back in my mother's day, educated women were under the impression that if a baby cried and his mother rushed to pick him up, she would spoil him, conditioning the baby to cry more." By the 1980s, when my wife Marie and I were raising our twin sons, that was still the prevalent philosophy about what to do with a baby who cried when being put to bed. We were advised to kiss our babies good-night, tiptoe out of their bedroom, ignore their heart-rending sobs when they heard us leave, come back in 10 minutes, wait for them to quiet down, tiptoe out again, and again ignore the resulting sobs. We felt horrible. Many other modern parents have shared our ordeal, and continue to share it.

In contrast, observers of children in hunter-gatherer societies commonly report that, if an infant begins crying, the parents' practice is to respond immediately. For example, if an Efe Pygmy infant starts to fuss, the mother or some other care-giver tries to comfort the infant within 10 seconds. If a !Kung infant cries, 88% of crying bouts receive a response (consisting of touching or nursing the infant) within 3 seconds, and almost all bouts receive a response within 10 seconds. Mothers respond to !Kung infants by nursing them, but many responses are by non-mothers (especially other adult women), who react by touching or holding the infant.

The result is that !Kung infants spend at most one minute out of each hour crying, mainly in crying bouts of less than 10 seconds. Because the responses of !Kung care-givers to crying by their infants are prompt and reliable, the total time that !Kung infants spend crying each hour is half that measured for Dutch infants. Many other studies show that one-year-old infants whose crying is ignored end up spending more time crying than do infants whose crying receives a response.

To settle once and for all the question of whether children whose crying is ignored turn out to be healthier adults than do children whose crying receives a prompt response, one would have to do a controlled experiment. The all-powerful experimenter would arbitrarily divide a society's households into two groups, and the parents of one group of children would be required to ignore their child's "needless" crying while the other group of parents would respond to crying within three seconds. Twenty years later, when the infants were adults, one could assess which group of children were more autonomous, secure in relationships, self-reliant, self-controlled, unspoiled, and endowed with other virtues emphasized by some modern educators and pediatricians.

Naturally, those well-designed experiments and rigorous assessments have not been carried out. One must instead fall back on the messy natural experiments and unrigorous anecdotes of comparing societies with different child-rearing practices. At least, one can conclude that the prompt responses of hunter-gatherer parents to infants crying do not consistently lead to children who end up conspicuously lacking in autonomy and self-reliance and other virtues. We shall return to the impressionistic answers that scholars have offered to this question of long-term outcomes.

Physical punishment

Related to those debates about spoiling a child by promptly responding to its crying are the familiar debates about spoiling a child by avoiding punishing it. There is great variation among human societies in their attitudes towards punishing children: variation within a given society from generation to generation, and variation between similar neighboring societies within the same generation. As for variation within the same society between generations, spanking of children was much more widely practised in the United States in my parents' generation than it is today. The German chancellor Bismarck commented that, even within a given family, spanked generations tend to alternate with non-spanked generations. That conforms to the experience of many of my American friends: those who were spanked as children swear that they will never inflict such barbaric cruelties on their own children, while those who were not spanked as children swear that it is healthier to administer a brief spanking than to practise the guilt manipulation and other behavioral controls that substitute for spanking, or to spoil kids entirely.

As for variation between contemporary neighboring societies, consider Western Europe today. Sweden forbids spankings; a Swedish parent who spanks a child can be charged with the criminal offense of child abuse. In contrast, many of my educated liberal German and British friends and American evangelical Christian friends believe that it is better to spank a child than not to spank. Spankers are fond of quoting the 17th-century English poet Samuel Butler ("Spare the rod and spoil the child") and the Athenian playwright Menander ("The man who has never been flogged has never been taught"). Similarly, in modern Africa the Aka Pygmies never beat or even scold their children, and they consider horrible and abusive the child-rearing practices of neighboring Ngandu farmers, who do beat their children.

Variation in physical punishment characterizes or characterized not only modern Europe and Africa but also other times and parts of the world. Within ancient Greece, Athenian children (despite Menander's dictum) ran around unchecked, while at the same time in Sparta everyone, not just a child's parents, could beat a child. In New Guinea, while some tribes do not even punish babies for brandishing sharp knives, I encountered an opposite extreme at a small village (Gasten) of a dozen huts around a clearing, where village life took place in full view of all the residents. One morning, I heard angry screaming, and I looked out to see what was happening. A mother was incensed at her daughter of about age eight, shouting at the daughter and hitting her, and the daughter was sobbing and holding her arms in front of her face to ward off the blows. Other adults were watching, and nobody was interfering. The mother got more and more furious. Finally, the mother went over to the edge of the clearing, bent down to pick up some object, came back to the child, and vigorously rubbed the object into the child's face, causing her daughter to scream uncontrollably in agony. It turned out that the object was a bunch of stinging nettle leaves. I don't know what the daughter had done to provoke this punishment, but the mother's behavior was evidently considered acceptable by all of the onlookers.

How can one explain why some societies practise physical punishment of children, while others don't? Much of the variation is evidently cultural and unrelated to differences in subsistence economy. For instance, I am unaware of differences between the economies of Sweden, Germany, and Britain, all of them industrialized agriculture-based societies speaking Germanic languages, that could explain why many modern Germans and British spank but Swedes don't. The New Guineans of both Gasten and of Enu's adoptive tribe are gardeners and swineherds, again without obvious differences to explain why physical punishment with nettles is acceptable at Gasten while even mild physical punishment is rare among Enu's adoptive people.

However, there does seem to be a broad trend: most hunter-gatherer bands do minimal physical punishment of young children, many farming societies do some punishment, and herders are especially likely to punish. One contributing explanation is that misbehavior by a hunter-gatherer child will probably hurt only the child and not anyone or anything else, because hunter-gatherers tend to have few valuable physical possessions. But many farmers, and especially herders, do have valuable material things, especially valuable livestock, so herders punish children to prevent serious consequences to the whole family—e.g., if a child fails to close the pasture gates, valuable cows and sheep can run away. More generally, compared to mobile societies of egalitarian hunter-gatherers, sedentary societies (e.g., most farmers and herders) have more power differences, more gender-based and age-based and individual inequality, more emphasis on learning deference and respect—and hence more punishment of children.

Here are some examples. Among hunter-gatherers, the Piraha, Andaman Islanders, Aka Pygmies, and !Kung practise little or no physical punishment. Daniel Everett relates the following story from his years of living among the Piraha. He became a father at the age of 19, and he came from a Christian background that practised physical punishment. One day, his daughter Shannon did something that he considered to merit a spanking. He grabbed a switch, told her to come to the next room where he would spank her, and she began yelling that she didn't need a spanking. The Pirahas came running at the sound of angry voices and asked him what he was doing. He didn't have a good answer to tell them, but he still recalled biblical injunctions about spanking children, so he told his daughter that he wouldn't spank her there in the presence of the Pirahas, but that she should go to the end of the airstrip and find another switch to be spanked with, and that he would meet her there in five minutes. As Shannon started on her way, the Pirahas asked her where she was going. Fully aware of what the Pirahas would think of her answer, she replied with glee, "My dad is going to hit me on the airstrip!" Out came Piraha children and adults to follow Daniel Everett as he was about to carry out this unthinkably barbaric behavior of hitting a child. He surrendered in defeat, leaving his smug daughter to celebrate her triumph. Piraha parents instead talk to their children respectfully, rarely discipline them, and do not use violence.

Similar attitudes prevail among most other hunter-gatherer groups studied. If one Aka Pygmy parent hits an infant, the other parent considers that ground for divorce. The !Kung explain their policy of not punishing children by saying that children have no wits and are not responsible for their actions. Instead, !Kung and Aka children are permitted to slap and insult parents. The Siriono practise mild punishment of a child that eats dirt or a taboo animal, by roughly picking up the child, but they never beat a child, whereas children are allowed to have temper tantrums in which they beat their father or mother as hard as possible.

Among farming peoples there is variation, with the most punitive being herders whose valuable livestock are at stake if a child looking after the livestock misbehaves. In some farming communities, discipline of children is lax, and they have few responsibilities and also few opportunities to damage valuable possessions, until they reach puberty. For example, among the people of the Trobriand Islands near New Guinea, who are farmers without livestock except for pigs, children are neither punished nor expected to obey. The ethnographer Bronislaw Malinowski wrote of the Trobriand Islanders, "Often . . . I would hear a youngster told to do this or that, and generally the thing, whatever it was, would be asked as a favor, though sometimes the request might be backed up by a threat of violence. The parent would either coax or scold or ask as from one equal to another. A simple command, implying the expectation of natural obedience, is never heard from parents to child in the Trobriands. . . . When I suggested, after some flagrant infantile misdeed, that it would mend matters for the future if the child were beaten or otherwise punished in cold blood, the idea appeared unnatural and immoral to my [Trobriand] friends."

A friend who has lived for many years among a herding people of East Africa told me that the herders' children there behave like little juvenile delinquents until the age of male circumcision, at which time they are expected to assume responsibilities. Then, following an initiation ceremony, boys begin herding the valuable cows, girls begin caring for siblings, and both begin to be disciplined. Among the Tallensi people of Ghana in West Africa, no one hesitates to punish a child who seems to deserve it, e.g., for dawdling while driving cattle. One Tallensi man pointed out to a visiting British anthropologist a scar that had resulted from his being severely whipped as a small boy. A Tallensi elder explained, "If you don't harass your child, he will not gain sense"—similar to Butler's dictum "Spare the rod and spoil the child."

Child autonomy

How much freedom or encouragement do children have to explore their environment? Are children permitted to do dangerous things, with the expectation that they must learn from their mistakes? Or are parents protective of their children's safety, and do parents curtail exploration and pull kids away if they start to do something that could be dangerous?

The answer to this question varies among societies. However, a tentative generalization is that individual autonomy, even of children, is a more cherished ideal in hunter-gatherer bands than in state societies, where the state considers that it has an interest in its children, does not want children to get hurt by doing as they please, and forbids parents to let a child harm itself. I write these lines just after I picked up a rental car at an airport. The recording that was broadcast to us passengers on the shuttle bus from the airport baggage claim to the rental car lot warned us, "Federal law requires children under five years of age or weighing under 80 pounds to be transported in a federally approved car seat." Hunter-gatherers would consider that warning to be none of the business of anyone other than the child and perhaps its parents and band members, but certainly not of a distant bureaucrat. At the risk of overgeneralizing, one could say that hunter-gatherers are fiercely egalitarian, and that they don't tell anyone, not even a child, to do anything. Generalizing or overgeneralizing further, small-scale societies appear to be not nearly as convinced as are we WEIRD moderns of the idea that parents are responsible for a child's development, and that they can influence how a child turns out.

That theme of autonomy has been emphasized by observers of many hunter-gatherer societies. For example, Aka Pygmy children have access to the same resources as do adults, whereas in the U.S. there are many adults-only resources that are off-limits to kids, such as weapons, alcohol, and breakable objects. Among the Martu people of the Western Australian desert, the worst offense is to impose on a child's will, even if the child is only three years old. The Piraha Indians consider children just as human beings, not in need of coddling or special protection. In Daniel Everett's words, "They [Piraha children] are treated fairly and allowance is made for their size and relative physical weakness, but by and large they are not considered qualitatively different from adults . . . the Pirahas have an undercurrent of Darwinism running through their parenting philosophy. This style of parenting has the result of producing very tough and resilient adults who do not believe that anyone owes them anything. Citizens of the Piraha nation know that each day's survival depends on their individual skills and hardiness. . . . The Pirahas' view that children are equal citizens of society means that there is no prohibition that applies to children but does not equally apply to adults and vice versa. . . . They have to decide for themselves to do or not to do what their society expects of them. Eventually they learn that it is in their best interests to listen to their parents a bit."

Some hunter-gatherer and small-scale farming societies don't intervene when children or even infants are doing dangerous things that may in fact harm them, and that could expose a Western parent to criminal prosecution. I mentioned earlier my surprise, in the New Guinea Highlands, to learn that the fire scars borne by so many adults of Enu's adoptive tribe were often acquired in infancy, when an infant was playing next to a fire, and its parents considered that child autonomy extended to a baby's having the right to touch or get close to the fire and to suffer the consequences. Hadza infants are permitted to grasp and suck on sharp knives (Plate 19). Here is an incident observed by Daniel Everett among the Piraha Indians: "We noticed that a [Piraha] toddler about two years old was sitting in the hut behind the man we were interviewing. The child was playing with a sharp kitchen knife, about nine inches in length. He was swinging the knife blade around him, often coming close to his eyes, his chest, his arm, and other body parts one would not like to slice off or perforate. What really got our attention, though, was that when he dropped the knife, his mother—talking to someone else—reached back nonchalantly without interrupting her conversation, picked up the knife, and handed it back to the toddler. No one told him not to cut himself or hurt himself with the knife. And he didn't, but I have seen other Piraha children cut themselves severely with knives."

Nevertheless, not all small-scale societies permit children to explore freely and do dangerous things. Variation in the freedom that children enjoy seems to me partly understandable from several considerations. Two are the considerations that I already discussed as accounting for more physical punishment among herders and farmers than among hunter-gatherers. While hunter-gatherer societies tend to be egalitarian, many farming and herding societies recognize different rights for men and women, or for younger and older people. The hunter-gatherer societies also tend to have fewer valuable possessions that a child could damage than do farmers and herders. Both of those considerations may contribute to hunter-gatherer children enjoying greater freedom to explore.

In addition, how much freedom children enjoy seems to depend partly on how dangerous the environment is, or is perceived to be. Some environments are relatively safe for children, but others are dangerous because of either environmental hazards or else dangers from people. Consider the following spectrum of environments, from the most dangerous to the least dangerous, paralleled by a range of child-rearing practices from adults severely restricting the freedom of young children to adults permitting young children to wander.

Among the most dangerous environments are the New World's tropical rainforests, which teem with biting, stinging, poisonous insects (army ants, bees, scorpions, spiders, and wasps), dangerous mammals (jaguars, peccaries, and pumas), large poisonous snakes (fer-de-lance and bushmasters), and stinging plants. No infant or small child left alone would survive for long in the Amazon rainforest. Hence, Kim Hill and A. Magdalena Hurtado write, "[Ache] infants under one year of age spend about 93% of their daylight time in tactile contact with a mother or father, and they are never set down on the ground or left alone for more than a few seconds . . . it is not until about three years of age that Ache children begin to spend significant amounts of time more than one meter from their mother. Even still, Ache children between three and four years of age spend 76% of their daylight time less than one meter away from their mother and are monitored almost constantly." As a result, Hill and Hurtado commented, Ache children don't learn to walk independently until they are 21 to 23 months old, 9 months later than American children. Ache children between three and five years of age are often carried piggyback in the forest by an adult, rather than being allowed to walk. Only when an Ache child is five years old does it begin to explore the forest on its own legs, but even then Ache children remain within 50 meters of an adult for most of the time.

Dangerous, but not quite as dangerous as the neotropical rainforest, are the Kalahari Desert, the Arctic, and the swamps of the Okavango Delta. !Kung children play in groups that are supervised casually but effectively by adults; the children are usually within eye or ear contact of adults in camp. In the Arctic one cannot allow children to run around freely, because of dangers from accidents that would result in exposure or freezing. Young girls in Southern Africa's Okavango Delta are permitted to catch fish with baskets, but they stay near shore because of danger from crocodiles, hippopotamuses, elephants, and buffaloes. These examples should be tempered, however, by mentioning that 4-year-old Aka Pygmy children, while they don't go off into the Central African rainforest by themselves, do go off with 10-year-old Aka children despite the dangers of leopards and elephants.

A less dangerous environment, where children can be given more freedom, is that of the Hadza in East Africa. It has leopards and other dangerous predators, as does the environment of the !Kung, but it differs from the !Kung environment in being hilly, so that it is possible to see greater distances, and parents can keep an eye on children playing at greater distances from a Hadza camp than from a !Kung camp. The New Guinea rainforests are also moderately safe: there are no dangerous mammals, many snakes are poisonous but they are rarely encountered, and the main danger is from other people. Hence I often see New Guinea children playing, walking, or canoeing by themselves, and my New Guinea friends tell me of spending much time in the forests by themselves as children.

Among the safest environments are Australia's deserts and Madagascar's forests. In recent times Australian deserts have harbored no mammals dangerous to humans. Like New Guinea, Australia has a reputation for poisonous snakes, but one rarely comes across them unless one goes looking for them. Hence Martu children in the Australian desert regularly go out on foraging trips unsupervised by adults. Similarly, Madagascar's forests harbor no large predators and few poisonous plants and animals, so children can safely go off by themselves in groups to dig yams.

Multi-age playgroups

On the American frontier, where population was sparse, the one-room schoolhouse was a common phenomenon. With so few children living within daily travel distance, schools could afford only a single room and a single teacher, and all children of different ages had to be educated together in that one room. But the one-room schoolhouse in the U.S. today is a romantic memory of the past, except in rural areas of low population density. Instead, in all cities, and in rural areas of moderate population density, children learn and play in age cohorts. School classrooms are age-graded, such that most classmates are within a year of each other in age. While neighborhood playgroups are not so strictly age-segregated, in densely populated areas of large societies there are enough children living within walking distance of each other that 12-year-olds don't routinely play with 3-year-olds. That norm of age cohorts applies not only to modern societies with state governments and schools, but also to populous pre-state societies, because of the same basic demographic fact: many children close in age, living in proximity. For example, many African chiefdoms have or had age cohorts, in which children close in age were initiated and circumcised at the same time, and (among the Zulu) boys of the same age formed military cohorts.

But demographic realities produce a different result in small-scale societies, which resemble one-room schoolhouses. A typical hunter-gatherer band numbering around 30 people will on the average contain only about a dozen pre-adolescent kids, of both sexes and various ages. Hence it is impossible to assemble separate age-cohort playgroups, each with many children, as is characteristic of large societies. Instead, all children in the band form a single multi-age playgroup of both sexes. That observation applies to all small-scale hunter-gatherer societies that have been studied.

In such multi-age playgroups, both the older and the younger children gain from being together. The young children gain from being socialized not only by adults by also by older children, while the older children acquire experience in caring for younger children. That experience gained by older children contributes to explaining how hunter-gatherers can become confident parents already as teen-agers. While Western societies have plenty of teen-aged parents, especially unwed teen-agers, Western teen-agers are suboptimal parents because of inexperience. However, in a small-scale society, the teen-agers who become parents will already have been taking care of children for many years (Plate 38).

For example, while I was spending some time in a remote New Guinea village, a 12-year-old girl named Morcy was designated to cook for me. When I returned to the village two years later, I found that Morcy had gotten married in the intervening time and was now, at the age of 14, holding her first child. I at first thought: surely there is a mistake about her age, and she really is 16 or 17? But Morcy's father was the man who kept the village birth and death record book, and he had recorded her date of birth himself. I then thought: how on earth can a girl only 14 years old be a competent mother? In the United States, it would even be forbidden by law for a man to marry such a young girl. But Morcy seemed to be dealing in a self-assured way with her child, no differently from older mothers at the village. I finally reflected that Morcy had already had years of experience in taking care of young children. At age 14, she was better qualified to be a parent than I had been when I became a father at age 49.

Another phenomenon affected by multi-age playgroups is premarital sex, which is reported from all well-studied small hunter-gatherer societies. Most large societies consider some activities as suitable for boys, and other activities as suitable for girls. They encourage boys and girls to play separately, and there are enough boys and girls to form single-sex playgroups. But that's impossible in a band where there are only a dozen children of all ages. Because hunter-gatherer children sleep with their parents, either in the same bed or in the same hut, there is no privacy. Children see their parents having sex. In the Trobriand Islands, Malinowski was told that parents took no special precautions to prevent their children from watching them having sex: they just scolded the child and told it to cover its head with a mat. Once children are old enough to join playgroups of other children, they make up games imitating the various adult activities that they see, so of course they have sex games, simulating intercourse. Either the adults don't interfere with child sex play at all, or else !Kung parents discourage it when it becomes obvious, but they consider child sexual experimentation inevitable and normal. It's what the !Kung parents themselves did as children, and the children are often playing out of sight where the parents don't see their sex games. Many societies, such as the Siriono and Piraha and New Guinea Eastern Highlanders, tolerate open sexual play between adults and children.

Child play and education

After the first night that I spent in a New Guinea Highland village, I woke up the next morning to hear the shouts of village boys playing outside my hut. Instead of playing hopscotch or pulling toy cars, they were playing tribal war. Each boy had a small bow, together with a quiver of arrows with tips of wild grass, which hurt but didn't injure a boy when he was struck. The kids were divided into two groups, shooting arrows at each other, a boy in each group advancing to come close to an "enemy" boy before firing an arrow at him, but bobbing and darting from side to side to avoid being hit himself, and quickly running back to attach a new arrow. It was a realistic imitation of an actual Highland war, except that the arrows were non-lethal, the participants were boys rather than men, and they belonged to the same village and were laughing.

This "game" that introduced me to life in the New Guinea Highlands is typical of so-called educational play of children around the world. Much child play is imitation of adult activities that the children see, or hear about in stories told by adults. The kids play for fun, but their play serves the function of letting them practise things that they will later have to do as adults. For instance, among the Dani people of the New Guinea Highlands, the anthropologist Karl Heider observed that educational play of children imitates everything that goes on in the world of Dani adults, except rituals reserved for adults. Dani games imitating adult life include fighting battles with grass spears; using spears or sticks to "kill" "armies" of berries, rolled realistically back and forth to imitate warriors advancing and retreating; target practice at hanging moss and at ant hives; hunting birds for fun; building imitation huts and imitation gardens with ditches; dragging around a flower attached to a string, as if it were a pig, and calling it by the Dani words meaning "pig-pig"; and gathering at night around a fire, watching a burning stick fall, and pretending that the person to whom the stick points will become one's future brother-in-law.

Whereas adult life and child's play in the New Guinea Highlands revolve around wars and pigs, adult life among the Nuer people in the Sudan revolves around cattle. Hence the games of Nuer children also center around cattle: children build toy kraals (cattle enclosures) out of sand, ashes, and mud, and they fill the toy kraals with toy mud figures of cattle, which they then play at herding. Among the Mailu people who live on the coast of New Guinea and use sail canoes and catch fish, games of children include sailing a toy canoe, using a toy net, and using a toy fish spear. Yanamamo Indian children in Brazil and Venezuela play at exploring the plants and animals of the Amazon rainforest in which they live. As a result, they become knowledgeable naturalists at an early age.

Among the Siriono Indians of Bolivia, an infant boy only three months old already receives a tiny bow and arrow from his father, although he will not be able to use it for several years. By the time the boy is 3, he begins shooting at non-living targets, then at insects, next at birds, then at age 8 the boy begins to accompany his father on hunting trips, and by age 12 the boy is a full-fledged hunter. By age 3, Siriono girls begin to play with a miniature spindle, spin, make baskets and pots, and help their mother at household tasks. The boy's bow and arrow and the girl's spindle are the only Siriono toys. The Siriono have no organized games equivalent to our games of tag or hide-and-seek, except that boys wrestle.

In contrast to all those "educational games" that imitate adult activities and prepare children for them, there are other Dani games that Karl Heider considered non-educational, in that they were not obviously training children to execute small versions of eventual adult activities. They included making figures out of string, making designs of knotted grass, somersaulting down a hill, and leading around a rhinoceros beetle by a leash made of a grass stalk forced into the hole made by breaking off the beetle's horns. These are examples of what is termed "child culture": children learning to get along with other children, and playing games that have nothing to do with becoming an adult. However, the line between educational and non-educational games can be blurred. For example, one Dani game of string figures consists of making two loops representing a man and a woman who meet from each side and "copulate," while leading a beetle on a leash could be considered practice for leading a pig on a leash.

A regular feature of the games of hunter-gatherer societies and the smallest farming societies is their lack of competition or contests. Whereas many American games involve keeping score and are about winning and losing, it is rare for hunter-gatherer games to keep score or identify a winner. Instead, games of small-scale societies often involve sharing, to prepare children for adult life that emphasizes sharing and discourages contests. An example is the game of cutting up and sharing a banana that Jane Goodale described for New Britain's Kaulong people and that I related on page 91.

Modern American society differs from traditional societies in the number, source, and claimed function of toys. American toy manufacturers heavily promote so-called educational toys to foster so-called creative play (Plate 18). American parents are taught to believe that manufactured store-bought toys are important to the development of their children. In contrast, traditional societies have few or no toys, and any toys that do exist are made either by the child itself or by the child's parents. An American friend who spent his childhood in rural Kenya told me that some of his Kenyan friends were very inventive, and used sticks and string to build their own small cars with wheels and axles (Plate 17). One day, my American friend and his Kenyan friend tried to harness a pair of giant Goliath beetles to pull a toy cart that they had built. The two boys spent a whole afternoon at their game, but despite hours of effort they could not get the two beetles to pull in coordination. When my friend returned as a teen-ager to the United States and watched American children playing with their plastic ready-made store-bought toys, he gained the impression that American children are less creative than Kenyan children.

In modern state societies, there is formal education: schools and after-hour classes, in which specially trained instructors teach children material set by school boards, as an activity separate from play. But education in small-scale societies is not a separate activity. Instead, children learn in the course of accompanying their parents and other adults, and of hearing stories told by adults and older children around the campfire. For instance, Nurit Bird-David wrote as follows about southern India's Nayaka people: "At a time where in modern societies children begin schooling, say at age 6, Nayaka children independently go hunting small game, visiting and staying with other families, free from supervision by their own specific parents, though not necessarily from adults. . . . Teaching, additionally, is done in a very subtle way. No formal instruction and memorizing here, no classes, no exams, no cultural sites [schools] in which packages of knowledge, abstracted from their context, are transmitted from one person to another. Knowledge is inseparable from social life."

As another example, among Africa's Mbuti Pygmies studied by Colin Turnbull, children imitate their parents by playing with a tiny bow and arrow, a strip of a hunting net, or a miniature basket (Plate 20), and by building a miniature house, catching frogs, and chasing a cooperative grandparent who agrees to pretend to be an antelope. "For children, life is one long frolic interspersed with a healthy sprinkle of spankings and slappings. . . . And one day they find that the games they have been playing are not games any longer, but the real thing, for they have become adults. The hunting is now real hunting; their tree climbing is in earnest search of inaccessible honey; their acrobatics on the swings are repeated almost daily, in other forms, in the pursuit of elusive game, or in avoiding the malicious forest buffalo. It happens so gradually that they hardly no-tice the change at first, for even when they are proud and famous hunters their life is still full of fun and laughter."

Whereas for small-scale societies education follows naturally from so-cial life, in some modern societies even the rudiments of social life require explicit education. For example, in parts of modern American cities where people do not know their neighbors, and where car traffic and potential kidnappers and a lack of sidewalks mean that children cannot safely walk to play with other kids, children have to be taught formally how to play with other children in classes termed "mommy and me classes." There, a mother or another care-giver brings her child to a classroom with a trained teacher and a dozen other children and their mothers. The chil-dren sit in an inner circle, the mothers and care-givers sit in an outer circle and gain experience of child play, and the children are taught how to take turns speaking, listening, and handing objects back and forth to other children. There are many features of modern American society that my New Guinea friends consider bizarre, but nothing astonished them more than being told that American children need specified places, times, and instruction in order to learn how to meet and play with each other.

Their kids and our kids

Finally, let's reflect on differences in child-rearing practices between small-scale societies and state societies. Of course, there is much variation among industrial state societies today in the modern world. Ideals and practices of raising children differ between the U.S., Germany, Sweden, Japan, and an Israeli kibbutz. Within any given one of those state societ-ies, there are differences between farmers, urban poor people, and the urban middle class. There are also differences from generation to genera-tion within a given state society: child-rearing practices in the U.S. today are unlike those prevalent in the 1930s.

Nevertheless, there are still some basic similarities among all of those state societies, and some basic differences between state and non-state societies. State governments have their own separate interests regarding the state's children, and those interests do not necessarily coincide with the interests of a child's parents. Small-scale non-state societies also have their own interests, but a state society's interests are more explicit, administered by more centralized top-down leadership, and backed up by well-defined enforcing powers. All states want children who, as adults, will become useful and obedient citizens, soldiers, and workers. States tend to object to having their future citizens killed at birth, or permitted to become burned by fires. States also tend to have views about the education of their future citizens, and about their citizens' sexual conduct. Those shared goals of states promote some convergence among states in their policies regarding children; the child-rearing practices of non-state societies vary over a much wider spectrum than do the practices of state societies. Within non-state societies, hunter-gatherer societies are subject to convergent pressures of their own: they share some basic similarities of child-rearing with each other, but as a group they differ from states as a group.

States do have military and technological advantages, and advantages of vastly larger populations, over hunter-gatherers. Throughout recent millennia, those advantages have enabled states to conquer hunter-gatherers, so that the modern world map is now divided completely among states, and few hunter-gatherer groups have survived. But even though states are much more powerful than hunter-gatherer bands, that doesn't necessarily imply that states have better ways of raising their children. Some child-rearing practices of hunter-gatherer bands may be ones that we could consider emulating.

Naturally, I'm not saying that we should emulate all child-rearing practices of hunter-gatherers. I don't recommend that we return to the hunter-gatherer practices of selective infanticide, high risk of death in childbirth, and letting infants play with knives and get burned by fires. Some other features of hunter-gatherer childhoods, like the permissiveness of child sex play, feel uncomfortable to many of us, even though it may be hard to demonstrate that they really are harmful to children. Still other practices are now adopted by some citizens of state societies, but make others of us uncomfortable—such as having infants sleep in the same bedroom or in the same bed as parents, nursing children until age three or four, and avoiding physical punishment of children.

But some other hunter-gatherer child-rearing practices may fit readily into modern state societies. It's perfectly feasible for us to transport our infants vertically upright and facing forward, rather than horizontally in a pram or vertically upright but facing backwards in a pack. We could respond quickly and consistently to an infant's crying, practise much more extensive allo-parenting, and have far more physical contact between infants and care-givers. We could encourage self-invented play of children, rather than discourage it by constantly providing complicated so-called educational toys. We could arrange for multi-age child playgroups, rather than playgroups consisting of a uniform age cohort. We could maximize a child's freedom to explore, insofar as it is safe to do so.

I find myself thinking a lot about the New Guinea people with whom I have been working for the last 49 years, and about the comments of Westerners who have lived for years in hunter-gatherer societies and watched children grow up there. A recurring theme is that the other Westerners and I are struck by the emotional security, self-confidence, curiosity, and autonomy of members of small-scale societies, not only as adults but already as children. We see that people in small-scale societies spend far more time talking to each other than we do, and they spend no time at all on passive entertainment supplied by outsiders, such as television, video games, and books. We are struck by the precocious development of social skills in their children. These are qualities that most of us admire, and would like to see in our own children, but we discourage development of those qualities by ranking and grading our children and constantly telling them what to do. The adolescent identity crises that plague American teen-agers aren't an issue for hunter-gatherer children. The Westerners who have lived with hunter-gatherers and other small-scale societies speculate that these admirable qualities develop because of the way in which their children are brought up: namely, with constant security and stimulation, as a result of the long nursing period, sleeping near parents for several years, far more social models available to children through allo-parenting, far more social stimulation through constant physical contact and proximity of caretakers, instant caretaker responses to a child's crying, and the minimal amount of physical punishment.

But our impressions of greater adult security, autonomy, and social skills in small-scale societies are just impressions: they are hard to measure and to prove. Even if these impressions are real, it's difficult to establish that they are the result of a long nursing period, allo-parenting, and so on. At minimum, though, one can say that hunter-gatherer rearing practices that seem so foreign to us aren't disastrous, and they don't produce societies of obvious sociopaths. Instead, they produce individuals capable of coping with big challenges and dangers while still enjoying their lives. The hunter-gatherer lifestyle worked at least tolerably well for the nearly 100,000-year history of behaviorally modern humans. Everybody in the world was a hunter-gatherer until the local origins of agriculture around 11,000 years ago, and nobody in the world lived under a state government until 5,400 years ago. The lessons from all those experiments in child-rearing that lasted for such a long time are worth considering seriously.

CHAPTER 6

The Treatment of Old People:
Cherish, Abandon, or Kill?

The elderly ▪ Expectations about eldercare ▪ Why abandon or kill? ▪ Usefulness of old people ▪ Society's values ▪ Society's rules ▪ Better or worse today? ▪ What to do with older people?

The elderly

While I was visiting a village on the Fijian island of Viti Levu, I fell into conversation with a local man who had visited the United States and told me his impressions. There were some features of American life that he admired or envied, but others that disgusted him. Worst of all was our treatment of the elderly. In rural Fiji old people continue to live in the village where they have spent their lives, surrounded by their relatives and life-long friends. They often reside in a house of their children, who take care of them, even to the point of pre-chewing and softening food for an old parent whose teeth have been worn down to the gum-line. In the United States, though, my Fijian acquaintance was outraged that many old people are sent to retirement homes where they are visited only occasionally by their children. He burst out accusingly to me, "You throw away your old people and your own parents!"

Among traditional societies, some accord their elderly even higher status than do Fijians, allowing the elderly to tyrannize their adult children, to control the society's property, and even to prevent young men from marrying until their 40s. Others accord their elderly even lower status than do Americans, starving or abandoning or actively killing them. Of course, there is much individual variation within any society: I have several American friends who put their parents into a retirement home and visit them once a year or never, and another friend who published his 22nd book on his 100th birthday and celebrated the occasion in the company of all of his children, grandchildren, and great-grandchildren, whom he also saw regularly throughout the year. But the range of variation among traditional societies in their normal practices of eldercare exceeds even the range of individual variation in the United States. I don't know any individual American whose devoted care of his aged parents goes as far as pre-chewing their food, nor any who has strangled his aged parents and been publicly commended as a good son for doing so. The lot of the elderly is widely acknowledged to be often miserable in the United States. Is there anything that we can learn from all that variation among traditional societies, both as to what we could emulate and what we should avoid?

Before I proceed, let me deal with two objections that are often raised. One is that there isn't a universal definition of the age at which one becomes "old": that, too, varies among societies and with one's personal perspective. In the United States the federal government in effect defines old age as beginning at age 65, when one becomes eligible for Social Security. When I was in my teens, I looked up to people in their late 20s as being seemingly at their peak of life and wisdom, people in their 30s as already middle-aged, and anyone from about 60 onwards as old. Now that I am 75 years old, I regard my 60s and early 70s as the peak of my own life, and old age as likely to start sometime around 85 or 90 depending on my health. In rural New Guinea, however, where relatively few people reach the age of 60, even 50-year-olds are regarded as old. I recall arriving at a village of Indonesian New Guinea where, when the local people learned that I was (then) 46 years old, they gasped out *"setengah mati!,"* meaning "half-dead," and they assigned a teen-aged boy to walk constantly beside me to ensure that I would not come to grief. Hence "old age" has to be defined by the standards of the local society, not by some arbitrary universal year count.

The other objection is related to that first objection. In countries where life expectancy is under 40, one might imagine that almost no one reaches old age as defined in the United States. Actually, in almost every New Guinea village where I have made inquiries, even if few people survive to 50 and anyone over 50 is considered a *lapun* (old man), I am still shown one or two people whose age can be estimated at over 70 by their memories of datable events (e.g., whether they were alive at the time of the great cyclone of 1910). They are likely to be lame, sight-impaired or blind, and dependent on relatives for food, but they nevertheless play (as we shall see) a vital role in the life of the village. Similar findings apply to other traditional peoples: Kim Hill and A. Magdalena Hurtado reconstructed genealogies of five forest-dwelling Ache Indians from Paraguay who died at the respective estimated ages of 70, 72, 75, 77, and 78, while Nancy Howell photographed a !Kung man whom she calculated to be 82 years old but who could still walk long distances when his group was moving camp, and still gathered much of his own food and built his own hut.

How can we account for the wide variation among societies in their norms for treating the elderly? Part of the explanation, we shall see, involves variation among societies in material factors that make the elderly more or less useful to the society, and that make it more or less feasible for younger people to support their elderly. The other part of the explanation involves variation among societies in cultural values, such as respect for the elderly, respect for privacy, emphasis on the family versus the individual, and self-reliance. These values are only partly predictable from the material factors that make old people useful or just a burden.

Expectations about eldercare

Let's start off with a naive expectation about eldercare. Although the expectation is obviously incomplete, formulating it will nevertheless help us by forcing us to ask why and in what respects it breaks down. A layperson with a rosy view of life might reason: parents and their children do and should love each other. Parents devote their best efforts to their kids and make sacrifices for them. Kids respect and are grateful to the parents who raised them. Hence we expect kids throughout the world to take good care of their old parents.

A naive evolutionary biologist might reach that same heart-warming conclusion by a different chain of reasoning. Natural selection is about passing on genes. The most direct way for people to pass on their genes is through their children. Hence natural selection should favor parents whose genes cause them to behave in ways that promote the survival and reproduction of their children. Similarly, cultural selection is about passing on learned behaviors, and parents serve as behavioral models for their children. It therefore makes sense for parents to make sacrifices for their kids, even to sacrifice their own lives, if they thereby promote the survival and reproductive success of their kids. Conversely, older parents are likely to have accumulated resources, status, knowledge, and skills that their kids haven't yet accumulated. Kids know that it's in their parents' genetic and cultural interests to help their kids by passing on those resources, status, knowledge, and skills. Therefore, kids reason, it's also in the kids' interest to take care of their elderly parents so that the parents can continue to help them. More generally, in a society of inter-related individuals, one expects the younger generation as a whole to take care of their elders, who share culture and many genes with members of the younger generation.

However, we know that these rosy predictions are only partly true. Yes, parents usually do take care of their children, who in turn often take care of their parents, and the younger generation as a whole often takes care of its elders. But these conclusions don't hold for at least some kids in most societies, nor for most kids in some societies. Why not? What was wrong with our reasoning?

Our naive error (which evolutionary biologists now avoid) was that we failed to consider conflicts of interest between generations. Parents shouldn't always make unlimited sacrifices, kids shouldn't always be grateful, love has its limits, and people aren't Darwinian calculating devices that constantly evaluate optimum transmission of their genes and culture and behave accordingly. All people, including old people, want a comfortable life for themselves, not just for their kids. There often are limits to the sacrifices that parents are willing to endure for their kids. Conversely, kids often are impatient to enjoy a comfortable life. They reason, quite correctly, that the more parental resources that the parents themselves consume, the fewer resources will remain available for the kids to enjoy. Even insofar as kids do behave instinctively as Darwinian calculating devices, natural selection teaches us that kids *shouldn't* always take care of their elderly parents. There are many circumstances under which kids can improve transmission of their own genes or cultures by being stingy to, abandoning, or even killing their parents.

Why abandon or kill?

In what sorts of society "should" (by this reasoning) and do children (and the younger generation in general) neglect, abandon, or kill their parents (and the older generation in general)? The many reported cases involve societies for which old people become a serious handicap endangering the whole group's safety. This situation arises under two different sets of circumstances. One set applies to nomadic hunter-gatherers who must shift camp from time to time. Without beasts of burden, the nomads have to carry everything on their backs: babies, children under the age of four unable to walk at the group's pace, weapons, tools, all other material possessions, and food and water for the journey. To add to that load old or sick people unable to walk at all is difficult or impossible.

The other set of circumstances arises in environments, especially Arctic regions and deserts, where severe food shortages periodically occur, and where food surpluses large enough to carry the group through the period of shortage cannot be accumulated. If there isn't enough food to keep everyone fit or just alive, the society must sacrifice its least valuable or least productive members; otherwise, everybody's survival will be endangered.

However, it is not the case that all nomads and Arctic and desert peoples sacrifice all of their elderly. Some groups (such as the !Kung and African Pygmies) seem more reluctant to do so than are other groups (such as the Ache, Siriono, and Inuit). Within a group, the treatment of a particular old person may depend on whether a close relative is available to care for and defend the old person.

How are burdensome old people jettisoned? At the risk of my using language that may appear unfeeling or gruesome, there are five methods that can be arranged in a sequence of increasingly direct action. The most passive method is merely to neglect old people until they die: to ignore them, give them little food, let them starve, let them wander off, or let them die in their own filth. For example, this method has been reported among the Inuit of the Arctic, the Hopi of the North American deserts, the Witoto of tropical South America, and Aboriginal Australians.

The next method, practised in various forms by the Lapps (Saami) of northern Scandinavia, the San of the Kalahari Desert, the Omaha and Kutenai Indians of North America, and the Ache Indians of tropical South America, is intentionally to abandon an old or sick person when the rest of the group shifts camp. A variant of this method among the Ache, reserved for old men (but not for old women, who are killed outright), is to take men out of the forest to a "white man's road" and leave them to walk off and never be heard from again. More often, a weak person is left in a shelter or in the camp being evacuated, and provided with some firewood, food, and water, so that if the abandoned person recovers strength, he or she can try to catch up with the rest of the group.

The anthropologist Allan Holmberg happened to be with a group of Bolivia's Siriono Indians when such an abandonment occurred. Here is his account of what took place: "The band decided to make a move in the direction of the Rio Blanco. While they were making preparations for the journey, my attention was called to a middle-aged woman who was lying sick in her hammock, too sick to speak. I inquired of the chief what they planned to do with her. He referred me to her husband, who told me that she would be left to die because she was too ill to walk and because she was going to die anyway. Departure was scheduled for the following morning. I was on hand to observe the event. The entire band walked out of the camp without so much as a farewell to the dying woman. Even her husband departed without saying goodbye. She was left with fire, a calabash of water, her personal belongings, and nothing more. She was too sick to protest." Holmberg himself was ill and went off to a mission station for medical treatment. When he came back to the campsite three weeks later, the woman was not there, so he followed a trail to the group's next campsite, where he found the woman's remains stripped to her bones by ants and vultures. "She had tried her utmost to follow the fortunes of the band, but had failed and had experienced the same fate that is accorded all Siriono whose days of utility are over."

A third method for disposing of the elderly, reported for the Chukchi and the Yakut of Siberia, the Crow Indians of North America, the Inuit, and the Norse, involves the older individual choosing or being encouraged to commit suicide, by jumping off a cliff, going out to sea, or seeking death in battle. The New Zealand physician and sailor David

Lewis related how an aging friend of his, the navigator Tevake from the Reef Islands in the Southwest Pacific Ocean, made a formal farewell and then set off to sea alone on a boat journey from which he did not return and evidently did not intend to return.

Whereas that third method constitutes unassisted suicide, the fourth method can be described either as assisted suicide or else as killing with the victim's cooperation, e.g., by strangling, stabbing, or burying alive. Old Chukchi people who submitted to voluntary death were praised and assured that they would receive one of the best dwelling places in the next world. The wife of the victim held his head on her knees, while two men on opposite sides pulled tight a rope around his neck. Among the Kaulong people of southwestern New Britain, strangling of a widow by her brothers or son immediately after her husband's death was routine until the 1950s. This act was an obligation that, although emotionally shattering for the executioner, was considered shameful to avoid. One Kaulong son described to Jane Goodale how his mother humiliated him into doing it: "When I hesitated, my mother stood up and spoke loudly so all could hear and said that the reason I hesitated was that I wished to have sex with her." Sick and old people in the Banks Islands begged their friends to end their suffering by burying them alive, and the friends did so as an act of kindness: "a man at Mota buried his brother, who was in extreme weakness from influenza; but he [the survivor] heaped the earth loosely over his [the victim's] head, and wept, and went from time to time to ask him whether he were still alive."

The final widespread method is to kill the victim violently without the victim's cooperation or consent, again by strangling or burying alive, or else by suffocating, stabbing, delivering an ax blow to the head, or breaking the neck or back. One Ache Indian man interviewed by Kim Hill and A. Magdalena Hurtado described his methods of killing old women (as mentioned above, old men were instead left to walk off): "I customarily killed old women. I used to kill my aunts [classificatory aunts] when they were still moving (alive). . . . I would step on them, then they all died, there by the big river. . . . I didn't used to wait until they were completely dead to bury them. When they were still moving I would break them [their backs or necks]. . . . I wouldn't care for old women; all by myself I would stick them [with his bow]."

Our reaction to these accounts of spouses, children, brothers or sisters, or fellow band members killing or abandoning an old or sick person is likely to be one of horror—just as is our reaction to the accounts in Chapter 5 of a mother killing her newborn baby if it is a twin or born damaged. But, just as in those cases of infanticide, we have to ask ourselves: what else could a nomadic society, or a society with not enough food for the whole group, do with its elderly? Throughout their lives, the victims have already watched old or sick people being abandoned or killed, and have probably already done it to their own parents. It is the form of death that they expect, and in which in many cases they cooperate. We are fortunate that we do not face that same ordeal ourselves as victim or suicide assister or killer, because we have the good fortune to live in societies with surplus food and medical care. As Winston Churchill wrote of the Japanese admiral Kurita, who had to choose between two equally awful courses of action in wartime, "Those who have endured a similar ordeal may judge him." In fact, many of you readers of this book have endured or will endure a similar ordeal yourselves, when you find yourself forced to decide whether to tell the physician caring for your aged or sick parent in failing health that the time has come to halt further aggressive medical intervention, or just to administer pain-killers, sedatives, and palliative care.

Usefulness of old people

What useful services can old people perform for traditional societies? From a cold-blooded adaptive perspective, societies in which old people do remain useful will tend to prosper if those societies care for their elderly. More often, of course, young people who care for their elders couch their reasons not in terms of that evolutionary advantage but in terms of love, respect, and obligation. However, when a group of hunter-gatherers is starving and debating whom they can afford to feed, cold-blooded considerations may be voiced explicitly. Of the services rendered by older people, the first ones that I shall mention are also performed by younger people but are still within the power of older people, while other services involve skills perfected by long experience and hence especially suitable to old people.

People eventually reach an age at which men can no longer spear to death a lion, and women can no longer trot miles with a heavy load to and from the mongongo nut grove. Nevertheless, there are other ways in which older people can continue to obtain food for their grandchildren and thereby ease the provisioning burden on their children and children-in-law. Ache men continue to hunt and gather into their 60s by concentrating on small animals, fruit, and palm products and breaking trail when the band shifts camp. Older !Kung men set animal traps, gather plant food, and join younger men on hunts in order to interpret animal tracks and propose strategies. Among Hadza hunter-gatherer women of Tanzania, the age group working the hardest consists of post-menopausal grandmothers (Plate 21), who spend on the average seven hours a day foraging for tubers and fruit—even though they no longer have dependent children of their own to feed. But they do have hungry grandchildren, and the more time that a Hadza grandmother spends foraging for food, the faster her grandchildren gain weight as a result. Similar benefits have been described for 18th- and 19th-century Finnish and Canadian farmers: analyses of church and genealogical records show that more children survive to adulthood if they have a living grandmother than if both grandmothers are dead, and that every decade that a post-menopausal woman survives past age 50 is associated with her children producing on the average two extra children of their own (presumably because of the grandmother's help).

Another service that older people can render even past the age of digging tubers seven hours a day is baby-sitting. That frees up the older person's children and children-in-law to spend more time foraging unencumbered for their own children, the grandchildren of the older person. !Kung grandparents often take care of their grandchildren uninterruptedly for several consecutive days, thereby enabling their children to undertake overnight hunting and gathering trips on which the grandchildren would be an encumbrance. A main reason that elderly Samoans give today for migrating to the United States is to care for their grandchildren, and thus to enable their children to hold jobs outside the house and to face fewer burdens inside the house.

Old people can make things for their grown children to use, such as tools, weapons, baskets, pots, and woven textiles (Plate 22). For example, older Semang hunter-gatherers of the Malay Peninsula were noted for making blowguns. This is an area where the elderly not only try to hang on to earlier abilities but are likely to excel: the best basket-makers and potters are often older people.

Other areas in which abilities grow with age include medicine, religion, entertainment, relationships, and politics. Traditional midwives and medicine men are often old, as are magicians and priests, prophets and sorcerers, and the leaders of songs, games, dances, and initiation rites. Older people enjoy a huge social advantage, insofar as they have spent a lifetime building up a network of relationships, into which they can then introduce their children. Political leaders are usually older people, so much so that the phrase "tribal elders" has become virtually a synonym for tribal leaders. That remains generally true even in modern state societies: for instance, the average age on taking office is 54 for American presidents and 53 for American Supreme Court justices.

But perhaps the most important function of older people in traditional societies is one that may not have occurred to readers of this book. In a literate society the main repositories of information are written or digital sources: encyclopedias, books, magazines, maps, diaries, notes, letters, and now the Internet. If we want to ascertain some fact, we look it up in a written source or else online. But that option doesn't exist for a pre-literate society, which must rely instead on human memories. Hence the minds of older people are the society's encyclopedias and libraries. Time and time again in New Guinea, when I am interviewing local people and ask them some question to which they are unsure of the answer, my informants pause and say, "Let's ask the old man [or the old woman]." Older people know the tribe's myths and songs, who is related to whom, who did what to whom when, the names and habits and uses of hundreds of species of local plants and animals, and where to go to find food when conditions are poor. Hence caring for older people becomes a matter of life or death, just as caring for one's hydrographic charts is a matter of life or death for modern boat captains. I'll illustrate this value of old people by the story of a case involving knowledge essential for a tribe's survival.

The story happened to me in 1976, on a Southwest Pacific island called Rennell. Because I had been sent to Rennell to prepare an environmental impact report for a proposed bauxite mine on the island, I wanted to find out how rapidly forests might regenerate after being cleared for mining, and which tree species were useful for timber, edible fruits, or other purposes. Middle-aged islanders proceeded to name for me 126 Rennell plant species in the Rennell language (*anu, gangotoba, ghai-gha-ghea, kagaa-loghu-loghu,* etc.). For each species, they explained whether its seeds and fruits were inedible to animals as well as to humans, or else eaten by birds and bats but not humans (naming the particular bird and bat species involved), or else edible to humans. Among those species eaten by humans, some were further distinguished as being "eaten only after the hungi kengi."

Never having heard of a hungi kengi, I ask what it was and how it turned normally inedible fruits into edible ones. In explanation, my informants brought me to a hut where they introduced me to the source of that information, a very old woman unable to walk unassisted. It turned out that *hungi kengi* was the Rennell name for the biggest cyclone to have hit the island in living memory, apparently around 1910 to judge from European colonial records. The old woman had at that time been a child not quite ready to be married, so she was probably in her late 70s or early 80s when I met her in 1976. The cyclone had flattened Rennell's forests, destroyed gardens, and threatened surviving islanders with starvation. Until new gardens could be planted and began producing, people had to resort to eating anything at all digestible, including not just the usual preferred wild fruit species but also fruits that would normally be ignored—i.e., the fruits identified for me as being "eaten only after the hungi kengi." That required knowledge about which of those second-choice fruits were non-poisonous and safe to eat, or had poisons that could be removed by some method of food preparation. Fortunately, at the time of the hungi kengi, there were islanders alive who remembered an earlier cyclone and how they had coped then. Now, this old woman was the last person alive in her village with that inherited experience and knowledge. If another big cyclone were to strike Rennell, her encyclopedic memory of which wild fruits to eat would be all that stood between her fellow villagers and starvation. Such stories about the overwhelming importance of old people's memories for their relatives' survival abound for pre-literate societies.

Society's values

Thus, much of the reason why societies do or don't care for their aged depends on how useful old people are. Another part of the reason depends on a society's values: whether old people are respected or scorned. Obviously, these two reasons are related: the more useful old people are, the more likely they are to be respected. But, as in so many other areas of human culture, the coupling between utility and values is a loose one: some societies emphasize respect for the aged more than do other societies that appear economically similar.

At least some respect for old people seems widespread among human societies. In the modern United States a relatively mild form of respect co-exists with some attitudes of devaluing: American children are often told to respect their elders, not to talk back to them, and to give up one's seat on a bus if one sees an old person standing. Respect for old people is stronger among the !Kung, in part because there are proportionately far fewer old !Kung than old Americans: barely 20% of !Kung born reach the age of 60, and they deserve admiration for having survived lions, accidents, diseases, raids, and other dangers inherent in the !Kung lifestyle.

An especially strong form of respect is the doctrine of filial piety associated with Confucius, traditionally prevalent in China, Korea, Japan, and Taiwan, and actually written into law until the laws were changed by Japan's constitution of 1948 and China's marriage law of 1950. According to Confucian doctrine, children owe absolute obedience to their parents, and disobedience or disrespect is considered despicable. Concretely, children (especially oldest sons) have a sacred duty to support parents in their old age. Even today, filial piety remains alive and well in East Asia, where (at least until recently) almost all elderly Chinese and three-quarters of elderly Japanese have lived with their children or family.

Another strong form of respect is the emphasis on family in southern Italy, Mexico, and many other societies. As described by Donald Cowgill, "The family is depicted as the core of the social structure and the source of an all-pervading influence over its members. . . . The honor of the family was crucial, and individual members were expected to support the

male authority, sacrifice for the family, respect parents, and avoid bringing shame on the family name. . . . [The family's oldest male took on a
godfather image as] a dominant authority who enforced conformity to
family goals and did not countenance divided allegiance. . . . within this
framework, there was only limited leeway for individual self-expression,
which in any case was to be subordinated to the family interest. . . .
Middle-aged children included elderly parents in the activities of their
nuclear families, and a majority rejected outright the notion of ever committing their parents to be placed in a nursing home."

These Confucian Chinese, southern Italians, and Mexican households
provide examples of a widespread phenomenon termed the "patriarchal"
family, whose main authority is vested in the family's oldest living male.
Other familiar examples include many or most contemporary herding
and other rural societies, and in the past the ancient Romans and Hebrews. To appreciate how patriarchal families are organized, think by contrast of the modern American living arrangements that many readers of
this book will take for granted, and that anthropologists term "neolocal."
That term means that a newly married couple establishes a new household
(hence "neolocal") separate from the household of either the groom's or
the bride's parents. The new household contains a nuclear family, consisting of just the married couple and (eventually) their dependent children.

While this arrangement seems normal and natural to us, it is exceptional by geographic and historical standards: only about 5% of traditional
societies have neolocal households. Instead, the commonest traditional
arrangement is the "patrilocal" household, meaning that a newly married
couple comes to live with the groom's parents or family. In that case, the
household unit consists not just of the nuclear family but of a wider family
extended either horizontally or vertically. Horizontal extensions (i.e.,
within the same generation as the patriarch) may include multiple wives
of the polygamous patriarch living within the same family compound,
plus the patriarch's unmarried sisters and perhaps some of his married
younger siblings as well. Vertical extensions to other generations assemble
within one house or compound the patriarch and his wife, one or more of
their married children, and the latters' children who are the patriarch's
grandchildren. Whether the extensions are horizontal or vertical or both,
the whole household is an economic, financial, social, and political unit,

all of its members live coordinated daily lives, and the patriarch is the primary authority.

Naturally, a patrilocal household lends itself to care for the elderly: they live in the same household as their children, they own and control the house or houses, and they enjoy economic and physical security. Of course, this arrangement doesn't guarantee that adult children *love* their elderly parents; their feelings may be ambivalent or dominated by fear and respect for authority, and the children may just be biding their time until they too can tyrannize their own adult children. A neolocal household makes care for the elderly more difficult, whatever children's feelings for their aged parents may be, because parents and children are physically separated.

At the opposite extreme from this strong status of the elderly in traditional patriarchial societies is their status in much of modern American society (with conspicuous exceptions among some immigrant communities that retain traditional values). To quote Cowgill's list of depressing attributes, "We associate old age with loss of usefulness, decrepitude, illness, senility, poverty, loss of sexuality, sterility, and death." Those views have practical consequences for the job opportunities and medical care of older people. Mandatory retirement ages were until recently widespread in the United States, and they are still widespread in Europe. Employers tend to consider older people as set in their ways and less manageable and teachable, hence employers prefer to invest in young employees who are considered more flexible and more easily trained. In an experimental study carried out by Joanna Lahey for Boston College's Center for Retirement Research, responses to false résumés sent to prospective employers and differing only in the applicants' names and ages revealed that a woman aged 35–45 applying for an entry-level job is 43% more likely to be called for an interview than an applicant 50–62 years old. The explicit hospital policy termed "age-based allocation of health care resources" is to give younger patients priority over older patients whenever health-care resources are limited, on the grounds that medical time, energy, and money should not be invested in saving elderly lives written off as "fragile and failing." Is it any surprise that Americans and Europeans, even already in their 30s, respond by investing much money of their own in measures to preserve a youthful appearance, such as hair dyeing and plastic surgery?

At least three sets of values, some of them shared with European society, contribute to this low status of the elderly in modern America. One set, emphasized by the sociologist Max Weber, is the work ethic, which Weber stressed in connection with John Calvin's form of the Protestant Revolution, and which Weber formulated especially with regards to Germany, but which is more broadly relevant to modern Western society. At the risk of reducing his long and complex books and articles to one sentence, Weber may be said to have viewed work as the central business of one's life, the source of one's status and identity, and good for one's character. It follows that retired elderly people who are no longer working lose their social status.

A more specifically American set of values is a cluster related to our emphasis on the individual. That individualism is the opposite of the emphasis on extended family discussed above for many other societies. An American's sense of self-worth is measured by his/her own achievements, not by the collective achievements of the extended family to which he/she belongs. We are taught to be independent and to rely on ourselves. Independence, individualism, and self-reliance are all praised as virtues, and the opposite traits of dependence, inability to stand on one's own feet, and inability to take care of oneself are disparaged. In fact, for Americans a dependent personality is a clinical diagnosis used by psychiatrists and psychologists, and labeled Mental Disorder number 301.6 by the American Psychiatric Association, to identify a condition requiring treatment, whose goal is to help the regrettably dependent individual achieve the American virtue of independence.

Also part of this American value cluster is our emphasis on individual privacy, an unusual concept by the standards of world cultures, most of which provide little individual privacy and don't consider it a desirable ideal. Instead, common traditional living arrangements consist of an extended family inside a single dwelling, or a group of huts or shelters around a single clearing, or a whole band sleeping in one communal shelter. Unthinkably to most modern Americans, even sex between a couple traditionally goes on with a minimum of privacy. The couple's hammock or mat is visible to other couples, and the couple's young children may be sharing the same mat but are merely expected to close their eyes. Our neolocal residence pattern, according to which children upon reaching the age of marriage set up their own private household, represents the opposite extreme from that traditional arrangement in which privacy is minimal.

Care for the elderly goes against all those interwoven American values of independence, individualism, self-reliance, and privacy. We accept a baby's dependence, because the baby has never been independent, but we struggle against the dependence of the elderly who have been independent for decades. But the cruel reality is that old people eventually reach a condition in which they can no longer live independently, cannot rely on their own abilities, and have no choice but to become dependent on others and to give up their long-cherished privacy. Dependency is at least as painful for the elderly person involved as for the middle-aged child who watches it happening to a formerly self-reliant parent. How many readers of this chapter have known an elderly person who insisted out of self-respect on trying to continue to live independently, until an accident (such as falling and breaking a hip, or being unable to get out of bed) made the continued independence impossible? American ideals push old Americans to lose self-respect, and push their younger care-givers to lose respect for them.

The remaining distinctively American value creating prejudice against the aged is our cult of youth. Of course, this isn't a completely arbitrary value that we happen to have adopted as a cultural preference for no good reason. It's indeed true that, in this modern world of rapid technological change, the recency of young adults' education makes their knowledge more up-to-date and useful for important things like jobs, and for mundane challenges of everyday life. I at age 75, and my 64-year-old wife, are reminded of this reality behind our cult of youth whenever we attempt to turn on our television set. We grew up accustomed to television sets with just three knobs, all located on the set itself: an on-off button, a volume control knob, and a channel selector knob. My wife and I can't figure out the 41-button remote now required just to turn on our modern television set, and we have to phone our 25-year-old sons to talk us through it if they don't happen to be at home with us. Another external factor favoring our cult of youth is the competitiveness of modern American society, which gives an advantage to younger people blessed with speed, endurance, strength, agility, and quick reflexes. Still another factor is that so many Americans are children of recent immigrants who were born and grew up abroad. Those children saw that their older parents couldn't speak English without an accent and actually did lack important knowledge about the functioning of American society.

That is, I don't deny that there are some valid reasons for modern Americans to value youth. However, our cult of youth spills over into spheres that seem arbitrary and, in some cases, seriously unfair. We tend to consider young people beautiful or handsome, but why should yellow, brown, or black hair be admired as more beautiful than silver or white hair? Television, magazine, and newspaper advertisements for clothing invariably depict young models; the thought of advertising a man's shirt or a woman's dress with a 70-year-old model seems strange—but why? An economist might answer that younger people change and buy clothes more often, and have less developed brand loyalty, than do older people. By that economic interpretation, the ratio of 70-year-old clothing models to 20-year-old clothing models should be roughly equal to the ratio of clothing purchases and brand changes by 70-year-olds to clothing purchases and brand changes by 20-year-olds. But the proportion of clothing purchases and brand changes by 70-year-olds surely isn't as close to zero as is the proportion of 70-year-old clothing models. Similarly, advertisements for soft drinks, beer, and new cars invariably feature young models (Plate 23), although old people also consume soft drinks and beer and buy cars. Instead, pictures of old people are used to sell adult diapers, arthritis drugs, and retirement plans (Plate 24).

These examples from the world of advertising may seem humorous, until you reflect that they are merely one expression of American ageism: our cult of youth, and our negative view of aging. It isn't a serious matter that 70-year-old models aren't employed to sell soft drinks, but it is indeed serious that older job applicants are routinely passed over for job interviews, and that older patients receive lower priority for limited resources of medical care. The soft drink and beer ads aimed at old as well as young viewers also illustrate that a negative view of age is not only held by young Americans but is also internalized by old Americans themselves. Surveys by Louis Harris and Associates showed that American people believe that the elderly are bored, closed-minded, dependent, isolated, lonely, narrow-minded, neglected, old-fashioned, passive, poor, sedentary, sexually inactive, sick, unalert, unproductive, morbidly afraid of death, in constant fear of crime, living the worst years of life—and spending a good deal of their time sleeping, sitting and doing nothing, or nostalgically dwelling upon their past. These views were held equally by old people polled and by young people polled, even though the individual old people polled claimed that they themselves didn't fit those stereotypes applying on the average to other old people.

Society's rules

We have now considered several sets of factors influencing why societies variously take better or worse care of their elderly: the society's ability to carry or feed them, their usefulness, and the society's values, which tend to reflect that usefulness but are also to some degree independent of usefulness. But these are all ultimate explanatory factors unlikely to come up for discussion in practical day-to-day decisions about old people, such as whether or not to cut for Grandpa a choice steak from today's antelope kill, even though he is no longer able to go hunting himself. The grandchild butchering the antelope doesn't refer then to a general principle of ultimate value, such as "You remember what foods to eat after a hungi kengi, so we'll reward your utility by giving you this steak." Instead, those practical decisions are made in accordance with the society's rules, which specify what to do in particular situations and ultimately reflect usefulness and values, but which let you divide an antelope quickly without philosophical discussions about hungi-kengis.

There is a host of such rules, varying among societies, to cover a host of choices. The rules empower the elderly to commandeer certain but not other resources. The rules are accepted by young people, who defer to the elderly and let them take the resources, even though there is a clear conflict of interest between young and old people for the resources, and even though the young are strong enough to snatch the resources. But they don't, and instead they agree to wait until they too are old and will be deferred to. Out of many possible sets of examples, I'll give just three.

A simple example involves food taboos, which ensure that certain foods are reserved for the elderly, in the belief (espoused by young and old alike) that the foods would endanger young people but that old people have acquired immunity to the danger with age. Every society has its own particular food taboos, which seem arbitrary to other societies, but taboos are widespread among traditional societies. For instance, young Omaha Indians inclined to break open animal bones in order to eat the rich marrow inside were warned by their wily elders that that would make them sprain their ankle, but that old people could safely eat marrow. Among the Iban of Borneo, old men enjoyed eating venison, but young men were forbidden to do so with the warning that it would make them as timid as deer. Old Siberian Chukchi drank reindeer milk but tabooed it for younger people, alleging that it was for the latters' protection because milk would make a young man impotent and would cause a young woman to develop flabby breasts.

A particularly elaborate set of food taboos was reported for the Aranda (alias Arunta) Aborigines near Alice Springs in the central Australian desert. The best foods were reserved for old people, especially old men, who spelled out the dire consequences that would befall young people if they foolishly ate those forbidden foods. Supposedly, eating a female bandicoot makes a young man bleed to death when he is circumcised; emu fat causes abnormal development of the penis; eating parrots makes a hollow develop on top of the head, and a hole in the chin; and wildcat causes painful foul-smelling sores to break out on the head and neck. Young women were warned of further dangers: eating female bandicoot stimulates continued menstrual blood flow, kangaroo tail causes premature aging and baldness, quail prevents development of the breasts, and brown hawk conversely makes the breasts swell up and burst without producing milk.

Another resource that old men in many societies succeed in monopolizing for themselves and tabooing for younger men is—younger women. The rules specify that older men should marry much younger women and have multiple wives, and that younger men should not expect to marry until they in turn reach the age of 40 or even older. The long list of traditional societies with such practices include the Akamba of East Africa, the Araucanian Indians of South America, the Bakong of West Africa, the Banks Islanders of the Southwest Pacific, the Berber of North Africa, the Chukchi of Siberia, the Iban of Borneo, the Labrador Inuit of Canada, the Xhosa of Southern Africa, and many Aboriginal Australian tribes. I encountered such a case among a tribe in the lowlands of North New

Guinea, when an old lame man named Yono pointed out to me a girl who looked to be less than 10 years old, and whom he said he had "marked" as his bride-to-be. He had made a down payment on her as a baby at her birth, had periodically made further payments to her parents, and now expected to marry her as soon as her breasts developed and she underwent her first menses.

As with food taboos and other privileges of the elderly, one has to ask why young people acquiesce in such rules and defer to the authority of the elderly. For young men, part of the reason is that they do so in the expectation that it will eventually be their turn. In the meantime, they hang around the campfire and seek opportunities for sexual satisfaction when the old husband is absent.

These two sets of examples of rules by which the elderly in many traditional societies ensure that they will be cared for—by food taboos, and by rigorously reserving young wives for old men—don't operate in modern industrial societies. Hence we find ourselves wondering why young people of those traditional societies tolerate such rules. My remaining set of examples will be much more familiar to this book's readers: the retention of property rights by the elderly. In modern societies today, just as in many traditional societies, most old people relinquish ownership of their property only through inheritance at the time that they die. Hence the threat, lurking in the background, of the elderly altering their wills contributes to the motivation of the young to care for their elders.

A mild example of this phenomenon operates for a !Kung band, whose rights to its land (the n!ore) are considered to be associated with the oldest band members, not with the band as a whole. More coercive examples are nearly ubiquitous among herding and farming societies: the senior generation, usually in the form of its patriarchal male, continues to own its land, livestock, and valuable possessions into old age, and most often until death. Hence the patriarch enjoys a commanding position to persuade his children to let him stay in the family house and to take care of him. For example, the Old Testament describes Abraham and other Hebrew patriarchs as owning many livestock in their old age. Old Chukchi men own reindeer; old Mongol men own horses; old Navajo own horses, sheep, cattle, and goats; and old Kazakhs own those same four livestock species plus camels. By controlling livestock, farmland, and (nowadays) other property and financial assets, older people hold strong leverage over the younger generation.

In many societies, the power that the old generation thereby exercises is so strong that the society's government becomes described as a "gerontocracy"—i.e., tyranny by the elderly. Examples include again the ancient Hebrews, many African herding societies, many Aboriginal Australian tribes, and (closer to home for my book readers) rural Ireland. As summarized by Donald Cowgill, "Here [in Ireland] it is customary for an older man to retain ownership and control of the family farm until very late in his life. Meanwhile his sons continue to work as unpaid family laborers, totally dependent upon the farmer for economic support and unable to marry because of the lack of an independent means of supporting a family. In the absence of a definite and unambiguous system of inheritance, the father may play one child against another, using the prospect of inheritance as 'a form of blackmail' to keep the children (in their 30's or 40's) submissive to his will. Ultimately he may turn the farm over to a son, being careful to reserve the 'west room'—the most spacious and best furnished—for himself and his wife and to provide for financial support for the rest of their lives."

In light of our own familiarity with the power that the elderly enjoy in our society through their property rights, we can now better understand our error in our initial surprise at the fact that the elderly in traditional societies succeed in enforcing food taboos and access to young wives. When I first heard of those customs, I found myself wondering, "Why doesn't an individual young tribesman just grab and eat food delicacies like marrow and venison, and marry a beautiful young woman of his choice rather than wait until age 40?" The answer is: he doesn't, for the same reason that young adults in our society rarely succeed in seizing property from their parents against the parents' will. Our young adults don't, because they would be opposed not just by their weak old parents but by our entire society that enforces the rules. And why don't all young tribesmen rise simultaneously in revolt and say, "We are changing the rules, so that from now on we young men can eat marrow"? Young tribesmen don't, for the same reason that all young Americans don't rise in revolt and change the inheritance rules: in any society it's a lengthy, difficult process to change the basic rules, old people have plenty of leverage for opposing rule changes, and learned deference and respect for the elderly don't vanish overnight.

Better or worse today?

Compared to the status of the elderly in traditional societies, what has changed today? One set of factors has changed enormously for the better, but many other factors have changed for the worse.

The good news is that older people enjoy on the average much longer lives, far better health, far more recreational opportunities, and far less grief from deaths of their children than at any previous time in human history. Life expectancy averaged over 26 First World countries is 79 years, with the highest expectancy being 84 years in Japan—approximately double the value in traditional societies. The well-known reasons for this surge in lifespan are public health measures (such as provision of clean drinking water, screening of windows, and immunizations) to combat infectious diseases—plus modern medicine, more efficient food distribution to combat famine (Chapters 8 and 11), and (believe it or not, even despite two world wars) proportionately reduced death tolls from war in societies with state government compared to traditional societies (Chapter 4). Thanks to modern medicine and means of travel, old people can now enjoy a much higher quality of life today than in the past. For example, I recently returned from a safari in Africa on which 3 of the 14 other participants were between 86 and 90 years old and still able to undertake moderate walks. Far more people live to see their great-grandchildren—57% of those American men and 68% of those American women who live past the age of 80—than in the past. Over 98% of First World babies survive infancy and childhood, while the proportion is as low as 50% in traditional societies. Hence the formerly common experience of grieving over the death of one's child is now rare in the First World.

Offsetting that good news is much bad news, some of it a straightforward consequence of demography. The ratio of old people to children and productive young workers has soared, because birth rates have dropped while survival rates of the elderly have risen. That is, the population pyramid is becoming inverted: we used to have lots of young people and few old people, but at present we have lots of old people and fewer babies. It's no consolation to us of the current generation to reflect that it won't be so bad 80 years from now, when today's shrinking cohort of babies finally becomes a shrinking cohort of the elderly. For instance, the percentage of the whole population that is at least 65 years old is now only 2% in the poorest countries, but 10 times higher in some First World countries. Never before has any human society had proportionally so many old people to deal with.

One obvious negative consequence of those demographic facts is that society's burden of supporting the elderly is heavier, because more older people require to be supported by fewer productive workers. That cruel reality lies at the root of the much-discussed looming crisis of funding the American Social Security system (and its European and Japanese counterparts) that provides pensions for retired workers. If we older people keep working, we prevent our children's and our grandchildren's generation from getting jobs, as is happening right now. If, instead, we older people retire and expect the earnings of the shrinking younger cohort to continue to fund the Social Security system and pay for our leisure, then the financial burden of the younger cohort is far greater than ever before. And if we expect to move in with them and let them privately support and care for us in their homes, they have other ideas. One wonders whether we are returning to a world where we shall be reconsidering choices about end of life made by traditional societies—such as assisted suicide, encouraged suicide, and euthanasia. In writing these words, I am certainly not recommending these choices; I am instead observing the increasing frequency with which these measures are being discussed, carried out, and debated by legislators and courts.

Another consequence of the population pyramid's inversion is that, insofar as older people continue to be valuable to society (e.g., due to their long and varied experience), any individual old person is less valuable because so many other old individuals offer that same value. That 80-year-old Rennell Island woman who remembered the hungi kengi would have been less useful if there had been a hundred other hungi kengi observers still alive.

Aging plays out differently for men and for women. While women in the First World enjoy on the average longer lives than do men, that of course means a much higher likelihood of a woman becoming a widow than of a man becoming a widower. For instance, in the U.S. 80% of older men are married and only 12% are widowers, while less than 40% of older women are married and over half are widows. That's partly because of longer female life expectancy, but also because men tend to be older than their wives at the time of marriage, and because widowed men are more likely to remarry (to considerably younger new wives) than are widowed women.

Traditionally, old people spent their final years living with the same group, or (in a sedentary society) in the same settlement or even in the same house, in which they had spent their adult lives or even their whole lives. There, they maintained the social ties that had supported them throughout their lives, including ties with surviving life-long friends and with at least some of their children. They generally had their sons or daughters or both living nearby, depending on whether the custom of their society was for a bride to move to the groom's parents or for the groom to move to the bride's parents upon marriage.

In the modern First World that constancy of social ties into old age has declined or disappeared. Under our own custom of neolocal residence, bride and groom don't live near either the groom's parents or the bride's parents, but they instead go off to establish a new separate residence of their own. That gives rise to the modern phenomenon known as the empty-nest syndrome. In the U.S. in the early 1900s, at least one parent of a couple often died before the youngest child's leaving home and thus never experienced an empty nest, and the duration of the empty nest for an average parent was less than two years. Now, most American parents will survive to experience an empty nest for more than a decade, often for many decades.

Old parents left to themselves in our empty-nest society are unlikely to find themselves still living near life-long friends. About 20% of the American population changes residence each year, so that either old parents, their friends, or probably both will have moved repeatedly since childhood. Common living circumstances for old people are that they go to live with one of their children, but thereby become cut off from their friends because their child has moved from the original family house; or they live by themselves as long as possible, with some friends nearby but not necessarily with their children nearby; or they live separately from both life-long friends and from children, in a retirement home, where they may or may not receive visits from their children. This is the situation that caused my Fijian acquaintance whom I quoted in the first paragraph to upbraid us with the accusation, "You throw away your old people and your own parents!"

Another factor contributing to the social isolation of the modern elderly besides neolocal residence and frequent shifts of residence is formal retirement from the labor force. This phenomenon became common only in the late 19th century. Until then, people just worked until their bodies or minds wore out. Now, retirement is almost universal as a policy in industrial countries, at an age ranging from 50 to 70, depending on the country (e.g., younger in Japan than in Norway) and on the profession (e.g., younger for commercial airline pilots than for college teachers). Three trends of modern industrial societies joined to favor retirement as a formal policy. One trend is our increased lifespan, such that many people live to an age at which they can no longer continue to work. There was no need to have formal policies mandating retirement at 60 or 70 in an era when average lifespan was less than 50 anyway. A second trend is increasing economic productivity, such that a workforce composed of a smaller fraction of the population has become capable of supporting a large fraction of the population no longer working.

The remaining modern trend favoring retirement is the various forms of social insurance to provide economic support for retired older people. Government-mandated or government-supported pensions arose in Germany under Chancellor Bismarck in the 1880s, spread in the following decades to other western and northern European countries and New Zealand, and reached the United States in 1935 with the passage of our Social Security Act. This is not to claim that mandatory retirement is an unmixed blessing: many people are required to retire at an arbitrary age (e.g., 65 or 60) when they would like to continue working, are capable of doing so, and may in fact be at their peak of productivity. But there seems no reason to object to people having at least the option of retiring, and having the government provide a mechanism (based on their own earnings during their working lifetime) for supporting them economically if they do choose to retire. However, one has to recognize and solve a new problem created by retirement: the problem of severing one's life-long work relationships, and thereby falling deeper into the social isolation already arising from neolocal residence and mobility.

Yet another modern institution that solves long-standing problems of the elderly while creating new problems is the specialized facilities where old people reside and are cared for separately from their families. While monasteries and convents took in some old people already in the distant past, the first known public old folks' home was established in Austria under Emperor Maria Theresa in 1740. Such facilities are of various types and go under different names, including retirement homes, retirement communities, nursing homes, and hospices. All of those facilities serve to deal with the modern demographic realities of more old people alive, fewer adult children potentially available to care for them, and most of those adult children working outside the house and unable to attend to an old person during the day. When facilities for the elderly work well, they can provide a new set of social relationships to replace the life-long ones lost when the old person moves into the facility. In many cases, however, they contribute to social isolation of the elderly by furnishing a place where aged parents can be left by their children and have their material needs met with more or less adequacy, but where their social needs are not met because their adult children (knowing that those material needs are being met) visit variously once a day, once a week, once a year, or never, within my circle of acquaintances.

Looming behind this increasing social isolation of the modern elderly is that they are perceived as less useful than were old people in the past, for three reasons: modern literacy, formal education, and rapid technological change. We now store knowledge in writing, and so literacy has virtually abolished the role of old people's memories as the formerly dominant means of storing knowledge. All functioning state societies support educational systems, and in the First World school attendance of children is nearly mandatory, so that old people as a group are no longer a society's teachers as well as no longer its memories. As regards technological obsolescence, the snail's pace of technological change in the past meant that technologies learned by a person in childhood were still being employed unchanged 70 years later, so that the technological skills of an old person remained useful. With our rapid pace of technological innovation today, technologies become outdated within a few years, and the training that old people received 70 years ago is useless. Just to mention an example from my own experience, when I was going to school in the 1940s and early 1950s, we employed four methods for multiplying numbers: memorizing multiplication tables, which we used to multiply small two-digit numbers and obtain exact answers; long-hand multiplication on paper to obtain exact answers, but tedious for numbers of more than four digits; slide rules, to obtain quick answers accurate to about three decimal places; and tables of logarithms, to obtain answers accurate to four or five decimal places fairly quickly. I became proficient at all four methods, but all of those skills of mine are now useless, because my sons' generation uses pocket calculators yielding answers accurate to seven decimal places within a few seconds. My abilities to build a vacuum-tube radio and to drive a manual-shift car have also become obsolete. Much else that I and my contemporaries learned in our youth has become equally useless, and much that we never learned has become indispensable.

What to do with older people?

In short, the status of old people in modern Western societies has changed drastically and paradoxically within the last century. We are still grappling with the resulting problems, which constitute a disaster area of modern life. On the one hand, people live longer, old people enjoy better physical health, and the rest of society can better afford to care for them than at any previous time in human history. On the other hand, old people have lost most of the traditional usefulness that they offered to society, and they often end up socially more miserable while physically healthier. Most of you readers of this book will face or already have faced these problems, either when you have to figure out what to do with your own aged parents, or when you become old yourself. What can we do? I shall offer a few suggestions from my personal observations, without pretending that they will solve this huge problem.

One suggestion involves a renewed importance of the traditional role of old people as grandparents. Until the Second World War, most American and European women of child-bearing age remained home and took care of their children. In recent decades young women have increasingly joined the workforce outside their homes, motivated by interest, economic necessity, or both. That creates the problem of child care familiar to so many young parents. While they attempt to cope by various combinations of baby-sitters and day-care facilities, difficulties with the reliability and quality of those expedients are common.

Grandparents offer advantages for solving the baby-sitter problem for modern working couples. Grandparents are highly motivated to care for their own grandchildren, experienced from having raised their own children, able to give quality one-on-one undivided attention to a child, unlikely to quit on short notice for a better job, willing to work for no pay, and not prone to complain about pay or bonuses. Within my own circle of friends are grandfathers and grandmothers retired from many work backgrounds—physicians, lawyers, professors, business executives, engineers, and others—who love being regular care-givers for their grandchildren, while their daughters, sons, sons-in-law, and daughters-in-law hold jobs outside the house. These older friends of mine have taken on roles equivalent to those of !Kung grandparents minding grandchildren in camp, freeing up their own children to go off hunting antelope and gathering mongongo nuts. It's a win-win situation for everyone involved: for the grandparents, the parents, and the child. But I must add a cautionary note: now that married couples often wait until their 30s or even their early 40s to become parents, the grandparents in turn may be in their late 70s or early 80s, and losing the stamina required to keep up with a young child all day long.

A second suggestion involves an upside to rapid technological and social change. While that change tends to make the skills of the elderly obsolescent in a narrow sense, it also makes their experience valuable in a broader sense, because that experience encompasses conditions unlike those prevailing today. If similar conditions should recur in the future, today's young adults will lack personal knowledge of dealing with them. Instead, the people with the most relevant experience may be the elderly. Our elderly are like the 80-year-old Rennell Island woman whom I met, survivor of the island's hungi kengi, whose knowledge of which fruits to eat under starvation conditions may seem useless and quaint—until the next hungi kengi strikes, when she alone will know how to cope.

Out of innumerable other possible examples illustrating that value of the memories of the elderly, I shall mention two vignettes from my own experience. First, the professor who was my tutor at college was born in 1902. I recall him telling me in 1956 how it felt to be growing up in an American city while horse-drawn transportation was being replaced by motor vehicles. My tutor and his contemporaries were at the time delighted by the change-over, because they saw that cars were making the city much cleaner (!) and quieter (!!), as horse manure and the clickety-clack of horses' hooves against the pavement disappeared from the streets. Today, when we associate motor vehicles with pollution and noise, my tutor's memories seem absurd, until we think of the broader message: technological change regularly brings unanticipated problems in addition to its anticipated benefits.

My other vignette took place when my then-22-year-old son Joshua and I discovered that our dinner companion at a hotel one evening was an 86-year-old ex-marine who had participated in (and was willing to talk about) the American assault on the beaches of Tarawa Atoll in the Southwest Pacific Ocean on November 20, 1943, against ferocious Japanese resistance. In one of the most fiercely contested amphibious landings of the Second World War, within three days and within an area of less than half of a square mile, 1,115 Americans and all except 19 of the 4,601 Japanese defenders were killed. I had never heard the story of Tarawa's horrors first-hand, and I hope that Joshua will never experience such horrors himself. But perhaps he and his generation will make better choices for our country if they have learned from survivors of the last world war over 65 years ago what it was like. These two vignettes illustrate why there are programs bringing together elderly people and high school students, for the students to hear and learn from vivid accounts of events that may prove to hold lessons for them.

My remaining suggestion is to understand and make use of the changes in people's strengths and weaknesses as they grow older. At the risk of overgeneralizing about a vast and complex subject without presenting supporting evidence, one can say that useful attributes tending to decrease with age include ambition, desire to compete, physical strength and endurance, capacity for sustained mental concentration, and powers of novel reasoning to solve circumscribed problems (such as the structure of DNA and many problems of pure mathematics, best left to scholars under the age of 40). Conversely, useful attributes tending to increase with age include experience of one's field, understanding of people and relationships, ability to help other people without one's own ego getting in the way, and powers of synthetic interdisciplinary thinking to solve complex problems involving multifaceted databases (such as the origin of species, biogeographic distributions, and comparative history, best left to scholars over the age of 40). These shifts in strengths result in many older workers choosing to devote more of their efforts to supervising, administering, advising, teaching, strategizing, and synthesizing. For instance, my farmer friends in their 80s spend less time on horseback and on tractors, more time making strategic decisions about the business of farming; my older lawyer friends spend less time in court, more time mentoring younger lawyers; and my older surgeon friends spend less time doing long or complex operations, and more time training young physicians.

The problem for society as a whole is to use older people for what they are good at and like to do, rather than requiring them to continue to put in the 60-hour work weeks of ambitious young workers, or else going to the opposite extreme of stupidly imposing policies of mandatory retirement at some arbitrary age (as remains regrettably widespread in Europe). The challenge for older people themselves is to be introspective, to notice the changes in themselves, and to find work utilizing the talents that they now possess. Consider two examples involving great musicians, both of them introspective honest people who spoke openly about what types of music they could or couldn't write in their old age (Plates 40, 41). The composer Richard Strauss's opera librettist, Stefan Zweig, described their first meeting, when Strauss was already 67 years old: "Strauss frankly admitted to me in the first hour of our meeting that he well knew that at 70 the composer's musical inspiration no longer possesses its pristine power. He could hardly succeed in composing symphonic works like *Till Eulenspiegel* and *Tod und Verklärung* [his masterpieces of his 20s and 30s] because pure music requires an extreme measure of creative freshness." But Strauss explained that he still felt inspired by situations and words, which he could still illustrate dramatically in music, because they spontaneously suggested musical themes to him. Hence his last composition, completed at age 84, and one of his greatest achievements, was his *Four Last Songs for Soprano and Orchestra,* with a subdued autumnal mood anticipating death, unostentatiously rich orchestration, and quotations from his own music of 58 years earlier. The composer Giuseppe Verdi intended to end his musical career with his sprawling grand operas *Don Carlos* and *Aida,* written respectively at ages 54 and 58. However, Verdi was persuaded by his publisher to write two more operas, *Otello* at age 74 and *Falstaff* at age 80, often considered his greatest works, but in a much more condensed, economical, subtle style than his earlier music.

Devising new living conditions for our elderly, appropriate to the changing modern world, remains a major challenge for our society. Many past societies made better use of their elderly, and gave them better lives, than we do today. We can surely find better solutions now.

PART FOUR

DANGER AND RESPONSE

CHAPTER 7

Constructive Paranoia

Attitudes towards danger ▪ A night visit ▪ A boat accident ▪ Just a
stick in the ground ▪ Taking risks ▪ Risks and talkativeness

Attitudes towards danger

On one of my first trips to New Guinea, when I was still inexperienced
and incautious, I spent a month with a group of New Guineans, studying
birds on a forest-covered mountain. After a week camped at low elevation
and inventorying birds there, I wanted to identify the bird species living
at higher elevation, so we moved our gear a few thousand feet up the
mountain. For the campsite at which we would be based for the next week,
I selected a gorgeous location in tall forest. It was on a long ascending
ridge at a point where the ridge flattened and became broader, offering lots
of gentle terrain nearby in which I could comfortably walk around and
watch birds. From a nearby stream, we could obtain water without having
to go far. The campsite was at one side of the flat ridge crest, overlooking
a steep drop-off into a deep valley over which I would be able to watch
soaring hawks, swifts, and parrots. As the place to erect our tents, I chose
the base of a glorious giant of a forest tree, with a thick straight trunk
covered with moss. Delighted at the prospect of spending a week in such
beautiful surroundings, I asked my New Guinea companions to build a
platform for our tents.

To my astonishment, they became agitated and refused to sleep there.
They explained that the tall tree was dead, so it might fall over on our camp
and kill us. Yes, I did see that the tree was dead, but I was still surprised

at their overreaction and objected, "It's a huge tree. It looks still solid. It's not rotten. No wind could blow it over, and there isn't wind here anyway. It will be years before this tree falls over!" But my New Guinea friends remained frightened. Rather than sleep in the shelter of a tent under that tree, they declared that they would instead sleep exposed out in the open, far enough away that the tree wouldn't hit and kill them if it fell.

I thought then that their fears were absurdly exaggerated and verged on paranoia. But as my months of camping in New Guinea forests went on, I noticed that, at least once on almost every day, I heard a tree falling somewhere in the forest. I listened to stories of New Guineans killed by tree-falls. I reflected that these New Guineans spent much of their lives camped in the forest—perhaps a hundred nights a year, or about 4,000 nights over their 40-year expected lifespan. I eventually carried out the math. If you do something that involves a very low probability of killing a person—say, just once in a thousand times that you do that something—but you do it a hundred times per year, then you are likely to die in about 10 years, instead of living out your expected lifespan of 40 years. That risk of falling trees doesn't deter New Guineans from going into the forest. But they do reduce the risk by being careful not to sleep under dead trees. Their paranoia makes perfect sense. I now think of it as "constructive paranoia."

My choice of this oxymoronic, seemingly unpleasant term for a quality that I admire is intentional. We normally use the word "paranoia" in a pejorative sense, to include greatly exaggerated and baseless fears. That's how New Guineans' reactions to camping under dead trees initially struck me, and it's true that usually a particular dead tree wouldn't fall on the particular night that a person chose to camp under it. But, in the long run, that seeming paranoia is constructive: it's essential to surviving under traditional conditions.

Nothing else that I have learned from New Guineans has affected me as deeply as that attitude. It's widespread in New Guinea, and reported in many other traditional societies around the world. If there is some act that carries a low risk each time, but if you're going to do it frequently, you had better learn to be consistently careful if you don't want to die or become crippled at a young age. That's an attitude that I've learned to adopt towards the low-risk but frequent hazards of American life, such as driving my car, standing in the shower, climbing a ladder to change a light bulb, walking up and down stairs, and walking on slippery sidewalks. My cautious behavior drives crazy some of my American friends, who consider it ridiculous. The Westerners who most share my constructive paranoia are three friends whose lifestyle made them, too, alert to the cumulative hazard of repeated low-risk events: one friend who piloted small airplanes, another who was an unarmed policeman on the streets of London, and a third who floats rubber rafts down mountain streams as a fishing guide. All three learned from examples of less cautious friends who were eventually killed after years of that job or activity.

Of course, not just New Guinea life but also Western life has its dangers, even if one isn't a pilot, bobby, or river guide. But there are differences between the perils of modern Western life and of traditional life. Obviously, the types of dangers are different: cars and terrorists and heart attacks for us, lions and enemies and falling trees for them. More significantly, the overall level of danger is much lower for us than for them: our average lifespan is double theirs, meaning that the average per-year risk that we face is only about half as great. The other significant difference is that the effects of many or most accidents that we Americans suffer can be repaired, whereas accidents in New Guinea are much more likely to prove crippling or fatal. On the sole occasion when I became incapacitated and unable to walk in the United States (from slipping on an icy Boston sidewalk and breaking my foot), I hobbled to a nearby pay phone to call my physician father, who picked me up and took me to a hospital. But when I injured my knee in the interior of Papua New Guinea's Bougainville Island and became unable to walk, I found myself stranded 20 miles inland from the coast, without any means to obtain outside help. New Guineans who break a bone can't get it set by a surgeon and are likely to end up with an improperly set bone that leaves them permanently impaired.

In this chapter I shall describe three incidents that befell me in New Guinea, and that illustrate constructive paranoia or the lack of it. At the time of the first incident, I was too inexperienced even to recognize signs of mortal danger nearby: I was operating as a normal Westerner, but in a traditional world that required a different mind-set. In the next event, over a decade later—the one that finally taught me to embrace constructive paranoia—I was forced to acknowledge that I had made a mistake that nearly cost me my life, while another, more cautious man facing the same choice at the same time didn't make my mistake and thus didn't experience the trauma of coming close to death. In the remaining incident, yet another decade later, I was with a New Guinea friend who reacted with constructive paranoia to a seemingly inconsequential detail that I had overlooked. He and I were never able to decide whether the apparently innocent stick on the ground that my friend spotted really did mark the presence of hostile people (as my friend feared), but I was impressed by his cautious attention to minutiae. In the following chapter I'll discuss the types of danger faced by traditional societies, and the ways in which people estimate, misestimate, and deal with danger.

A night visit

One morning, I set out from a large village with a group of 13 New Guinea Highlanders to reach an isolated small village several days' walk away. The region was in the foothill altitudinal zone with New Guinea's lowest population densities, below the elevation of the densely populated Highland valleys suitable for intensive cultivation of sweet potatoes and taro, above the lowland elevations where sago palms grow well and fresh-water fish are plentiful, and in the altitudinal range with the highest incidence of cerebral malaria. I was told before setting out that our journey would take about three days, and that we would be constantly in forests that were completely uninhabited. The whole region had a very sparse population and had come only a few years previously under government control. Warfare had been occurring until recently, and endocannibalism (eating of one's dead relatives) was reported as still being practised. Some of my New Guinea companions were local, but most of them came from another district of the Highlands and knew nothing about this district.

The first day's walk was not bad. Our route wound around the slopes of a mountain, gradually gained in elevation to cross a ridge, and then began to descend again along the course of the river. But the second day was one of the most grueling hikes of my career in New Guinea. It was already drizzling when we broke camp at 8:00 A.M. There was no trail: instead, we waded along a mountain torrent, climbing up and down over huge slippery boulders. Even for my New Guinea friends, accustomed to rugged Highland terrain, the route was a nightmare. By 4:00 P.M. we had descended over 2,000 vertical feet along the river and were exhausted. We pitched camp in the rain, erected our tents, cooked our rice and tinned fish for dinner, and went to sleep while the rain continued.

The details of the layout of our two tents are relevant for understanding what happened during that night. My New Guinea friends slept under a large tarpaulin stretched over a central raised horizontal ridge-pole, and pulled down taut to the ground along both sides parallel to the ridge-pole, like an inverted V in cross-section. The tarpaulin's two ends were open; one could walk into or out of the tarpaulin at its front and back ends, and the ridge-pole was high enough that one could stand up under the tarpaulin's center. My own tent was a bright green Eureka pup-tent stretched over a light metal frame, and with a large front door flap and a small rear window flap both of which I zipped closed. My tent's front door faced one of the two open ends (the "front") of the New Guineans' large tarpaulin, and was just a few yards away from it. Anyone walking out of the front of their tarpaulin would come first to the closed front door of my tent, then walk along the side of my tent, and finally pass my tent's rear with its closed window flap. But to someone unfamiliar with Eureka pup-tents, it would have been unclear whether the actual entrance after unzipping a flap was the closed front door or the rear with a closed window. I slept with my head towards the rear and my feet towards the front door, but I would have been invisible from the outside of my tent because its walls were not transparent. The New Guineans kept a fire going inside their tarpaulin for warmth.

All of us quickly fell asleep, worn out from the long grueling day. I have no idea how much later it was that I became awakened by a soft sound of footsteps and a sense of the ground shaking from someone walking nearby. The sound and motion stopped, evidently because the unknown person was standing near the rear of my tent, near my head. I assumed that one of my 13 companions had just come out of the large tarpaulin shelter to urinate. It did seem strange that he had not gone out of the rear of the tarpaulin away from my tent for privacy, but had instead turned towards my tent, walked along its length, and was now standing at my tent's rear and near my head. But I was sleepy, attributed no significance to where he had chosen to urinate, and dozed off. Within a short time I was awakened again, this time by voices from the shelter of the New Guineans who were talking, and by bright light from their fire, which they had stirred up. That wasn't unusual; New Guineans often do wake up periodically during the night and talk. I called out asking them to be more quiet, and I went back to sleep. And that was the entirety of the apparently meaningless incident at night, as I experienced it.

When I woke up the next morning, I opened the front door flap of my tent and greeted the New Guineans under their tarpaulin a few yards away, starting to cook breakfast. They told me that their voices and their stirring up the fire at night had been caused by several of them being awakened by the presence of a strange man standing at the open front of their tarpaulin. When the stranger realized that he was being watched, he made a gesture, visible in the firelight, of stretching out one arm horizontally and letting its hand droop downwards at the wrist. At that gesture, some of the New Guineans called out in fear (for reasons that I shall mention in a moment). Their calling out was what I had sleepily mistaken as the noise of their talking during the night. At the sound of their calling, others of the New Guineans awoke and sat up. The strange man then ran off into the rainy night. My New Guinea friends pointed out some barefoot footprints in the wet mud where the man had stood. But I don't recall my friends saying anything that alarmed me.

It was indeed unexpected to me that anyone would come at night in the rain to our camp in the middle of an uninhabited stretch of forest. However, I had become accustomed to the fact that things unexpected to me did often happen in New Guinea, and I had never felt that I was in any personal danger from any New Guinean. After we finished breakfast and folded up our tents, we resumed our journey, now on its third day. Our route climbed out of the awful river bed and followed a broad clear path through beautiful tall forests along the river bank. I felt as if I were walking in awe inside a high Gothic cathedral. I strolled on alone ahead of my New Guinea friends, in order to identify birds that hadn't already been disturbed by them, and to enjoy in solitude the magical cathedral-like forests. It was only when I finally reached a larger river below the village that was our final destination that I sat down to wait for my friends to catch up. It turned out that I had walked a long distance ahead of them.

Our 10-day stay at the isolated small village was so interesting in its own way that I forgot about the incident of the prowler at night. When it finally became time to return to the large village from which we had set out, the local men among my 13 New Guinea friends proposed that we return by a completely different route, which they said bypassed the awful wading in a river. That new route proved to be a good dry trail going through forests. It took us only two days to get back to the large village, instead of the agonizing three days of our march out. I still have no idea why our local guides had inflicted the route with the grueling wading of the stream on themselves, as well as on the rest of us.

Subsequently, I recounted our adventures to a missionary who had been living in the area for several years, and who had also visited the isolated small village. In the following years I came to know better two of the local men who had been our guides on that trek. From the accounts of the missionary and of the two New Guineans, I learned that the prowler at night was well known in that district—as a crazy, dangerous, powerful sorcerer. He once threatened to kill the missionary with his bow and arrow, and once actually tried to do so with a spear at the same isolated village that I had visited, laughing as he jabbed his spear in earnest. He was reported to have killed numerous local people, including two of his wives, and also his eight-year-old son just because the boy ate a banana without his father's permission. He behaved like a true paranoid, unable to distinguish reality from his imagination. Sometimes he lived in a village with other people, but at other times he lived alone in the area of forest where we had camped on that night, and where he had killed women who made the mistake of going there.

Despite the man being so obviously crazy and dangerous, local people didn't dare interfere with him, because they feared him as a great sorcerer. The gesture that he made at night when detected by my New Guinea friends—outstretched arm with drooping wrist—conventionally symbolizes to New Guineans in that area the cassowary, New Guinea's largest bird, which is believed to be actually a powerful magician who can turn himself into a bird. The cassowary is flightless, a distant relative of ostriches and emus, weighs 50 to 100 pounds, and terrifies New Guineans because it has stout legs with razor-sharp claws that it uses to disembowel dogs or people when attacked. That extended-arm, drooping-wrist gesture made by the sorcerer at night is believed to work powerful magic, and it mimics the shape of the neck and head of the cassowary held in the position when the bird is about to attack.

What was that sorcerer intending to do when he came into our camp that night? While your guess is as good as mine, his aims were probably not friendly. He knew or could infer that the green pup-tent would have a European inside it. As for why he came to the back rather than to the front door of my tent, I guess that that was either because he wanted not to be detected by the New Guineans in their shelter facing my tent's front door as he tried to get into my tent, or because he was confused by my tent's structure and mistook the back (with its small window flap zipped closed) for the front with its large door. If I had had the experience of New Guinea then that I do now, I would have practised constructive paranoia and screamed to my nearby New Guinea friends as soon as I heard and felt footsteps near the rear of my tent. I certainly wouldn't have walked alone, far ahead of my New Guinea friends, on the next day. In retrospect, my behavior was stupid and put me in danger. But I didn't know enough then to read the warning signs and to exercise constructive paranoia.

A boat accident

In the second incident, my New Guinea friend Malik and I were on an island off Indonesian New Guinea and wanted to get ourselves and our gear to the New Guinea mainland, separated from the island by a strait a dozen miles wide. Around 4:00 P.M. on a clear afternoon, slightly more than two hours before sunset, we joined four other passengers in a wooden canoe about 30 feet long, driven by two outboard motors mounted on the stern and with a crew of three young men. The four other passengers were not New Guineans: instead, they were a Chinese fisherman working on the New Guinea mainland, plus three men from the Indonesian islands of Ambon, Ceram, and Java respectively. The canoe's cargo and passenger space was covered by a plastic awning about four feet high, stretched over a framework, loosely attached to each side of the canoe, and extending from about 4 feet in front of the stern forward to 10 feet behind the canoe's prow. The three crew sat in the stern at the motors, and Malik and I sat just in front of them, facing the rear. With the awning over us and at our sides, there was little outside that we could see. The four other passengers sat at our backs, towards the canoe's prow.

The canoe set off, and the crew soon had the engines up to full speed, through waves several feet high. A little water splashed into the canoe under the awning, then a little more, and the other passengers began groaning good-naturedly. As some more large quantities of water splashed in, one of the crew began bailing water immediately in front of me out the loose sides of the awning. More large quantities of water came in, soaking the luggage stored towards the front of the canoe. I put my binoculars for protection inside the small yellow knapsack that I was holding in my lap, and that contained my passport, money, and all of my field notes wrapped inside a plastic bag. Over the roar of the engines and the crashing of the waves, Malik and the other passengers began to shout loudly, now no longer good-naturedly, at the driver, telling him to slow down or turn back. (This and all the rest of the conversations during this whole incident were in the Indonesian language, the official language and the lingua franca of Indonesian New Guinea.) But he didn't slow down, and more water splashed in. The accumulated weight of water was now causing the canoe to ride so low that water began pouring in over the sides.

The next few seconds, as the canoe settled lower into the ocean, were a blur that I can't reconstruct in detail. I was now scared that I would be trapped under the canoe's plastic awning as it sank. Somehow, I and everyone else managed to get out of the canoe into the ocean; I don't know whether some of us towards the rear jumped out of the open rear space not covered by the awning, or whether we instead crawled out under the awning's sides, and whether the passengers in front of us crawled out under the awning or scrambled to the open space in front or to the rear of the awning. Malik told me afterwards that the crew got out of the canoe first, then I got out, then Malik.

The next minute was even more of a panicked blur for me. I was wearing heavy hiking boots, a long-sleeved shirt, and shorts, and found myself in the water several yards from the canoe, which had capsized and was now bottom up. The weight of my hiking boots was dragging me underwater. My initial thought was a vivid, frightened "what is there that I can hold on to to keep myself afloat?" Near me, someone was clinging to a yellow life preserver, which I tried to grab in my panic, but the other person pushed me away. From my position now floating in the water, the waves seemed high. I had swallowed some water. While I can swim for short distances in a calm swimming pool, I wouldn't have been able to swim or float for many minutes through waves. I felt overwhelmed by fear that there was nothing to keep me afloat: our luggage and the canoe's gas tank floating nearby weren't buoyant enough to support my weight, the inverted canoe hull was now low in the water, and I feared that even it would sink. The island from which we had set out appeared to be several miles distant, another island seemed equally distant, and no other boat was in sight.

Malik swam over to me, grabbed the collar of my shirt, and pulled me back to the canoe. For the next half-hour he stood on the submerged upside-down engine and clung to the canoe's stern, while I clung nearby to the rear of the canoe's left side, with Malik keeping a grip on my neck. I stretched my arms out over the hull's round smooth underside, merely to steady myself, because the hull offered nothing for my hands to grasp. Occasionally I reached out my right hand to grip a submerged part of the engine, but that kept my head low above the water, which splashed into my face. Instead, for most of the time, my only grip holding me to the canoe was with my feet, which were somehow inserted in or hooked onto the left side's sunken gunwale. Now that the canoe was upside down and my feet were on the gunwale, the gunwale's depth below the water was such that my head was not far above the surface of the water, and occasionally a wave washed over me. Some piece of wood or awning was loose on the gunwale and rubbed and hurt my knee with each wave. I asked Malik to hold me while I untied my boot laces with one hand and then took off and threw away the heavy boots that were dragging me down.

From time to time I turned around to look at the waves coming towards me, and to brace myself for especially big waves. Often, one of my legs lost its grip on the gunwale, leaving me to rotate helplessly on the other leg that was still on the gunwale. Several times I lost my grip with both legs, was swept loose, paddled back or was pulled back by Malik, and in panic tried to regain my leg grip on the gunwales. During the entire time since the capsizing, the struggle to survive from one wave to the next had been all-consuming. I had the sense that there was no pause in the struggle.

Each wave threatened to shake me loose. Each time that I did get shaken loose, there was a panicked struggle to get back to the canoe and to get a grip again. I was often gasping from water in my face.

Because Malik's stance on the engine seemed more secure than my foot grip on the gunwales, I eventually moved from the canoe's side to its stern and stood with one leg on the submerged engine next to Malik, leaning forward and resting my arms on the round hull. Then I found and grabbed with my right hand some wooden bars attached to the hull, probably a partially broken piece of gunwale. This was the first good handhold that I had had since the canoe capsized. Standing on the engine and leaning forwards over the hull had the advantage that it kept my head higher above the waves than when I had been standing on the more deeply submerged gunwale, but it had the disadvantage that it placed more strain on my leg and was more tiring.

We didn't seem to be drifting any closer to the two islands visible in the distance. I knew that I wouldn't be able to stay afloat for more than a minute if the canoe, already floating low in the water, sank. I asked Malik if the canoe was just being held up by trapped air under the hull and was at risk of sinking if that air somehow came out, but he answered that the canoe timbers themselves would float. There was nothing that I could do except to hold on, react to each wave, wait (for what?), and watch. I kept asking Malik whether he was OK—probably just to assure myself that I was OK.

Luggage floated out from underneath the canoe. Some of it had been lashed to the canoe and stayed floating near the prow, including my own three suitcases. But other luggage was loose and drifted away, including my red rucksack, my green duffel bags, and Malik's luggage. It flashed through my mind that the most important thing was to save my life, and that what happened to my luggage was trivial by comparison. I nevertheless found myself slipping into my usual what-if mode of mulling over how I would deal with problems that arise in the course of travel. If I lost my passport, I thought, I could always get another one, though it would be a big mess to have to go to the nearest American embassy in Indonesia's capital 1,600 miles away. If I lost all my money and traveler's checks, I wasn't sure if I had a separate record of my traveler's check numbers, and that record would be in my drifting or floating luggage anyway. If we did get rescued, I would have to borrow a lot of money in order to fly to Indonesia's capital and get a new passport: how and from whom could I borrow money? My most important possessions—that passport, money, and traveler's checks, plus my bird notes from the whole trip—were in my yellow knapsack, which I had been holding in my lap in the canoe and didn't see now. If I didn't succeed in retrieving my knapsack, perhaps I could at least reconstruct from memory the bird lists for the main sites that I had visited. Then I realized that it was absurd to be thinking about my passport, money, and bird lists, when I didn't know if I was going be alive an hour from now anyway.

The scene of our struggles was paradoxically beautiful. There was a cloudless blue sky overhead, lovely tropical islands were visible from afar, and birds were flying. Even with the distraction of my struggle for survival, I continued to identify the birds: there were Lesser Crested Terns (or were they Greater Crested?), possibly a smaller species of tern, and one Striated Heron. But, for the first time in my life, I was in a situation where I didn't know if I would live. I couldn't acknowledge my own feelings about the prospect of death. Instead, I reflected on how upset my mother and my fiancée would be if I died. I recited to myself the telegram that I imagined my mother receiving: "We are sorry to have to tell you that your son Jared drowned in the Pacific Ocean yesterday."

At some point I told myself that, if I did survive, I should stop obsessing about things in life less important than survival. What would I do differently with the rest of my life if I did survive this accident? One thought was to devote myself to having children, about which I had been uncertain. (Afterwards, I did decide to have children.) Would I ever return to New Guinea if I survived? The risks of New Guinea—risks associated with boats like this, with crashes of the small planes on which I depended for travel, and with injuries or illnesses that could leave me physically incapacitated in a remote mountain range—all those risks weren't worth just obtaining a list of birds for yet another previously unexplored mountain. Perhaps this would be the end of my New Guinea career, even if I did survive.

But I then reminded myself that I had more immediate problems than to figure out what I would do if I survived. I recalled that one of my locked suitcases floating lashed to the canoe's prow contained two folded-up air mattresses and two air pillows, which would be excellent life preservers if inflated. I asked Malik to ask one of the men perched on the canoe's prow to open the suitcase and extract the mattresses and pillows. I dug the suitcase key out of my pocket and passed it to Malik, to pass on to one of the men on the prow. But no one did open my suitcase, for reasons that I never learned.

The canoe's other seven people besides Malik and me—the other four passengers and three crew—were now all sitting on or clinging to the front of the canoe's upside-down hull. The Ceram passenger made several dives under the canoe to look for anything useful, and he succeeded in pulling out the canoe's three life preservers, which he gave to the seven people at the front. No one did anything to help Malik and me. The Ambon passenger was weeping and repeating, "I can't swim, we are going to die!" The Javan passenger was reciting prayers. The Chinese fisherman said that he was afraid of rain and big waves if we were still afloat and alive after sunset; "God help us then!" he added. Malik said that, if we were not rescued within the hour or so remaining before sunset, there would be no hope for us, because the direction of the ocean currents was carrying us out to sea away from land, and we would not survive the night. I didn't think seriously of what would happen to us if we were not rescued before sunset, except to reflect how hard it had already been to be wet, shivering, and clinging to the rolling hull for an hour in daylight, and how much harder it would be to continue to do so for 12 hours at night in the dark. But the three crew and the Ceram man seemed secure and relaxed. One of them was singing, one or two of them occasionally swam near the hull, and the Ceram man sat on the hull eating a big fruit called a durian, of which passengers had brought several and which were now floating loose.

We kept looking around us for other boats. None were visible, except for some sails far off towards the New Guinea mainland. After around 5:30 P.M., an hour before sunset, we saw three small sails of sailing canoes coming from the mainland on a course that would carry them past us but in the distance. One of my fellow passengers took a stick, mounted a shirt on it, stood up on the canoe's hull, and waved the stick and shirt to catch the attention of whoever was in the sailing canoes. The Ceram man asked me to take off my blue shirt, which Malik then mounted on another stick and waved while he too stood up. All of us kept shouting "Tolong!" (Indonesian for "help"), but we were far out of hearing range of the sailing canoes in the distance.

I was still standing on the upside-down engine underwater at the stern. It at least offered a secure platform for my feet, whereas the other seven people sitting or standing on the smooth round hull in front of me, and now joined by Malik as well, had nothing to grip. But I knew that I was not going to be able to stand uncomfortably on the engine all night, because my leg was already starting to cramp. I shouted out to Malik to ask him whether he thought that I would be more secure sitting forward on the hull with him and the other passengers than standing on the engine, and he answered, "Yes." For me to get from the stern to the front of the boat meant traversing an area of hull much more insecure than either the stern or the front: it required walking along the round hull of the pitching canoe. I climbed from the engine onto the hull, stood up, and tried walking forwards. I quickly fell off into the sea, scrambled back onto the hull, eventually reached a position just behind the Chinese fisherman, and sat astride the hull immediately behind him. This had some disadvantages: there was nothing for either my hands or my feet to grip, I had to shift my body as the hull rolled, a few times I fell off into the sea and had to scramble back on, and I began to shiver because my body was now completely in the air rather than partly in the warm sea. It was ironical to be at risk of hypothermia in the tropical lowlands: while I would have felt hot if I had been dry, being instead constantly splashed and wet and wind-exposed left me chilled. But my head was now high above the waves, I was not standing on the engine and developing leg cramps, and I thought that I could maintain my new position for longer than the position in which I had been standing at the stern.

As the sun dropped lower towards the horizon, two of the three crew took two of the three life preservers and swam off towards the island, miles in the distance, from which we had set out, saying that they were going to fetch help. It still wasn't clear whether the three sailing canoes in the distance were on a path that would pass far ahead of us, where they couldn't see or hear us, or whether any of them was getting closer. The remaining men on our hull pointed to the sun, concerned with how many minutes remained before sunset, and with whether we would be visible into the sun or back-lit by the sun from the sailing canoes. Besides the sailing canoes, we saw a motor launch and possibly one other boat, but they were very far away.

Now, the sail of the nearest sailing canoe seemed to be getting bigger. Enough of the canoe was now visible to make it likely that the canoe must also have seen us and was actually getting closer. When it was about 100 yards away from us, the canoe stopped and dropped its sail. In the canoe there was just one man, who paddled towards us. We could now see that the canoe was a small one, only about 10 feet long, riding very low in the sea, with perhaps only six inches of freeboard. As the little canoe came alongside us, without discussion the two men on our capsized hull nearest the canoe, the Ambon man who couldn't swim and the Javanese, jumped into it. The little canoe couldn't safely hold anyone else, and its boatman paddled off. As it did so, it became clear that the second of the three canoes was approaching, and it too dropped sail at a distance of 100 yards. It was larger than the first canoe, and in it were two men, who paddled towards us. When it came close, this time there was discussion between those two men and our group, and among the people in our group, as to how many people the sailing canoe could hold, and who they would be. At first, the two men in the sailing canoe proposed to take only two or three of us, because they were concerned about their own canoe's low freeboard and risk of being swamped, but they finally agreed to take four of the five of us left on our hull. We agreed among ourselves that the person to remain on our hull would be the third crew member, who retained our remaining life preserver.

As I stepped into the sailing canoe, Malik asked me where my passport was. I replied that it was in my yellow knapsack, possibly still in the airspace under our hull. The Ceram man who had already dived repeatedly under the hull to retrieve the life preservers now dived again, came out with my yellow knapsack, and passed it to me. The sailing canoe then pushed off from our capsized hull, with six people in it: one of its two crew members in front and the other in back, and behind the front crewman the Chinese fisherman, me, Malik, and the Ceram man in that sequence. I had periodically looked at my wristwatch, which to my surprise was still working despite its immersion in seawater. The time was 6:15 P.M., 15 minutes before sunset. We had been in the water or on our capsized canoe for two hours.

It soon grew dark. Our two rescuers paddled towards the nearest land in the distance, which happened to be the island from which we had set out that afternoon. The sailing canoe rode very low in the water, with just a few inches of freeboard, and one of the men sitting behind me bailed constantly. I reflected that this little, heavily loaded canoe could also tip over, but that we probably were safe now. I didn't feel any relief or strong feelings; this was all just happening to me, as if I were an emotionless observer.

As our canoe paddled on, we heard voices in the water to our left. I guessed that it might be the voices of our motor canoe's two crew members who had swum off with life preservers. However, one of my companions could understand better than could I what the voices were shouting in Indonesian. It turned out that the shouts were from the three people in the first rescue canoe (its pilot, and our Ambon and Javan passengers), which was sinking, having taken on too much water from being overloaded. The freeboard of our own rescue canoe was too low for us to pick up another person. Someone in our canoe shouted something back to the three men in the water, and our rescuers paddled on, leaving them to their fates.

I don't know how long it took us to return to the island: perhaps an hour. As we approached it, we saw big waves breaking and a fire on the beach, and we wondered what the fire meant. In front of me I heard a conversation in Indonesian between the Chinese fisherman and the canoe paddler in the prow, including repeatedly the Indonesian words *empat pulu ribu* (meaning "40,000"). The Chinese fisherman, who had retrieved a small bag of his from our overturned canoe, opened his bag, took out money, and gave it to the paddler. I assumed at the time that the paddler was tired and wanted to land us at that nearby beach with the fire, and that the fisherman was offering him 40,000 Indonesian rupiah as an inducement to take us further to the island's main dock. But Malik told me later that what the paddler actually said was this: "If you don't give me 10,000 rupiah [about $5] for each of the four of you now, I will take you back to your capsized canoe and leave you there."

Our rescue canoe rounded a point of the island and came into a sheltered bay where campfires were burning on the beach. Behind us in the dark, we heard a motor and saw a motorboat with a bright light come up slowly behind us. Our little canoe stopped in shallow water, and Malik, the Chinese fisherman, the Ceram man, and I stepped out and waded to and climbed into the motorboat, which by coincidence turned out to be a fishing boat belonging to the family of the Chinese fisherman. It had been out fishing, happened to see our two crewmen who had swum off with the two life preservers, picked them up, searched for and found our capsized canoe, and picked up the floating luggage still attached to the canoe (including my suitcases but none of Malik's luggage). We stayed in the motorboat as it slowly headed towards the New Guinea mainland. We told the motorboat drivers about the three men from the first capsized rescue canoe whom we had heard shouting in the water. However, when we reached the approximate location where we had heard them, the motorboat went straight on and did not circle or shout. Malik told me later that the drivers explained that the three men from the capsized rescue canoe had probably somehow reached shore.

The motorboat ride to the mainland took about an hour and a half. I was shirtless and shivering. We landed around 10:00 P.M., to find a crowd awaiting us at the mainland dock, the news of our accident having somehow preceded us. Among that crowd, my attention was instantly drawn to a small elderly woman, possibly a Javan from her appearance. In my life I have never seen such an expression of extreme emotion on the face of anyone, except for actors in movies. She seemed to be overwhelmed by a mixture of grief, horror, and disbelief at something awful that had happened, and by utter exhaustion. The woman came out of the crowd and began questioning us. It turned out that she was the mother of the Javan man who had been in the first sailing canoe that had capsized.

I spent the following day at a small guesthouse, rinsing saltwater out of my suitcases and their contents. While my equipment—my binoculars, tape recorders, altimeters, books, and sleeping bag—was ruined and unsalvageable, I was able to rescue my clothes. Malik lost everything that he had brought with him. Under local conditions, we had no recourse against the canoe crew whose negligent motor operation had caused the accident.

On the following evening I climbed onto the roof of a nearby building around 6:00 P.M. in order to re-experience how rapidly the daylight had faded at sunset. Near the equator, daylight fades much more rapidly than in the temperate zones, because the sun sets vertically rather than at an

angle sloping to the horizon. At 6:15 P.M., the time when we had been rescued on the previous day, the sun was just above the horizon, and its light
was growing dimmer. Sunset came at 6:30 P.M., and by 6:40 P.M. it was
much too dark for someone in another boat to have distinguished us and
our capsized canoe even at a distance of only a few hundred yards. We had
had a close escape and been rescued just in time.

As I came down from the roof in the dark, I was feeling helpless and
still unable to grasp what those reckless crewmen had done to me. I had
lost valuable equipment, and I had almost lost my life. My fiancée, my
parents, my sister, and my friends had almost lost me. My knees were raw
and scarred from being rubbed with each wave against the gunwale as I
gripped it. All of that because of the recklessness of three young men who
should have known better, drove too fast in high waves, ignored all the
water splashing into the canoe, refused to slow down or stop when repeatedly asked to do so, swam off with two of the three life preservers, never
apologized, and never showed the slightest regret for the anguish and loss
that they had actually inflicted on us, and for how close they had come to
killing us. Those bastards!

While wallowing in these thoughts, I came across a man on the ground
level of the building onto whose roof I had climbed to view the sunset. I
fell into conversation with him and told him why I had gone up onto the
roof and what had happened to us on the previous day. He answered that,
coincidentally, he had also been on the same island the previous day, and
had also wanted to go to the mainland. He had looked at the canoe that
we hired, with its big engines, seen the young crewmen and their cocky
and laughing behavior, and watched how they gunned the engines and
handled the canoe coming in to shore to await passengers. He had had
much experience of boats. He had decided that he didn't want to risk his
life with that crew and boat, and had waited for a larger and slower boat
to go to the mainland.

That reaction of his jolted me. So, I hadn't been helpless after all! The
cocky crew weren't the only people who had come close to throwing away
my life. I was the one who had stepped into their canoe; no one had forced
me to do it. The accident had ultimately been my responsibility. It had
been completely within my power to prevent it from happening to me.
Instead of asking why the crew had been so stupid, I should have been

asking myself why I had been so stupid. The man who had chosen to wait for a larger boat had exercised New Guinea–style constructive paranoia, and he had thereby escaped being traumatized and nearly killed. I should have exercised constructive paranoia myself, and I would now do so for the rest of my life.

Just a stick in the ground

The most recent of the three episodes related in this chapter unfolded many years after my canoe accident had convinced me of the virtues of constructive paranoia. Out of New Guinea's lowlands rise many separate isolated mountain ranges, which are interesting to biologists because they resemble "islands" of montane habitats surrounded by a "sea" of lowlands, as far as the distributions of species confined to montane habitats are concerned. The higher elevations of most of the isolated mountain ranges are uninhabited by people. There are two possible means to reach those high elevations in order to survey their birds and other animals and plants. One is to be flown directly by helicopter to high elevations, but it is difficult to obtain a helicopter for charter in New Guinea, and even harder to locate a clear area for landing a helicopter on a forest-covered New Guinea mountain. The other method is to find a village close enough to the mountain that one can bring one's gear to the village by plane, helicopter, or boat, and then walk from the village to climb the mountain. The difficulties of New Guinea terrain are such that it is impractical to carry one's gear to a mountain camp more distant than about five miles from a village. A further practical problem is that, for many of the isolated peaks, available maps don't show the location and elevation of the highest peak or the nearest village; one instead has to obtain that geographic information by a survey flight.

One particular mountain range interested me because, although it was reported to be not especially high, it was isolated. Hence at the end of one of my trips to New Guinea, while I was starting to plan the next year's trip, I chartered a small plane to fly a survey along the entire length of that mountain range, and I identified its highest peak. There was no village within at least 25 miles of the peak in any direction, and no garden clearing or any other signs of human presence nearby. That ruled out reaching the peak from the village and required instead a helicopter-based operation, which in turn required finding a natural clearing at which to land a helicopter. (Some helicopters can hover over the forest canopy while passengers and cargo are being lowered by winch through the canopy to the ground, but that requires special helicopters and training.) While one's first impression of New Guinea forests is of an unbroken expanse of green trees, one does encounter occasional natural clearings at landslides where an earthquake has shaken down a patch of forest, or at a marsh, a dried-up pond, the bank of a river or pond, or a dry mud volcano. On this survey flight I was delighted to spot a huge landslide clearing, about two and a half miles from the peak and several thousand feet lower in elevation. By New Guinea standards, that's much too far to establish a camp at the landslide and to be able to walk daily to the peak to observe birds. Instead, it would be necessary to fly our gear by helicopter into a first camp at the landslide, then to clear a trail and carry the gear ourselves to a second campsite in forest close to the peak: hard work, but nevertheless feasible.

With that problem of finding a helicopter landing site potentially solved, the other problem involved obtaining permission and help from local New Guinean land-owners. But how was I to do that, when there were no signs of humans anywhere near the peak? Whom should I contact? I knew from personal experience that there were nomads moving around at low elevation in the eastern part of the range. There were reports, but there was no definite information, that related nomads might range further west near the peak, but I hadn't spotted any signs of their presence from the plane. I also knew from experience that nomads living in isolated mountain ranges remain mostly or entirely at low elevation, where their staple food of sago palm grows. At high elevation there isn't enough food to support a resident human population. At most, nomads might make occasional hunting trips to higher elevations above the altitudinal ceiling for sago palms, but I had been in several mountain ranges where the nomads don't even do that, and where animals living at high elevation are tame because they have never seen humans and never been hunted.

My failure to locate any signs of nomads near my intended peak had two consequences. First, it meant that I hadn't found any New Guineans who would claim to own the mountain, and from whom to ask permission. Second, in my New Guinea fieldwork I need local people to make and run a camp, clear trails, and help me find and identify birds, but here there were no local people available. That second problem was one that I could solve just by bringing New Guineans whom I already knew from another part of New Guinea. The potential huge problem was the first one of permission.

In New Guinea, every bit of land is claimed by some group, even if they never visit the land. An absolute no-no in New Guinea is to trespass on someone's land without permission. The consequences of being caught trespassing include being robbed, murdered, and/or raped. I have been in several unpleasant situations when I did ask permission from the most nearby people, who did claim to own the area that I wanted to visit and who gave me their permission, only for me to find on going there that some other group claimed to own the area and was outraged to find me there without *their* permission. Compounding the danger was that, in this case, I would not just be coming myself, but would also be bringing several New Guineans from another part of New Guinea. That would be considered even more infuriating to local land-owners: New Guineans, unlike me, might be there to steal women and pigs and to settle land.

What would I do if, after I was dropped by helicopter at this landslide, and after the helicopter flew off and left me for three weeks, I did encounter nomads? My helicopter would have to make several shuttle flights to bring my supplies and my co-workers to the landslide, thereby advertising my presence. If there were any nomads at all within miles, they would hear and see the helicopter, figure out that it was landing there, and come track us down. Making things even worse in this situation: the nomads in this area, if there were any, might be "uncontacted," i.e., might never have seen a white man or missionary or government official. First contact with previously uncontacted tribal peoples is terrifying. Neither side knows what the other side wants or will do. It is difficult or impossible to communicate peaceful intent by sign language to previously uncontacted people whose language one does not know, even if they wait long enough to let you try to communicate. The risk is that they won't wait; they may be terrified or furious, panic, and immediately start shooting with bows and arrows. What would I do if I were found by nomads?

After that survey flight, I went back to the U.S. to plan a helicopter-based expedition to that landslide and that summit the following year. Practically every night of that intervening year, while drifting off to sleep, I ran through my head scenarios imagining what I might do if I did encounter nomads there in the forest. In one scenario, I would sit down and hold out my hands to show that I had no weapon and was non-threatening, force a smile, reach into my knapsack to pull out a chocolate bar and eat a piece myself to show that it was non-poisonous and edible, and offer them the rest of the bar. But—they might get angry immediately, or they might panic when they saw me fumbling in my knapsack, as if to take out a gun. Or, in another scenario, I would start imitating calls of local New Guinea birds, to show that I was there just to study birds. That's often a good ice-breaker with New Guineans. But they might just think that I was crazy, or trying to work bird-related sorcery on them. Or, if I was with the New Guineans whom I had flown in, and together we encountered a single nomad, perhaps we could somehow induce him to stay at our camp, we'd make friends with him, I'd start to learn his language, and we'd induce him not to go off and bring back some of his fellow nomads before we got picked up and left in our helicopter several weeks later. But—how would we induce one terrified nomad to stay in our camp for several weeks, with these other New Guinean trespassers?

I had to recognize that none of these happy-ending scenarios that I imagined was even remotely plausible. That realization didn't make me abandon the whole project. It still seemed most likely that we simply wouldn't encounter any nomads, because we hadn't seen any signs of any huts from the air, and because my previous experience was that lowland nomads usually don't visit summits of mountains. But when I finally did go back to New Guinea a year later to carry out the planned exploration of the summit, I still didn't have a plan that I was convinced would work if we did encounter nomads.

Finally came the day, a year later, when the project was ready to begin. I assembled four New Guinea friends from mountains several hundred miles away, and half a ton of supplies, to fly in a chartered small airplane to the closest available airstrip, a small dirt strip at a village 37 miles south of the peak that was our target. As we flew along the foothills of the mountain range, we spotted eight huts scattered along rivers at the base of the hills in the eastern part of the range, but the last hut was still 23 miles east of our peak. On the following day our chartered small helicopter arrived at the airstrip to shuttle us in four runs into the big landslide clearing that we had seen on our previous trip. The first flight took two of the New Guineans, plus a tent and axes and some food to sustain them in case of an accident such that the helicopter could not return for a while. After just an hour, the helicopter came back to our airstrip with a note from them reporting exciting news. In flying around the peak, they had discovered a campsite location much better than the big landslide: a little landslide only two-thirds of a mile from the peak, and at higher elevations than the bigger landslide. That meant that we would be able to travel back and forth between our camp and the peak within a few hours, without any need to carry our gear from the big landslide and establish a closer camp. Two more helicopter flights brought the other two New Guineans and more supplies from the airstrip to the selected campsite.

The last helicopter flight carried me and the rest of our supplies to the campsite. During the flight I looked down carefully from the helicopter for any signs of people. About 10 miles north of the airstrip and still 27 miles south of the peak was another village on a small river. Soon after that village, I spotted two isolated huts, presumably belonging to nomads, still lying in the flat lowlands before we reached the first of a series of ridges leading up to the mountain range. Once we reached the ridges, there were no further signs of humans whatsoever: no huts, no gardens, no anything else. In New Guinea a distance of 27 miles from our campsite over rough terrain might as well be on the other side of the ocean, as far as our risks of unwanted visitors were concerned. Perhaps we were in luck, and perhaps these mountains really were uninhabited and unvisited!

The helicopter circled our planned campsite, where I could see the four New Guineans waving below. The clearing proved to be a small steep-sided gully whose slopes had apparently collapsed in a landslide (probably triggered by one of the frequent earthquakes in that region), such that the floor of the gully was dirt bare of vegetation, perfect for landing a helicopter. Apart from that small landslide and the big distant landslide that had been our original target, everything else within sight was covered by forests. The pilot and I landed and unloaded our last cargo, then I went up in the helicopter again and asked the pilot to head for the nearby peak so that we could plan where to make a trail. From the head of our gully, we could see a ridge leading straight to the peak, but not so steeply as to present problems. The peak itself was very steep for its top 200 vertical feet and might be a difficult scramble to climb. But there were still absolutely no signs of people or huts or gardens. The helicopter then dropped me at our campsite and flew off, agreeing to pick us up again 19 days later.

That was an act of faith on our part: from what we saw of the terrain, it would have been utterly impossible to walk back to the airstrip 37 miles distant. While I had brought along a small radio, in that hilly terrain my radio could not receive or transmit messages from or to the helicopter base 150 miles away. Instead, as a precaution in case of an accident or ill- ness requiring an emergency evacuation, I arranged for a small airplane whose scheduled flight path took it not too far from our campsite to devi- ate from its path and circle our camp every five days. We could try to talk with the pilot by radio to confirm that we were OK, and we agreed that we would place a bright red air mattress on the landslide if we did have an emergency.

We spent all of the second day constructing our camp. Our happiest discovery was that there were still no signs of people: if nomads had been alerted by our helicopter to try to track us down, it wasn't happening yet. Large birds were flying in and out of the gully, undisturbed by our pres- ence a few dozen yards away. That suggested that the birds were unafraid of people, and provided further evidence that nomads didn't visit this area.

On the third day I was at last ready to climb to the peak, following my New Guinea friends Gumini and Paia, who were cutting trail. Initially, we climbed 500 feet up out of our landslide gully onto the ridge, which bore a small patch of grass and shrubs with low trees, I assumed because of an older landslide that was now becoming overgrown. Climbing along the ridge, we soon entered closed forest and worked our way upwards in an easy climb. Bird-watching was now exciting, as I began to see and hear montane species, including a couple of uncommon and little-known ones such as the Perplexing Scrub-Wren and the Obscure Honeyeater. When we finally reached the summit pyramid, it was indeed very steep, as it had appeared from the air. But we were able to pull ourselves up it by holding on to tree roots. On its top I spotted a White-breasted Fruit-Dove and a

Hooded Pitohui, two montane species that were absent below. Apparently this peak was just high enough to support a few individuals of each species. But I hadn't met some other montane species that are common and noisy at this elevation elsewhere in New Guinea: perhaps they really were absent because the area of this mountain was too small to support a viable population of them. I sent Paia back to camp, while Gumini and I walked slowly down our trail, birding as we went.

So far, I was delighted and relieved. Everything was going well. The problems that I had feared hadn't materialized. We had succeeded in finding a landing place for our helicopter in the forest, made a comfortable camp, and cleared an easy short trail to the summit. Best of all, we had found no signs of visits by nomads. The 17 days remaining to us would be ample time to establish which montane bird species were present and which weren't. Gumini and I descended our new trail in good spirits and emerged from the forest into the small open patch that I had taken to be an old landslide clearing on the ridge above our camp.

Suddenly, Gumini stopped, bent over, and stared closely at something on the ground. When I asked what he found so interesting, he just said, "Look," and he pointed. What he was pointing to was nothing more than a small stalk or tree seedling a couple of feet high, with a few leaves on it. I told him, "That's just a very young tree. See, there are lots of other young trees growing up here in this clearing. What's so special about this one?"

Gumini answered, "No, it's not a young tree. It's a stick stuck in the ground." I disagreed: "What makes you think so? It's just a seedling growing up out of the ground." In reply, Gumini grasped it and pulled. It lifted out easily, without the need for any effort to break or pull out roots. When he had lifted it out, we saw that there were no roots at the base of the stick, which was broken off cleanly. I thought that perhaps Gumini's pulling had snapped its roots, but he dug down around the hole left by the stick and showed me that there weren't any broken-off roots. It must instead be a broken-off small stick inserted into the ground, as he had insisted. How had it gotten there and become inserted?

We both looked overhead at the small trees 15 feet tall above us. I suggested, "A branch must have broken off that tree overhead, and fallen down and gotten stuck in the ground." But Gumini objected, "If that branch broke and fell, it's not likely to have landed with the broken-off end pointing exactly down and the leaves pointing up. And it's a light branch, not heavy enough to drive itself several inches into the ground. It looks to me like some person broke it off and inserted it with the sharp broken end into the ground and the leaves upwards, as a sign."

I felt a shiver and my skin flushing on the back of my neck, as I thought of Robinson Crusoe cast ashore on his supposedly uninhabited island, suddenly coming across a human footprint. Gumini and I sat down, picked up and held the stick, and looked around us. For an hour we sat there, talking to each other about the possibilities. If a person really did this, why isn't there any other sign of human activity, just this broken stick? If a person did plant it, how recently was he here to do it? It wasn't today, because the leaves are already slightly wilted. But it wasn't a long time ago either, because the leaves are still green, not shriveled and dry. Is this open area really an overgrown landslide clearing as I had assumed? Maybe, instead, it's an old garden that has become overgrown. I kept coming back to my belief that a nomad would not have walked in there a few days ago from a hut 27 miles away, broken and planted a stick, and walked off without leaving any other signs. Gumini kept insisting that a broken stick wasn't likely to insert itself into the ground, so as to mimic what a person does.

We walked back the short distance into camp, where the other New Guineans were, and told them what we had found. Nobody else had seen any hint of human presence. Now that I had gotten into this paradise about which I had been dreaming for a year, I wasn't going to put out the red mattress as an emergency sign for evacuation on the first overflight three days later, just because there was one unexplained stick in the ground. That would be carrying constructive paranoia too far. There was probably some natural explanation for that stick, I told myself. Maybe it really had happened to fall vertically with enough force to insert itself, or maybe we had overlooked its roots broken off when we pulled it out. But Gumini was an experienced woodsman, one of the very best whom I had met in New Guinea, and he wasn't likely to misread signs.

All that we could do was to be very careful, remain alert for other signs of people, and not do anything else to give away our presence to any nomads who might be lurking nearby. Our four noisy helicopter flights to establish our camp could be expected to have tipped off any nomad within dozens of miles. We would probably soon know if there were any. As precautions, we didn't yell to each other from a distance. I made a point of being especially quiet when I went below camp to bird-watch at low elevation where any nomads were most likely to be. So that our campfire smoke wouldn't give away our presence from afar, we reserved making a big fire for our main cooking until after dark. Eventually, after we found some large monitor lizards prowling around our camp, I asked my New Guinea friends to make bows and arrows for defense. They complied, but only half-heartedly—perhaps because freshly cut green wood wouldn't make a good bow and arrow, or because four green bows and arrows in the hands of just my four New Guineans wouldn't be of much use if there really were a band of angry nomads around.

As the days went on, no more mysterious broken sticks turned up, and there were no suspicious signs of humans. Instead, we saw tree kangaroos during the day, unafraid and not running away at the sight of us. Tree kangaroos are New Guinea's largest native mammals and the first target of native hunters, so in inhabited areas they quickly become shot out. Surviving individuals learn to be active only at night and are very shy and flee if seen. We also encountered unafraid cassowaries, New Guinea's biggest flightless bird, which is also a prime target of hunters and also rare and very shy in areas with people. The big pigeons and parrots in the area were also unafraid. Everything pointed to this being a location whose animals had never experienced human hunters or visitors.

When our helicopter came back and evacuated us on schedule 19 days after we had arrived, the mystery of the broken stick was still unresolved. We had seen no other possible signs of humans than that one stick. In retrospect, I think it's unlikely that nomads from the lowlands many miles away climbed up thousands of feet, made a garden, came back a year or two later, planted one stick by coincidence a couple of days before our arrival so that the leaves were still green, and left no other trace of themselves. While I can't explain how that stick got there, my guess is that Gumini's constructive paranoia was in this case unjustified.

But I can certainly understand how Gumini acquired his attitude. His area had come under government control recently. Until then, traditional fighting had been going on. Paia, 10 years older than Gumini, had grown up making stone tools. In Gumini's and Paia's society, people who weren't super-attentive to signs of strangers in the forest didn't live long. It does no harm to be suspicious of sticks not readily explained naturally, to spend an hour examining and discussing each one, and then to remain alert for other sticks. Before my canoe accident, I would have dismissed Gumini's reaction as exaggerated, just as I had dismissed as exaggerated the reactions of New Guineans to the dead tree under which I had camped earlier in my New Guinea career. But I had now spent enough time in New Guinea to understand Gumini's reaction. It's better to pay attention 1,000 times to sticks that turn out to have fallen naturally into an unnatural-looking position, than to make the fatal mistake of ignoring one stick that really did get placed by strange humans. Gumini's constructive paranoia was an appropriate reaction of an experienced, cautious New Guinean.

Taking risks

While the underlying caution that I term constructive paranoia has struck me frequently among New Guineans, I don't want to leave the misimpression that they are thereby paralyzed and hesitant to act. To begin with, there are cautious and incautious New Guineans, just as there are cautious and incautious Americans. Then, too, the cautious ones are perfectly able to weigh risks and to act. They do some things that they know are risky, but that they nevertheless choose to do repeatedly and with appropriate care. That's because doing those things is essential for their obtaining food and succeeding in life, or because they place value on doing them. I'm reminded of a line attributed to the great hockey player Wayne Gretzky, about the risks of attempting difficult hockey shots that might miss the net: "100% of the shots you don't take don't go in!"

My New Guinea friends would understand Gretzky's quip, and would add two footnotes to it. First, a closer analogy with traditional life would be if you were actually penalized for missing a shot—but you would still take shots, albeit more cautiously. Second, a hockey player can't wait forever for the perfect opportunity to take a shot, because a hockey game has a time limit of one hour. Similarly, traditional lives include time limits: you'll die of thirst within a few days if you don't take risks in finding water, you'll starve within a few weeks if you don't take risks in obtaining food, and you'll die within less than a century no matter what you do. In fact, traditional lifespans are on the average considerably shorter than those of modern First World people, because of uncontrollable factors such as diseases, droughts, and enemy attacks. No matter how cautious a person in a traditional society is, he or she is likely to die before age 55 anyway, and that may mean having to tolerate higher risk levels than in First World societies with an average lifespan of 80—just as Wayne Gretzky would have to take more shots if a hockey game lasted only 30 minutes instead of one hour. Here are three examples of calculated risks that traditional people accept but that horrify us:

!Kung hunters, armed with nothing more than small bows and poisoned arrows, wave sticks and shout to drive groups of lions or hyenas off of animal carcasses. When a hunter succeeds in wounding an antelope, the small arrow does not kill by impact: instead, the prey runs off, the hunters track it, and by the time that the prey has collapsed from the slow-acting poison's effect many hours or a day later, lions or hyenas are likely to have found the carcass first. Hunters who are not prepared to drive those predators off carcasses are guaranteed to starve. Few things impress me as more suicidal than the thought of walking up to a group of feasting lions while shaking a stick to intimidate them. Nevertheless, !Kung hunters do it dozens of times a year, for decades. They attempt to minimize their risks by challenging sated lions with visibly bulging bellies and likely to be ready to retreat, and by not challenging hungry or emaciated lions that evidently just discovered the carcass and are likely to stand their ground.

Women in the Fore area of New Guinea's Eastern Highlands move from their natal village to their husband's village at the time of marriage. When married women later go back to their natal village to visit their parents and other blood relatives, they may travel either with their husbands or else alone. In traditional times of chronic warfare, a woman's traveling alone involved the risk of her being raped or killed while traversing enemy territory. Women attempted to minimize those risks by seeking protection from other relatives living in the territory traversed. However, the dangers and the protection were both difficult to predict. A woman might be attacked in revenge for a killing carried out a generation ago; or her protectors might be outnumbered by those seeking revenge, or might acknowledge justice in the demand for revenge.

For instance, the anthropologist Ronald Berndt related the story of a young woman named Jumu, from Ofafina village, who went to marry a man at Jasuvi. For Jumu later to return with her child to visit her parents and brothers at Ofafina required traversing the Ora district, where a woman named Inusa had recently been killed by Ofafina men. Hence Jumu's Jasuvi in-laws advised her to seek protection from an Ora male relative named Asiwa, who also happened to be a brother's son of the dead Inusa. Unfortunately, after finding Asiwa in his garden, Jumu was detected by some Ora men, who tricked and pressured Asiwa into allowing one of them to rape Jumu in Asiwa's presence, and then killed Jumu and her child. Asiwa was apparently only half-hearted in his efforts to protect Jumu, because he felt that the killing of Jumu and her child constituted legitimate revenge for Inusa's killing. As for why Jumu made what proved to be the fatal mistake of entrusting herself to Asiwa's protection, Berndt commented, "Fighting, revenge, and counter-revenge are so commonplace that people become accustomed to this state of affairs." That is, Jumu was unwilling to abandon forever the hope of seeing her parents again, and she accepted and tried to minimize the risks involved.

My remaining example of the delicate balance between constructive paranoia and knowingly accepting risks involves Inuit hunters. An important Inuit method of hunting seals in the winter involves standing, sometimes for hours, over one of the seal's breathing holes in a shelf of sea ice, in the hopes that a seal will surface at that hole for a quick breath and can then be harpooned. This technique poses the risk that the ice shelf may break off and drift out to sea, leaving the hunter stranded on the ice and facing likely death from ice break-up and drowning, exposure, or starvation. It would be much safer for hunters to remain on land and not place themselves at that risk. But that in turn would make death from starvation probable, because land hunting offers no rewards to match killing seals at breathing holes. While Inuit hunters attempt to select ice shelves unlikely to break off, even the most careful hunter cannot predict shelf break-off with certainty, and other hazards of Arctic life result in a short average lifespan for traditional Inuit hunters. That is, if a hockey game lasted only 20 minutes, one would have to risk taking shots even if missed shots were penalized.

Risks and talkativeness

Finally, I would like to speculate about a possible connection between two features of traditional life: its risks, and what I have experienced as the talkativeness of traditional peoples. Ever since my first trip to New Guinea, I have been impressed by how much more time New Guineans spend talking with each other than do we Americans and Europeans. They keep up a running commentary on what is happening now, what happened this morning and yesterday, who ate what and when, who urinated when and where, and minute details of who said what about whom or did what to whom. They don't merely fill the day with talk: from time to time through the night they wake up and resume talking. That makes it difficult for a Westerner like me, accustomed to nights spent in uninterrupted sleep and not punctuated with conversations, to get a good night's rest in a hut shared with many New Guineans. Other Westerners have similarly commented on the talkativeness of the !Kung, of African Pygmies, and of many other traditional peoples.

Out of innumerable examples, here is one that stuck in my mind. One morning during my second trip to New Guinea, I was in a camp tent with two New Guinea Highland men, while other men from the camp were out in the forest. The two men belonged to the Fore tribe and were talking to each other in the Fore language. I had been enjoying learning the Fore language, and the men's conversation was sufficiently repetitive and about a subject for which I had already acquired vocabulary that I was able to follow much of what they were saying. They were talking about the Highland staple food of sweet potato, for which the Fore word is isa-awe. One of the men looked at the large pile of sweet potatoes in the corner of the tent, assumed an unhappy expression, and said to the other man, "Isa-awe kampai." ("There aren't any sweet potatoes.") They then counted how many isa-awe the pile actually contained, using the Fore counting system that mapped objects against the 10 fingers of the two hands, then against the 10 toes, and finally against a series of points along the arms. Each man related to the other how many isa-awe he himself had eaten that morning. Then they compared notes on how many isa-awe the "red man" had eaten that morning (i.e., me: the Fore referred to Europeans as *tetekine*, literally "red man," rather than as "white man"). The man who had spoken first now said that he was hungry for isa-awe, although he had eaten breakfast only an hour ago. The conversation went on to estimate how much longer that pile of isa-awe would last, and when the red man (me again) would buy some more isa-awe. There was nothing unusual about that conversation: it stands out in my mind only because it indelibly reinforced my memory of the Fore word *isa-awe*, and because I was struck at the time by how long the men were able to continue a conversation consisting of variants just on the single theme of isa-awe.

We may feel inclined to dismiss such talking as "mere gossip." But gossip fulfills functions for us, and for New Guineans as well. One function in New Guinea is that traditional people have none of the means of passive entertainment to which we devote inordinate time, such as television, radio, movies, books, video games, and the Internet. Instead, talking is the main form of entertainment in New Guinea. Another function of New Guinea talking is to maintain and develop social relationships, which are at least as important to New Guineans as they are to Westerners.

In addition, I think that their constant stream of conversation helps New Guineans to cope with life in the dangerous world around them. Everything gets discussed: minute details of events, what has changed since yesterday, what might happen next, who did what, and why they did it. We get most of our information about the world around us from the media; traditional New Guineans get all their information from their own observations and from each other. Life is more dangerous for them than it is for us. By talking constantly and acquiring as much information as possible, New Guineans try to make sense of their world, and to prepare themselves better to master life's dangers.

Of course, conversation serves that same function of risk avoidance for us as well. We, too, talk, but we have less need of talk, because we face fewer dangers and have more sources of information. I'm reminded of an American friend whom I'll call Sara, and whom I admired for her own efforts to cope with a dangerous world around her. Sara was a single mother, working full-time, living on a modest salary, and struggling to pay for her young son's needs and her own needs. As a smart and sociable person, she was interested in meeting the right man to become a partner for her, a father for her son, a protector, and an economic contributor.

For a single mother, the world of American men is full of dangers that are difficult to assess accurately. Sara had encountered her share of men who proved to be dishonest or violent. That didn't discourage her from continuing to date. However, like !Kung hunters who don't give up when they find lions on a carcass, but who use all their experience to assess quickly the dangers posed by those particular lions, Sara had learned to size up men quickly and to be alert for small signs of danger. She regularly spent much time talking with women friends in similar situations, in order to share experiences of men and other opportunities and risks of life, and so they could help each other make sense of their observations.

Wayne Gretzky would understand why Sara kept exploring men, despite many missed shots. (I'm pleased to be able to report that Sara finally did make a happy second marriage, with a good man who was a single father when she met him.) And my New Guinea friends would understand Sara's constructive paranoia, and all the time that she devoted to rehearsing with her friends the details of her daily life.

CHAPTER 8

Lions and Other Dangers

Dangers of traditional life ▪ Accidents ▪ Vigilance ▪ Human violence ▪ Diseases ▪ Responses to diseases ▪ Starvation ▪ Unpredictable food shortages ▪ Scatter your land ▪ Seasonality and food storage ▪ Diet broadening ▪ Aggregation and dispersal ▪ Responses to danger

Dangers of traditional life

The anthropologist Melvin Konner spent two years living with !Kung hunter-gatherers in a remote area of Botswana's Kalahari Desert, far from any roads or towns. The nearest town was a small one with few motor vehicles, such that a car appeared along the road through town on the average only every minute or so. Yet when Konner brought a !Kung friend named !Khoma to the town, the man was terrified at the prospect of having to cross the road, even when no car was visible in either direction. This was a man whose lifestyle in the Kalahari involved driving lions and hyenas off the carcasses of game animals.

Sabine Kuegler, the German missionary couple's daughter who grew up with her parents among the Fayu tribe in Indonesian New Guinea's swamp forests, where there are also no roads or motor vehicles or towns, related a similar reaction. At the age of 17 she finally left New Guinea to attend boarding school in Switzerland. "There were unbelievably many cars here, and they roared along so unbelievably fast! . . . Every time that we had to cross the street without a traffic light, I began to sweat. I couldn't estimate the cars' speed, and I was panicked that I would be run over. . . . Cars raced by from both directions, and when there was a small gap in the traffic, my friends ran across the street. But I stayed there, as if turned to stone. . . . For five minutes I kept standing at the same place. My fear was just too great. I walked a huge detour until I finally found a street-crossing with a traffic light. From then on, all my friends knew that they had to plan crossing the street with me far in advance. To this day, I'm still afraid of rushing traffic in cities." Yet Sabine Kuegler had become accustomed to watching out for wild pigs and crocodiles in New Guinea swamp forests.

These two similar stories illustrate several points. People in every society face dangers, but the particular dangers differ among societies. Our perceptions of both unfamiliar risks and familiar ones are often unrealistic. Konner's !Kung friend and Sabine Kuegler were both correct, in that cars actually are the number-one danger in Western life. But American college students and women voters, asked to rank life's dangers, both rated nuclear power as more dangerous than cars, despite nuclear power (even including the death tolls from the two atomic bombs dropped at the end of World War II) having actually killed only a tiny fraction of the number of people that cars have killed. American college students also rate pesticides as extremely risky (close behind guns and smoking, in their opinion), and surgery as relatively safe, whereas in reality surgery is more dangerous than pesticides.

One could add that traditional lifestyles are overall more dangerous than the Western lifestyle, as expressed in a much shorter lifespan. That difference, though, is mostly recent. Before effective state government began around 400 years ago to reduce the impact of famines, and especially before public health measures and then antibiotics largely overcame infectious diseases less than 200 years ago, lifespans in European and American state societies were no higher than in traditional societies.

What, really, are the main dangers in traditional life? We shall see that lions and crocodiles are only part of the answer. As for reactions to dangers, we modern people sometimes respond rationally by adopting measures effective at minimizing the dangers, but in other cases we respond "irrationally" and ineffectively, e.g. by denial, or else by prayer and other religious practices. How do traditional peoples respond to dangers? I shall discuss what seem to me to be the four main groups of dangers faced by traditional peoples: environmental hazards, human violence, infectious and parasitic diseases, and starvation. The first two of those groups are still major problems in modern Western societies, the third and especially the fourth less so (although they are still important in other parts of the modern world). Then I'll briefly mention ways in which our assessments of risks are distorted, such that we overreact to pesticides and underreact to surgery.

Accidents

When we imagine the dangers facing traditional societies, our first association is likely to be with lions and other environmental hazards. In reality, for most traditional societies environmental dangers rank only third as a cause of death, behind disease and human violence. But environmental dangers exert a bigger effect on people's behavior than do diseases, because for environmental dangers the relation between cause and effect is much quicker and more easily perceived and understood.

Table 8.1 lists the main reported causes of accidental death or injury for seven traditional peoples for whom summaries are available. All seven live in or near the tropics and practise at least some hunting and gathering, but two (New Guinea Highlanders and the Kaulong) obtain most of their calories by farming. Obviously, different traditional peoples must face different dangers related to their different environments. For instance, drowning and being carried out to sea on an ice floe are risks for the Inuit of the Arctic coast but not for the !Kung of the Kalahari Desert, while being struck by a toppling tree and being bitten by a poisonous snake are risks for Aka Pygmies and the Ache but not for the Inuit. Falling into a collapsing underground cavern is a risk for the Kaulong but for none other of the seven tabulated groups, because only the Kaulong live in an environment with many thinly roofed sinkholes. Obviously too, Table 8.1 lumps together the differences between sexes and age classes within a society: accidents kill more men than women among the Ache, the !Kung, and many other peoples, not only because hunting animals by men poses more dangers than does plant gathering by women, but also because men tend to be more risk-seeking than are women. But Table 8.1 still suffices to suggest some conclusions.

Table 8.1. Causes of accidental death and injury

Ache (Paraguay)	1. Poisonous snakes. 2. Jaguars, lightning, getting lost. 3. Tree-fall, falling from tree, infected insect bites and thorn scratches, fire, drowning, exposure, cut by ax.
!Kung (Southern Africa)	1. Poisoned arrows. 2. Fire, large animals, poisonous snakes, falling from tree, infected thorn scratch, exposure. 3. Getting lost, lightning.
Aka Pygmies (Central Africa)	Falling from tree, tree-fall, large animals, poisonous snakes, drowning.
New Guinea Highlands	1. Fire, tree-fall, infected insect bites and thorn scratches. 2. Exposure, getting lost.
Fayu (New Guinea lowlands)	Scorpions and spiders, poisonous snakes, pigs and crocodiles, fire, drowning.
Kaulong (New Britain)	1. Tree-fall. 2. Falling from tree, drowning, cut by ax or knife, collapse of underground cavern.
Agta (Philippines)	Tree-fall, falling from tree, drowning, hunting and fishing accidents.

We note first that Table 8.1 makes no mention of the main causes of accidental death in modern Westernized societies: in descending sequence of death toll, we are killed by cars (Plate 44), alcohol, guns, surgery, and motorcycles, of which none except occasionally alcohol is a hazard for traditional peoples. One might wonder whether we have merely traded our old hazards of lions and tree-falls for our new hazards of cars and alcohol. But there are two other big differences between environmental hazards in modern societies and in traditional societies besides the particular hazards involved. One difference is that the cumulative risk of accidental death is probably lower for modern societies, because we exert far more control over our environment even though it does contain new hazards of our own manufacture such as cars. The other difference is that, thanks to modern medicine, the damage caused by our accidents is much more often repaired before it kills us or inflicts life-long incapacity. When I broke a tendon in my hand, a surgeon splinted my hand, which healed and regained full function within six months, but some New Guinea friends who experienced tendon and bone breaks ended up with no or improper healing and were crippled for life.

Those two differences are part of the reason why traditional people so willingly abandon their jungle lifestyle, admired in the abstract by Westerners, who don't have to live that lifestyle themselves. For instance, those differences help explain why so many Ache Indians give up the freedom of their lives as forest hunters and settle on reservations, degrading as that may seem to outsiders. Similarly, an American friend of mine traveled halfway around the world to meet a recently discovered band of New Guinea forest hunter-gatherers, only to discover that half of them had already chosen to move to an Indonesian village and put on T-shirts, because life there was safer and more comfortable. "Rice to eat, and no more mosquitoes!" was their short explanation.

As you read through the seven sets of entries of Table 8.1, you'll see some common themes of dangers that are serious for many or most traditional peoples, but that are rare or surprising for us moderns. Wild animals are indeed a major threat for traditional peoples (Plate 43). For example, jaguars cause 8% of deaths of adult Ache men. Lions, leopards, hyenas, elephants, buffalo, and crocodiles do kill Africans, but the animal that kills more Africans than any other is the hippopotamus. !Kung and African Pygmies are killed, bitten, scratched, and gored not just by big carnivores but also by antelope and other injured prey that they hunt. While we are horrified at the idea of !Kung hunters driving prides of lions from carcasses, the !Kung recognize that the most dangerous lion is in fact a lone beast too old, sick, or wounded to catch swift prey and reduced to attacking humans.

Poisonous snakes also rank high as a hazard for the tropical peoples of Table 8.1. They cause 14% of deaths of adult Ache men (i.e., more than jaguars), and even more loss of limbs. Almost every adult Yanomamo and Ache man has been bitten at least once. Ranked even more often as dangerous are trees, as a result both of trees or branches falling on people in the forest (remember my own experience that I described at the start of Chapter 7), and of people climbing a tree to hunt or to gather fruit or honey and falling out of the tree (Plate 42). Domestic fires for warmth are a bigger risk than bush fires, such that most New Guinea Highlanders and !Kung acquire burn scars from sleeping next to a fire as an adult or playing next to it as a baby.

Death from exposure to cold and/or wet weather is a danger outside the tropics, and at high altitudes in New Guinea and elsewhere in the tropics. Even for the Ache living in Paraguay near the Tropic of Capricorn, winter temperatures can drop below freezing, and an Ache caught out in the forest at night without a fire is at risk of dying. On one of New Guinea's highest mountains, while I was hiking well prepared and warmly dressed in freezing rain and gale-force winds at an altitude of 11,000 feet, I met a group of seven New Guinea schoolchildren who had foolishly set out that morning in clear weather, wearing shorts and T-shirts, to cross the mountain. By the time that I encountered them several hours later, they were shivering uncontrollably, stumbling, and barely able to speak. Local men with me, who shepherded them to a shelter, pointed out to me a nearby rock pile behind which a group of 23 men had sought shelter in bad weather in a previous year and had ended up dying there of exposure. Drowning and being struck by lightning are other environmental hazards for traditional as well as modern peoples.

The !Kung, New Guineans, Ache, and many other foraging peoples are legendary for their ability to follow tracks, read clues in the environment, and detect a barely indicated trail. Nevertheless, even they, and especially their children, occasionally make mistakes, get lost, and may be unable to find their way back to camp before nightfall, with fatal consequences. Friends of mine were involved in two such tragedies in New Guinea, one in which a boy walking with a group of adults wandered off and was never found despite exhaustive searches that same day and on the following days, the other in which an experienced strong man became lost on a mountain in the late afternoon, could not reach his village, and died of exposure in the forest at night.

Still other causes of accidents are our own weapons and tools. The arrows used by !Kung hunters are smeared with a potent poison, with the result that an accidental scratch by an arrow is the most serious cause of hunting accidents for the !Kung. Traditional people around the world accidentally cut themselves with their own knives and axes, as do modern cooks and woodsmen.

Less heroic and much commoner than lions or lightning as causes of accidental death or injury are humble insect bites and thorn scratches. In the humid tropics any bite or scratch—even one from a mere gnat, leech, louse, mosquito, or tick—is likely to become infected, and to develop if untreated into an incapacitating abscess. For example, once when I revisited a New Guinea friend named Delba with whom I had spent several weeks hiking through the forest two years previously, I was shocked to find him house-bound and unable to walk at all, as the result of a simple scratch that had become infected, and that then responded quickly to antibiotics that I carried but that New Guinea villagers don't have. Ants, bees, centipedes, scorpions, spiders, and wasps not only bite or scratch but also inject poisons that are sometimes fatal. Along with falling trees, stinging wasps and biting ants are the dangers that my New Guinea friends fear most in the forest. Some insects lay an egg under one's skin, from which hatches a larva that produces a huge and permanently disfiguring abscess.

While these causes of accidents in traditional societies are varied, they yield some generalizations. Serious consequences of accidents include not just death itself but also, even if one survives, the possibility of temporarily or permanently decreased physical effectiveness, resulting in impaired capacity to provide for one's children and other relatives, decreased resistance to diseases, crippling, and limb amputation. It's these "minor" consequences, not the risk of death, that make my New Guinea friends and me so afraid of ants, wasps, and infected thorn scratches. A poisonous snake bite that the victim survives may still cause gangrene and leave the victim paralyzed, maimed, or having lost the bitten arm or leg.

Just like the omnipresent risk of starvation to be discussed later in this chapter, environmental hazards influence people's behavior far more than one might guess from the number of deaths or injuries caused. In fact, the number of deaths may be low precisely because so much behavior is invested in combating the hazards. For instance, lions and other big carnivores account for only 5 out of 1,000 !Kung deaths, and this might mislead one to the erroneous conclusion that lions are not a big factor in !Kung life. In reality, that low death toll reflects the profound influence of lions on !Kung life. New Guineans, living in an environment without dangerous carnivores, hunt at night; the !Kung don't, both because it then becomes difficult to detect dangerous animals and their tracks, and because dangerous carnivores themselves are more active at night. !Kung women always go foraging in groups, constantly make noise and talk loudly to ensure that animals do not encounter them by surprise, look for tracks, and avoid running (because it incites a predator to attack). If a predator is seen in the vicinity, the !Kung may restrict their travel out of camp for a day or two.

Most accidents—those caused by animals, snakes, falling trees, falling out of a tree, bush fires, exposure, getting lost, drowning, insect bites, and thorn scratches—are associated with going out to forage for or to produce food. Most accidents could thus be avoided by staying home or in camp, but then one would acquire no food. Hence environmental dangers illustrate the modified Wayne Gretzky principle: If one takes no shots, then one will miss no shots but one is also guaranteed to score no goals. Traditional foragers and farmers, even more than Wayne Gretzky, must balance hazards against the overriding need for a steady stream of scores. Similarly, we modern city-dwellers could avoid the major hazard of urban life, car accidents, by staying home and not exposing ourselves to thousands of other drivers roaring unpredictably at 60 to 100 miles per hour along the freeways. But the jobs and shopping of most of us depend on driving. Wayne Gretzky would say: If no drives, then no pay check and no food.

Vigilance

How do traditional peoples respond to their reality of living lives always at danger from environmental hazards? Their responses include the constructive paranoia that I explained in Chapter 7, religious responses that I'll discuss in Chapter 9, and several other practices and attitudes.

The !Kung are constantly vigilant. While out foraging or walking through the bush, they watch and listen for animals and people, and they examine tracks in the sand to deduce what animal or person made the tracks, in which direction it was traveling, at what speed, how long ago, and whether or how they should modify their plans as a result. Even while in camp they must remain vigilant, despite the deterrence value of people and noise and fires, because animals sometimes enter camps, especially snakes. If the large poisonous snake known as the black mamba is seen in a camp, the !Kung are likely to abandon the camp rather than try to kill the snake. That might seem to us an overreaction, but the black mamba is one of Africa's most dangerous snakes because of its large size (up to eight feet), quick movements, long fangs, and potent neurotoxic venom; most bites are fatal.

In any dangerous environment, accumulated experience teaches rules of behavior to minimize the risks, rules worth following even if an outsider considers it overreacting. What Jane Goodale wrote about the outlook of the Kaulong people in the rainforests of New Britain could apply equally well to traditional peoples elsewhere, with just substitutions of the specific examples: "Prevention of accidents is important, and the knowledge of how, when, and under what circumstances any particular endeavor should or should not be undertaken is necessary to personal success and survival. Significantly, innovation in any technique or in behavior relating to the natural environment is considered to be extremely dangerous. There is a rather narrow range of correct behavior, beyond which there is the distinct and oft-stated danger of the sudden opening of the ground under one's feet, the falling of a tree as one walks underneath, or the sudden rise of flood waters while one is attempting to cross over the other bank. For example, I was told to stop skipping stones on the surface of our river ('a flood will come up'); not to play with fire ('the ground will open up,' or 'the fire will burn you, and not cook your food'); not to call the name of cave bats while hunting them ('the cave will collapse'); and many other 'don'ts' with similar sanctions carried out by the natural environment." The same attitude underlies the philosophy of life that a New Guinea friend summed up for me: "Everything happens for a reason, so one must be cautious."

A common Western reaction to danger that I have never, ever, encountered among experienced New Guineans is to be macho, to seek or enjoy dangerous situations, or to pretend to be unafraid and try to hide one's own fear. Marjorie Shostak noted the lack of those same Western macho attitudes among the !Kung: "Hunts are often dangerous. The !Kung face danger courageously, but they do not seek it out or take risks for the sake of proving their courage. Actively avoiding hazardous situations is considered prudent, not cowardly or unmasculine. Young boys, moreover, are not expected to conquer their fear and act like grown men. To unnecessary risks, the !Kung say, 'But a person could die!' "

Shostak went on to describe how a 12-year-old !Kung boy named Kashe and his cousin and his father recounted a successful hunt in which the father had speared a large gemsbok, an antelope that defended itself with long razor-sharp horns. When Shostak asked Kashe whether he was helping his father with the kill, Kashe laughed and proudly answered, "No, I was up in a tree!" "His smile became an easy laugh. Puzzled, I asked again, and he repeated that he and his cousin had climbed a tree as soon as the animal had stopped running and had stood its ground. I teased him, saying everyone would have gone hungry if the animal had been left to him and his cousin. He laughed again and said, 'Yes, but we were so scared!' There was no hint of embarrassment or of a need to explain what might have been seen, in our culture, as behavior lacking in courage. . . . There would be plenty of time for him to learn to face dangerous animals and to kill them, and there was no doubt in his mind (or his father's, to judge from the expression on *his* face), that he would, one day. When I questioned the father, he beamed, 'Up in the tree? Of course. They're only children. They could have gotten hurt.' "

New Guineans, !Kung, and other traditional peoples relate to each other long stories of dangers encountered, not only for entertainment in the absence of television and books, but also for their educational value. Kim Hill and A. Magdalena Hurtado give some examples from Ache campfire conversations: "Stories of accidental death are sometimes told in the evening when band members relate the day's events to things that happened in the past. Children are fascinated by these stories and probably learn invaluable lessons about the dangers of the forest, which aid in their own survival. One boy died when he forgot to pinch the head of a palm larva before swallowing it. The jaws of the larva clamped onto his throat and he choked to death. Several times an adolescent boy strayed too far from the adult men while hunting and was either never seen again or found dead several days later. One hunter who was digging an armadillo burrow fell into the hole head first and suffocated. Another fell out of a tree almost 40 m [meters] to his death while he was trying to recover an arrow that he had shot at a monkey. One small girl fell into a hole left by a bottle tree that had rotted away and broke her neck. Several men were attacked by jaguars. Some of their remains were found and others simply vanished. A boy was bitten on the head by a poisonous snake in the camp at night while he slept. He died the next day. One old woman was killed by a falling tree chopped by an adolescent girl for firewood. Henceforth the girl became known as 'Falling Firewood,' a nickname that reminded her daily of her misdeed. One man was bitten by a coati and later died of the wound. In a similar incident a hunter was bitten on the wrist in 1985. His main arteries and veins were punctured and he certainly would have died if he had not received modern medical attention. A small girl fell in a river while crossing on a log bridge and was swept away. . . . Finally, in an event that seems a stroke of truly random bad luck, six people in one band were killed when a lightning bolt struck the camp during a storm."

Human violence

Traditional societies exhibit much variation in their frequency and forms of death by human violence, which usually ranks as either the leading or (after illness) the second-leading cause of death. A significant factor underlying this variation is the degree of state or outside interference in suppressing or discouraging violence. Types of violence can be somewhat arbitrarily dichotomized into either war (discussed in Chapters 3 and 4) or homicide, where war in its clearest form is defined as collective fighting between different groups, while homicide is defined as killings of individuals within a group. However, this dichotomy becomes blurred when one has to decide whether killings between neighboring groups usually on friendly terms should be counted as in-group homicide or out-group war. Further ambiguities involve which types of killings to count: for instance, published tabulations of Ache violence include infanticide and senilicide, but published !Kung tabulations don't, and different authors hold different opinions about the frequency of infanticide among the !Kung. The choice of victims, and the relation between the victim and the killer, also vary greatly among societies. For example, Ache victims of violence were mainly infants and children, while !Kung victims were mainly adult men.

!Kung studies of violence are instructive for several reasons. Initial accounts of the !Kung by anthropologists described them as peaceful and non-violent, so much so that a popular book published in 1959, early in the history of modern !Kung studies, was entitled *The Harmless People*. During three years of residence among the !Kung in the 1960s, Richard Lee observed 34 fights leading to blows but no killings, and informants told

him that there actually were no killings during those years. Only after Lee
had been in the area for 14 months and come to know his informants better were they willing to talk to him about past killings. When they did
start talking, by cross-checking accounts of different informants Lee was
able to assemble a reliable list of names and sex and age of killers and
victims, the relation between killer and victim, and the circumstances,
motive, season, time of day, and weapons used for 22 killings between 1920
and 1969. That list did not count cases of infanticide and senilicide, which
Lee believed to be rare, but Nancy Howell's interviews of !Kung women
suggest that infanticide did occur. Lee concluded that those 22 cases represented the total number of deaths by violence in his study area between
1920 and 1969.

All 22 of those !Kung killings should surely be considered homicides
rather than wars. In some cases the victim and the killer were within the
same camp, while in other cases they were in different camps, but no killing involved a group of people from one camp seeking to kill a group of
people from another camp (i.e., "war"). In fact, there was no reported
event at all suggestive of a war among the !Kung in Lee's area during the
period 1920–1969. But the !Kung did say that they used to have raiding
expeditions, apparently similar to the witnessed "wars" of other traditional peoples, during the generation of the grandparents of the oldest
living !Kung—i.e., before Tswana herders began making annual visits to
the !Kung and trading with them in the 19th century. We saw in Chapter
4 that visits of traders to the Inuit also had the effect of suppressing Inuit
war, even though neither the traders with the Inuit nor those with the
!Kung purposely suppressed war. Instead, the Inuit themselves abandoned
war in their own self-interest in order to have more opportunities to profit
from trade, and the !Kung may have done the same.

As for the rate of !Kung homicide, 22 killings over the course of 49
years works out to less than 1 homicide every 2 years. That sounds utterly
trivial to readers of urban American newspapers, who can open the newspaper on any randomly chosen day and read about all the murders committed in their city within the last 24 hours. The main explanation for this
difference is of course that the base population within which murders can
occur is millions of people for an American city, but only about 1,500
people for the !Kung population surveyed by Lee. Referred to that base

population, the homicide *rate* for the !Kung works out to 29 homicides per 100,000 person-years, which is triple the homicide rate for the United States and 10 to 30 times the rates for Canada, Britain, France, and Germany. One might object that the United States calculation excludes violent deaths in war, which would yield a higher rate for the United States. However, the !Kung rate also doesn't include deaths in !Kung "wars" (i.e., their raiding expeditions that ended over a century ago), whose number is completely unknown for the !Kung but is known to be high for many other traditional peoples.

The figure of 22 !Kung homicides in 49 years is instructive for another reason as well. One homicide every 27 months means that, for an anthropologist carrying out a field study of a people lasting one year, the odds are against any homicide occurring during that period, and the anthropologist would consider the people as peaceful. Even if the anthropologist were resident there for five years, a period long enough for a killing to be likely to occur given !Kung homicide rates, the killing would be very unlikely to take place under the eyes of the anthropologist, whose assessment of the frequency of violence would depend on whether his informants chose to tell him about it. Similarly, although the United States ranks as the most homicidal society in the First World, I have never personally witnessed a homicide, and I have heard only a few first-hand accounts of homicides within my circle of acquaintances. Nancy Howell's calculations suggest that violence was the second-leading cause of !Kung death, behind infectious and parasitic diseases, but ahead of degenerative diseases and accidents.

It is also instructive to consider why violent deaths ended recently among the !Kung. The last homicide reported to Lee occurred in the spring of 1955, when two !Kung men killed a third !Kung man. The two killers were arrested by the police, put on trial, and jailed, and did not return to their home area. This event occurred only three years after the first instance in which the police intervened to jail a !Kung killer. From 1955 until Lee published his analysis in 1979, there was no further homicide in his study area. This course of events illustrates the role of control by a strong state government in reducing violence. That same role also becomes obvious from central facts of the colonial and post-colonial history of New Guinea in the last 50 years: namely, the steep decrease in violence following establishment of Australian and Indonesian control of remote areas of eastern and western New Guinea respectively, previously without state government; the continued low level of violence in Indonesian New Guinea under maintained rigorous government control there; and the eventual resurgence of violence in Papua New Guinea after Australian colonial government gradually yielded to less rigorous independent government. That tendency for violence to decrease under state government control does not deny the fact that traditional societies have non-violent means of resolving most of their disputes successfully before the disputes become violent (Chapter 2).

Details of the 22 !Kung homicides were as follows. All of the killers, and 19 of the 22 victims, were adult men aged 20 to 55; only 3 of the victims were women. In all cases the !Kung killer knew the victim, who was a distant relative; the !Kung lacked completely the killings of strangers common in the United States in the course of robberies or road rage. All killings took place publicly in camps, in the presence of other people. Only 5 of the 22 !Kung killings were premeditated. For example, in one dramatic case around 1948, a notorious and possibly psychotic killer named /Twi, who had already killed two men, was ambushed and shot with a poisoned arrow by a man named /Xashe. The wounded /Twi still managed to stab a woman named //Kushe in the mouth with a spear and shot //Kushe's husband N!eishi in the back with a poisoned arrow, before many gathered people shot poisoned arrows at /Twi until he looked like a porcupine, then stabbed his dead body with spears. The other 17 !Kung killings, however, unfolded during spontaneous fights. For instance, a fight broke out at N≠wama when one man refused to let another man marry the younger sister of the first man's wife. In the resulting big argument that exploded, the husband shot an arrow at his sister-in-law; the sister-in-law's suitor and his father and brother, and the husband and his allies, shot arrows and spears at each other; and, amidst several parallel fights, the suitor's father was mortally wounded by a poisoned arrow in the thigh plus a spear in the ribs.

Most of the !Kung killings (15 out of 22) were parts of feuds in which one killing led to another and then to yet another over the course of up to 24 years; such cycles of retaliatory killings also characterize traditional war (Chapters 3 and 4). Among motives for !Kung killings other than that one of revenge for a previous killing, adultery is the one most often mentioned. For example, a husband whose wife had slept with another man attacked and wounded the adulterer, who then managed to kill the husband. Another cuckolded husband stabbed and killed his wife with a poisoned arrow, then fled the area and never returned.

As for other small-scale societies, some are less violent than the !Kung (e.g., Aka Pygmies, the Siriono), while others are or were more violent (e.g., the Ache, Yanomamo, Greenland and Iceland Norse). During the time that the Ache were still living in the forest as hunter-gatherers before 1971, violence was the commonest cause of death, exceeding even diseases. More than half of Ache violent deaths were at the hands of non-Ache Paraguayans, but killings of Ache by other Ache still accounted for 22% of Ache deaths. In marked contrast to the pattern of !Kung violence directed exclusively against adult !Kung, most (81%) of Ache homicide victims were children or infants—e.g., children (predominantly girls) killed to accompany a dead adult into the grave, children who were killed or who died of neglect after the death or desertion of their father, or infants killed because they were born separated by only a short birth interval from their next older sibling. Also in contrast to the !Kung, the commonest form of in-group killings of adult Ache was not a spontaneous fight with whatever weapons happened to be at hand, but instead a ritualized and pre-planned fight with clubs specially made for the occasion. As is true for the !Kung, state intervention has greatly decreased levels of violence among the Ache: since they began increasingly living on reservations after 1977 and came under the direct or indirect influence of the Paraguayan state, killings of adult Ache by other Ache have ceased, and Ache killings of their children and infants have decreased.

How do people in traditional societies without state government and police protect themselves against the constant danger of violence? A large part of the answer is that they adopt many forms of constructive paranoia. One widespread rule is to beware of strangers: routinely to attempt to kill or drive off a stranger detected on your territory, because the stranger may have come to scout out your territory or to kill a member of your tribe. Another rule is to beware of the possibility of treachery by supposed allies, or (conversely) to practise pre-emptive treachery against potentially fickle allies. For instance, a tactic of Yanomamo warfare is to invite people of a neighboring village to come to a feast at one's own village, and then to kill them when they have set down their weapons and are eating. Don Richardson reports that the Sawi people of southwestern New Guinea honor treachery as an ideal: better than killing an enemy outright is to convince an enemy of your friendship, to invite the enemy many times over the course of months to visit you and partake of your food, and then to watch his terror when you declare, just before killing him, "Tuwi asonai makaerin!" (We have been fattening you with friendship for the slaughter!)

Still another tactic to reduce the risk of attack is that the locations of villages are commonly chosen for the purpose of defense or maintaining a good view over the surroundings. For instance, New Guinea mountain villages are typically located on hilltops, and many late-phase Anasazi settlements in the southwestern United States were in sites accessible only by a ladder that could be pulled up to cut off the entrance. While these locations oblige the inhabitants to carry water for long distances uphill from the river in the valley bottom below, that effort is considered preferable to the risk of being surprised by an attack at a riverside valley location. As population density or as fighting increases, people tend to shift from living in dispersed unprotected huts to aggregating for defense in large palisaded villages.

Groups protect themselves by building a network of alliances with other groups, and individuals ally themselves with other individuals. A function of the constant talking that has struck me in New Guinea, and that has struck other visitors to other traditional societies, is to learn as much as possible about each individual in one's universe of contact, and to monitor people's activities constantly. Especially good sources of information are women who were born into one's own group, and who were then sent in marriage to another group, in the common traditional living pattern termed patrilocal residence (i.e., brides moving to join their husband's group, rather than new husbands moving to join their wife's group). Such married women often warn their blood relatives in their natal society that their husbands and other relatives by marriage are planning an attack. Finally, just as endless evening campfire conversations about accidents serve not just to entertain but also to educate children (and everyone else) about environmental risks, endless conversations about raids and people alert listeners to dangers arising from people, as well as providing gripping entertainment.

Diseases

Depending on the particular traditional society, diseases collectively rank as either the leading danger to human life (e.g., among the Agta and !Kung, where they accounted respectively for an estimated 50%–86% and 70%–80% of all deaths) or as the second most important danger after violence (e.g., among the Ache, among whom "only" one-quarter of deaths under conditions of forest life were due to illness). It must be added, though, that malnourished people become more susceptible to infection, and that food shortage is thus a contributing factor to many deaths whose cause is recorded as infectious disease.

Among diseases, the relative importance of different categories of disease for traditional peoples varies greatly with lifestyle, geographic location, and age. In general, infectious diseases are most important among infants and young children and remain important at all ages. Parasitic diseases join infectious diseases in importance in childhood. Diseases associated with worm parasites (such as hookworm and tapeworm) and insect-born protozoan parasites (such as malaria and the agent causing sleeping sickness) are more of a problem for peoples of warm tropical climates than for peoples of the Arctic, deserts, and cold mountaintops, where the worms themselves and the protozoa's insect vectors have difficulty surviving in the environment. Later in life, degenerative diseases of bones, joints, and soft tissue—such as arthritis, osteoarthritis, osteoporosis, bone fractures, and tooth wear—rise in importance. The much more physically demanding lifestyle of traditional peoples than of modern couch potatoes makes the former more susceptible than the latter to such degenerative diseases at a given age. Conspicuously rare or absent among traditional peoples are all of the diseases responsible for most deaths in the First World today: coronary artery disease and other forms of atherosclerosis, stroke and other consequences of hypertension, adult-onset diabetes, and most cancers. I shall discuss the reasons for this striking difference between First World and traditional health patterns in Chapter 11.

Only within the last two centuries have infectious diseases receded in importance in the First World as causes of human death. The reasons for those recent changes include appreciation of the importance of sanitation; the installation of clean water supplies by state governments, the introduction of vaccination, and other public health measures; the growth of scientific knowledge of microbes as the agents of infectious disease, permitting rational design of effective counter-measures; and the discovery and design of antibiotics. Poor hygiene permitted (and still permits today) the transmission of infectious and parasitic diseases among traditional peoples, who often use the same water supply for drinking, cooking, bathing, and washing, defecate nearby, and do not understand the value of washing one's hands before handling food.

Just to mention an example of hygiene and disease that impressed me personally, on a trip to Indonesia during which I spent most of each day bird-watching alone on forest trails radiating from a campsite shared with Indonesian colleagues, I was disconcerted to discover that I was experiencing sudden attacks of diarrhea at an hour varying unpredictably from day to day. I racked my brain to figure out what I was doing wrong, and what could account for the variation of the attacks' timing. Finally, I made the connection. Each day, a wonderfully kind Indonesian colleague, who felt responsible for my well-being, came out from camp and followed my trail of that day until he encountered me, to make sure that I hadn't had an accident or gotten lost. He handed me some biscuits that he had thoughtfully brought from camp as a snack, chatted with me for a few minutes to satisfy himself that all was well with me, and returned to camp. One evening, I suddenly realized that my diarrhea attack each day began about half an hour after my kind friend had met me and I had eaten his biscuits on that day: if he met me at 10:00 A.M., my attack came at 10:30, and if he met me at 2:30 P.M., it came at 3:00 P.M. From the next day onwards, I thanked him for his biscuits, disposed of them inconspicuously after he had turned back, and never had any more attacks. The problem had originated with my friend's handling of the biscuits rather than with the biscuits themselves, of which we kept a supply in their original cellophane packets at our camp, and which never made me ill when I opened the packet myself. Instead, the cause of the attacks must have been intestinal pathogens transmitted from my friend's fingers to the biscuits.

The prevalent types of infectious diseases differ strikingly between small populations of nomadic hunter-gatherers and family-level farming societies on the one hand, and large populations of modern and recently Westernized societies plus traditional densely populated Old World farming societies on the other hand. Characteristic diseases of hunter-gatherers are malaria and other arthropod-transmitted fevers, dysentery and other gastrointestinal diseases, respiratory diseases, and skin infections. Lacking among hunter-gatherers, unless they have been recently infected by Western visitors, are the feared infectious diseases of settled populations: diphtheria, flu, measles, mumps, pertussis, rubella, smallpox, and typhoid. Unlike the infectious diseases of hunter-gatherers, which are present chronically or else flare up and down, those diseases of dense populations run in acute epidemics: many people in an area become sick within a short time and quickly either recover or die, then the disease vanishes locally for a year or more.

The reasons why those epidemic diseases could arise and maintain themselves only in large human populations have emerged from epidemiological and microbiological studies of recent decades. Those reasons are that the diseases are efficiently transmitted, have an acute course, confer lifetime immunity on victims who survive, and are confined to the human species. The diseases become transmitted efficiently from a sick person to nearby healthy people by microbes that a patient excretes onto his skin from oozing pustules, that a patient ejects into the air by coughing and sneezing, or that enter nearby water bodies when a patient defecates. Healthy people become infected by touching a patient or an object handled by the patient, breathing in the patient's exhaled breath, or drinking contaminated water. The disease's acute course means that, within a few weeks of infection, a patient either dies or recovers. The combination of efficient transmission and acute course means that, within a short time, everybody in a local population has become exposed to the disease and is now either dead or recovered. The lifetime immunity acquired by survivors means that there is no one else alive in the population who could contract the disease until some future year, when a new crop of unexposed babies has been born. Confinement of the disease to humans means that there is no animal or soil reservoir in which the disease could maintain itself: it dies out locally and cannot come back until an infection spreads again from a distant source. All of those features in combination mean that these infectious diseases are restricted to large human populations, sufficiently numerous that the disease can sustain itself within the population by moving constantly from one area to another, locally dying out but still surviving in a more distant part of the population. For measles the minimum necessary population size is known to be a few hundred thousand people. Hence the diseases can be summarized as "acute immunizing crowd epidemic infectious diseases of humans"—or, for short, crowd diseases.

The crowd diseases could not have existed before the origins of agriculture around 11,000 years ago. Only with the explosive population growth made possible by agriculture did human populations reach the high numbers required to sustain our crowd diseases. The adoption of agriculture enabled formerly nomadic hunter-gatherers to settle down in crowded and unsanitary permanent villages, connected by trade with other villages, and providing ideal conditions for the rapid transmission of microbes. Recent studies by molecular biologists have demonstrated that the microbes responsible for many and probably most of the crowd diseases now confined to humans arose from crowd diseases of our domestic animals such as pigs and cattle, with which we came into regular close contact ideal for animal-to-human microbe transfer only upon the beginnings of animal domestication around 11,000 years ago.

Of course, the absence of crowd diseases from small populations of hunter-gatherers does not mean that hunter-gatherers are free from infectious diseases. They do have infectious diseases, but their diseases are different from the crowd diseases in four respects. First, the microbes causing their diseases are not confined to the human species but are shared with animals (such as the agent of yellow fever, shared with monkeys) or else capable of surviving in soil (such as the agents causing botulism and tetanus). Second, many of the diseases are not acute but chronic, such as leprosy and yaws. Third, some of the diseases are transmitted inefficiently between people, leprosy and yaws again being examples. Finally, most of the diseases do not confer permanent immunity: a person who has recovered from one bout of a disease can contract the same disease again. These four facts mean that these diseases can maintain themselves in small human populations, infecting and re-infecting victims from animal and soil reservoirs and from chronically sick people.

Hunter-gatherers and small farming populations are not immune to crowd diseases; they are merely unable to maintain crowd diseases by themselves. In fact, small populations are, tragically, especially susceptible to crowd diseases when they become infected by a visitor from the outside world. Their enhanced susceptibility is due to the fact that at least some of the crowd diseases tend to have higher fatality rates in adults than in children. In dense urban First World populations everyone (until recently) became exposed to measles as a child, but in a small isolated population of hunter-gatherers the adults have not been exposed to measles and are likely to die of it if it arrives. There are many horror stories of Inuit, Native American, and Aboriginal Australian populations being virtually wiped out by epidemic diseases introduced through European contact.

Responses to diseases

For traditional societies, diseases differ from the other three major types of dangers as regards people's understanding of the underlying mechanisms, and hence of effective cures or preventive measures. When someone is injured or dies from an accident, violence, or hunger, the cause and underlying process are clear: the victim was hit by a falling tree, struck by an enemy's arrow, or starved by insufficient food. The appropriate cure or preventive measure is equally clear: don't sleep under dead trees, watch out for enemies or kill them first, and ensure a reliable food supply. However, in the case of diseases, sound empirical understanding of causes, and science-based preventive measures and cures, achieved notable success only within the last two centuries. Until then, state societies as well as traditional small-scale societies suffered heavy tolls from disease.

This is not to say that traditional peoples have been completely helpless at preventing or curing diseases. The Siriono evidently understand that there is a connection between human feces and diseases such as dysentery and hookworm. A Siriono mother promptly cleans up her infant's feces when it defecates, stores the feces in a basket, and eventually dumps the basket's contents far away in the forest. But even the Siriono are not rigorous in their hygiene. Anthropologist Allan Holmberg relates watching a Siriono infant unobserved by his mother defecate, lie in his feces, smear them over himself, and put them into his mouth. When his mother finally noticed what was going on, she put her finger into the baby's mouth, removed the feces, wiped but didn't bathe the filthy baby, and resumed eating herself without washing her hands. Piraha Indians let their dogs eat off the plates from which they themselves are simultaneously eating: that's a good way to acquire canine germs and parasites.

By trial and error, many traditional peoples identify local plants which they believe help cure particular ailments. My New Guinea friends frequently point out to me certain plants which they say that they use to treat malaria, other fevers, or dysentery or to induce miscarriage. Western ethnobotanists have studied this traditional pharmacological knowledge, and Western pharmaceutical companies have extracted drugs from these plants. Nevertheless, the overall effectiveness of traditional medical knowledge, interesting as it is, tends to be limited. Malaria is still one of the commonest causes of illness and death in New Guinea's lowlands and hills. It was only when scientists established that malaria is caused by a protozoan of genus *Plasmodium* transmitted by mosquitoes of genus *Anopheles,* and that it can be cured by various drugs, that the percentage of New Guinea lowlanders suffering malaria attacks could be reduced from around 50% to below 1%.

Views of disease causes, and resulting attempted preventive measures and cures, differ among traditional peoples. Some but not all peoples have specialized healers, termed "shamans" by Westerners, and given specific epithets by the people involved. The !Kung and the Ache often view illness fatalistically, as something that is due to chance and can't be helped. In other cases the Ache offer biological explanations: e.g., that fatal intestinal illnesses of children are due to weaning and eating solid food, and that fevers are caused by eating bad meat, too much honey, honey unmixed with water, too many insect larvae, or other dangerous foods, or by exposure to human blood. Each of these explanations may sometimes be correct, but they don't serve to protect the Ache from a high death rate from disease. The Daribi, Fayu, Kaulong, Yanomamo, and many other peoples blame some illnesses on a curse, magic, or a sorcerer, to be countered by raiding, killing, or paying the responsible sorcerer. The Dani, Daribi, and !Kung attribute other illnesses to ghosts or spirits, with whom !Kung healers attempt to mediate by going into a trance. The Kaulong, Siriono, and many other peoples seek moral and religious explanations for illnesses: i.e., the victim brought the illness on himself by an oversight, committing an offense against nature, or violating a taboo. For instance, the Kaulong attribute respiratory illnesses of men to pollution by women, when a man has made the dangerous mistake of coming into contact with an object polluted by a woman menstruating or giving birth, or when a man has walked under any fallen tree or bridge or has drunk from a river (because a woman might have walked on the tree, over the bridge, or through the river). Before we Westerners look down on those Kaulong theories of male respiratory disease, we should reflect on the frequency with which our own cancer victims seek to identify their moral responsibility or the cause for their cancer, whose specific cause is as obscure to us as is the cause of male respiratory illness to the Kaulong.

Starvation

In February 1913, as the British explorer A. F. R. Wollaston was descending in good spirits through New Guinea montane forests after having succeeded in reaching the snow line on New Guinea's highest mountain, he was horrified to find two recently dead bodies in his path. Over the next two days, which he described as among the most awful of his life, he encountered over 30 more bodies of New Guinea mountain people, mostly women and children, singly or in groups of up to five, lying in rough shelters along the track. One group consisting of a dead woman and two dead children included a still-living small girl about three years old, whom he carried to his camp and fed with milk but who died within a few hours. Into camp came another group of a man, a woman, and two children, of whom all except one of the children expired. The whole group, already chronically malnourished, had exhausted their supplies of sweet potatoes and pigs and found no wild food to eat in the forest except the hearts of some palm trees, and the weaker ones apparently died of starvation.

Compared to accidents, violence, and disease, which are frequently recognized and mentioned as causes of death in traditional societies, death due to starvation as witnessed by Wollaston receives much less mention. When it does occur, it is likely to involve mass deaths, because people in small-scale societies share food, so that either no one starves or else many people do simultaneously. But starvation is greatly underappreciated as a contributing cause of death. Under most circumstances, when people become seriously malnourished, something else occurs to kill them before they die purely of starvation and nothing else. Their body resistance fails, they become susceptible to illness, and they are recorded as dying of a disease from which a healthy person would have recovered. As they become physically weak, they become more prone to accidents such as falling from a tree or drowning, or to being killed by healthy enemies. The pre-occupation of small-scale societies with food, and the diverse and elaborate measures to which they resort to ensure their food supply and which I shall explain in the following pages, testify to their omnipresent concern with starvation as a major risk of traditional life.

Furthermore, food shortage takes the form not only of starvation in the sense of insufficient calories, but also shortages of specific vitamins (causing diseases such as beriberi, pellagra, pernicious anemia, rickets, and scurvy), specific minerals (causing endemic goiter and iron-deficiency anemia), and protein (causing kwashiorkor). Those specific deficiency diseases are more frequent among farmers than among hunter-gatherers, whose diets tend to be more varied than those of farmers. Like calorie starvation, specific deficiency diseases are likely to contribute to someone being recorded as dying of an accident, violence, or infectious disease before the person dies of the deficiency disease alone.

Starvation is a risk that affluent First World citizens don't even think about, because our access to food remains the same, day after day, from season to season, and year after year. Of course, we have some particular foods that are seasonal and available for just a few weeks a year, such as freshly harvested local cherries, but the total available amount of food is essentially constant. For small-scale societies, however, there are unpredictably good or bad days, some season each year when food is predictably short and to which people look forward with foreboding, and unpredictably good or bad years. As a result, food is a major and almost constant subject of conversation. I was initially surprised that my Fore friends spent so much time talking about sweet potatoes, even after they had just eaten to satiation. For the Siriono Indians of Bolivia, the overwhelming preoccupation is with food, such that two of the commonest Siriono expressions are "My stomach is empty" and "Give me some food." The significance of sex and food is reversed between the Siriono and us Westerners: the Sirionos' strongest anxieties are about food, they have sex virtually whenever they want, and sex compensates for food hunger, while our strongest anxieties are about sex, we have food virtually whenever we want, and eating compensates for sexual frustration.

Unlike us, many traditional societies, especially ones in arid or Arctic environments, face frequent predictable and unpredictable food shortages, and their risk of famine is far higher than ours. The reasons for this difference are clear. Many traditional societies have few or no stored food surpluses on which to fall back, either because they can't produce surpluses to store, or because a hot wet climate would cause food to spoil quickly, or because their lifestyle is nomadic. Those groups that actually could store surplus food risk losing it to raiders. Traditional societies are threatened by local food failures because they can integrate food resources only over a small area, whereas we First World citizens ship food over our whole country and import it from the most distant countries. Without our motorized vehicles, roads, railroads, and ships, traditional societies can't transport food long distances and can acquire it only from near neighbors. Traditional societies lack our state governments that organize food storage, transport, and exchange over large areas. Nevertheless, we shall see that traditional societies have many other ways of coping with the risk of famine.

Unpredictable food shortages

The shortest time scale and smallest spatial scale of variation in tribal food supply involve day-to-day variation in individual hunting success. Plants don't move around and can be gathered more or less predictably from one day to the next, but animals do move, so that any individual hunter risks bagging no animal on any given day. The solution to that uncertainty adopted almost universally by hunter-gatherers is to live in bands including several hunters who pool their catch to average out the large day-to-day fluctuations in catch for each individual hunter. Richard Lee described that solution from his own experience with the !Kung of Africa's Kalahari Desert, but he was also generalizing for hunter-gatherers of all continents and all environments when he wrote: "Food is never consumed alone by a family; it is always (actually or potentially) shared out with members of a living group or band of up to 30 (or more) members. Even though only a fraction of the able-bodied foragers go out each day, the day's returns of meat and gathered foods are divided in such a way that every member of the camp receives an equitable share. The hunting band or camp is a unit of sharing." His principle of pooling and averaging among hunter-gatherers also applies to many small-scale herding and farming societies, such as the Sudan's Nuer people studied by E. E. Evans-Pritchard, who share meat, milk, fish, grain, and beer: "Although a household owns its own food, does its own cooking, and provides independently for the needs of its members, men, and much less, women and children, eat in one another's homes to such an extent that, looked at from outside, the whole community is seen to be partaking of a joint supply. Rules of hospitality and conventions about the division of meat and fish lead to a far wider sharing of food than a bare statement of the principles of ownership would suggest."

The next longer and larger scale of variation in food supply involves unpredictable variation in food availability affecting a whole local group. A spell of cold wet weather lasting a few days makes it unrewarding and dangerous for Ache Indians to go out hunting, and leaves them not only hungry but also at risk of cold exposure and respiratory infections. Ripening of the local crop of plantains and peach palm fruits, which are staple plant foods for Yanomamo Indians, occurs unpredictably: there is either none to eat, or else a local superabundance. The millet crop of the Nuer may be ruined by drought, elephants, heavy rain, locusts, or weaverbirds. Severe droughts that cause famine afflict !Kung hunter-gatherers unpredictably in about one out of four years, and are uncommon but feared among Trobriand Island farmers. Frosts kill the staple sweet potato crop in about 1 out of 10 years among New Guinea Highland farmers at high elevation. Destructive cyclones strike the Solomon Islands at irregular intervals of one to several decades.

Small-scale societies attempt to cope with these unpredictable local food failures in several ways that include shifting camp, storing food in their own bodies, agreements between different local groups, and scattering land for food production. The simplest solution for nomadic hunter-gatherers not tied to fixed gardens, and faced with local food scarcity, is to move to another location where food availability is at the moment higher. As for fattening up whenever possible, if problems of food rotting or of enemy raiders prevent you from storing food in a larder or container, you can at least store it as your own body fat, which won't rot and can't be stolen. In Chapter 11 I'll give examples of small-scale societies that gorge, when food is abundant, to a degree unbelievable to Westerners, except for those few of us who have competed in hot-dog-eating contests. People thereby fatten themselves and become better able to survive subsequent times of food scarcity.

While gorging may help you carry yourself through a few weeks of food scarcity, it won't protect you against a year of starvation. One long-term solution is to make reciprocal agreements with neighboring groups about sharing food when one group's area has enough food and another group's area is suffering from a food shortage. Local food availability fluctuates with time in any area. But two areas located a sufficient distance apart are likely to have fluctuations in food availability that are out of phase. That opens the door for your group to reach a mutually advantageous agreement with another group, such that they allow you onto their land or send you food when they have enough food but you don't, and your group returns the favor when it's the other group that's short of food.

For example, in the area of the Kalahari Desert occupied by the !Kung San, rainfall in a given month varies by up to a factor of 10 between different sites. The result, in Richard Lee's words, is that "the desert may be blooming in one area and a few hours' walk away, the land may still be parched." As one example, Lee compared monthly rainfall at five sites in the Ghanzi district for 12 months from July 1966 to June 1967. The total rainfall for the year varied by less than a factor of 2 between sites, but rainfall in a given month varied among sites from no rainfall at all to 10 inches. The site of Cume had the highest annual rainfall but was nevertheless the driest of the five sites in May 1967 and the second driest in November 1966 and February 1967. Conversely, Kalkfontein had the lowest annual rainfall, but it was the second-wettest site in March 1967 and again in May 1967. Hence for any site, a group confined to that site would be certain to experience droughts and food shortages at certain times, but could usually find some other group whose site was wet and flourishing—provided that the two groups had agreed to help each other in times of need. In fact, such generalized reciprocity is essential to the !Kung's ability to survive in their locally unpredictable desert environment.

Reciprocity (punctuated occasionally by hostility) is widespread among traditional societies. Trobriand Island villages distribute food between villages to even out local food shortages. Among the Iñupiat of northern Alaska, individual families in times of local famine moved to live with relatives or partners in another district. The most important fruits consumed by South America's Yanomamo Indians come from groves of peach palm trees and plantain trees, both of which (especially the former) produce harvests more abundant than a local group can consume by itself. The fruits spoil after ripening and cannot be stored, so they have to be eaten while ripe. When a local group finds itself with a surplus, it invites neighbors to come for a feast, in the expectation that those neighbors will reciprocate when they in turn produce a food surplus.

Scatter your land

The other common long-term solution to the unpredictable risk of a local food shortage is to scatter your land-holdings. I encountered this phenomenon in New Guinea when, while out bird-watching one day, I stumbled across a New Guinea friend's garden clearing in the middle of forest a mile northeast of his village, and several miles from his other gardens scattered to the south and west of his village. What on earth did he have in mind, I asked myself, when he chose that isolated location for his new garden? It seemed so inefficient to commit himself to a waste of travel time, and the garden's remoteness made it hard to protect from marauding pigs and thieves. But New Guineans are smart and experienced gardeners. If you see them doing something that you initially don't understand, there usually turns out to be a reason. What was his motive?

Other Western scholars and development experts have been equally puzzled by other cases of field scattering elsewhere in the world. The example most often discussed involves medieval English peasants, who tilled dozens of tiny scattered plots. To modern economic historians, that was "obviously" a bad idea because of the resulting wasted travel and transport time and inevitable unplowed strips between plots. A similar modern case of field scattering by Andean peasant farmers near Lake Titicaca, studied by Carol Goland, provoked development experts to write in exasperation, "The peasants' cumulative agricultural efficiency is so appalling . . . that our amazement is how these people even survive at all. . . . Because inheritance and marriage traditions continually fragment and scatter a peasant's fields over numerous villages, the average peasant spends three-quarters of his day walking between fields that sometimes measure less than a few square feet." The experts proposed land-swapping among farmers in order to consolidate their holdings.

But Goland's quantitative study in the Peruvian Andes showed that there really is method to such apparent madness. In the Cuyo Cuyo district, the peasant farmers whom Goland studied grow potatoes and other crops in scattered fields: on the average 17 fields, up to a maximum of 26 fields, per farmer, each field with an average size of only 50 by 50 feet. Because the farmers occasionally rent or buy fields, it would be perfectly possible for them in that way to consolidate their holdings, but they don't. Why not?

A clue noticed by Goland was the variation in crop yield from field to field, and from year to year. Only a small part of that variation is predictable from the environmental factors of field elevation, slope, and exposure, and from work-related factors under the peasants' control (such as their effort in fertilizing and weeding the field, seed density, and planting date). Most of that variation is instead unpredictable, uncontrollable, and somehow related to the local amount and timing of rain for that year, frosts, crop diseases, pests, and theft by people. In any given year there are big differences between yields of different fields, but a peasant can't predict which particular field is going to produce well in any particular year.

What a Cuyo Cuyo peasant family has to do at all costs is to avoid ending up at the end of any year with a low harvest that would leave the family starving. In the Cuyo Cuyo area, farmers can't produce enough storable food surpluses in a good year to carry them through a subsequent bad year. Hence it is not the peasant's goal to produce the highest possible time-averaged crop yield, averaged over many years. If your time-averaged yield is marvelously high as a result of the combination of nine great years and one year of crop failure, you will still starve to death in that one year of crop failure before you can look back to congratulate yourself on your great time-averaged yield. Instead, the peasant's aim is to make sure to produce a yield above the starvation level in every single year, even though the time-averaged yield may not be highest. That's why field scattering may make sense. If you have just one big field, no matter how good it is on the average, you will starve when the inevitable occasional year arrives in which your one field has a low yield. But if you have many different fields, varying independently of each other, then in any given year some of your fields will produce well even when your other fields are producing poorly.

To test this hypothesis, Goland measured the yields of all the fields of 20 families—488 individual fields in all—in each of two successive years. She then calculated what each family's total crop yield, pooled over all their fields, would have been if, while still cultivating the same total field area, they had concentrated all their fields at one of their actual locations, or if instead they had scattered their fields at 2, 3, 4, etc. up to 14 different ones of the actual locations. It turned out that, the more numerous were the scattered locations, the lower was the calculated time-averaged yield, but also the lower was the risk of ever dropping below the starvation yield level. For instance, a family that Goland labeled family Q, which consisted of a middle-aged husband and wife and a 15-year-old daughter, was estimated to need 1.35 tons of potatoes per acre of land per year in order to avoid starvation. For that family, planting at just a single location would have meant a high risk (37%!) of starving in any given year. It would have been no consolation to family Q, as they sat starving to death in a bad year such as arrives about once in every three years, to reflect that that choice of a single location gave them the highest time-averaged yield of 3.4 tons per acre, more than double the starvation level. Combinations of up to six locations also exposed them to the risk of occasional starvation. Only if they planted seven or more locations did their risk of starvation drop to zero. Granted, their average yield for seven or more locations had dropped to 1.9 tons per acre, but it never dropped below 1.5 tons per acre, so they never starved.

On the average, Goland's 20 families actually planted two or three more fields than the number of fields that she calculated that they had to plant in order to avoid starvation. Of course, that field scattering did force them to burn more calories while walking and transporting things between their scattered fields. However, Goland calculated that the extra calories thereby burned up were only 7% of their crop calorie yields, an acceptable price to pay for avoiding starvation.

In brief, through long experience, and without using statistics or mathematical analyses, Goland's Andean peasants had figured out how to scatter their land just enough to buffer them against the risk of starvation from unpredictable local variation in food yields. The peasants' strategy fits the precept "Don't put all your eggs in one basket." Similar considerations probably also explain field scattering by medieval English peasants. The same considerations may explain why the Lake Titicaca peasants so harshly criticized by exasperated agricultural development researchers for appalling inefficiency were actually smart, and why it was actually the researchers' land-swapping advice that was appalling. As for my New Guinea friend whose isolated garden several miles from his other gardens initially puzzled me, his people mentioned five reasons for scattering their gardens: to reduce the risks of all their gardens simultaneously being devastated by a wind-storm, crop disease, pigs, or rats, and to obtain a wider variety of crops by planting at three different elevations in different climatic zones. Those New Guinea farmers are similar to Goland's Andean farmers, except for planting fewer but larger gardens (on the average, 7 gardens with a range from 5 to 11 for the New Guineans, instead of 17 fields with a range from 9 to 26 for the Andean farmers).

Far too many American investors forget the difference, recognized by peasant farmers around the world, between maximizing time-averaged yields and making sure that yields never drop below some critical level. If you are investing money that you are sure you won't need soon, just to spend in the distant future or for luxuries, it's appropriate to aim to maximize your time-averaged yield, regardless of whether yields become zero or negative in occasional bad years. But if you depend on your investment earnings to pay current expenses, your strategy should be that of the peasants: make sure that your annual earnings always remain above the level necessary for your maintenance, even if that means having to settle for a lower time-averaged yield. As I write these lines, some of the smartest investors in the United States are suffering the consequences of ignoring that difference. Harvard University has the largest endowment, and has had the highest time-averaged endowment earnings rate, of any American university. Its endowment managers became legendary for their skill, success, and willingness to explore profitable types of investments previously shunned by conservative university investment managers. The salary of a Harvard manager was linked to the long-term average growth rate of the portion of Harvard's portfolio for which that manager was responsible. Unfortunately, Harvard's investment income is not reserved for luxuries or a rainy day but contributes about half of the operating budget of Harvard College. During the worldwide financial meltdown of 2008–2009, Harvard's endowment principal and income crashed, as did so many other investments aimed at maximizing long-term yields, so Harvard was forced to impose a hiring freeze and to postpone indefinitely its billion-dollar plan for a new science campus. In retrospect, Harvard's managers should have followed the strategy practised by so many peasant farmers (Plate 45).

Seasonality and food shortage

We have been discussing how traditional peoples cope with the danger of starvation arising from unpredictable fluctuations in food supply. Of course, there are also predictable seasonal fluctuations. Inhabitants of the temperate zones are familiar with the differences between spring, summer, fall, and winter. Even today, when food storage and long-distance food transport have evened out most seasonal variation in food availability in supermarkets, local fresh fruits and vegetables still become available on a predictable schedule. For example, near my home in Los Angeles is a farmers' market that stocks only locally grown seasonal produce, such as asparagus in April and May, cherries and strawberries in May and June, peaches and apricots in June and July, squashes from July through January, and persimmons from October through January. In the temperate zones of North America and Eurasia, availabilities of other foods besides fresh fruits and vegetables also used to fluctuate seasonally, until modern storage and transport eliminated the fluctuations. There was an abundance of meat in the fall, when farm animals were culled and slaughtered; of milk in the spring and summer, when cows and sheep gave birth; of fish such as salmon and herring, which have predictable times of fish runs up rivers and along the coast; and of hunted migratory wild animals such as reindeer and bison at certain seasons.

As a result, some months of the temperate-zone year were times of plenty, and other months were predictable lean times when people knew that stored food might run out and that they would at least have to tighten their belts and at worst risk starvation. For the Greenland Norse, that lean season came each year at the end of winter, when they were close to eating up the cheese, butter, and dried meat stored from the previous year, but when their cows and sheep and goats had not yet given birth and so were not yet producing milk, the herds of migratory harp seals had not yet arrived along the coast, and the resident common seals had not yet landed on beaches to give birth. It appears that the inhabitants of one of Norse Greenland's two settlements all starved to death at the end of such a winter around 1360.

Americans, Europeans, and other residents of the temperate zones tend to assume that tropical regions, especially near the equator, lack seasonality. While temperature is of course much less variable from month to month in the tropics than in the temperate zones, most tropical areas do have marked wet seasons and dry seasons. For instance, the town of Pomio in Papua New Guinea lies only a few hundred miles south of the equator, is very wet (260 inches of rain a year), and receives 6 inches of rain even in the driest month. However, the wettest months at Pomio (July and August) are 7 times wetter than the driest months (February and March), and that has big consequences for food availability and living conditions at Pomio. Hence people resident at low latitudes or even on the equator face predictable lean seasons, just as do traditional temperate-zone peoples. In many cases that lean season falls during the local dry season, which variously comes during the months of September and October for the !Kung of the Kalahari and for the Daribi people in the hills of Papua New Guinea, December to February for Mbuti Pygmies of the Congo's Ituri Forest, and January for the Kaulong people of New Britain. But some other low-latitude peoples experience instead a lean season during their wettest months, which are December to March for the Ngarinyin Aborigines of Northwest Australia, and June to August for the Nuer of the Sudan.

Plate 29. First contact: Ishi, the last surviving Yahi Indian from California, on August 29, 1911, the day that he emerged from hiding and entered Euro-American society. He was terrified and exhausted, and expected to be killed. (Page 398)

Plate 30. First contact between New Guinea Highlanders, who had never previously seen a European, and the Australian miner Dan Leahy, in the Chuave area in 1933. (Pages 2, 4, and 58)

Plate 31. First contact: a New Guinea Highlander weeps in terror at his first sight of a European, during the 1933 Leahy Expedition. (Pages 2 and 58)

Plate 32. Traditional trade: a canoe of New Guinea traders, carrying goods to be given to traditional trade partners in return for other goods. (Page 60)

Plate 33. Modern trade: a professional store-keeper, selling manufactured goods to anyone who enters the store, in return for the government's money. (Page 61)

Plate 34. A modern border between nations: a Chinese trader presenting his passport and visa to a Russian police officer near the Russia-China border. (Page 37)

Plate 35. Ellie Nesler, a California woman tried for killing a man charged with sexually abusing her son. Any parent will understand Ellie's outrage. But the essence of state justice is that government would collapse if citizens took justice into their own hands. (Page 98)

Plate 36. Traditional warfare: Dani tribesmen fighting with spears in the Baliem Valley of the New Guinea Highlands. The highest one-day death toll in those wars occurred on June 4, 1966, when northern Dani killed face-to-face 125 southern Dani, many of whom the attackers would personally have known (or known of). The death toll constituted 5% of the southerners' population. (Chapter 3)

Plate 37. Modern warfare: the Hiroshima atomic bomb cloud of August 6, 1945. The American soldiers who dropped the bomb did not personally know their victims and did not look them in the face as they were killing them. The 100,000 Japanese killed at Hiroshima represent the highest one-day death toll in modern warfare, and constituted 0.1% of Japan's population at that time. That is, large modern populations are associated with high absolute death tolls in modern warfare, but the methods of traditional warfare can result in much higher proportional death tolls. (Pages 127 and 142)

Plate 38. Traditional transport of children commonly places the child in immediate physical contact with the care-giver, vertically erect, looking forward, and thus seeing the same field of view as the care-giver. This is a Pume Indian baby from Venezuela being carried by an older sister. (Pages 185, 188, and 201)

Plate 39. Modern transport of children often removes the child from physical contact with the care-giver, and places the child looking backwards and reclining horizontally rather than vertically erect. This is an American baby being pushed in a baby carriage by its mother. (Page 184)

Plates 40 and 41. The composers Richard Strauss (left) and Giuseppe Verdi (below) learned how to make the best use of their musical talents as they changed with age. The results were among their greatest compositions: Strauss's *Four Last Songs*, and Verdi's operas *Otello* and *Falstaff*, completed at ages 84, 74, and 80, respectively. (Page 239)

Plate 42. Traditional dangers: a man climbing a tree to harvest açaí berries in Brazil. Falling out of a tree, or being struck by a falling tree, is a major hazard in many traditional societies. (Page 280)

Plate 43. Traditional dangers: a large crocodile that was killed after it had killed people in Indonesia. Wild animals are major hazards in most traditional societies. (Page 280)

Plate 44. Modern dangers: car crashes are a major hazard of modern life. (Page 279)

Plate 45. Risk management: Harvard University's endowment principal and income crashed during the worldwide financial meltdown of 2008–2009. Harvard's investment managers should have followed the risk management strategy of peasant farmers, who maximize long-term time-averaged yields only insofar as that is compatible with maintaining yields above a certain critical level. (Page 307)

Plate 46. A dowser, a person who claims that rotation of a forked stick can reveal the presence of hidden underground water for land-owners wanting to know where to dig a well. Dowsers illustrate our tendency to resort to rituals in situations whose outcomes are hard to predict. (Page 342)

Plate 47. Vanishing languages: Sophie Borodkin (died January 2008), the last speaker of Eyak, a distinctive Native American language formerly spoken in Alaska. (Page 397)

Table 8.2. Traditional food storage around the world

EURASIA	
Eurasian herders	Dairy products: butter, cheese, skyr, fermented milk.
European farmers	Wheat and barley, salted or dried fish, dairy products, potatoes and other tubers, pickled vegetables, beer, oil.
Korea	Kimchi: pickled fermented cabbage, turnip, cucumber. Pickled, salted, or fermented fish and shrimp.
Ainu (Japan)	Nuts, dried and frozen fish, dried venison, root starch.
Nganasan (Siberia)	Smoked, dried, or frozen reindeer meat. Rendered goose fat.
Itenm'i (Kamchatka)	Dried and fermented fish.
AMERICAS	
Most Native American farmers	Dried maize.
Northern Plains Indians	Pemmican: dried bison meat, rendered fat, and dried berries.
Andes	Freeze-dried meat and tubers and fish.
Inuit	Frozen whale meat, frozen or dried caribou meat, seal oil.
Northwest Coast Indians	Dried and smoked salmon, rendered candlefish oil, dried berries.
Great Basin Shoshone	Mesquite pod starch, pine nuts, dried meat.
Inland Northern California Indians	Acorn meal, dried salmon.
AFRICA	
Nuer	Millet, beer.
PACIFIC	
East Polynesia	Fermented taro and breadfruit. Dried bananas and starch.
Maori (New Zealand)	Bird meat, heated and sealed with fat. Tubers.
Trobriand Islands (New Guinea)	Yams.
New Guinea lowlands	Sago starch and dried fish.
New Guinea Highlands	Tubers. Sweet potatoes stored as live pigs.
Australian Aborigines	Wild grass seed cakes.

Traditional peoples dealt with predictable seasonal food shortages in three main ways: storing food, broadening their diet, and dispersing and aggregating. The first of these methods is routine in modern society: we store food in refrigerators, deep freezers, cans, bottles, and dried packages. Many traditional societies as well set aside food surpluses accumulated during a season of food abundance (such as fall harvest time in the temperate zones), and consumed that food during a season of food scarcity (such as temperate-zone winters). Food storage was practised by sedentary societies living in markedly seasonal environments with alternating seasons of food abundance and food deficits. It was uncommon among nomadic hunter-gatherers with frequent changes of camp, because they couldn't carry much food with them (unless they had boats or dog-drawn sleds), and the risk of pilferage by animals or other humans made it unsafe for them to leave food unguarded at one camp and to plan to return later. (However, some hunter-gatherers, such as Japan's Ainu, Pacific Northwest Coast Indians, the Great Basin Shoshone, and some Arctic peoples, were sedentary or seasonally sedentary and stored large quantities of food.) Even among sedentary peoples, some living in small family groups stored little food because they were too few to defend a larder against raiders. Food storage was more widespread in cold temperate regions than in the hot wet tropics, where food spoils quickly. **Table 8.2** gives examples.

The main practical problem to be overcome in storing food is to prevent the food from rotting through decomposition by microorganisms. Because microbes, like all other living creatures, require mild temperatures and water, many methods of food storage involve keeping food cold (not an option in the tropics before the development of refrigerators) or else drying food. Some foods are sufficiently low in water content in their natural form that they can be stored for months or even years, as is or else after just light drying. Those foods include many nuts, cereals, some roots and tubers such as potatoes and turnips, and honey. Most of those foods are stored in containers or larders built for the purpose, but many root crops can be "stored" or banked by the simple method of leaving them in the ground for months until they are required.

However, many other foods, such as meat and fish and juicy fruits and berries, have sufficiently high water content that they require extensive drying by means such as placing them on racks in the sun or smoking them over fires. For instance, smoked salmon, now a delicate luxury, used to be a staple prepared in large quantities by Pacific Northwest Coast Indians. Dried bison meat, combined with fat and dried berries to store as a mixture known as pemmican, was similarly a staple on the North American Great Plains. Andean Indians dried large quantities of meat, fish, potatoes, and oca by freeze-drying (alternately freezing and sun-drying).

Still other dried foods are obtained by taking a moist raw starting-material and extracting the nutritious component without most of the original water. Familiar modern examples of such foods are olive oil made from olives, cheese made from milk, and flour made from wheat. Traditional Mediterranean peoples, Eurasian herders, and Eurasian farmers respectively have been preparing and storing those same products for thousands of years. Rendering fat to extract it in a form with low water content was widely practised by Maori bird hunters of New Zealand, Native American bison hunters, and Arctic hunters of marine mammals. Pacific Northwest Coast Indians rendered fat from a species of smelt so oily that its English name is candlefish because when dried the fish can be burned like a candle. The staple food of the New Guinea lowlands is sago starch, obtained by extracting the starch from the pith of sago palms. Polynesians and Japan's Ainu similarly extracted starch from roots, as did the Great Basin Shoshone Indians from mesquite pods.

Numerous other methods of food preservation didn't involve drying. A simple method in Arctic and northern European areas with sub-zero winter temperatures was to freeze food in the winter and bury it in the ground or in subterranean ice-filled chambers where the food would remain frozen into the next summer. I stumbled upon a vestige of that practice when, as a university student at Cambridge, England, I went on a sight-seeing drive through the East Anglian countryside with British friends with whom I shared the hobby of spelunking (exploring caves). While we were chatting with a local land-owner, he invited us to see a strange building on his land whose purpose nobody understood. It proved to be a brick dome constructed of beautifully set courses of old brick, and with a locked door that our new acquaintance opened for us. Inside, we saw in front of us a brick-lined vertical hole 10 feet in diameter, with a wooden ladder disappearing into it, and so deep that we couldn't see a bottom.

On the following weekend, we returned with our cave-explorers' belaying ropes, acetylene torches, helmets, and single-piece overalls. Of course, we were hoping for a deep shaft, side galleries, and a forgotten treasure hoard. As the only American and the lightest member of our group, I was the one selected by my British friends to be the first to risk descending the rotting wooden ladder. To my disappointment, the ladder reached a dirt floor at a depth of only 30 feet, with neither side galleries, treasure, nor any other hint of function except for more beautiful courses of old brick. On my return to Cambridge that evening, I recounted our mysterious discovery over dinner. One of my table companions, an elderly engineer who spent his weekends taking walks through the countryside, exclaimed, "That's obviously an ice-house!" He told me that such buildings used to be regular features of British estates until refrigerators began to supplant them in the late 19th century. They were excavated to a depth far below the warm surface soil layer, were filled with food and blocks of ice in the winter, and maintained food frozen into the next summer. The quantity of food that our re-discovered ice-house must have been capable of holding was huge.

Another traditional method of food preservation is to boil food so as to kill microbes, then to seal the container while it is still hot and sterile. As recently as World War II, American city-dwellers were urged by the United States government to spare food supplies for our soldiers by patriotically planting backyard victory gardens and storing the boiled produce in air-tight vacuum jars. In the house in Boston where I grew up, my parents maintained a basement room that my mother filled with jars of tomatoes and cucumbers harvested in the autumn, and that my parents and sister and I consumed throughout the winter. My childhood was repeatedly punctuated by explosions of the antiquated pressure cooker in which my mother boiled produce before jarring it, spraying vegetable mush over our kitchen ceiling. New Zealand Maoris similarly preserved meat by cooking it and transferring it still hot into containers sealed with melted fat that kept out microbes. Without knowing about microbes, Maoris somehow discovered this method.

The remaining class of methods preserves food without either drying or freezing or boiling, by pickling and/or fermenting with substances that prevent microbial growth. These substances include salt or vinegar added to the food, or else alcohol, vinegar, or lactic acid developing during fermentation of the food itself. Examples include beer, wine, and other alcoholic beverages; the Korean staple of kimchee served with every Korean meal, and commonly including cabbage, turnips, and cucumbers fermented in brine; the fermented mare's milk of Asian herders; Polynesia's fermented taro and breadfruit; and the fermented fish of Kamchatka's Itenm'i people.

Finally, one can achieve the purpose of storing surplus food by converting it into some non-food item that is convertible back into food during a subsequent hungry season. Farmers in our modern cash economy do this by selling their produce for money when they harvest or slaughter, banking the money, and eventually converting the money back into other foods at a supermarket. Pig husbandry by New Guinea Highlanders in effect constitutes food banking, because the staple Highland crop of sweet potatoes can be stored as is for only a few months. However, by feeding sweet potatoes to pigs and waiting several years before slaughtering the pigs, Highlanders bank the sweet potatoes, transform them into pig meat, and effectively preserve them for much longer than a few months.

Diet broadening

Another strategy besides food storage for coping with seasonal food scarcity is to broaden one's diet and consume foods scorned during seasons of food plenty. In Chapter 6 I mentioned an example from Rennell Island, where people classify edible wild plants in two categories: those eaten normally, and those eaten only in desperation after a cyclone destroyed gardens. But Rennell Islanders usually obtain most of their plant food from gardens, and their classification of wild plants is not elaborate. Preferences for wild plant foods are classified much more finely among the !Kung, because traditionally they were hunter-gatherers and did not farm. They name at least 200 local wild plant species, of which they consider at least 105 edible, and which they divide along a preference hierarchy with at least six categories. Most preferred are plants that are superabundant, widely distributed, available in all months of the year, easy to collect, tasty, and considered nutritious. Number one in the hierarchy, because it meets all of these criteria, is the mongongo nut, which provides nearly half of all plant calories consumed by the !Kung and is rivaled in popularity only by meat. Lower in preference are plants that are scarce, found only locally, available only in certain months, unpleasant-tasting, hard to digest, or considered un-nutritious. When the !Kung move to a new camp, they begin by collecting mongongo nuts and their 13 other favorite plant species, until these become depleted in the vicinity. The !Kung then have to move down their food preference ladder and content themselves with less and less desirable foods. In the hot dry months of September and October, when the least food is available, the !Kung stoop to collecting fibrous tasteless roots that are ignored at other times of year, and that now are dug out and eaten without enthusiasm. About 10 species of trees exude edible resins that are rated low, considered hard to digest, and collected only incidentally as the occasion arises. At the bottom of the ladder are foods eaten only a few times a year, such as an abundant fruit thought to cause nausea and hallucinations, and meat from cows that died from eating toxic leaves. Lest you think that these food preference ladders of the !Kung are irrelevant to the lives of modern First World citizens, many Europeans adopted similar practices during the food shortages of World War II: for example, British friends told me of eating mice then, which they served up as creamed mouse.

Within 300 miles east of the !Kung, at population densities 100 times those of the !Kung, are Gwembe Tonga farmers. When the farmers' crops fail, the farmers' high numbers place much greater pressure on the environment's wild plants than do the relatively few !Kung, and so the Tonga have to reach farther down the preference ladder than do the !Kung. They then consume 21 plant species that also occur in the !Kung area but that the !Kung don't even consider edible. One of those plants is an acacia tree whose abundant seed pods are toxic. The !Kung could collect tons of those pods each year but choose not to. However, at times of famine the Tonga do collect them and soak, boil, and leach them for a day to wash out the toxins, then eat the pods.

My last example of diet broadening comes from the Kaulong people of the island of New Britain, for whom garden-grown taro is the staple food and pig meat is ceremonially important. What the Kaulong call *taim bilong hanggiri* in Tok Pisin (i.e., "time belong hunger") is the local dry season of October through January, when little food is available from gardens. At that time the Kaulong go into the forest to hunt, collect insects and snails and small animals, and gather wild plants about which they are understandably unenthusiastic. One of those plants is a toxic wild nut that has to be prepared by soaking it for several days to leach out its poison. Another of those second-choice plants is a wild palm tree whose trunk is roasted and eaten, and which at other times of year is scorned as pig food.

Aggregation and dispersal

Along with food storage and diet broadening, the remaining traditional solution to the problem created by a predictable season of food scarcity is to follow an annual cycle of population movement, aggregation, and dispersal. When food resources are few and concentrated in a few areas, people gather to live at those areas. At favorable times of year when resources are widely and uniformly distributed, people spread out over the landscape.

A familiar European example is that farmers in the Alps spend the winter at their farmhouses in the valleys. In the spring and summer they follow the growth of new grass and the melting of snow cover up the mountain slopes, to take their flocks of cows and sheep to alpine pastures. Similar seasonal cycles of aggregation and dispersal occur among many other farming societies around the world, and among many hunter-gatherer societies including Aboriginal Australians, Inuit, Pacific Northwest Coast Indians, Great Basin Shoshone, !Kung, and African Pygmies. The times of population concentration during the lean season provide the opportunity for annual ceremonies, dances, initiations, marriage negotiations, and other occasions of group social life. The following two examples illustrate how these cycles unfold for the Shoshone and the !Kung.

The Great Basin Shoshone Indians of the western United States live in an extremely seasonal desert environment whose summers are dry and hot (day temperatures over 90° or even 100° Fahrenheit), winters are cold (temperatures often below freezing all day), and most of the low precipitation (under 10 inches per year) falls in the winter as snow. The main foods consumed during the winter, which is the season of food scarcity, are stored pine nuts and mesquite starch. In the fall people concentrate at pine groves to harvest, process, and store large quantities of nuts within a short time. Groups of between 2 and 10 related families then spend the winter in a camp at a nut grove with a source of water. In the spring, as warming temperatures bring a resumption of plant growth and animal activity, the camps break up into nuclear families that spread out over the landscape to higher and lower elevations. The widespread and varied food resources during the summer enable the Shoshone to expand greatly their diet: they forage for seeds, roots, tubers, berries, nuts, and other plant food; they gather grasshoppers, fly larvae, and other insect food; they hunt rabbits, rodents, reptiles, and other small animals, plus deer, mountain sheep, antelope, elk, and bison; and they fish. At the end of the summer they gather again at their pine groves and group winter camps. In another desert environment, this one in southern Africa, the !Kung similarly follow an annual cycle dictated by water availability and food resources dependent on water. They concentrate at the few permanent waterholes during the dry season, and spread out over 308 less reliable or seasonal water sources during the wet season.

Responses to danger

Finally, now that we've discussed traditional dangers and responses to those dangers, let's compare actual measures of danger (in whatever way it is measured) with our responses (i.e., how much we worry about dangers, and how extensively we defend ourselves against them). A naive expectation might be that we are completely rational and informed, and that our reactions to various dangers are proportional to their seriousness as measured by the number of people that each type of danger actually kills or injures each year. This naive expectation isn't upheld, for at least five sets of reasons.

First, the annual number of people killed or injured by a certain type of danger may be low precisely because we are so aware of it and go to such great efforts to minimize our risk. If we were fully rational, perhaps a better measure of danger than the actual annual number of deaths inflicted (easy to count up) would be the annual numbers of deaths that would have been inflicted if we hadn't taken counter-measures (hard to estimate). Two examples stand out among those that we have discussed in this chapter. Few people in traditional societies normally die of famine, precisely because so many of a society's practices are organized so as to reduce the risk of dying of famine. Few !Kung are killed each year by lions, not because lions aren't dangerous, but instead because they are indeed so dangerous that the !Kung take elaborate measures to protect themselves against lions: don't leave camp at night, constantly scan the environment for tracks and signs of lions while out of camp during the day, constantly talk loudly and travel in groups while women are out of camp, watch out for old or injured or hungry or solitary lions, and so on.

A second reason for the mismatch between actual danger and our acceptance of risk is a modified version of the Wayne Gretzky principle: our willingness to expose ourselves to danger increases steeply with the potential benefits from the dangerous situation. The !Kung drive lions off carcasses with meat on which to feast, but they don't drive lions off resting places without carcasses. Most of us wouldn't enter a burning house just for the fun of it, but would do so to rescue our child trapped in the house. Many Americans and Europeans and Japanese are now making agonizing reappraisals of the wisdom of building nuclear power stations, because on the one hand Japan's Fukushima nuclear station accident emphasizes the dangers of nuclear power, and on the other hand those dangers are offset by the benefits of reducing global warming by reducing coal, oil, and gas power generation.

Third, people systematically misestimate risks—at least in the Western world, where psychologists have made extensive studies of the phenomenon. When Americans are asked about dangers today, they are likely first to mention terrorists, plane crashes, and nuclear accidents, even though those three dangers combined have killed far fewer Americans over the last four decades combined than do cars, alcohol, or smoking in any single year. When Americans' rankings of risks are compared with actual annual deaths caused (or with probability of death per hour of the risky activity), it turns out that people greatly overrate the risk of nuclear reactor accidents (ranked as the number-one danger by American college students and women voters), and also overrate the risks of DNA-based technologies, other new chemical technologies, and spray cans. Americans underrate the risks of alcohol, cars, and smoking, and (to a lesser extent) of surgery, home appliances, and food preservatives. Underlying these biases of ours are that we especially fear events beyond our control, events with the potential for killing lots of people, and situations involving new, unfamiliar, or hard-to-assess risks (hence our fear of terrorists, plane crashes, and nuclear reactor accidents). Conversely, we are inappropriately accepting of old familiar risks that appear to be within our control, that we accept voluntarily, and that kill individuals rather than groups of people. That's why we underrate the risks of driving cars, alcohol, smoking, and standing on step-ladders: we choose to do those things, we feel that we control them, and we know that they kill other people, but we think that they won't kill us because we consider ourselves careful and strong. As Chauncey Starr expressed it, "We are loath to let others do unto us what we happily do to ourselves."

Fourth, some individuals accept, or even seek and enjoy, danger more than do other individuals. Such people include recreational skydivers, bungee-jumpers, compulsive gamblers, and race-drivers. Databases compiled by insurance companies confirm our intuitive sense that men seek out danger more than do women, and that male risk-seeking peaks in one's twenties and then declines with age. I recently returned from a visit to Africa's Victoria Falls, where the enormous one-mile-wide Zambezi River drops 355 feet into a narrow crack drained by an even narrower gorge into a pool (appropriately called the Boiling Pot) through which plunges the river's entire volume. The roar of the falls, the blackness of the rock walls, the mist filling the entire crack and gorge, and the churning of the water below the falls suggest what the entrance to hell must be like, if there is a hell. Just over the Boiling Pot, the gorge is traversed by a bridge across which pedestrians can walk between the countries of Zambia and Zimbabwe, whose border is formed by the river. From that bridge, tourists so inclined bungee-jump into the black, roaring, spray-filled gorge. As I watched the scene, I could not bring myself even to walk towards the bridge, and I reflected that I couldn't have bungee-jumped there even if I were told that that was the only way to save the lives of my wife and children. But we were later visited by one of my son's 22-year-old classmates, a young man named Lee, who did bungee-jump into that gorge, by plunging head-first off the bridge with a rope tied to his ankles. I was astonished at Lee's voluntarily paying to do something so terrifying that I would have paid all my life's savings in order to avoid doing it—until I reflected on some equally horrible experiences that I had chosen to undergo as a student cave-explorer at that same age of 22, when I was equally risk-seeking.

Finally, some societies are more tolerant of accepting risks than other, more conservative societies. Such differences are familiar among First World societies and have been observed among Native American tribes and among New Guinea tribes. Just to mention one current example: during recent military operations in Iraq, American soldiers have been described as more risk-taking than French and German soldiers. Speculative explanations for this difference include the lessons learned by France and Germany from the slaughter of almost 7,000,000 of their citizens during the two world wars in often foolishly risky military operations; and the founding of modern American society by emigrants from other lands who were willing to accept the risks of uprooting themselves to move to a strange new homeland, leaving behind risk-averse countrymen in their land of origin.

Thus, all human societies face dangers, although different types of dangers lie in store for peoples at different localities or with different lifestyles. I worry about cars and step-ladders, my New Guinea lowland friends about crocodiles and cyclones and enemies, and the !Kung about lions and droughts. Each society has adopted a spectrum of measures for mitigating the particular hazards that it recognizes. But we citizens of WEIRD societies don't always think as clearly as we should about the dangers that we face. Our obsession with the dangers of DNA technologies and spray cans would better be focused on the homely hazards of cigarettes and cycling without helmets. Whether traditional peoples make similar misestimates of their lives' dangers remains to be studied. Are we WEIRD moderns especially prone to misestimate risks because we get most of our information second-hand from television and other mass media that emphasize sensational but rare accidents and mass deaths? Do traditional peoples estimate risks more accurately because they instead learn only from the first-hand experiences of themselves, their relatives, and their neighbors? Can we learn to think more realistically about dangers?

PART FIVE

RELIGION, LANGUAGE, AND HEALTH

CHAPTER 9

What Electric Eels Tell Us About
the Evolution of Religion

Questions about religion ▪ Definitions of religion ▪ Functions and
electric eels ▪ The search for causal explanations ▪ Supernatural
beliefs ▪ Religion's function of explanation ▪ Defusing anxiety ▪
Providing comfort ▪ Organization and obedience ▪ Codes of behavior
towards strangers ▪ Justifying war ▪ Badges of commitment ▪
Measures of religious success ▪ Changes in religion's functions

Questions about religion

"In the beginning, all people lived around a great ironwood tree in the
jungle, speaking the same language. One man whose testes were enormously swollen from infection with a parasitic worm spent his time sitting on a branch of the tree, so that he could rest his heavy testes on the
ground. Out of curiosity, animals of the jungle came up and sniffed at his
testes. Hunters then found the animals easy to kill, and everyone had
plenty of food and was happy.

"Then, one day, a bad man killed a beautiful woman's husband, in order to get the woman for himself. Relatives of the dead husband attacked
the murderer, who was defended in turn by his own relatives, until the
murderer and his relatives climbed into the ironwood tree to save themselves. The attackers tugged on the lianas hanging from one side of the
tree, in order to pull the tree's crown down towards the ground and get at
their enemies.

"Finally, the lianas snapped in half, causing the tree to spring back with
tremendous force. The murderer and his relatives were hurled out of the
tree in many directions. They landed so far away, in so many places, that
they never found each other again. With time, their languages became

more and more different. That is why people today speak so many separate languages and cannot understand each other, and why it is hard work for hunters to catch animals for food."

That story is told by a tribal people in northern New Guinea. The story exemplifies a widespread class of myths called origin myths, familiar to us through accounts of the Garden of Eden and the Tower of Babel in the Bible's book of Genesis. Despite those parallels with Judeo-Christian religions, traditional New Guinea societies, like other small-scale societies, lacked churches, priests, and sacred books. Why is that tribal belief system so reminiscent of Judeo-Christian religions in its origin myth, yet so different in other respects?

Virtually all known human societies have had "religion," or something like it. That suggests that religion fulfills some universal human need, or at least springs from some part of human nature common to all of us. If so, what is that need, or that part of human nature? And what really defines "religion"? Scholars have been debating these and related questions for centuries. For a belief system to constitute a religion, must it include belief in a god or gods or some supernatural forces, and does it necessarily include anything else? When, in human evolutionary history, did religion appear? Human ancestors diverged from the ancestors of chimpanzees around 6,000,000 years ago. Whatever religion is, we can agree that chimps don't have it, but was there already religion among our Cro-Magnon ancestors and our Neanderthal relatives of 40,000 years ago? Were there different historical stages in the development of religions, with creeds like Christianity and Buddhism representing a more recent stage than tribal belief systems? We tend to associate religion with humanity's noble side, not with its evil side: why, then, does religion sometimes preach murder and suicide?

These questions posed by religion are especially interesting in the context of this book, devoted to exploring the whole spectrum of human societies, from small-scale or ancient to populous or modern. Religion is an area where traditional institutions still thrive within otherwise modern societies: the world's major religions today arose between 1,400 and over 3,000 years ago, in societies much smaller and more traditional than the ones that still espouse those religions today. Religions nevertheless vary with the scale of society, and that variation cries out for explanation. In addition, most readers of this book, and I, question our personal religious beliefs (or lack thereof) at some point in our lives. When we do, understanding of the different things that religion has meant to different people may help us find answers that fit us as individuals.

For individuals and for societies, religion often involves a huge investment of time and resources. To mention just a few examples, Mormons are expected to contribute 10% of their income to their church. It's estimated that traditional Hopi Indians devote an average of one out of three days to religious ceremonies, and that one-quarter of the population of traditional Tibet consisted of monks. The fraction of resources in medieval Christian Europe devoted to building and staffing churches and cathedrals, supporting the many orders of monasteries and nunneries, and underwriting crusades must have been large. To borrow a phrase from economists, religion thus incurs "opportunity costs": those investments of time and resources in religion that could have been devoted instead to obviously profitable activities, such as planting more crops, building dams, and feeding larger armies of conquest. If religion didn't bring some big real benefits to offset those opportunity costs, any atheistic society that by chance arose would be likely to outcompete religious societies and take over the world. So why hasn't the world become atheistic, and what are those benefits that religion evidently brings? What are the "functions" of religion?

To a believer, such questions about religion's functions may seem nonsensical or even offensive. A believer might respond that religion is nearly universal among human societies simply because there really is a God, and that the ubiquity of religion no more requires discovering its supposed functions and benefits than does the ubiquity of rocks. If you are such a believer, let me invite you to imagine, just for a moment, an advanced living creature from the Andromeda galaxy, who races around the universe at a velocity far exceeding the speed of light (considered impossible by us humans), visits the universe's trillions of stars and planets, and studies the diversity of life in the universe, with metabolisms variously powered by light, other forms of electromagnetic radiation, heat, wind, nuclear reactions, and inorganic or organic chemical reactions. Periodically, our Andromedan visits Planet Earth, where life evolved to utilize energy only from light and from inorganic and organic chemical reactions. For a brief period between about 11,000 BC and September 11, AD 2051,

Earth was dominated by a life form that called itself humans and that clung to some curious ideas. Among those ideas: that there is an all-powerful being, called God, which has a special interest in the human species rather than in the millions of trillions of other species in the universe, and which created the universe, and which humans often picture as similar to a human except for being omnipotent. Of course the Andromedan recognized those beliefs to be delusions worthy of study rather than of credence, because the Andromedan and many other living creatures had already figured out how the universe really had been created, and it was absurd to imagine that any all-powerful being would be especially interested in or similar to the human species, which was much less interesting and advanced than billions of other life forms existing elsewhere in the universe. The Andromedan also observed that there were thousands of different human religions, most of whose adherents believed their own religion to be true and all the other religions to be false, and that suggested to the Andromedan that all were false.

But this belief in such a god was widespread among human societies. The Andromedan understood the principles of universal sociology, which had to provide an explanation for why human societies persisted despite the huge drain of time and resources that religion imposed on individuals and societies, and despite religion's motivating individuals to inflict on themselves painful or suicidal behaviors. Obviously, the Andromedan reasoned, religion must bring some compensating benefits; otherwise, atheistic societies not burdened by those time and resource drains and those suicidal impulses would have replaced religious societies. Hence if you, my readers, find it offensive to inquire about the functions of your own religion, perhaps you would be willing for a moment to step back and inquire about the functions of New Guinea tribal religions, or to place yourself in the frame of mind of the Andromedan visitor and inquire about human religions in general.

Definitions of religion

Let's begin by defining religion, so that we can at least agree about what phenomenon we are discussing. Which features are shared by all religions, including Christianity and tribal religions along with the polytheism of classical Greece and Rome, and are necessary and sufficient to identify a phenomenon as a religion rather than as some related but different phenomenon (such as magic, patriotism, or a philosophy of life)?

Table 9.1. Some proposed definitions of religion

1. "Human recognition of superhuman controlling power and especially of a personal God entitled to obedience." (*Concise Oxford Dictionary*)

2. "Any specific system of belief and worship, often involving a code of ethics and a philosophy." (*Webster's New World Dictionary*)

3. "A system of social coherence based on a common group of beliefs or attitudes concerning an object, person, unseen being, or system of thought considered to be supernatural, sacred, divine or highest truth, and the moral codes, practices, values, institutions, traditions, and rituals associated with such belief or system of thought." (*Wikipedia*)

4. "Religion, in the broadest and most general terms possible, . . . consists of the belief that there is an unseen order, and that our supreme good lies in harmoniously adjusting ourselves thereto." (William James)

5. "Social systems whose participants avow belief in a supernatural agent or agents whose approval is to be sought." (Daniel Dennett)

6. "A propitiation or conciliation of superhuman powers which are believed to control nature and man." (Sir James Frazer)

7. "A set of symbolic forms and acts which relate man to the ultimate conditions of his existence." (Robert Bellah)

8. "A system of beliefs and practices directed toward the 'ultimate concern' of a society." (William Lessa and Evon Vogt)

9. "The belief in superhuman beings and in their power to assist or to harm man approaches universal distribution, and this belief—I would insist—is the core variable which ought to be designated by any definition of religion. . . . I shall define 'religion' as 'an institution consisting of culturally patterned interaction with culturally postulated superhuman beings.'" (Melford Spiro)

10. "The common element of religion cross-culturally is a belief that the highest good is defined by an unseen order combined with an array of symbols that assist individuals and groups in ordering their lives in harmony with this order and an emotional commitment to achieving that harmony." (William Irons)

11. "A religion is a unified system of beliefs and practices relative to sacred things, that is to say, things set apart and forbidden—beliefs and practices which unite into one single moral community called a Church, all those who adhere to them." (Émile Durkheim)

12. "Roughly, religion is (1) a community's costly and hard-to-fake commitment (2) to a counterfactual and counterintuitive world of supernatural agents (3) who master people's existential anxieties, such as death and deception." (Scott Atran)

Table 9.1. *(continued)*

13. "A religion is: (1) a system of symbols which acts to (2) establish powerful, pervasive and long-lasting moods and motivations in men by (3) formulating conceptions of a general order of existence and (4) clothing these conceptions with such an aura of factuality that (5) the moods and motivation seem uniquely realistic." (Clifford Geertz)

14. "Religion is a social institution that evolved as an integral mechanism of human culture to create and promote myths, to encourage altruism and reciprocal altruism, and to reveal the level of commitment to cooperate and reciprocate among members of the community." (Michael Shermer)

15. "A religion we will define as a set of beliefs, practices and institutions which men have evolved in various societies, so far as they can be understood, as responses to those aspects of their life and situation which are believed not in the empirical-instrumental sense to be rationally understandable and/or controllable, and to which they attach a significance which includes some kind of reference to the relevant actions and events to man's conception of the existence of a 'supernatural' order which is conceived and felt to have a fundamental bearing on man's position in the universe and the values which give meaning to his fate as an individual and his relations to his fellows." (Talcott Parsons)

16. "Religion is the sigh of the oppressed creature, the heart of a heartless world, and the soul of soulless conditions. It is the opium of the people." (Karl Marx)

Table 9.1 lists 16 different definitions proposed by scholars of religion. Definitions numbers 11 and 13, by Émile Durkheim and Clifford Geertz respectively, are the ones most frequently quoted by other scholars. It will be obvious that we are not even close to agreement on a definition. Many of these definitions are written in a convoluted style similar to the language used by lawyers in drafting a contract, and that warns us that we are treading on hotly contested ground.

As a fallback position, could we skirt the problem of defining religion in the same way that we often skirt the problem of defining pornography, by saying, "I can't define pornography, but I nevertheless know it when I see it!"? No, unfortunately even that fallback position won't work; scholars don't agree about whether to recognize some widespread and well-known movements as religions. For instance, there have been long-standing debates among scholars of religion about whether Buddhism, Confucianism, and Shintoism should be counted as religions; the current trend is to count Buddhism but not Confucianism, although Confucianism was usually counted a decade or two ago; Confucianism is now instead usually termed a way of life or a secular philosophy.

These difficulties in defining religion are instructive. They warn us that the phenomena that we lump together as religions contain several different components, which are variously strong, weak, or virtually absent in different religions, different societies, and different stages of the evolution of religions. Religion shades into other phenomena, which possess some but not all of the attributes usually associated with religion. That's why there is disagreement over whether Buddhism, usually counted as one of the world's four biggest religions, really is a religion at all or is "just" a philosophy of life. The components commonly attributed to religions fall into five sets: belief in the supernatural, shared membership in a social movement, costly and visible proofs of commitment, practical rules for one's behavior (i.e., "morality"), and belief that supernatural beings and forces can be induced (e.g., by prayer) to intervene in worldly life. As we shall see, though, it would not make sense to define religion by the combination of all five of those attributes, nor to label as non-religion a phenomenon lacking one or more of them, because one would thereby exclude some branches of movements widely recognized as religions.

The first of these five attributes is the basis of the definition of religion that I offered to my University of California undergraduate students when I first taught a course in cultural geography. I proposed, "Religion is the belief in a postulated supernatural agent for whose existence our senses can't give us evidence, but which is invoked to explain things of which our senses do give us evidence." This definition has two virtues: belief in supernatural agents is indeed one of the most widespread characteristics of religion; and explanation, as we shall discuss later, was among the main origins and early functions of religions. Most religions do postulate the existence of gods, spirits, and other agents that we term "supernatural" because they or their provable consequences can't be perceived directly in the natural world. (Throughout this chapter, I shall repeatedly use the word "supernatural" in that neutral sense, without any of the pejorative connotations sometimes associated with the word.) Many religions go further and postulate the existence of an entire parallel supernatural world—often, a heaven, a hell, or another afterlife to which we ourselves shall be transferred after our death in this natural world. Some believers are so convinced of the existence of supernatural agents that they insist that they have seen, heard, or felt spirits or ghosts.

But I soon realized that my definition was inadequate, for reasons that are also instructive. Belief in supernatural agents characterizes not only religions but also phenomena that no one would consider religious—such as belief in fairies, ghosts, leprechauns, and aliens in UFOs. Why is it religious to believe in gods, but not necessarily religious to believe in fairies? (Hint: believers in fairies don't meet on a specified day each week to perform certain rituals, don't identify themselves as a community of fairy-believers separate from fairy-skeptics, and don't offer to die in defense of their belief in fairies.) Conversely, some movements that everyone considers to be religions don't require belief in supernatural agents. Numerous Jews (including rabbis), Unitarians, Japanese people, and others are agnostics or atheists but still consider themselves, and are considered by others, to belong to a religion. The Buddha did not associate himself with any gods and claimed that he was "merely" teaching a path to enlightenment that he had discovered.

A big failing in my definition was that it omitted a second attribute of religions: they are also social movements of people who identify themselves as sharing deeply held beliefs. Someone who believes in a god and in a long list of other doctrines that he invented, and who devotes part of every Sabbath to sitting in a room by himself, praying to that god, and reading a book that he has written himself but shown to no one else, doesn't qualify as practising a religion. The closest actual equivalent to such a person is hermits who live in isolation and devote themselves to prayer. But those hermits arose from a community of believers who provided the hermits' beliefs, and who may continue to support and visit the hermits. I'm not aware of hermits who devised their own religion from scratch, went off into the desert to live alone, and refused food offerings and discouraged visitors. If someone should show me such a hermit, I would define him as a non-religious hermit or else as a misanthrope, while others might consider him to be a typical religious hermit except for failing the test of sociality.

A third attribute of many religions is that their adherents make costly or painful sacrifices that convincingly display to others the adherents' commitment to the group. The sacrifice may be of time: e.g., interrupting other activities five times per day to face towards Mecca and pray, or spending part of every Sunday in church, or spending years memorizing a complex ritual, prayers, and songs (possibly requiring learning another language), or devoting two years to missionary activities as a young adult (expected of Mormons), or joining a crusade or a pilgrimage or visiting Mecca at one's own expense. The sacrifice may be of money or property donated to the church. One may offer a valuable domestic animal: one sacrifices to God one's own lamb, not some captured wild animal that cost nothing. Or the sacrifice may be of one's bodily comfort or integrity, by fasting, chopping off a finger joint, circumcising or subincising (splitting lengthwise) the penis, or spilling one's blood by cutting one's nose or tongue or penis or inside the throat or other body part. All of those costly public or painful displays serve to convince other believers that one is serious in one's commitment to their religion and will even sacrifice one's life if necessary. Otherwise, if I merely shouted "I'm a Christian!," I might be lying for personal advantage (as some prisoners do in the hopes of gaining parole), or to save my life. While the second and third attributes (i.e., a social movement and costly sacrifices) seem to me necessary conditions for a movement to count as a religion, they're not sufficient conditions by themselves. There are also non-religious social movements sharing deeply held beliefs and demanding costly sacrifices of their adherents, such as patriotism.

The next-to-last attribute of religions is that belief in gods and other postulated supernatural agents has practical consequences for how people should behave. Those rules of behavior may variously take the form of laws, moral codes, taboos, or obligations, depending on the type of society. While virtually all religions have such rules of behavior, it is not the case that rules of behavior stem only from religion: modern secular state governments, countless non-religious groups, and atheistic or agnostic citizens also have their own rules.

Finally, many religions teach that supernatural agents not only reward virtuous rule-obeying people and punish evil-doers and rule-breakers, but also can be induced by prayers, donations, and sacrifices to intervene on behalf of mortal petitioners.

Thus, religion involves a constellation of five sets of attributes, which vary in strength among the world's religions (including traditional religions). We may use this constellation to understand the differences between religion and several related phenomena that share some but not all of the attributes of religion. Patriotism and ethnic pride resemble religion in being social movements distinguishing their adherents from outsiders, demanding sacrifice (even of one's life) as a display of one's commitment, and celebrated in rituals and ceremonies such as (for Americans) Independence Day, Thanksgiving Day, and Memorial Day. Unlike religion, patriotism and ethnic pride do not teach belief in supernatural agents. Sports fans, like religious believers, form social groups of adherents (e.g., Boston Red Sox fans) distinct from adherents of other social groups (e.g., New York Yankee fans) but don't espouse supernatural agents, don't demand great sacrifices as proof of affiliation, and don't regulate a broad range of moral behavior. Marxism, socialism, and other political movements do attract committed groups of adherents (like religions), motivate adherents to die for their ideals, and may have broad moral codes, but don't rely on the supernatural. Magic, sorcery, superstition, and water-witching (the belief that underground water can be located by a divining rod) do involve belief in supernatural agents with consequences for everyday behavior. However, magic, superstition, and related phenomena do not serve as defining attributes of committed social groups akin to believers: there are not groups of believers in the dangers of black cats who meet every Sunday to re-affirm their separateness from non-believers in the dangers of black cats. Perhaps the grayest borderline area involves movements such as Buddhism, Confucianism, and Shintoism, about which there are varying degrees of uncertainty whether they constitute religions or else philosophies of life.

Functions and electric eels

Religion is nearly universal in humans, but nothing even remotely resembling it has been described in animals. Nevertheless, we can inquire about—indeed, we have to wonder about—the origins of religion, just as we wonder about the origins of other uniquely human traits such as art and spoken language. Six million years ago, our ancestors were apes that surely lacked religion; by the time that the first written documents appeared around 5,000 years ago, there was already religion. What happened in the intervening 5,995,000 years? What were religion's antecedents in animals and in human ancestors, and when and why did it arise?

A method termed the functional approach has been the commonest framework adopted by scholars of religion since they began studying it scientifically almost 150 years ago. They ask: what functions does religion fulfill? They note that religion often imposes heavy costs on individuals and societies, such as impelling many people to live celibate lives and to forgo having children, to go to the effort and expense of building huge pyramids, to kill one's valuable domestic animals and occasionally even one's own child and oneself, and to spend much time repeating the same words over and over again. Religion must have functions and bring benefits to offset those heavy costs; otherwise, it wouldn't have come into being and couldn't be maintained. What human problems did the invention of religion solve? A brief summary of the functional approach might be to assert something like this: religion was invented in order to carry out certain functions and solve certain problems, such as maintaining social order, comforting anxious people, and teaching political obedience.

Another approach, emerging more recently from the field of evolutionary psychology, objects: religion surely didn't evolve and wasn't consciously invented for any specific purpose or to solve any specific problem. It wasn't the case that some budding chief got a brilliant idea one day and invented religion from scratch, foreseeing that he could more easily hold his subjects in sway if he convinced them of religious reasons to build a pyramid. Nor is it likely that a psychologically attuned hunter-gatherer, concerned that his fellow tribesmen had become too depressed by a recent death to go hunting, made up a story about the afterlife in order to console them and give them new hope. Religion instead probably arose as a by-product of some other capacities of our ancestors and of their own animal ancestors, and those capacities had unforeseen consequences and gradually acquired new functions as they developed.

To an evolutionary biologist like myself, there is no contradiction between these two different approaches to the origin of religion, in effect postulating two stages. Biological evolution itself similarly proceeds in two stages. First, variation between individuals is generated by mutations and recombinations of genes. Second, because of natural selection and sexual selection there are differences among the resulting variant individuals in how they survive, reproduce, and pass on their genes to the next generation. That is, some of those variant individuals turn out to perform functions and to solve life's problems better than do other variant individuals. A functional problem (e.g., surviving in a colder climate) isn't solved by an animal realizing that it needs thicker fur, nor by cold climates stimulating mutations for a thicker fur. Instead, something (in the case of biological evolution, the mechanisms of molecular genetics) creates something else (in this case, an animal with thicker or thinner fur), and some life conditions or environmental problems (in this case, cold temperatures) endow some but not others of those variant animals with a useful function. Thus, gene mutations and recombinations provide the origins of biological diversity, while natural selection and sexual selection sieve that starting material by the criterion of function.

Similarly, evolutionary psychologists assert that religion is a by-product of features of the human brain that arose for reasons other than building pyramids or comforting bereaved relatives. To an evolutionary biologist, that's plausible and unsurprising. Evolutionary history is chock-full of by-products and mutations that were initially selected for one function and then developed further and became selected to fulfill another function. For example, creationists skeptical of the reality of evolution used to point to electric eels that electrocute their prey with 600-volt shocks, and then argued that a 600-volt eel could never have arisen from a normal no-volt eel by natural selection, because the necessary intermediate stages of low-voltage eels couldn't electrocute any prey and wouldn't be good for anything. In fact, it turns out that 600-volt eels evolved through changes of function, as a by-product of electric field detection and electricity generation in normal fish.

Many fish have skin sense organs sensitive to electric fields in the environment. Those fields can be either of physical origin (e.g., from ocean currents or from the mixing of waters of different salinities), or else of biological origin (from the electrical triggering of animals' muscle contractions). Fish possessing such electric-sensitive sense organs can employ them for two functions: to detect prey, and to navigate through the environment, especially in muddy water and under nighttime conditions where eyes are of little use. The prey reveal themselves to the animals' electric field detector by having a much higher electrical conductivity than does fresh water. That detection of environmental electric fields may be termed passive electrodetection; it does not require any specialized electricity-generating organs.

But some fish species go further and generate their own low-voltage electric fields, which let them detect objects not only by an object's own electric field, but also by its modification of the electric field set up by the fish. Organs specialized to generate electricity evolved independently in at least six separate lineages of fish. Most electrical organs are derived from the electricity-generating membranes of muscles, but one fish species develops its electric organs from nerves. The zoologist Hans Lissmann furnished the first compelling proof of such active electrodetection, after much inconclusive speculation by others. Lissmann conditioned electric fish, by food rewards, to distinguish an electrically conducting object from a non-conducting object of identical appearance, such as a conducting metal disk versus an identical-looking non-conducting plastic or glass disk. While I was working in a Cambridge University laboratory near the building in which Lissmann was doing his studies, a friend of Lissmann told me a story illustrating the sensitivity of electrodetection by electric fishes. Lissmann noticed that a captive electric fish that he was maintaining in his laboratory got excited around the same time in the late afternoon of every weekday. He eventually realized that it was because his female technician was getting ready to go home at that hour, stepped behind a screen, and combed her hair, which set up an electric field that the fish could detect.

Low-voltage fish use their electricity-generating organs and their skin electrodetectors for improved efficiency of two different functions, both shared with the many fish possessing electrodetectors but lacking electricity-generating organs: prey detection and navigation. Low-voltage fish also use each other's electric impulses for a third function, that of communicating with each other. Depending on the pattern of the electric impulses, which varies among species and individuals, a fish can extract information and thereby recognize the species, sex, size, and individual (strange or familiar) of fish generating the impulses. A low-voltage fish also communicates social messages to other fish of its species: in effect, it can electrically say, "This is my territory, you get out," or "Me Tarzan, you Jane, you turn me on, it's time for sex."

Fish generating a few volts could not only detect prey but could also use their shocks for a fourth function: to kill small prey, like minnows. More and more volts let one kill bigger and bigger prey, until one arrives at a 600-volt eel six feet long that can stun a horse in the river. (I remember this evolutionary history all too vividly, because I started to do my Ph.D. thesis on electricity generation by electric eels. I got so absorbed in the molecular details of electricity generation that I forgot the end results, and I impulsively grabbed my first eel to start my first experiment—with a shocking outcome.) High-volt fish can also use their powerful discharges for two more functions: to defend themselves against would-be predators, by blasting the attacker; and to hunt by "electrofishing," i.e., attracting prey to the electrically positive end of the fish (the anode), a technique also used by commercial fishermen who however have to generate electricity with batteries or generators rather than with their own bodies.

Now, let's go back to those skeptical creationists who object that natural selection could never have produced a 600-volt eel from a normal no-volt eel, supposedly because all the necessary intermediate stages of low-volt electric organs would have been useless and wouldn't have helped their owners survive. The answer to the creationist is that killing prey with a 600-volt shock wasn't the original function of electric organs, but arose as a by-product of an organ initially selected for other functions. We've seen that electrical organs acquired six successive functions as natural selection ramped up their output from nothing to 600 volts. A no-volt fish can do passive electrodetection of prey and can navigate; a low-volt fish can perform those same two functions more efficiently, and can also electrocommunicate; and a high-volt fish can electrocute prey, defend itself, and carry out electrofishing. We shall see that human religion topped electric eels by traversing seven rather than just six functions.

The search for causal explanations

From which human attributes might religion similarly have arisen as a by-product? A plausible view is that it was a by-product of our brain's increasingly sophisticated ability to deduce cause, agency, and intent, to anticipate dangers, and thereby to formulate causal explanations of predictive value that helped us survive. Of course animals also have brains and can thereby deduce some intent. For instance, a Barn Owl detecting a mouse by sound in complete darkness can hear the mouse's footsteps, calculate the mouse's direction and speed, thereby deduce the mouse's intent to continue running in that direction at that speed, and pounce at just the correct time and place to intersect the mouse's path and capture the mouse. But animals, even our closest relatives, have far less reasoning ability than do humans. For example, to the African monkeys known as vervet monkeys, ground-dwelling pythons are major predators. The monkeys have a special alarm call that they give at the sight of a python, and they know enough to jump up into a tree if warned by the python alarm call of another monkey nearby. Astonishingly to us, though, those smart monkeys don't associate the sight of the python's track in the grass with the danger that a python may be nearby. Contrast those weak reasoning abilities of monkeys with the abilities of us humans: we have been honed by natural selection for our brains to extract maximum information from trivial cues, and for our language to convey that information precisely, even at the inevitable risk of frequent wrong inferences.

For instance, we routinely attribute agency to other people besides ourselves. We understand that other people have intentions like ourselves, and that individuals vary. Hence we devote much of our daily brain activity to understanding other individual people and to monitoring signs from them (such as their facial expressions, tone of voice, and what they do or don't say or do), in order to predict what some particular individual may do next, and to figure out how we can influence her to behave in a way that we want. We similarly attribute agency to animals: !Kung hunters approaching a prey carcass on which lions are already feeding look at the lions' bellies and behavior to deduce whether the lions are sated and will let themselves be driven off, or whether they are still hungry and will stand their ground. We attribute agency to ourselves: we notice that our own actions have consequences, and if we see that behaving in one way brings success and another doesn't, we learn to repeat the action associated with success. Our brain's ability to discover such causal explanations is the major reason for our success as a species. That's why, by 12,000 years ago, before we had agriculture or metal or writing and were still hunter-gatherers, we already had by far the widest distribution of any mammal species, spread from the Arctic to the equator over all of the continents except Antarctica.

We keep trying out causal explanations. Some of our traditional explanations made the right predictions for reasons that later proved to be scientifically correct; some made the right predictions for the wrong reason (e.g., "avoid eating that particular fish species because of a taboo," without understanding the role of poisonous chemicals in the fish); and some explanations made wrong predictions. For example, hunter-gatherers overgeneralize agency and extend it to other things that can move besides humans and animals, such as rivers and the sun and moon. Traditional peoples often believe those moving inanimate objects to be, or to be propelled by, living beings. They may also attribute agency to non-moving things, such as flowers, a mountain, or a rock. Today we label that as belief in the supernatural, distinct from the natural, but traditional peoples often don't make that distinction. Instead, they come up with causal explanations whose predictive value they observe: their theory that the sun (or a god carrying the sun in his chariot) marches daily across the sky fits the observed facts. They don't have independent knowledge of astronomy to convince them that belief in the sun as an animate agent is a supernatural error. That isn't silly thinking on their part: it's a logical extension of their thinking about undoubtedly natural things.

Thus, one form in which our search for causal explanations overgeneralizes and leads straightforwardly to what today we would term supernatural beliefs consists of attributing agency to plants and non-living things. Another form is our search for consequences of our own behavior. A farmer wonders what he did differently this time to cause a formerly high-yielding field to have a poor yield this year, and Kaulong hunters wonder what a particular hunter did to cause him to fall into a hidden sinkhole in the forest. Like other traditional peoples, the farmers and the hunters rack their brains for explanations. Some of their explanations we now know to be scientifically correct, while others we now consider to be unscientific taboos. For instance, Andean peasant farmers who don't understand coefficients of variation nevertheless scatter their crops among 8 to 22 fields (Chapter 8); they may traditionally have prayed to the rain gods; and Kaulong hunters are careful not to call out the names of cave bats while hunting bats in areas with sinkholes. We have now become convinced that field scattering is a scientifically valid method to ensure yields above some minimum value, and that prayers to rain gods and taboos on calling bat names are scientifically invalid religious superstitions, but that's the wisdom of hindsight. To the farmers and hunters themselves, there isn't a distinction between valid science and religious superstition.

Another arena for over-pursuit of causal explanations is theories of illness. If someone gets sick, the victim and her friends and relatives search for an explanation of the illness just as they would for any other important happening. Was it due to something that the sick person did (e.g., drinking from a certain water source), or neglected to do (e.g., washing her hands before eating, or asking a spirit for help)? Was it because of something that someone else did (e.g., another sick person sneezing on her, or a sorcerer working magic on her)? Like traditional people, we First World citizens in the era of scientific medicine continue to seek satisfying explanations for illness. We have come to believe that drinking from a certain water source or not washing one's hands before eating does provide a valid explanation for illness, and that not asking a spirit for help doesn't. It's not enough to be told that you got stomach cancer because you inherited variant 211 of the PX2R gene; that's unsatisfying and leaves you helpless; maybe instead it was because of your diet. Traditional people seek cures for illness, just as we do today when doctors' cures fail. Often those traditional cures do appear to be beneficial for many possible reasons: most illnesses cure themselves anyway; many traditional plant remedies do prove to have pharmacological value; the shaman's bedside manner relieves the patient's fear and may provide a placebo-based cure; assigning a cause to an illness, even if it's not the right cause, makes the patient feel better by letting him adopt some action rather than waiting helplessly; and if the victim does die, it may mean that he sinned by violating a taboo, or that a powerful sorcerer was responsible who must be identified and killed.

Still another form of our search for causal explanations is to seek explanations for events about which modern science just gives us the unsatisfying answer "It has no explanation, stop trying to find an explanation." For instance, a central problem in most organized religions is the problem of theodicy, the theme of the book of Job: if a good and omnipotent god exists, then why does evil happen in the world? Traditional peoples, ready to discuss for an hour the explanation of a broken stick in the ground, will surely not fail to discuss why a good person apparently obeying the society's rules nevertheless became injured, defeated, or killed. Did he break a taboo, or do evil spirits exist, or were the gods angry? People will also surely not fail to try to explain why someone who an hour ago was breathing, moving, and warm is now cold and not breathing or moving, like a stone: is there a part of the person, called a spirit, that has escaped and entered a bird or is now living somewhere else? Today, you might object that those are searches for "meaning" rather than for explanations, and that science provides only explanations, and that you should either turn to religion for meaning or else acknowledge that your thirst for meaning is meaningless. But everybody in the past, and still most people today, want their demand for "meaning" answered.

In short, what we now term religion may have arisen as a by-product of the human brain's increasing sophistication at identifying causal explanations and at making predictions. For a long time there wouldn't have been a recognized distinction between the natural and the supernatural, or between religion and the rest of life. As for when "religion" arose in the course of human evolution, I would guess: very gradually, as our brain became more sophisticated. Over 15,000 years ago, Cro-Magnons were already sewing tailored clothing, inventing new tools, and creating superb paintings of polychrome animals and humans on the walls of the Lascaux, Altamira, and Chauvet caves, in deep chambers where the paintings would have been visible only by candlelight, and which fill many modern visitors with religious awe (Plate 25). Whether or not arousing awe was the actual intent of the prehistoric painters, they surely had sufficiently modern brains to be capable of holding beliefs qualifying as religious. As for our Neanderthal relatives, for whom there is evidence that they decorated with ocher pigments and buried their dead—maybe. It seems to me safe to assume that our ancestors have had religious beliefs for at least the 60,000-year-plus history of behaviorally modern *Homo sapiens,* and perhaps for much longer.

Table 9.2. Examples of supernatural beliefs confined to particular religions

1. There is a monkey god who travels thousands of kilometers at a single somersault. (Hindu)

2. You can obtain benefits from the spirits by spending four days in a lonely place without food and water and cutting off a finger joint from your left hand. (Crow Indians)

3. A woman who had not been fertilized by a man became pregnant and gave birth to a baby boy, whose body eventually after his death was carried up to a place called heaven, often represented as being located in the sky. (Catholic)

4. A shaman, who is paid for his efforts, sits in a house in dim light together with all of the village's adults, who close their eyes. The shaman goes to the bottom of the ocean, where he pacifies the sea goddess who had been causing misfortunes. (Inuit)

5. To determine whether a person accused of adultery is guilty, force-feed a poisonous paste to a chicken. If the chicken does not die, that means that the accused person was innocent. (Azande)

6. Men who sacrifice their lives in battle for the religion will be carried to a heaven populated by beautiful virgin women. (Islam)

7. On Tepeyac Hill north of Mexico City in 1531, the Virgin Mary appeared to a Christianized Indian, spoke to him in Nahuatl (the Aztec language, at that time still widely spoken there), and enabled him to pick roses in a desert area where roses normally can't grow. (Mexican Catholic)

8. On a hilltop near Manchester Village in western New York State on September 21, 1823, the Angel Moroni appeared to a man named Joseph Smith and revealed to him buried golden plates awaiting translation as a lost book of the Bible, the Book of Mormon. (Mormon)

9. A supernatural being gave a chunk of desert in the Middle East to the being's favorite group of people, as their home forever. (Jewish)

10. In the 1880s God appeared to a Paiute Indian named Wovoka during a solar eclipse, and informed him that in two years buffalo would again fill the plains and white men would vanish, provided that Indians took part in a ritual called the Ghost Dance.

Supernatural beliefs

Virtually all religions hold some supernatural beliefs specific to that religion. That is, a religion's adherents firmly hold beliefs that conflict with and cannot be confirmed by our experience of the natural world, and that appear implausible to people other than the adherents of that particular religion. **Table 9.2** offers a sample of such beliefs, to which innumerable other examples could be added. No other feature of religion creates a bigger divide between religious believers and modern secular people, to whom it staggers the imagination that anyone could entertain such beliefs. No other feature creates a bigger divide between believers in two different religions, each of whom firmly believes its own beliefs but considers it absurd that the other religion's believers believe those other beliefs. Why, nevertheless, are supernatural beliefs such universal features of religions?

One suggested answer is that supernatural religious beliefs are just ignorant superstitions similar to supernatural non-religious beliefs, illustrating only that the human brain is capable of deceiving itself into believing anything. We can all think of supernatural non-religious beliefs whose implausibility should be obvious. Many Europeans believe that the sight of a black cat heralds misfortune, but black cats are actually rather common. By repeatedly tallying whether or not a one-hour period following or not following your observation of a black cat in an area with high cat density did or did not bring you some specified level of misfortune, and by applying the statistician's chi-square test, you can quickly convince yourself that the black-cat hypothesis has a probability of less than 1 out of 1,000 of being true. Some groups of New Guinea lowlanders believe that hearing the beautiful whistled song of the little bird known as the Lowland Mouse-Babbler warns us that someone has recently died, but this bird is among the commonest species and most frequent singers in New Guinea lowland forests. If the belief about it were true, the local human population would be dead within a few days, yet my New Guinea friends are as convinced of the babbler's ill omens as Europeans are afraid of black cats.

A more striking non-religious superstition, because people today still invest money in their mistaken belief, is water-witching, also variously known as dowsing, divining, or rhabdomancy. Already established in Europe over 400 years ago and possibly also reported before the time of Christ, this belief maintains that rotation of a forked twig carried by a practitioner called a dowser, walking over terrain whose owner wants to know where to dig a well, indicates the location and sometimes the depth of an invisible underground water supply (Plate 46). Control tests show that dowsers' success at locating underground water is no better than random, but many land-owners in areas where geologists also have difficulty at predicting the location of underground water nevertheless pay dowsers for their search, then spend even more money to dig a well unlikely to yield water. The psychology behind such beliefs is that we remember the hits and forget the misses, so that whatever superstitious beliefs we hold become confirmed by even the flimsiest of evidence through the remembered hits. Such anecdotal thinking comes naturally; controlled experiments and scientific methods to distinguish between random and non-random phenomena are counterintuitive and unnatural, and thus not found in traditional societies.

Perhaps, then, religious superstitions are just further evidence of human fallibility, like belief in black cats and other non-religious superstitions. But it's suspicious that costly commitments to belief in implausible-to-others religious superstitions are such a consistent feature of religions. The investments that the 10 groups of adherents listed in Table 9.2 make or made to their beliefs are far more burdensome, time-consuming, and heavy in consequences to them than are the actions of black-cat-phobics in occasionally avoiding black cats. This suggests that religious superstitions aren't just an accidental by-product of human reasoning powers but possess some deeper meaning. What might that be?

A recent interpretation among some scholars of religion is that belief in religious superstitions serves to display one's commitment to one's religion. All long-lasting human groups—Boston Red Sox fans (like me), devoted Catholics, patriotic Japanese, and others—face the same basic problem of identifying who can be trusted to remain as a group member. The more of one's life is wrapped up with one's group, the more crucial it is to be able to identify group members correctly, and not to be deceived by someone who seeks temporary advantage by claiming to share your ideals but really doesn't. If that man carrying a Boston Red Sox banner, whom you had accepted as a fellow Red Sox fan, suddenly cheers when the New York Yankees hit a home run, you'll find it humiliating but not life-threatening. But if he's a soldier next to you in the front line and he drops his gun (or turns it on you) when the enemy attacks, your misreading of him may cost you your life.

That's why religious affiliation involves so many costly displays to demonstrate the sincerity of your commitment: sacrifices of time and resources, enduring of hardships, and other costly displays that I'll discuss later. One such display might be to espouse some irrational belief that contradicts the evidence of our senses, and that people outside our religion would never believe. If you claim that the founder of your church had been conceived by normal sexual intercourse between his mother and father, anyone else would believe that too, and you've done nothing to demonstrate your commitment to your church. But if you insist, despite all evidence to the contrary, that he was born of a virgin birth, and nobody has been able to shake you of that irrational belief after many decades of your life, then your fellow believers will feel much more confident that you'll persist in your belief and can be trusted not to abandon your group.

Nevertheless, it's not the case that there are no limits to what can be accepted as a religious supernatural belief. Scott Atran and Pascal Boyer have independently pointed out that actual religious superstitions over the whole world constitute a narrow subset of all the arbitrary random superstitions that one could theoretically invent. To quote Pascal Boyer, there is no religion proclaiming anything like the following tenet: "There is only one God! He is omnipotent. But he exists only on Wednesdays." Instead, the religious supernatural beings in which we believe are surprisingly similar to humans, animals, or other natural objects, except for having superior powers. They are more far-sighted, longer-lived, and stronger, travel faster, can predict the future, can change shape, can pass through walls, and so on. In other respects, gods and ghosts behave like people. The god of the Old Testament got angry, while Greek gods and goddesses became jealous, ate, drank, and had sex. Their powers surpassing human powers are projections of our own personal power fantasies; they can do what we wish we could do ourselves. I do have fantasies of hurling thunderbolts that destroy evil people, and probably many other people share those fantasies of mine, but I have never fantasized existing only on Wednesdays. Hence it doesn't surprise me that gods in many religions are pictured as smiting evil-doers, but that no religion holds out the dream of existing just on Wednesdays. Thus, religious supernatural beliefs are irrational, but emotionally plausible and satisfying. That's why they're so believable, despite at the same time being rationally implausible.

Religion's function of explanation

Religion has changed its functions with time over the course of the history of human societies. Two of its oldest functions have variously decreased or almost disappeared among citizens of Westernized societies today. Conversely, several of its major modern functions scarcely existed in small-scale hunter-gatherer and farming societies. Four functions that were formerly weak or non-existent rose to peak importance and have now been declining again. These changes of religion's functions during its evolution are similar to the changes of function of many biological structures (such as fish electric organs) and forms of social organization during biological evolution.

I shall now discuss what are proposed by various scholars as seven major functions of religion, to conclude by asking whether religion is becoming obsolete or is likely to survive and, if the latter, which functions will sustain its persistence. I'll consider these seven functions roughly in the inferred sequence of their appearance and disappearance during the history of societal evolution, starting with functions prominent early in human history but less so now, and ending with functions originally absent but prominent recently or now.

An original function of religion was explanation. Pre-scientific traditional peoples offer explanations for everything they encounter, of course without the prophetic ability to distinguish between those explanations that scientists today consider natural and scientific, and those others that scientists now consider supernatural and religious. To traditional peoples, they are all explanations, and those explanations that subsequently became viewed as religious aren't something separate. For instance, the New Guinea societies in which I have lived offer many explanations for bird behavior that modern ornithologists consider perceptive and still accurate (e.g., the multiple functions of bird calls), along with other explanations that ornithologists no longer accept and now dismiss as supernatural (e.g., that songs of certain bird species are voices of former people who became transformed into birds). Origin myths, like those of tribal people and of the book of Genesis, are widespread to explain the existence of the universe, people, and language diversity. The ancient Greeks, who identified correct scientific explanations for many phenomena, incorrectly invoked gods as supernatural agents to explain sunrises, sunsets, tides, winds, and rain. Creationists, and the majority of Americans today, still invoke God as a "First Cause" who created the universe and its laws and thus accounts for their existence, and who also created every plant and animal species, including the human species. But I'm not aware of creationists continuing to evoke God to explain every sunrise, tide, and wind. Many secular people today, while attributing to God the universe's origin and its laws, accept that the universe, once thus created, has thereafter run with little or no divine interference.

In modern Western society, religion's original explanatory role has increasingly become usurped by science. The origins of the universe as we know it are now attributed to the Big Bang and the subsequent operation of the laws of physics. Modern language diversity is no longer explained by origin myths, such as the Tower of Babel or the snapping of the lianas holding the New Guinea ironwood tree, but is instead considered as adequately explained by observed historical processes of language change, as I shall discuss in Chapter 10. Explanations of sunrises, sunsets, and tides are now left to astronomers, and explanations of winds and rain are left to meteorologists. Bird songs are explained by ethology, and the origin of each plant and animal species, including the human species, is left to evolutionary biologists to interpret.

For many modern scientists, the last bastion of religious explanation is God-as-First-Cause: science seemingly can have nothing to say about why the universe exists at all. From my freshman year at Harvard College in 1955, I recall the great theologian Paul Tillich defying his class of hyper-rational undergraduates to come up with a scientific answer to his simple question: "Why is there something, when there could have been nothing?" None of my classmates majoring in the sciences could give Tillich any answer. But they in turn would have objected that Tillich's own answer "God" consisted merely of putting a name on his lack of an answer. In fact, scientists are working now on Tillich's question and have proposed answers.

Defusing anxiety

The next function of religion that I'll discuss is another one that was probably strongest in early societies: religion's role in defusing our anxiety over problems and dangers beyond our control. When people have done everything realistically within their power, that's when they are most likely to resort to prayers, rituals, ceremonies, donations to the gods, consulting oracles and shamans, reading omens, observing taboos, and performing magic. All of those measures are scientifically ineffective at producing the desired result. However, by preserving the fiction and convincing ourselves that we are still doing something, aren't helpless, and haven't given up, we at least feel in charge, less anxious, and able to go on to make our best effort.

Our craving for relief from feeling helpless is illustrated by a study of religious Israeli women, carried out by anthropologists Richard Sosis and W. Penn Handwerker. During the 2006 Lebanon War the Hizbollah launched Katyusha rockets against the Galilee region of northern Israel, and the town of Tzfat and its environs in particular were hit by dozens of rockets daily. Although siren warnings while rockets were en route alerted Tzfat residents to protect their own lives by taking refuge in bomb shelters, they could do nothing to protect their houses. Realistically, that threat from the rockets was unpredictable and uncontrollable. Nevertheless, about two-thirds of the women interviewed by Sosis and Handwerker recited psalms every day to cope with the stress of the rocket attacks. When they were asked why they did so, a common reply was that they felt compelled "to do *something*" as opposed to doing nothing at all. Although reciting psalms does not actually deflect rockets, it did provide the chanters with a sense of control as they went through the semblance of taking action. (Of course, they themselves did not give that explanation; they did believe that reciting psalms can protect one's house from destruction by a rocket.) Compared to women in the same community who did not recite psalms, the psalm reciters had less difficulty falling asleep, had less difficulty concentrating, were less inclined to bursts of anger, and felt less anxious, nervous, tense, and depressed. Thus, they really did benefit, by reducing the risk that natural anxiety over uncontrollable danger would cause them to endanger themselves in a different way by doing something foolish. As all of us who have been in situations of unpredictable and uncontrollable danger know, we do become prone to multiply our problems by thoughtlessness if we can't master our anxiety.

This function of religion, at its peak already in early religious societies, would have decreased as societies increased their control over life's course, through state government growing stronger and decreasing the frequency of violence and other dangers, states becoming increasingly able to avert famines by distributing stored food, and (in the last two centuries) the development of science and technology. But it's hardly the case that traditional people were largely helpless. Instead, they impress us with their ability to use their observations and their experience so as to leave as little room for chance as possible. For instance, New Guineans and other traditional farmers know dozens of varieties of sweet potatoes or other crops, where and how best to grow each one, and how to weed, fertilize, mulch, drain, and irrigate. When !Kung men and other hunters go hunting, they study and interpret animal tracks, thereby estimate the number and distance and speed and direction of movement of their prey, and observe the behavior of other animal species that provide clues to prey presence. Fishermen and sailors without compasses or other instruments can still navigate by understanding movements of the sun and stars, winds, ocean currents, reflections on clouds, seabirds, ocean bioluminescence, and other indicators of position. All peoples post defenses and remain alert against enemy attacks, and form alliances and plan ambushes to attack the enemy first.

But for traditional peoples, even more than for us moderns, there are limits to their effectiveness, and large areas beyond their control. Crop yields are affected by unpredictable droughts, rainfall, hail, wind storms, cold temperatures, and insect pests. There is a large role of chance in the movements of individual animals. Most illnesses lie beyond traditional control because of the limits of traditional medical knowledge. Like the Israeli women who recited psalms but couldn't control the paths of the rockets, much also remains beyond the control of traditional peoples after they have done their best. They, and we, rebel against remaining inactive and doing nothing. That makes them and us anxious, feeling helpless, prone to make mistakes, and unable to put out our best efforts. That's where traditional peoples, and still often we today, resort to prayer, rituals, omens, magic, taboos, superstitions, and shamans. Believing that those measures are effective, they and we become less anxious, calmer, and more focused.

One example, studied by the ethnographer Bronislaw Malinowski, comes from the Trobriand Islands near New Guinea, where villagers catch fish in two types of locations requiring different fishing methods: in the sheltered, calm inner lagoon, where one dumps poison into a patch of water and then just picks up the stunned or dead fish; and in the open sea, spearing or netting fish while paddling a canoe through waves and surf. Lagoon fishing is safe, easy, and offers predictable yields; open-sea fishing is dangerous and unpredictable, with large bonanzas if a shoal of fish happens to be running at that particular time and place, but with little profit and much personal risk if one doesn't happen to encounter a shoal that day. The islanders perform elaborate magical rituals before embarking on open-sea fishing in order to secure safety and success, because much doubt remains even after they have laid the best plans based on experience. But no magic is associated with lagoon fishing: one merely sets out and does it, without uncertainty or anxiety about the predictable result.

Another example is provided by !Kung hunters, whose expertise seems to leave nothing to chance. Little !Kung boys start playing with tiny bows and arrows from the time that they can walk, and begin hunting with their fathers when they reach adolescence. At evening campfires men recount over and over their previous hunts, listen to each other's stories about who saw what animals where in recent days, and plan the next hunt accordingly. During the hunt itself they remain attuned to sights and sounds of animals and of birds whose behavior may betray the presence of animals, as well as scrutinizing tracks to learn what animal passed by, and where it is likely to be found and to be heading now. One might imagine that these masters of desert hunting skills would have no need for magic. In fact, though, when hunters set out in the morning, there is always a big element of anxiety-provoking uncertainty about where prey will happen to be on that particular morning.

Some !Kung men deal with their anxiety by consulting oracle disks supposed to prophesy what direction will be most promising, and what prey they should be prepared for. Those disks are sets of five or six thin circles of antelope leather graded in diameter from two to three inches, each with its own name and with a recognizable top and bottom. Each man owns a set. A man stacks the disks on the palm of his left hand with the largest disk on top, shakes and blows on the disks, asks a question in a loud ritualized voice, then throws the disks on a garment spread on the ground. A diviner interprets the pattern of disks on the ground according to features that include whether or not they overlap, and which disks land top up or bottom up. The interpretation of the pattern seems to follow few fixed rules, except that disks 1 through 4 landing upside down predict the successful killing of a game animal.

Of course the disks don't tell the !Kung anything that they don't already know. !Kung men understand so much about animal behavior that their hunting plan has a good chance of proving successful, whatever the pattern of the disks. Instead, the disk pattern seems to be interpreted imaginatively like a Rorschach test, and serves to psych men up for a day of hunting. The disk ritual is useful in helping them reach agreement about pursuing one direction; choosing one direction, any direction, and sticking to it are preferable to becoming distracted by arguments.

For us today, prayer and ritual and magic are less widespread, because science and knowledge play a larger role in the success of our endeavors. But there remains much that we still can't control, and many endeavors and dangers where science and technology don't guarantee success. That's where we, too, resort to prayers, offerings, and rituals. Prime examples in the recent past have been prayers for safe completion of sea voyages, bountiful harvests, success in war, and especially healing from disease. When doctors can't predict a patient's outcome with high probability, and especially when doctors admit that they are helpless, that's when people are especially likely to pray.

Two specific examples illustrate for us the association between rituals or prayers on the one hand, and uncertain outcome on the other hand. Gamblers in a game of chance often follow their own personal rituals before throwing the dice, but chess-players don't have such rituals before moving a piece. That's because dice games are known to be games of chance, but there is no role of chance in chess: if your move costs you the game, you have no excuses, it was entirely your own fault for not foreseeing your opponent's response. Similarly, farmers wanting to drill a well to find underground water often consult dowsers in western New Mexico, where the area's local geological complexity results in big unpredictable variation in the depth and quantity of underground water, such that not even professional geologists can predict accurately from surface features the location and depth of underground water. In the Texas Panhandle, though, where the water table lies at a uniform depth of 125 feet, farmers merely drill a well to that depth at a site nearest to where the water is needed; no one uses dowsers, although people are familiar with the method. That is, New Mexico farmers and dice players deal with unpredictability by resorting to rituals just as do Trobriand ocean fishermen and !Kung hunters, while Texas Panhandle farmers and chess-players dispense with rituals just as do Trobriand lagoon fishermen.

In short, religious (and also non-religious) rituals are still with us to help us deal with anxiety in the face of uncertainty and danger. However, this function of religion was much more important in traditional societies facing greater uncertainty and danger than do modern Westernized societies.

Providing comfort

Let's now turn to a function of religion that must have expanded over the last 10,000 years: to provide comfort, hope, and meaning when life is hard. A specific example is to comfort us at the prospect of our own death and at the death of a loved one. Some mammals—elephants are a striking example—appear to recognize and mourn the death of a close companion. But we have no reason to suspect that any animal except us humans understands that, one day, it too will die. We would inevitably have realized that that fate lay in store for us as we acquired self-consciousness and better reasoning power, and began to generalize from watching our fellow band members die. Almost all observed and archaeologically attested human groups demonstrate their understanding of death's significance by not just discarding their dead but somehow providing for them by burial, cremation, wrapping, mummification, cooking, or other means.

It's frightening to see someone who was recently warm, moving, talking, and capable of self-defense now cold, motionless, silent, and helpless. It's frightening to imagine that happening to us, too. Most religions provide comfort by in effect denying death's reality, and by postulating some sort of afterlife for a soul postulated as associated with the body. One's soul together with a replica of one's body may go to a supernatural place called heaven or some other name; or one's soul may become transformed into a bird or another person here on Earth. Religions that proclaim an afterlife often go further and use it not just to deny death but also to hold out hope for something even better awaiting us after death, such as eternal life, reunion with one's loved ones, freedom from care, nectar, and beautiful virgins.

In addition to our pain at the prospect of death, there are many other pains of life for which religion offers comfort in various ways. One way is to "explain" a suffering by declaring it not to be a meaningless random event but to possess some deeper meaning: e.g., it was to test you for your worthiness for the afterlife, or it was to punish you for your sins, or it was an evil done to you by some bad person whom you should hire a sorcerer to identify and kill. Another way is to promise that amends will be made to you in the afterlife for your suffering: yes, you suffered here, but never fear, you will be rewarded after your death. Still a third way is to promise not only that will your suffering be offset in a happy afterlife, but also that those who did you evil will have a miserable afterlife. While punishing your enemies on Earth gives you only finite revenge and satisfaction, the eternal exquisite tortures that they will suffer after death in Dante's Inferno will guarantee you all the revenge and satisfaction that you could ever long for. Hell has a double function: to comfort you by smiting your enemies whom you were unable to smite yourself here on Earth; and to motivate you to obey your religion's moral commands, by threatening to send you too there if you misbehave. Thus, the postulated afterlife resolves the paradox of theodicy (the co-existence of evil and a good God) by assuring you not to worry; all scores will be settled later.

This comforting function of religion must have emerged early in our evolutionary history, as soon as we were smart enough to realize that we'd die, and to wonder why life was often painful. Hunter-gatherers do often believe in survival after death as spirits. But this function expanded greatly later with the rise of so-called world-rejecting religions, which assert not only that there is an afterlife, but that it's even more important and long-lasting than this earthly life, and that the overriding goal of earthly life is to obtain salvation and prepare you for the afterlife. While world rejection is strong in Christianity, Islam, and some forms of Buddhism, it also characterizes some secular (i.e., non-religious) philosophies such as Plato's. Such beliefs can be so compelling that some religious people actually reject the worldly life. Monks and nuns in residential orders do so insofar as they live, sleep, and eat separately from the secular world, although they may go out into it daily in order to minister, teach, and preach. But there are other orders that isolate themselves as completely as possible from the secular world. Among them were the Cistercian order, whose great monasteries at Rievaulx, Fountains Abbey, and Jerveaulx in England remain England's best-preserved monastic ruins because they were erected far from towns and hence were less subject to plunder and re-use after they were abandoned. Even more extreme was the world rejection practiced by a few Irish monks who settled as hermits in otherwise uninhabited Iceland.

Small-scale societies place much less emphasis on world rejection, salvation, and the afterlife than do large-scale, more complex and recent societies. There are at least three reasons for this trend. First, social stratification and inequality have increased, from egalitarian small-scale societies to large complex societies with their kings, nobles, elite, rich, and members of highly ranked clans contrasting with their mass of poor peasants and laborers. If everybody else around you is suffering as much as you are, then there is no unfairness to be explained, and no visible example of the good life to which to aspire. But the observation that some people have much more comfortable lives and can dominate you takes a lot of explaining and comforting, which religion offers.

A second reason why large, complex societies emphasize comforting and the afterlife more than do small-scale societies is that archaeological and ethnographic evidence shows that life really did become harder as hunter-gatherers became farmers and assembled in larger societies. With the transition to agriculture, the average daily number of work hours increased, nutrition deteriorated, infectious disease and body wear increased, and lifespan shortened. Conditions deteriorated even further for urban proletariats during the Industrial Revolution, as work days lengthened, and as hygiene, health, and pleasures diminished. Finally, as we shall discuss below, complex populous societies have more formalized moral codes, more black-and-white emphasis on good and evil, and bigger resulting problems of theodicy: why, if you yourself are behaving virtuously and obeying the laws, do law-breakers and the rest of the world get away with being cruel to you?

All three of these reasons suggest why the comforting function of religion has increased in more populous and recent societies: it's simply that those societies inflict on us more bad things for which we crave comfort. This comforting role of religion helps explain the frequent observation that misfortune tends to make people more religious, and that poorer social strata, regions, and countries tend to be more religious than richer ones: they need more comforting. Among the world's nations today, the percentage of citizens who say that religion is an important part of their daily lives is 80%–99% for most nations with per-capita gross domestic products (GDP) under $10,000, but only 17%–43% for most nations with per-capita GDP over $30,000. (That doesn't account for high religious commitment in the rich U.S., which I'll mention in the next paragraph.) Even within just the U.S., there appear to be more churches and more church attendance in poorer areas than in richer areas, despite the greater resources and leisure time available to build and attend churches in richer areas. Within American society, the highest religious commitment and the most radical Christian branches are found among the most marginalized, underprivileged social groups.

It may initially seem surprising that religion has been maintaining itself or even growing in the modern world, despite the rise in two factors already mentioned as undermining religion: science's recent usurpation of religion's original explanatory role; and our increased technology and societal effectiveness reducing dangers that lie beyond our control and thus inviting prayer. That religion nevertheless shows no signs of dying out may be due to our persistent quest for "meaning." We humans have always sought meaning in our lives that can otherwise seem meaningless, purposeless, and evanescent, and in a world full of unpredictable unfortunate events. Now along comes science, seeming to say that "meaning" isn't meaningful, and that our individual lives really are meaningless, purposeless, and evanescent except as packages of genes for which the measure of success is just self-propagation. Some atheists would maintain that the problem of theodicy doesn't exist; good and evil are just human definitions; if cancer or a car crash kills X and Y but not A and B, that's just a random catastrophe; there isn't any afterlife; and if you've suffered or been abused here on Earth, it won't be fixed for you in the afterlife. If you respond to those atheists, "I don't like to hear that, tell me it's not true, show me some way in which science has its own way of providing meaning," those atheists' response would be "Your request is in vain, get over it, stop looking for meaning, there isn't any meaning—it's just that, as Donald Rumsfeld said of looting during the war in Iraq, 'Stuff happens!' " But we still have our same old brains that crave meaning. We have several million years of evolutionary history telling us, "Even if that's true, I don't like it and I'm not going to believe it: if science won't give me meaning, I'll look to religion for it." That's probably a significant factor in the persistence and even growth of religion in this century of growth in science and technology. It may contribute part—surely not all, but perhaps part—of the explanation for why the United States, the country with the most highly developed scientific and technological establishment, is also the most religious among wealthy First World countries. The greater gulf between rich and poor people in the U.S. than in Europe may be another part of the explanation.

Organization and obedience

The remaining four features of religion that I'll discuss—standardized organization, preaching political obedience, regulating behavior towards strangers by means of formal moral codes, and justifying wars—were absent in small-scale societies, appeared with the rise of chiefdoms and states, and have declined again in modern secular states. A defining feature of modern religions that we take for granted is standardized organization. Most modern religions have full-time priests, alias rabbis, ministers, imams, or whatever else they may be called, who receive either a salary or else life's necessities. Modern religions also have churches (alias temples, synagogues, mosques, etc.). Within any given sect, all of its churches use a standardized sacred book (Bible, Torah, Koran, etc.), rituals, art, music, architecture, and clothing. A practising Catholic who has grown up in Los Angeles and visits New York City can celebrate Sunday mass in a New York Catholic church and find all those features familiar. In religions of small-scale societies, on the other hand, all of those features either aren't standardized (rituals , art, music, clothing) or don't exist at all (full-time priests, dedicated churches, sacred books). While small-scale societies may have their shamans, and some of those shamans may receive fees or gifts, the shamans are not full-time professionals: they have to hunt, gather, and grow crops like every other able-bodied adult in their band or tribe.

Historically, those organizational features of religion arose to solve a new problem emerging as ancient human societies became richer, more populous, and both obliged and enabled to become more centralized. Band and tribal societies are too small and unproductive to generate food surpluses that could feed full-time priests, chiefs, tax collectors, potters, shamans, or specialists of any sort. Instead, every adult has to acquire his or her own food by hunting, gathering, or farming himself or herself. Only larger and more productive societies generate surpluses that can be used to feed chiefs and other leaders or craft specialists, none of whom grow or hunt food.

How did such a diversion of food come about? A dilemma results from the confluence of three self-evident facts: populous societies are likely to defeat small societies; populous societies require full-time leaders and bureaucrats, because 20 people can sit around a campfire and reach a consensus but 20,000,000 people cannot; and full-time leaders and bureaucrats must be fed. But how does the chief or king get the peasants to tolerate what is basically the theft of their food by classes of social parasites? This problem is familiar to the citizens of any democracy, who ask themselves the same question at each election: what have the incumbents done since the last election to justify the fat salaries that they pay themselves out of the public coffers?

The solution devised by every well-understood chiefdom and early state society—from ancient Egypt and Mesopotamia, through Polynesian Hawaii, to the Inca Empire—was to proclaim an organized religion with the following tenets: the chief or king is related to the gods, or even is a god; and he or she can intercede with the gods on behalf of the peasants, e.g., to send rain or to ensure a good harvest. The chief or king also renders valuable services by organizing the peasants to construct public works, such as roads, irrigation systems, and storehouses that benefit everybody. In return for those services, the peasants should feed the chief and his priests and tax collectors. Standardized rituals, carried out at standardized temples, serve to teach those religious tenets to the peasants so that they will obey the chief and his lackeys. Also fed by food collected from the peasants are armies obedient to the chief or king, with which the chief can conquer neighboring lands and thereby acquire more territory for the benefit of his peasants. Those armies bring two further advantages to the chief: wars against neighbors may enlist the energy of ambitious young nobles who might otherwise scheme to overthrow the chief; and the armies are ready to put down revolts by the peasants themselves. As early theocratic states evolved into the empires of ancient Babylon and Rome and commandeered more and more food and labor, the architectural trappings of state religions became more elaborate. That's why Karl Marx viewed religion as the opium of the people (Table 9.1), and an instrument of class oppression.

Of course, within recent centuries in the Judeo-Christian world, this trend has been reversed, and religion is much less than before the handmaiden of the state. Politicians and the upper classes now rely on means other than assertions of divinity to persuade or coerce all of us peasants. But the fusion of religion and state persists in some Muslim countries, Israel, and (until recently) Japan and Italy. Even the United States government invokes God on its currency and places official chaplains in Congress and in the armed forces, and every American president (whether Democrat or Republican) intones "God bless America" at the close of speeches.

Codes of behavior towards strangers

Yet another attribute of religion that became important in state societies but that didn't exist in the smallest societies was to dictate moral concepts of behavior towards strangers. All major world religions teach what is right, what is wrong, and how one should behave. But this link between religion and morality is weaker or absent, especially as regards behavior towards strangers, in the New Guinea societies of which I have experience. Instead, social obligations there depend heavily on relationships. Because a band or tribe contains only a few dozen or a few hundred individuals respectively, everyone knows everyone else and their relationships. One owes different obligations to different blood relatives, to relatives by marriage, to members of one's own clan, and to fellow villagers belonging to a different clan.

Those relationships determine, for example, whether you may refer to people by their names, marry them, or demand that they share their food and house with you. If you get into a fight with another tribe member, everyone else in the tribe is related to or knows both of you and pulls you apart. The problem of behaving peacefully towards unfamiliar individuals doesn't arise, because the only unfamiliar individuals are members of enemy tribes. Should you happen to meet an unfamiliar person in the forest, of course you try to kill him or else to run away; our modern custom of just saying hello and starting a friendly chat would be suicidal.

Thus, a new problem arose by around 7,500 years ago, when some tribal societies evolved into chiefdoms comprising thousands of individuals—a far greater number than any single person can know by name and relationship. Emergent chiefdoms and states faced big problems of potential instability, because the old tribal rules of behavior no longer sufficed. If you encountered an unfamiliar member of your chiefdom and fought with him according to tribal rules of behavior, a brawl would result as your relatives jumped in on your side and his relatives jumped in on his side. A death in such a brawl would spark efforts by the victim's relatives to kill one of the murderer's relatives in revenge. What's to save the society from collapsing in an incessant orgy of brawls and revenge murders?

The solution to this dilemma of large societies is the one used in our own society, and documented in all chiefdoms and early states for which we have information. Rules of peaceful behavior apply between all members of the society, regardless of whether some individual whom you encounter is familiar to you or a stranger. The rules are enforced by the political leaders (chiefs or kings) and their agents, who justify the rules by a new function of religion. The gods or supernatural agents are presumed to be the authors of the rules, codified in formal codes of morality. People are taught from childhood onward to obey the rules, and to expect severe punishment for breaking them (because now an attack on another person is also an offense against the gods). Prime examples familiar to Jews and Christians are the Ten Commandments.

In recent secularized societies, such rules of moral behavior within society have moved beyond their religious origins. The reasons why atheists, as well as many believers, now don't kill their enemies derive from values instilled by society, and from fear of the potent hand of the law rather than fear of the wrath of God. But from the rise of chiefdoms until the recent rise of secular states, religion justified codes of behavior and thereby enabled people to live harmoniously in large societies where one encounters strangers frequently. Religion's function in permitting strangers to live peacefully together, and its function in teaching the masses to obey their political leaders, constitute the twin aspects of the often-discussed roles of religion in maintaining social order. As Voltaire remarked cynically, "If God did not exist, he would have to be invented." Depending on one's perspective, these roles of religion have been regarded as either positive (promoting social harmony) or negative (promoting exploitation of the masses by oppressive elites).

Justifying war

Another new problem faced by emergent chiefdoms and states, but not by the bands and tribes of previous history, involved wars. Because tribes primarily use relationship by blood or marriage, not religion, to justify rules of conduct, tribesmen face no moral dilemmas in killing members of other tribes with whom they have no relationship. But once a state invokes religion to require peaceful behavior toward fellow citizens with whom one has no relationship, how can a state convince its citizens to ignore those same precepts during wartime? States permit, indeed they command, their citizens to steal from and kill citizens of other states against which war has been declared. After a state has spent 18 years teaching a boy "Thou shalt not kill," how can the state turn around and say "Thou must kill, under the following circumstances," without getting its soldiers hopelessly confused and prone to kill the wrong people (e.g., fellow citizens)?

Again, in recent as well as in ancient history, religion comes to the rescue with a new function. The Ten Commandments apply only to one's behavior toward fellow citizens within the chiefdom or state. Most religions claim that they have a monopoly on the truth, and that all other religions are wrong. Commonly in the past, and all too often today as well, citizens are taught that they are not merely permitted, but actually obliged, to kill and steal from believers in those wrong religions. That's the dark side of all those noble patriotic appeals: for God and country, *por Dios y por España, Gott mit uns,* etc. It in no way diminishes the guilt of the current crop of murderous religious fanatics to acknowledge that they are heirs to a long, widespread, vile tradition.

The Bible's Old Testament is full of exhortations to be cruel to heathens. Deuteronomy 20:10–18, for example, explains the obligation of the Israelites to practice genocide: when your army approaches a distant city, you should enslave all its inhabitants if it surrenders, and kill all its men and enslave its women and children and steal their cattle and everything else if it doesn't surrender. But if it's a city of the Canaanites or Hittites or any of those other abominable believers in false gods, then the true God commands you to kill everything that breathes in the city. The book of Joshua describes approvingly how Joshua became a hero by carrying out those instructions, slaughtering all the inhabitants of over 400 cities. The book of rabbinical commentaries known as the Talmud analyzes the potential ambiguities arising from conflicts between those two principles of "Thou shalt not kill [believers in thine own God]" and "Thou must kill [believers in another god]." For instance, according to some Talmudic commentators, an Israelite is guilty of murder if he intentionally kills a fellow Israelite; is innocent if he intentionally kills a non-Israelite; and is also innocent if he kills an Israelite while throwing a stone into a group consisting of nine Israelites plus one heathen (because he might have been aiming at the one heathen).

In fairness, this outlook is more characteristic of the Old Testament than of the New Testament, whose moral principles have moved far in the direction of defining one's dealings with anyone—at least in theory. But in practice, of course, some of history's most extensive genocides were committed by European Christian colonialists against non-Europeans, relying for moral justification on the New as well as the Old Testament.

Interestingly, among New Guineans, religion is never invoked to justify killing or fighting with members of an out-group. Many of my New Guinea friends have described to me their participation in genocidal attacks on neighboring tribes. In all those accounts, I have never heard the slightest hint of any religious motive, of dying for God or the true religion, or of sacrificing oneself for any idealistic reason whatsoever. In contrast, the religion-supported ideologies that accompanied the rise of states instilled into their citizens the obligation to obey the ruler ordained by God, to obey moral precepts like the Ten Commandments only with respect to fellow citizens, and to be prepared to sacrifice their lives while fighting against other states (i.e., heathens). That's what makes societies of religious fanatics so dangerous: a tiny minority of their adherents (e.g., 19 of them on September 11, 2001) die for the cause, and the whole society of fanatics thereby succeeds at killing far more of its perceived enemies (e.g., 2,996 of them on September 11, 2001). Rules of bad behavior toward out-groups reached their high point in the last 1,500 years, as fanatical Christians and Muslims inflicted death, slavery, or forced conversion on each other and on the heathen. In the 20th century, European states added secular grounds to justify killing millions of citizens of other European states, but religious fanaticism is still strong in some other societies. *Islam. Just say it.*

Badges of commitment

Secular people remain puzzled and troubled by several features of religion. Foremost among those are its regular association with irrational supernatural beliefs, such that each religion has a different set of such beliefs and adheres firmly to them but dismisses most such beliefs of other religions; its frequent promotion of costly, even self-mutilating or suicidal behaviors that would seem to make people less rather than more disposed to be religious; and its apparent basic hypocrisy of preaching a moral code and often claiming universality, while at the same time excluding many or most people from application of that code and urging the killing of them. How can these troubling paradoxes be explained? There are two solutions that I have found useful.

One solution is to recognize the need for adherents of a particular religion to display some reliable "badge" of commitment to that religion. Believers spend their lives with each other and constantly count on each other for support, in a world where many or most other people adhere to other religions, may be hostile to your own religion, or may be skeptical about all religions. Your safety, prosperity, and life will depend on your identifying correctly your fellow believers, and on your convincing them that they can trust you just as you trust them. What proofs of your and their commitment are believable?

To be believable, the proofs must be visible things that no one would or could fake for treacherous gain of temporary advantage. That's why religious "badges" are always costly: high commitments of time to learn and regularly practise rituals, prayers, and songs and to undertake pilgrimages; high commitments of resources, including money, gifts, and sacrificed animals; publicly espousing rationally implausible beliefs that others will ridicule as silly; and publicly undergoing or displaying signs of painful permanent body mutilation, including cutting and bleeding sensitive parts of one's body, disfiguring operations on one's genitals, and self-amputation of finger joints. If you see that someone has made those expensive commitments with lifelong consequences, then they've convinced you much more effectively than if they merely told you, "Trust me, I'm with you, I'm wearing the right sort of hat (but I might have bought it cheaply yesterday and might discard it tomorrow)." For essentially the same reason, evolutionary biologists recognize that many animal signals as well (such as a peacock's tail) have evolved to be costly, precisely because that makes them believable. When a female peahen sees a male peacock with a big tail displaying to her, she can be sure that such a male, capable of growing and surviving with such a big tail, really must have better genes and be better nourished than a male pretending to be superior but with just a small tail.

An interesting example of how religion fosters group cooperation and commitment comes from survival rates of American communes. Throughout the history of the United States continuing into modern times, people have experimented with forming communes where people can live together with other people chosen as sharing their ideals. Some of those communes share religious ideals, and others are non-religiously motivated; many non-religious communes were formed in the U.S. in the 1960s and 1970s. But all communes are subject to financial, practical, social, sexual, and other pressures, and to competition from the attractions of the outside world. The vast majority of communes disband, whether gradually or explosively, within the lifetimes of their founders. For example, in the 1960s one friend of mine was a co-founder of a commune in a beautiful, peaceful, but remote area of Northern California. Gradually, though, the other founder members drifted away because of the isolation, boredom, social tensions, and other reasons, until my friend was the last person left. She still lives there, but now just as a single person, no longer a member of a commune.

Richard Sosis compared the fates of several hundred religious and secular American communes founded in the 19th and early 20th centuries. Almost all eventually dissolved, except for the extremely successful colonies of the religious group known as Hutterites: all 20 Hutterite colonies that were in Sosis's sample survived. Leaving aside those Hutterite colonies, 199 sampled colonies eventually disbanded or died out, always preceded by a loss of faith in the group's ideology, and sometimes also by natural disasters, death of a charismatic leader, or hostility of outsiders. However, the annual probability of dissolution was four times higher for the secular communes than for the religious communes. Evidently, religious ideologies are more effective than secular ideologies at persuading members to maintain a possibly irrational commitment, to refrain from deserting even when it would make rational sense to do so, and to deal with the constant challenges of living in a community that holds property in common and that is at high risk of being abused by free-riding members. In Israel as well, where for many decades there have been both religious kibbutzim and a much greater number of secular kibbutzim, the religious kibbutzim have been more successful than the secular ones in every year, despite the high costs imposed on religious kibbutzim by their religious practices (e.g., abstaining from all labor one day a week).

Measures of religious success

The other solution that I have found useful for resolving religion's paradoxes is the approach of evolutionary biologist David Sloan Wilson. He notes that a religion serves to define a human group competing with other human groups espousing different religions. The most straightforward measure of a religion's relative success is its number of adherents. Why does the world today hold over a billion Catholics, about 14,000,000 Jews, and no Albigensian Manichaeans (members of a formerly numerous Christian sect believing in the dual existence of evil and good supernatural forces locked in eternal struggle)?

Wilson proceeds by recognizing that a religion's number of adherents depends on the balance between several processes tending to increase the number of adherents and several processes tending to decrease that number. The number of adherents is increased by believers giving birth to children and successfully raising their children in that faith, and by conversions of adherents of other religions or previously non-religious people. The number is decreased by deaths of adherents, and by losses of adherents to conversion to other religions. One might pause at this point and say, "Of course, that's obvious, so what?—how does that help me understand why Catholics believing in Christ's resurrection outnumber Jews who don't?" The power of Wilson's approach is that it provides a framework for examining separate effects of a religion's beliefs or practices on those various processes increasing or decreasing the number of adherents. Some of the results are straightforward, while others are subtle. It turns out that religions practise widely different strategies for achieving success.

For example, the American religion known as the Shaker movement was for a period in the 19th century very successful, despite demanding celibacy of its believers and thus lacking completely the commonest method by which religions propagate themselves (by having children). The Shakers achieved their success entirely by winning converts for many decades. At the opposite extreme, Judaism has persisted for several thousand years despite not seeking converts. Not surprisingly, Christianity and Islam, which do proselytize, have far more adherents than does Judaism, but Judaism has nevertheless persisted because of other factors contributing to its demographic growth: relatively high birth rates, low death rates except at times of persecution, emphasis on education to generate economic opportunities, strong mutual help, and low losses by conversion of Jews to other religions. As for Albigensian Manichaeans, their disappearance was only indirectly due to their belief that the forces of evil and of good are locked in eternal struggle. It wasn't the case that that belief discouraged Albigensians from having children, or that it was so implausible as to prevent their winning converts. Instead, that belief was anathema to mainstream Catholics, who declared a holy war against the Albigensians, eventually besieged and captured their stronghold, and burned all remaining Albigensians there to death.

More subtle reasons emerge from Wilson's framework for answering one of the biggest questions of Western religious history. Why, among the innumerable tiny Jewish sects competing with each other and with non-Jewish groups within the Roman Empire in the first century AD, did the one of them that became Christianity emerge as the dominant religion three centuries later? In late Roman times Christianity's distinctive features contributing to this outcome included its active proselytizing (unlike mainstream Judaism), its practices promoting having more babies and enabling more of them to survive (unlike contemporary Roman society), its opportunities for women (in contrast to Judaism and Roman paganism at that time, and to later Christianity), its social institutions resulting in lower death rates of Christians than of Romans from plagues, and the Christian doctrine of forgiveness. That doctrine, which is often misunderstood as the simplistic notion of indiscriminately turning the other cheek, actually proves to be part of a complex, context-dependent system of responses ranging from forgiveness to retaliation. Under certain circumstances, experimental tests carried out by playing simulation games show that forgiving someone who has done you one wrong may really be the response most likely to gain you advantages in the future.

Another example of the use of Wilson's framework involves the success of Mormonism, which has been among the most rapidly growing religions of the last two centuries. Non-Mormons tend to doubt the claim I cited earlier, by Mormonism's founder Joseph Smith, that the angel Moroni appeared to him on September 21, 1823, to reveal golden plates buried on a hilltop near Manchester village in western New York State and awaiting translation (Table 9.2). Non-Mormons also doubt the sworn statements of 11 witnesses (Oliver Cowdery, Christian Whitmer, Hiram Page, and 8 others) who claimed to have seen and handled the plates. Hence non-Mormons may wonder: how have those apparently implausible claims led to the explosive growth of Mormonism?

Wilson's approach involves realizing that a religion's success in increasing its number of adherents does not depend on whether its tenets happen to be true, but instead on whether those tenets and associated practices motivate the religion's adherents to conceive and successfully rear children, win converts, constitute a smoothly functioning society, or do all of those things. In Wilson's words, "Even massively fictitious beliefs can be adaptive, as long as they motivate behaviors that are adaptive in the real world. . . . Factual knowledge is not always sufficient by itself to motivate an adaptive behavior. At times a symbolic belief system that departs from factual reality fares better."

In the case of Mormonism, its tenets and practices have been outstandingly successful at promoting demographic growth. Mormons tend to have many children. They form a strongly supportive and interdependent society offering a full and satisfying social life and incentives to work. They emphasize proselytizing; young Mormons are expected to devote up to two years of their lives to winning converts, either overseas or else near home. Mormons are expected to pay to their church an annual tithe equaling 10% of their income (in addition to paying the usual U.S. federal, state, and local taxes). These high demands for commitment of time and resources guarantee that those who choose to become or remain Mormons take their faith seriously. As for the supposed implausibility of the statements of Joseph Smith and his 11 witnesses about divine revelations via the golden plates—what, really, is the difference between those statements and the biblical accounts of divine revelations to Jesus and to Moses, except for millennia of elapsed time and our differing skepticisms derived from our different upbringings?

What does Wilson have to say about the basic hypocrisy common among religions, in preaching noble moral principles while urging the killing of believers in other religions? Wilson's response is that a religion's success (or its "fitness," to use the language of evolutionary biology) is relative and can be defined only by comparison with the successes of other religions. Whether one likes it or not, religions can increase, and often have increased, their "success" (defined as the number of their adherents) by killing or forcibly converting adherents of other religions. As Wilson writes, "Whenever I strike up a conversation about religion, I am likely to receive a litany of evils perpetrated in God's name. In most cases, these are horrors committed by religious groups against other groups. How can I call religion adaptive in the face of such evidence? The answer is 'easily,' as long as we understand fitness in relative terms. It is important to stress that a behavior can be explained from an evolutionary perspective without being morally condoned."

Changes in religion's functions

Let's finally return to my initial question about the functions and definition of religion. We now see why religion is so difficult to define: because it has changed its functions as it has evolved, just as have electric organs. In fact, it has changed functions even more than have electric organs, which have adopted only six functions, compared with the seven functions variously characterizing religions **(Figure 9.1)**. Of those seven functions, four were entirely absent at one stage of religion's history, and five were still present but in

Figure 9.1 Religion's functions changing through time

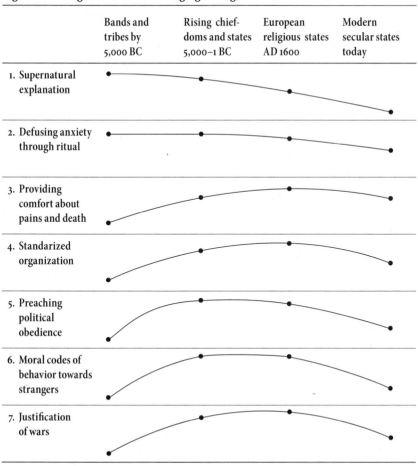

	Bands and tribes by 5,000 BC	Rising chief-doms and states 5,000–1 BC	European religious states AD 1600	Modern secular states today
1. Supernatural explanation				
2. Defusing anxiety through ritual				
3. Providing comfort about pains and death				
4. Standarized organization				
5. Preaching political obedience				
6. Moral codes of behavior towards strangers				
7. Justification of wars				

decline at another stage. Two functions had already appeared and were at their peak by the time of the emergence of intelligent questioning humans before 50,000 BC, and have been in steady decline in recent millennia: supernatural explanation (in steeper decline), and defusing anxiety about uncontrollable dangers through ritual (in gentler decline). The other five functions were absent (four of them) or weak (the fifth) in early intelligent humans, rose to a peak in chiefdoms and early states (three of them) or late Renaissance states (two of them), and have declined somewhat or sharply since that peak.

Those shifts of function make it harder to define religion than to define electric organs, because electric organs at least all share the trait of setting up detectable electric fields in the surrounding medium, whereas there is no single characteristic shared by all religions. At the risk of coming up with yet another definition to add to those of Table 9.1, I'd now propose: "Religion is a set of traits distinguishing a human social group sharing those traits from other groups not sharing those traits in identical form. Included among those shared traits is always one or more, often all three, out of three traits: supernatural explanation, defusing anxiety about uncontrollable dangers through ritual, and offering comfort for life's pains and the prospect of death. Religions other than early ones became co-opted to promote standardized organization, political obedience, tolerance of strangers belonging to one's own religion, and justification of wars against groups holding other religions." That definition of mine is at least as tortured as the most tortured definitions already in Table 9.1, but I think that it corresponds to reality.

What about religion's future? That depends on what shape the world will be in 30 years from now. If living standards rise all around the world, then religion's functions numbers 1 and 4–7 of Figure 9.1 will continue to decline, but functions 2 and 3 seem to me likely to persist. Religion is especially likely to continue to be espoused for claiming to offer meaning to individual lives and deaths whose meaning may seem insignificant from a scientific perspective. Even if science's answer to the search for meaning is true, and if religion's meaning is an illusion, many people will continue not to like science's answer. If, on the other hand, much of the world remains mired in poverty, or if (worse yet) the world's economy and living standards and peace deteriorate, then all functions of religion, perhaps even supernatural explanation, may undergo a resurgence. My children's generation will experience the answers to these questions.

CHAPTER 10

Speaking in Many Tongues

Multilingualism ▪ The world's language total ▪ How languages evolve ▪ Geography of language diversity ▪ Traditional multilingualism ▪ Benefits of bilingualism ▪ Alzheimer's disease ▪ Vanishing languages ▪ How languages disappear ▪ Are minority languages harmful? ▪ Why preserve languages? ▪ How can we protect languages?

Multilingualism

One evening, while I was spending a week at a mountain forest campsite with 20 New Guinea Highlanders, conversation around the campfire was going on simultaneously in several different local languages plus two lingua francas of Tok Pisin and Motu, as commonly happens when a group of New Guineans from different tribes happens to be gathered. I had already become accustomed to encountering a new language approximately every 10 or 20 miles as I walked or drove through the New Guinea Highlands. I had just come from the lowlands, where a New Guinea friend had told me how five different local languages were spoken within a few miles of his village, how he had picked up those five languages as a child just by playing with other children, and how he had learned three more languages after he began school. And so, out of curiosity that evening, I went around the campfire circle and asked each man to name each language that he "spoke," i.e., knew well enough to converse in.

Among those 20 New Guineans, the smallest number of languages that anyone spoke was 5. Several men spoke from 8 to 12 languages, and the champion was a man who spoke 15. Except for English, which New Guineans often learn at school by studying books, everyone had acquired all of his other languages socially without books. Just to anticipate your likely question—yes, those local languages enumerated that evening really were mutually unintelligible languages, not mere dialects. Some were tonal like Chinese, others were non-tonal, and they belonged to several different language families.

In the United States, on the other hand, most native-born Americans are monolingual. Educated Europeans commonly know two or three languages, sometimes more, having learned in school the languages other than their mother tongue. The linguistic contrast between that New Guinea campfire and modern American or European experience illustrates widespread differences between language use in small-scale societies and in modern state societies—differences that will increase in coming decades. In our traditional past, as is still true in modern New Guinea, each language had far fewer speakers than do the languages of modern states; probably a higher proportion of the population was multilingual; and second languages were learned socially beginning in childhood, rather than by formal study later in schools.

Sadly, languages are now vanishing more rapidly than at any previous time in human history. If current trends continue, 95% of the languages handed down to us from the tens of thousands of years of history of behaviorally modern humans will be extinct or moribund by the year 2100. Half of our languages will actually have become extinct by then, most of the remainder will be dying languages spoken only by old people, and only a small minority will be "live" languages still being transmitted from parents to children. Languages are disappearing so rapidly (about one every nine days), and there are so few linguists studying them, that time is running out even to describe and record most languages before they disappear. Linguists face a race against time similar to that faced by biologists, now aware that most of the world's plant and animal species are in danger of extinction and of disappearing even before they can be described. We do hear much anguished discussion about the accelerating disappearance of birds and frogs and other living species, as our Coca-Cola civilization spreads over the world. Much less attention has been paid to the disappearance of our languages, and to their essential role in the survival of those indigenous cultures. Each language is the vehicle for a unique way of thinking and talking, a unique literature, and a unique view of the world. Hence looming over us today is the tragedy of the impending loss of most of our cultural heritage, linked with the loss of most of our languages.

Why are languages vanishing at such a catastrophic rate? Does it really matter? Is our current plethora of languages good or bad for the world as a whole, and for all those traditional societies still speaking languages now at risk of vanishing? Many of you readers may presently disagree with what I just said, about language loss being a tragedy. Perhaps you instead think that diverse languages promote civil war and impede education, that the world would be better off with far fewer languages, and that high language diversity is one of those features of the world of yesterday that we should be glad to be rid of—like chronic tribal warfare, infanticide, abandonment of the elderly, and frequent starvation.

For each of us as individuals, does it do us good or harm to learn multiple languages? It certainly takes much time and effort to learn a language and become fluent in it; would we be better off devoting all that time and effort to learning more obviously useful skills? I think that the answers emerging to these questions about the value of traditional multilingualism, both to societies and to individuals, will intrigue you readers, as they intrigued me. Will this chapter convince you to bring up your next child to be bilingual, or will it instead convince you that the whole world should switch to speaking English as quickly as possible?

The world's language total

Before we can tackle those big questions, let's start with some preamble about how many languages still exist today, how they developed, and where in the world they are spoken. The known number of distinct languages still spoken or recently spoken in the modern world is around 7,000. That huge total may astonish many readers, because most of us could name only a few dozen languages, and the vast majority of languages are unfamiliar to us. Most languages are unwritten, spoken by few people, and spoken far from the industrial world. For example, all of Europe west of Russia has fewer than 100 native languages, but the African continent and the Indian subcontinent have over 1,000 native languages each, the African countries of Nigeria and Cameroon 527 and 286 languages respectively, and the small Pacific island nation of Vanuatu (area less than 5,000 square miles) 110 languages. The world's highest language diversity is on the island of New Guinea, with about 1,000 languages and an unknown but apparently large number of distinct language families crammed into an area only slightly larger than Texas.

Of those 7,000 languages, 9 "giants," each the primary language of 100 million or more people, account for over one-third of the world's population. In undoubted first place is Mandarin, the primary language of at least 700 million Chinese, followed by Spanish, English, Arabic, Hindi, Bengali, Portuguese, Russian, and Japanese in approximately that sequence. If we relax our definition of "big languages" to mean the top 70 languages—i.e., the top 1% of all languages—then we have encompassed the primary languages of almost 80% of the world's people.

But most of the world's languages are "little" languages with few speakers. If we divide the world's nearly 7 billion people by 7,000 languages, we obtain 1 million people as the average number of speakers of a language. Because that average is distorted by the 100-million-plus speakers of just 9 giant languages, a better measure of a "typical" language is to talk about the "median" number of speakers—i.e., a language such that half of the world's languages have more speakers, and the other half have fewer speakers. That median number is only a few thousand speakers. Hence half of the world's languages have under a few thousand speakers, and lots of them have between only 60 and 200 speakers.

But such discussions of numbers of languages, and numbers of language speakers, force us to confront the question that I anticipated in describing my New Guinea campfire language poll at the beginning of this chapter. What's the difference between a distinct language and a mere dialect of another language? Speech differences between neighboring populations intergrade completely; neighbors may understand 100%, or 92%, or 75%, or 42%, or nothing at all of what each other says. The cut-off between language and dialect is often arbitrarily taken at 70% mutual intelligibility: if neighboring populations with different ways of speaking can understand over 70% of each other's speech, then (by that definition) they're considered just to speak different dialects of the same language, while they are considered as speaking different languages if they understand less than 70%.

But even that simple, arbitrary, strictly linguistic definition of dialects and languages may encounter ambiguities when we try to apply it in practice. One practical difficulty is posed by dialect chains: in a string of neighboring villages ABCDEFGH, each village may understand both villages on either side, but villages A and H at opposite ends of the chain may not be able to understand each other at all. Another difficulty is that some pairs of speech communities are asymmetrical in their intelligibility: A can understand most of what B says, but B has difficulty understanding A. For instance, my Portuguese-speaking friends tell me that they can understand Spanish-speakers well, but my Spanish-speaking friends have more difficulty understanding Portuguese.

Those are two types of problems in drawing a line between dialects and languages on strictly linguistic grounds. A bigger problem is that languages are defined as separate not just by linguistic differences, but also by political and self-defined ethnic differences. This fact is expressed in a joke that one often hears among linguists: "A language is a dialect backed up by its own army and navy." For instance, Spanish and Italian might not pass the 70% test for being ranked as different languages rather than mere dialects: my Spanish and Italian friends tell me that they can understand most of what each other says, especially after a little practice. But, regardless of what a linguist applying this 70% test might say, every Spaniard and Italian, and everybody else, will unhesitatingly proclaim Spanish and Italian to be different languages—because they have had their own armies and navies, plus largely separate governments and school systems, for over a thousand years.

Conversely, many European languages have strongly differentiated regional forms that the governments of their country emphatically consider mere dialects, even though speakers from the different regions can't understand each other at all. My north German friends can't make heads or tails of the talk of rural Bavarians, and my north Italian friends are equally at a loss in Sicily. But their national governments are adamant that those different regions should not have separate armies and navies, and so their speech forms are labeled as dialects and don't you dare mention a criterion of mutual intelligibility.

Those regional differences within European countries were even greater 60 years ago, before television and internal migration began breaking down long-established "dialect" differences. For example, on my first visit to Britain in the year 1950, my parents took my sister Susan and

me to visit family friends called the Grantham-Hills in their home in the
small town of Beccles in East Anglia. While my parents and their friends
were talking, my sister and I became bored with the adult conversation
and went outside to walk around the charming old town center. After
turning at several right angles that we neglected to count, we realized that
we were lost, and we asked a man on the street for directions back to our
friends' house. It became obvious that the man didn't understand our
American accents, even when we spoke slowly and (we thought) distinctly.
But he did recognize that we were children and lost, and he perked up
when we repeated the words "Grantham-Hill, Grantham-Hill." He responded with many sentences of directions, of which Susan and I couldn't
decipher a single word; we wouldn't have guessed that he considered himself to be speaking English. Fortunately for us, he pointed in one direction, and we set off that way until we recognized a building near the
Grantham-Hills' house. Those former local "dialects" of Beccles and other
English districts have been undergoing homogenization and shifts towards BBC English, as access to television has become universal in Britain
in recent decades.

By a strictly linguistic definition of 70% intelligibility—the definition
that one has to use in New Guinea, where no tribe has its own army or
navy—quite a few Italian "dialects" would rate as languages. That redefi-
nition of some Italian dialects as languages would close the gap in linguistic diversity between Italy and New Guinea slightly, but not by much. If
the average number of speakers of an Italian "dialect" had equaled the
4,000 speakers of an average New Guinea language, Italy would have
10,000 languages. Aficionados of the separateness of Italian dialects might
credit Italy with dozens of languages, but no one would claim there to be
10,000 different languages in Italy. It really is true that New Guinea is
linguistically far more diverse than is Italy.

How languages evolve

How did the world end up with 7,000 languages, instead of our all sharing
the same language? Already for tens of thousands of years before language
spread by the Internet and Facebook, there has been ample opportunity

for language differences to disappear, because most traditional peoples have had contact with neighboring peoples, with whom they intermarry and trade, and from whom they borrow words and ideas and behaviors. Something must have caused languages, even in the past and under traditional conditions, to diverge and to remain separate, in the face of all that contact.

Here's how it happens. Any of us over the age of 40 has observed that languages change even over the course of just a few decades, with some words dropping out of use, new words being coined, and pronunciation shifting. For instance, whenever I revisit Germany, where I lived in 1961, young Germans notice that they have to explain to me some new German words (e.g., the new word *Händi* for cell phones, which didn't exist in 1961), and that I still use some old-fashioned German words that have been going out of use since 1961 (e.g., *jener/jene* for "that/those"). But young Germans and I can still mostly understand each other well. Similarly, you American readers under the age of 40 may not recognize some formerly popular English words like "ballyhoo," but in compensation you daily use the verb "to Google" and the participle "Googling," which didn't exist in my childhood.

After a few centuries of such independent changes in two geographically separate speech communities derived from the same original speech community, the communities develop dialects that may pose difficulties for each other to understand: e.g., the modest differences between American and British English, the bigger differences between the French of Quebec and of metropolitan France, and the still bigger differences between Afrikaans and Dutch. After 2,000 years of divergence, the speech communities have diverged so much as to be no longer mutually intelligible, although to linguists they are still obviously related—such as the French and Spanish and Romanian languages derived from Latin, or the English and German and other Germanic languages derived from proto-Germanic. Finally, after about 10,000 years, the differences are so great that most linguists would assign the languages to unrelated language families without any detectable relationships.

Thus, languages evolve differences because different groups of people independently develop different words and different pronunciations over the course of time. But the question remains why those diverged languages don't merge again when formerly separated people spread out and re-contact each other at speech boundaries. For instance, at the modern boundary between Germany and Poland, there are Polish villages near German villages, but the villagers still speak a local variety of either German or of Polish, rather than a German-Polish mish-mash. Why is that so?

Probably the main disadvantage of speaking a mish-mash involves a basic function of human language: as soon as you start to speak to someone else, your language serves as an instantly recognizable badge of your group identity. It's much easier for wartime spies to don the enemy's uniform than to imitate convincingly the enemy's language and pronunciation. People who speak *your* language are *your* people: they'll recognize you as a compatriot, and they'll support you or at least not be immediately suspicious of you, whereas someone speaking a different language is apt to be regarded as a potentially dangerous stranger. That instant distinction between friends and strangers still operates today: just see how you (my American readers) react the next time that you're in Uzbekistan, and you finally to your relief hear someone behind you speaking English with an American accent. The distinction between friends and strangers was even more important in the past (Chapter 1), often a matter of life and death. It's important to speak the language of at least some community, so that there will be some group that considers you as "our own." If you instead speak a mish-mash near a speech boundary, both groups may understand much of what you say, but neither group will consider you "one of our own," and you can't count on either group to welcome and protect you. That may be why the world's speech communities have tended to remain thousands of separate languages, instead of the whole world speaking one language or forming one dialect chain.

Geography of language diversity

Languages are distributed unevenly around the world: about 10% of the world's area contains half of its languages. For instance, at the low-end extreme of language diversity, the world's three largest countries—Russia, Canada, and China, each with an area of millions of square miles—have only about 100, 80, and 300 native languages respectively. But at the high-end extreme of language diversity, New Guinea and Vanuatu, with areas of only 300,000 and 4,700 square miles respectively, have about 1,000 and 110 native languages. That means that one language is spoken over an average area of about 66,000, 49,000, and 12,000 square miles in Russia, Canada, and China respectively, but only over 300 and 42 square miles respectively in New Guinea and Vanuatu. Why is there such enormous geographic variation in language diversity?

Linguists recognize ecological, socio-economic, and historical factors apparently contributing to the answer. Language diversity—e.g., the number of native languages per 1,000 square miles of area—correlates with numerous potentially explanatory factors, but these factors are in turn correlated with each other. Hence one has to resort to statistical methods, such as multiple regression analysis, to tease out which factors have primary effects actually causing language diversity to be high or low, and which other factors have just apparent effects mediated by their correlations with those primary factors. For example, there is a positive correlation between Rolls-Royce car ownership and lifespan: Rolls-Royce owners live on the average longer than do people who don't own Rolls-Royces. That's not because Rolls-Royce ownership directly improves survival, but because Rolls-Royce owners tend to have lots of money, which enables them to pay for the best health care, which is the actual cause of their long lifespans. When it comes, though, to correlates of linguistic diversity, there isn't yet a corresponding agreement about the actual underlying causes.

The four closest ecological correlations of language diversity are with latitude, climate variability, biological productivity, and local ecological diversity. First, language diversity decreases from the equator towards the poles: all other things being equal, tropical areas hold more languages than do equivalent areas at higher latitudes. Second, at a given latitude language diversity decreases with climate variability, whether the variability consists of regular within-year seasonal variation or of unpredictable between-year variation. For instance, language diversity is higher in tropical rainforests that are wet all year round than in adjacent more seasonal tropical savannahs. (This factor of seasonality could account at least in part, through the correlation between latitude and seasonality, for the higher language diversities in the less seasonal tropics than in strongly seasonal high latitudes.) Third, language diversity tends to be higher in more productive environments (e.g., higher in rainforests than in deserts), though again at least some of that effect could be because of a tendency for deserts and many other unproductive environments to be strongly seasonal. Finally, language diversity is high in ecologically diverse areas and tends especially to be higher in rugged mountainous areas than in flat areas.

These four ecological relationships are just correlations, not explanations. Suggested underlying explanations involve human population size, mobility, and economic strategies. First, a speech community's viability increases with its number of people: a language spoken by only 50 people is more likely to disappear, due to its speakers all dying or abandoning their language, than is a language spoken by 5,000 people. Hence regions with a lower biological productivity (supporting fewer people) tend to support fewer languages, and to require more area for the speakers of each language. A viable population in Arctic or desert regions needs tens of thousands of square miles to support itself, while a few hundred square miles would be ample in productive landscapes. Second, the more constant is the environment between seasons and between years, the more self-sufficient and sedentary can a speech community be within a small area, without much need to move periodically or to trade for necessities with other peoples. Finally, an ecologically diverse area can support many different language communities, each with its own specific subsistence economy adapted to a different local ecology: for instance, a mountainous area can support mountain herders, hill farmers, lowland river fishermen, and lowland savannah pastoralists at different elevations and in different habitats.

Ecological factors thus already tell us several reasons why small New Guinea has 5–10 times more languages than does huge Russia, Canada, or China. New Guinea lies within a few degrees of the equator, so its people experience only slight variations in climate. The New Guinea landscape is wet, fertile, and productive. New Guineans don't move much or at all with seasons or from year to year; they can meet all of their subsistence needs within a small area; and they don't have to trade except for salt, stone for tools, and luxuries like shells and feathers. New Guinea is rugged and ecologically diverse, with mountains up to 16,500 feet, rivers, lakes, seacoasts, savannahs, and forests. One could object that China and Canada have even higher mountains and offer a larger range of elevations than does New Guinea. But New Guinea's tropical location means that New Guineans can live year-round and farm at high population densities up to elevations of 8,000 feet, while high elevations in China and Canada are seasonally freezing and support only low human population densities (in Tibet) or no people at all.

In addition to those ecological factors, there are also socio-economic and historical factors contributing to differences in language diversity around the world. One such factor is that hunter-gatherer speech communities consist of fewer individuals but may cover larger areas than farmer speech communities. For instance, Aboriginal Australia was traditionally inhabited entirely by hunter-gatherers occupying an average of 12,000 square miles per language, while neighboring New Guinea supported mostly farmers occupying only 300 square miles per language. Within Indonesian New Guinea, I worked in areas supporting nearby both farmers (in the Central Highlands) and hunter-gatherers (in the Lakes Plains), with about two dozen languages for each lifestyle. The average hunter-gatherer language there had only 388 speakers, while the average farmer language had 18,241 speakers. The main reason for the small speech communities of hunter-gatherers is low food availability, hence low human population densities. Within the same environment, population densities of hunter-gatherers are 10 to 100 times lower than those of farmers, because much less food is available to hunter-gatherers, able to eat only that tiny fraction of wild plant species that is edible, than to farmers, who convert the landscape into gardens and orchards of edible plants.

A second socio-economic factor related to language diversity is political organization: language diversity decreases, and language communities increase in population and in area, with increasing political complexity from bands to states. For instance, the United States today, a large state with a single dominant coast-to-coast language, has a population about 30 times what was the population of the entire world at a time when the world still consisted entirely of hunter-gatherer bands and tribes with thousands of languages. The dominant U.S. language of English has largely replaced the hundreds of different local languages formerly spoken five centuries ago in what is now the national territory of the U.S. when it was divided among Native American bands, tribes, and chiefdoms. Underlying this trend is the fact, discussed in the Prologue, that increasing political complexity becomes necessary as a society increases in population—because a society of a few dozen people can make decisions in a group meeting without a leader, but a society of millions requires leaders and bureaucrats to operate. States expand their own languages at the expense of the languages of conquered and incorporated groups. That language expansion is partly a matter of state policy for the purposes of administration and national unity, and partly a spontaneous matter of individual citizens adopting the national language in order to obtain economic and social opportunities for themselves.

The remaining factor is a historical one whose various outcomes include the just-mentioned decrease in language diversity with increasing political complexity. World regions have repeatedly been swept by "language steamrollers," in which one group enjoying some advantage of population numbers, food base, or technology exploits that advantage to expand at the expense of neighboring groups, imposing its own language on the region and replacing previous local languages by driving out or killing their speakers or converting them to speaking the invader's language. The most familiar steamrollers are those associated with expansions of powerful states over stateless peoples. Recent examples have included European expansions replacing native languages of the Americas, the British conquest of Australia replacing Aboriginal Australian languages, and the Russian expansion over the Ural Mountains to the Pacific Ocean replacing native Siberian languages. In the past, as well, there have been historically documented state-driven steamrollers. The Roman Empire's expansion over the Mediterranean basin and most of Western Europe extinguished Etruscan, Continental Celtic languages, and many other languages. The expansion of the Inca Empire and its predecessors similarly spread the Quechua and Aymara languages over the Andes.

Less familiar to non-linguists are the steamrollers driven by expansions of pre-literate farmers over the lands of hunter-gatherers, and inferred from linguistic and archaeological rather than historical evidence. Well understood ones include the expansions of Bantu and Austronesian farmers, which largely replaced the former languages of hunter-gatherers in subequatorial Africa and Island Southeast Asia respectively. There were also steamrollers in which hunter-gatherers overran other hunter-gatherers, driven by improved technology: e.g., the expansion of the Inuit 1,000 years ago eastwards across the Canadian Arctic, based on technological advances such as dog sleds and kayaks.

A consequence of these several types of historical expansions is that some world regions containing few geographic barriers have repeatedly been overrun by linguistic steamrollers. The immediate result is very low linguistic diversity, because an invading language sweeps away pre-existing linguistic diversity. With time, the invading language differentiates into local dialects and then into separate languages, but all of them still closely related to each other. An early stage in this process is illustrated by the Inuit expansion of 1,000 years ago; all eastern Inuit people from Alaska to Greenland still speak mutually intelligible dialects of a single language. The Roman and Bantu expansions of 2,000 years ago represent a slightly later stage: the various Italic languages (such as French, Spanish, and Romanian) are very similar but no longer mutually intelligible, as is also true of the hundreds of closely related Bantu languages. At a still later stage, the Austronesian expansion that began around 6,000 years ago has by now generated a thousand languages falling into eight branches, but still sufficiently similar that there is no doubt about their relationship.

Contrasting with those easily overrun areas that Johanna Nichols terms "language spread zones" are what she terms "residual zones" or refugia: mountainous and other areas that are difficult for states and other outsiders to overrun, where languages survive and diffentiate for long times, and hence where unique language groups survive. Famous examples are the Caucasus Mountains, with 3 unique language families plus a few recently invaded languages belonging to three other widespread families; northern Australia, to which 26 of Aboriginal Australia's 27 language families are confined; Indian California, with about 80 languages variously classified into somewhere between 6 and 22 families; and, of course, New Guinea, with its 1,000 languages classified in dozens of families.

We thus have several more reasons why New Guinea leads the world in number of languages and of language families. In addition to the ecological reasons previously mentioned—little seasonal variation, sedentary populations, a productive environment supporting high human population densities, and great ecological diversity supporting many co-existing human groups with different subsistence strategies—we now have some socio-economic and historical factors as well. Those include the facts that traditional New Guinea never developed state government, so there was never a state steamroller to homogenize linguistic diversity; and that, as a result of New Guinea's highly dissected mountainous terrain, the steamroller probably caused by the spread of Highlands farming (that associated with the so-called Trans–New Guinea language phylum) was unable to eliminate dozens of older New Guinea language phyla.

Traditional multilingualism

Those are the reasons why the modern world inherited 7,000 languages from the traditional world until yesterday, and why language communities of hunter-gatherers and small-scale farmers without state government contained many fewer speakers than do modern state societies. What about bilingualism and multilingualism? Are traditional societies more, less, or equally often bilingual compared to modern state societies?

The distinction between bilingualism (or multilingualism) and monolingualism proves even more difficult to define and more arbitrary than is the distinction between a language and a dialect. Should you count yourself as bilingual only if you can converse fluently in a second language besides your mother tongue? Should you count languages in which you can converse clumsily? What about languages that you can read but not speak—e.g., Latin and classical Greek for those of us who learned those languages at school? And what about languages that you can't speak, but that you can understand when spoken by others? American-born children of immigrant parents often can understand but not speak their parents' language, and New Guineans often distinguish between languages that they can both speak and understand, and languages that they say that they can only "hear" but not speak. Partly because of this lack of agreement on a definition of bilingualism, we lack comparative data on the frequency of bilingualism around the world.

Nevertheless, we don't have to throw up our hands in despair and ignore the subject, because there is much anecdotal information about bilingualism. Most native-born Americans with English-speaking parents are effectively monolingual for obvious reasons: in the United States there is little need, and for most Americans little regular opportunity, to speak a second language; most immigrants to the U.S. learn English; and most English-speaking Americans marry English-speaking spouses. Most European countries have only a single official national language, and most native-born Europeans with native-born parents learn only that national language as pre-school children. However, because European countries are all much smaller in area and (today) much less self-sufficient economically, politically, and culturally than is the United States, most educated Europeans now learn additional languages in school by formal instruction and often achieve fluency. Shop assistants in many Scandinavian department stores wear pins on their jackets showing the flags of the various languages in which they are competent to help foreign customers. Nevertheless, this widespread multilingualism in Europe is a recent phenomenon that has resulted from mass higher education, post–World War II economic and political integration, and the spread of English-language mass media. Formerly, monolingualism was widespread in European nation-states, as in other state societies. The reasons are clear: state speech communities are huge, often millions of speakers; state societies favor the state's own language for use in government, education, commerce, the army, and entertainment; and (as I'll discuss below) states have potent intentional and unintentional means of spreading their state language at the expense of other languages.

In contrast, multilingualism is widespread or routine in traditional small-scale non-state societies. The reasons are again simple. We have seen that traditional language communities are small (a few thousand speakers or less) and occupy small areas. Immediately neighboring communities often speak different languages. People regularly encounter and have to deal with speakers of other languages. To trade, to negotiate alliances and access to resources, and (for many traditional people) even to obtain a spouse and to communicate with that spouse requires being not merely bilingual but multilingual. Second and further languages are learned in childhood and in the home or socially, not through formal instruction. In my experience, fluency in five or more languages is the rule among traditional New Guineans. I shall now supplement those New Guinea impressions of mine with brief accounts from two continents: Aboriginal Australia and tropical South America.

Aboriginal Australia was occupied by about 250 different language groups, all of them subsisting by hunting-gathering, with an average of about a thousand speakers per language. All reliable reports describe most traditional Aboriginals as being at least bilingual, and most as knowing many languages. One such study was carried out by anthropologist Peter Sutton in the Cape Keerweer area of the Cape York Peninsula, where the local population of 683 people was divided into 21 clans, each with a different form of speech and averaging 33 people per clan. Those speech forms are classified into five languages plus about seven dialects, so that the average number of speakers is about 53 per speech form, or 140 per language. Traditional Aborigines in the area spoke or understood at least five different languages or dialects. In part because speech communities are so tiny, and in part because of a preference for linguistic exogamy (marrying someone whose primary language is not one's own), 60% of marriages are between partners speaking different languages, another 16% are between speakers of different dialects of the same language, and only 24% are within the same dialect. That is despite the fact that neighboring clans tend to be linguistically similar, so that mere propinquity would lead to marriages being made within the same dialect if it were not for that preference for seeking geographically and linguistically more remote partners.

Because many social groups at Cape Keerweer involve speakers of different languages, conversations are often multilingual. It is customary to begin a conversation in the language or dialect of the person whom you are addressing, or (if you are a visitor) in the language of the host camp. You may then switch back to your own language, while your partners reply in their own languages, or you may address each person in his/her own language, your choice of language thereby indicating whom you are addressing at the moment. You may also switch languages depending on the implicit message that you wish to convey: e.g., one choice of language means "You and I have no quarrel," another means "You and I do have a quarrel but I wish to cool it," still another means "I am a good and socially proper person," and yet another means "I will insult you by talking to you disrespectfully." It is likely that such multilingualism was routine in our hunter-gatherer past, just as it still is today in traditional areas of New Guinea, and for the same underlying reasons: tiny speech communities, hence frequent linguistic exogamy, and daily encounters and conversations with speakers of other languages.

The other pair of studies, by Arthur Sorensen and Jean Jackson, is from the Vaupés River area on the border between Colombia and Brazil in the northwest Amazon Basin. About 10,000 Indians, speaking about 21 different languages of four different language families, are culturally similar in gaining their livelihood by farming, fishing, and hunting along rivers in tropical rainforests. Like Cape Keerweer Aborigines, Vaupés River Indians are linguistically exogamous but much more strictly so: in over a thousand marriages studied by Jackson, only one may possibly have been within a language group. While boys remain as adults in their parents' longhouse in which they grew up, girls from other longhouses and language groups move to their husband's longhouse at the time of marriage. A given longhouse contains women marrying in from several different language groups: three, in the case of a longhouse studied intensively by Sorensen. All children learn both their father's and their mother's languages already from infancy, then learn the languages of the other women of the longhouse. Hence everyone in the longhouse knows the four longhouse languages (that of the men, and those of the three language groups of the women), and most also learn some other languages from visitors.

Only after Vaupés River Indians have come to know a language well by hearing and passively acquiring vocabulary and pronunciation do they start speaking it. They carefully keep languages separate and work hard to pronounce each language correctly. They told Sorensen that it took them one or two years to learn a new language fluently. High value is placed on speaking correctly, and letting words from other languages creep into one's conversation is considered shameful.

These anecdotes from small-scale societies on two continents and on New Guinea suggest that socially acquired multilingualism was routine in our past, and that the monolingualism or school-based multilingualism of modern state societies is a new phenomenon. But this generalization is only tentative and subject to limitations. Monolingualism may have characterized small-scale societies in some areas of low language diversity or recent language expansions, as at high latitudes or among the Inuit east of Alaska. The generalization remains based on anecdotes and on expectations derived from traditionally small language communities. Systematic surveys employing some standard definition of multilingualism are needed to place this conclusion on a firmer foot.

Benefits of bilingualism

Let's now ask whether that traditional multilingualism or bilingualism brings net benefit, net harm, or neither to bilingual individuals compared with monolingual individuals. I'll describe some fascinating and recently discovered practical advantages of bilingualism that may impress you more than the usual claim that learning a foreign language enriches your life. I'll discuss here only the effects of bilingualism for individuals: I'll defer to a later section the corresponding question about whether bilingualism is good or bad for a society as a whole.

Among modern industrial countries, bilingualism is a subject of debate especially in the United States, which has been incorporating a large fraction of non-English-speaking immigrants into its population for over 250 years. A frequently expressed view in the U.S. is that bilingualism is harmful, especially for children of immigrants, who are thereby hindered in negotiating the prevalently English-speaking culture of the U.S. and will be better off not learning their parents' language. This view is widely held not only by native-born Americans but also by first-generation immigrant parents: e.g., by my grandparents and by my wife's parents, who diligently avoided speaking together in Yiddish and Polish respectively in the presence of their children, in order to make sure that my parents and my wife would learn only English. Additional bases for this view on the part of native-born Americans include fear and suspicion of things foreign, including foreign languages; and a concern on the part of both native-born and immigrant parents that it may be confusing for children to be exposed simultaneously to two languages, and that their mastery of language would be faster if they were exposed to just one language. That reasoning is a legitimate concern: a child learning two languages must learn twice as many speech sounds, words, and grammatical structures as a monolingual child; the bilingual child has only half as much time to devote to each language; and so the bilingual child (it is feared) may end up speaking two languages poorly, instead of speaking one language well.

In fact, studies carried out in the U.S., Ireland, and Wales until the 1960s did report that bilingual children were significantly disadvantaged linguistically compared to monolingual children, learned command of language more slowly, and ended up with smaller vocabularies in each language. But it was eventually realized that that interpretation was confounded by other variables correlated with bilingualism in those studies. In the U.S. more than in other countries, bilingualism is associated with poverty. When American bilingual children were compared with American monolingual English-speaking children, the latter tended to be from more affluent communities, to be attending better schools, and to have more educated and wealthy parents working at higher occupational levels and with larger vocabularies. Those correlates of bilingualism alone might have accounted for the lower language skills of the bilingual children.

More recent studies in the U.S., Canada, and Europe control for those other variables, by comparing bilingual and monolingual children attending the same school and matched for parental socio-economic status. It turns out that bilingual children and monolingual children matched in other respects pass milestones of language acquisition (e.g., age to say first word, first sentence, or to acquire a 50-word vocabulary) at the same age. Depending on the study, either bilingual and monolingual children end up as adults with essentially the same vocabulary size and word-retrieval rate, or else the monolingual children end up with a slight advantage (vocabulary up to 10% larger in their sole language). However, it would be misleading to summarize this result by saying, "Monolingual children end up with a slightly larger vocabulary: 3,300 versus only 3,000 words." Instead, the result is, "Bilingual children end up with a much larger vocabulary: a total of 6,000 words, consisting of 3,000 English words plus 3,000 Chinese words, instead of 3,300 English words and no Chinese words."

Studies to date have not demonstrated generalized cognitive differences between bilingual and monolingual people. It is not the case that one group is on the average smarter or thinks more quickly than the other group. Instead, there appear to be specific differences, such as (perhaps) slightly faster word retrieval and ability to name objects on the part of monolinguals (because they don't have the problem of selecting among different names, all correct but in different languages familiar to them). Among these specific differences, the most consistently established to date involves what cognitive scientists term "executive function," and that difference is in favor of bilinguals.

To understand the meaning of executive function, picture a person doing anything at all, e.g., crossing a street. Reflect that we are constantly bombarded by sensory information in many modalities, including sight, sound, smell, touch, and taste, plus our own thoughts. Into the pedestrian's senses flood the sight of billboards and of clouds overhead, the sounds of people talking and birds singing, the smells of the city, the touch sensation of the pedestrian's feet on the pavement and of his arms swinging at his sides, and thoughts of what his wife said to him at breakfast that morning. If he were not crossing a street, the pedestrian would concentrate on the words of people or on the sight of billboards or on his wife's most recent words. When crossing a street, though, his survival requires that he concentrate on the sights and sounds of cars approaching at different speeds from both directions, and on the feeling of his feet stepping off the curb. That is, to do anything at all in life requires inhibiting 99% of one's sensory input and thoughts at any moment, and paying attention to the 1% of input relevant to the task currently at hand. That brain process of executive function, also known as cognitive control, is believed to reside in the brain area known as the pre-frontal cortex. It's what permits you to pay selective attention, to avoid being distracted, to concentrate on solving a problem, to shift between tasks, and to call up and use the word or bit of information needed at the moment out of your huge stockpile of words and information. That is, executive control is a big deal: it's crucial to our functioning competently. In children, executive control develops especially over the course of the first five or so years of life.

Bilingual people have a special issue of executive control. Monolingual people hearing a word compare it with their single stock of words, and when uttering a word they draw it from their single stock. But bilingual people must and do keep their languages separate. Every time they hear a word pronounced, they must instantly know according to which set of arbitrary rules to interpret the meaning of those sounds: for instance, a

Spanish/Italian bilingual has learned that the sounds *b-u-rr-o* mean "donkey" in Spanish but "butter" in Italian. Every time bilinguals wish to say something, they must call up the words from the language being used in the current conversation, and not from their other language. Multilingual people participating in a group bilingual conversation, or Scandinavian shop assistants, must switch those arbitrary rules every few minutes or even more often.

The importance of executive control for multilingual people was brought home to me by a disconcerting failure of it on my part. When I went to work in Indonesia in 1979 and began learning the Indonesian language, I had already lived for extended periods in Germany, Peru, and Papua New Guinea, and I had become comfortable at speaking German, Spanish, or Tok Pisin without confusing those languages with each other or with English. I had also learned some other languages (especially Russian) but had never lived in their countries long enough to gain experience of speaking them continually. When I was initially talking with Indonesian friends, I was astonished to discover that my intention of pronouncing an Indonesian word often resulted in my uttering the Russian word with the same meaning, despite the Indonesian and Russian languages being completely unrelated! I had evidently learned to separate English, German, Spanish, and Tok Pisin into four well-controlled pigeonholes, but I was still left with an undifferentiated fifth pigeonhole equivalent to "language other than English, Spanish, German, and Tok Pisin." Only after more time in Indonesia was I able to inhibit the stock of Russian words lurking out of control in my mind and ready to creep into my Indonesian conversations.

In short, bilingual or multilingual people have constant unconscious practice in using executive control. They are forced to practise it whenever they speak, think, or listen to other people talking—i.e., constantly throughout their waking hours. In sports, art performance, and other arenas of life, we know that skills improve with practice. But: which are the skills that practice of bilingualism improves? Does bilingualism merely develop bilinguals' specific skill at switching between languages, or is bilingualism more generally useful to them?

Recent studies have devised tests to explore this question by comparing problem-solving by bilingual and monolingual people ranging from

3-year-old children to 80-year-old adults. The overall conclusion is that bilinguals of all those ages have an advantage at solving only a specific type of problem. But it is a broad specific problem: solving tasks that are confusing because the rules of the task change unpredictably, or because there are misleading and irrelevant but glaringly obvious cues that must be ignored. For instance, children are shown a series of cards depicting either a rabbit or a boat that is either red or blue, and that does or doesn't have a gold star. If a gold star is present, children must remember to sort the cards by color; if a gold star is absent, they must remember to sort the cards by the object depicted. Monolingual and bilingual subjects are equally successful at such games as long as the rule remains the same from trial to trial (e.g., "sort by color"), but monolinguals have much more difficulty than bilinguals at accommodating to a switch in rules.

As another example of a test, children sit in front of a computer screen on which either a red square suddenly flashes on the left of the screen or else a blue square flashes on the right of the screen. The keyboard below the screen includes a red key and also a blue key, and the child must push the key with the same color as the flashing square. If the red key is on the left of the keyboard and the blue key is on the right—i.e., in the same relative position as the flashing square of the same color on the screen—then bilinguals and monolinguals perform equally well. But if the positions of the red and blue keys are reversed to create confusion—i.e., if the red key is on the left side of the keyboard but the blue flashing square is the one on the left side of the screen—then bilinguals perform better than monolinguals.

It was initially expected that this advantage of bilinguals at tests involving rule changes or confusing information would apply only to tasks involving verbal cues. However, the advantage proves to be broader, and to apply also to non-verbal cues of space, color, and quantity (as in the two examples that I just described). But this hardly means that bilinguals are better than monolinguals at everything: the two groups tend to perform equally well at tasks without rule changes to be attended to, and without misleading cues to be ignored. Nevertheless, life is full of misleading information and changing rules. If bilinguals' advantage over monolinguals in these trivial games also applies to the abundance of confusing or shifting real-life situations, that would mean a significant advantage for bilinguals.

One interesting recent extension of these comparative tests is to infants. One might imagine that it would be meaningless or impossible to test "bilingual infants": infants can't speak at all, they can't be described as bilingual or monolingual, and they can't be asked to perform tests by sorting cards and pushing keys. In fact, infants develop the ability to discriminate speech that they hear long before they can speak themselves. One can test their powers of discrimination by watching whether they can learn to orient differently to two different sounds. It turns out that newborn infants, who have had no exposure to any of the world's languages, can discriminate between many consonant and vowel distinctions used in one or another of the world's languages, whether or not it happens to be their "native" language (which they haven't heard except from inside the womb). Over the course of their first year of life, as they hear speech around them, they lose that initial ability of theirs to discriminate non-native distinctions that they aren't hearing around them, and they sharpen their ability to discriminate native distinctions. For instance, the English language discriminates between the two liquid consonants *l* and *r*, while the Japanese language doesn't; that's why native Japanese people speaking English sound to native English-speakers as if they are mispronouncing "lots of luck" as "rots of ruck." Conversely, the Japanese language discriminates between short and long vowels, while the English language doesn't. However, newborn Japanese infants can discriminate between *l* and *r*, and newborn English infants can discriminate between short and long vowels, but each loses that ability over the first year of life because the distinction carries no meaning.

Recent studies have concerned so-called crib bilinguals: i.e., infants whose mother and father differ from each other in native language, but whose mother and father have both decided to speak her or his own language to the infant already from day 1, so that the infant grows up hearing two languages rather than just one language. Do crib bilinguals already gain over monolinguals the advantage in executive function, enabling them to deal better with rule switches and confusing information, that is apparent after the child can actually speak? And how does one test executive function in a pre-verbal infant?

A recent ingenious study by the scientists Ágnes Kovács and Jacques Mehler, carried out in the Italian city of Trieste, compared seven-month "monolingual" infants with infants "bilingual" in Italian plus either Slovenian, Spanish, English, Arabic, Danish, French, or Russian (i.e., hearing one language from their mother and the other language from their father). The infants were trained, conditioned, and rewarded for correct behavior by being shown a cute picture of a puppet popping up on the left side of a computer screen; the infants learned to look in the direction of the puppet and evidently enjoyed it. The test consisted of pronouncing to the infant a nonsense trisyllable with the structure AAB, ABA, or ABB (e.g., *lo-lo-vu, lo-vu-lo, lo-vu-vu*). For only one of the three structures (e.g., *lo-lo-vu*) did the puppet appear on the screen. Within 6 trials, on hearing *lo-lo-vu* both "monolingual" and "bilingual" infants learned to look towards the left side of the screen to anticipate the appearance of the cute puppet. Then the experimenter changed the rules and made the puppet appear on the right side (not on the left side) of the screen, in response not to the nonsense word *lo-lo-vu* but to *lo-vu-lo*. Within 6 trials, the "bilingual" infants had unlearned their previous lesson and had learned the new correct response, but the "monolingual" infants even after 10 trials were still looking at the now-wrong side of the screen on hearing the now-wrong nonsense word.

Alzheimer's disease

One can extrapolate from these results, and speculate that bilingual people may have an advantage over monolingual people in negotiating our confusing world of changing rules, and not merely in the trivial tasks of discriminating *lo-lo-vu* from *lo-vu-lo*. However, you readers will probably require evidence of more tangible benefits before you make the commitment to babble consistently in two different languages to your infant children and grandchildren. Hence you will be much more interested to learn about reported advantages of bilingualism at the opposite end of the lifespan: old age, when the devastating tragedy of Alzheimer's disease and other senile dementias lies in store for so many of us.

Alzheimer's disease is the commonest form of dementia of old age, affecting about 5% of people over the age of 75, and 17% of those over the age of 85. It begins with forgetfulness and a decline of short-term memory, and it proceeds irreversibly and incurably to death within about 5 to 10 years. The disease is associated with brain lesions, detectable by autopsy or (in life) by brain-imaging methods, including brain shrinkage and accumulation of specific proteins. All drug and vaccine treatments to date have failed. People with mentally and physically stimulating lives—more education, more complex jobs, stimulating social and leisure activities, and more physical exercise—suffer lower rates of dementia. However, the long latency period of up to 20 years between the beginning of protein build-up and the later appearance of Alzheimer's symptoms raises questions of cause and effect about the interpretation of these findings concerning stimulating lives: does stimulation itself really decrease Alzheimer's symptoms, or were those individuals instead able to lead stimulating lives precisely because they were not suffering from early stages of protein build-up, or because of genetic advantages that also protected them against Alzheimer's disease? In the hope that stimulating lives might be a cause rather than a result of reduced disease processes, older people afraid of developing Alzheimer's disease are sometimes urged to play bridge, play challenging online games, or solve Sudoku puzzles.

Intriguing results of the last few years suggest a protective effect of life-long bilingualism against Alzheimer's symptoms. Among 400 patients studied at clinics in Toronto, Canada, mostly in their 70s, and with a probable diagnosis of Alzheimer's disease (or other dementias in a few cases), bilingual patients showed their first symptoms at an age 4 or 5 years older than did monolingual patients. Life expectancy in Canada is 79, hence a delay of 4–5 years for people in their 70s translates into a 47% decrease of probability that they will develop Alzheimer's symptoms at all before they die. The bilingual and monolingual patients were matched in occupational status, but the bilingual patients had received on the average *lower* (not higher) levels of education. Because education is associated with lower incidence of Alzheimer's symptoms, this means that differences in education could not explain the lower incidence of symptoms in the bilingual patients: their lower incidence was *despite* their having received less education. A further intriguing finding was that, for a given level of cognitive impairment, bilingual patients had *more* brain atrophy revealed by brain-imaging methods than did monolingual patients. Expressing this differently, bilingual patients suffer less cognitive impairment than do monolingual patients with the same degree of brain atrophy: bilingualism offers partial protection against the consequences of brain atrophy.

The protection afforded by bilingualism does not raise the same uncertainties of interpretation about cause versus effect raised by the apparent protection offered by education and stimulating social activities. The latter might be results rather than causes of early stages of Alzheimer's lesions; and genetic factors predisposing one to seek education and social activities might also protect one against Alzheimer's disease. But whether one becomes bilingual is determined in early childhood, decades before the earliest Alzheimer's brain lesions develop, and regardless of one's genes. Most bilingual people become bilingual not through any decision or genes of their own, but through the accident of growing up in a bilingual society, or of their parents emigrating from their native land to a land with a different language. Hence the reduced Alzheimer's symptoms of bilinguals suggest that bilingualism itself protects against Alzheimer's symptoms.

How might this be? A short answer is the aphorism "Use it or lose it." Exercising most body systems improves their function; failing to exercise them lets their function deteriorate. This is the reason why athletes and artists practise. It's also the reason why Alzheimer's patients are encouraged to play bridge or online games, or to solve Sudoku puzzles. But bilingualism is the most constant practice possible for the brain. Whereas even a bridge or Sudoku fanatic can play bridge or solve Sudoku puzzles for only a fraction of a day, bilingual people impose extra exercise on their brain every second of their waking hours. Consciously or unconsciously, their brain is constantly having to decide, "Shall I speak, think, or interpret sounds spoken to me according to the arbitrary rules of language A, or of language B?"

Readers will share my personal interest in some unanswered but obvious further questions. If one extra language offers some protection, do two extra languages offer more protection? If so, does the protection increase in direct proportion to the number of languages, or else more steeply or less steeply? For instance, if bilingual people get four years of protection from their one extra language, does a New Guinean, an Aboriginal Australian, a Vaupés River Indian, or a Scandinavian shopkeeper speaking five languages (four beyond her first language) still get just 4 years of protection, or does she get 4 × 4 = 16 years of protection, or (if juggling four extra languages is much more than four times more taxing than juggling just one extra language) does she even get 50 years of protection? If you had the misfortune that your parents didn't raise you as a crib bilingual, and that you didn't learn a second language until you began high school at age 14, can you ever catch up to crib bilinguals in the benefits obtained? Both of these questions will be of theoretical interest to linguists, and of practical interest to parents wondering how best to raise their children. All of this suggests that bilingualism or multilingualism may bring big practical advantages to bilingual individuals, beyond the less practical advantages of a culturally enriched life, and regardless of whether language diversity is good or bad for the world as a whole.

Vanishing languages

The world's 7,000 languages are enormously diverse in a wide range of respects. For instance, one day while I was surveying birds in jungle around Rotokas village in the mountains of the Pacific island of Bougainville, the villager guiding me and naming local birds for me in the Rotokas language suddenly exclaimed *"Kópipi!"* as he pointed out the most beautiful bird song that I had ever heard. It consisted of silver-clear whistled tones and trills, grouped in slowly rising phrases of two or three notes, each phrase different from the previous one, and producing an effect like one of Franz Schubert's deceptively simple songs. The singer proved to be a species of long-legged short-winged warbler previously unknown to Western science.

As I talked with my guide, I gradually realized that the music of Bougainville's mountains included not only the *kópipi*'s song but also the sound of the Rotokas language. My guide named one bird for me after another: *kópipi, kurupi, vokupi, kopikau, kororo, keravo, kurue, vikuroi. . . .* The only consonant sounds from those names are *k, p, r,* and *v.* Later, I learned that the Rotokas language has only 6 consonant sounds, the fewest of any known language in the world. English, by comparison, has 24, while the now-extinct Ubykh language of Turkey had about 80. Somehow, the people of Rotokas, living in a tropical rainforest on the highest mountain of the Southwest Pacific Ocean east of New Guinea, have managed to build a rich vocabulary and communicate clearly while relying on fewer basic sounds than any other people in the world.

But the music of their language is now disappearing from Bougainville's mountains, and from the world. The Rotokas language is just 1 of 18 languages spoken on an island roughly three-quarters the size of the American state of Connecticut. At last count it was spoken by only 4,320 people, and that number is declining. With its vanishing, a 30,000-year experiment in human communication and cultural development will come to an end. That vanishing exemplifies the impending tragedy of the loss not just of the Rotokas language, but of most of the world's other languages. Only now are linguists starting seriously to estimate the world rate of language loss, and to debate what to do about it. If the present rate of language disappearance continues, then by the year 2100 most of the world's current languages will either already be extinct, or else will be moribund languages spoken only by old people and no longer being transmitted from parents to children.

Of course, language extinction isn't a new phenomenon that began only 70 years ago. We know from ancient written records, and we infer from distributions of languages and peoples, that languages have been going extinct for thousands of years. From Roman authors and from scraps of writing on ancient monuments and coins in the territory of the former Roman Empire, we know that Latin replaced Celtic languages formerly spoken in France and Spain, and replaced Etruscan, Umbrian, Oscan, Faliscan, and other languages within Italy itself. Preserved ancient texts in Sumerian, Hurrian, and Hittite attest to now-vanished languages spoken several thousand years ago in the Fertile Crescent. The spread of the Indo-European language family into western Europe, beginning within the last 9,000 years, eliminated all the original languages of Europe except for the Basque language of the Pyrenees. We infer that African Pygmies, Philippine and Indonesian hunter-gatherers, and ancient Japanese people spoke now-vanished languages replaced by Bantu languages, Austronesian languages, and the modern Japanese language respectively. Far more languages must have vanished without a trace.

Despite all that evidence for past extinctions of languages, modern language extinctions are different because of their greatly increased rate.

Extinctions of the last 10,000 years left us with 7,000 languages today, but extinctions of the next century or so will leave us with only a few hundred. That record-high rate of language extinction is due to the homogenizing influences of the spreads of globalization and of state government over the whole world.

As an illustration of the fates of most languages, consider Alaska's 20 native Inuit and Indian languages. The Eyak language, formerly spoken by a few hundred Indians on Alaska's south coast, had declined by 1982 to two native speakers, Marie Smith Jones and her sister Sophie Borodkin (Plate 47). Their children speak only English. With Sophie's death in 1992 at the age of 80, and Marie's death in 2008 at the age of 93, the language world of the Eyak people reached its final silence. Seventeen other native Alaskan languages are moribund, in the sense that not a single child is learning them. Although they are still spoken by older people, they too will meet the fate of Eyak when the last of those speakers dies, and almost all of them have fewer than a thousand speakers each. That leaves only two native Alaskan languages still being learned by children and thus not yet doomed: Siberian Yupik, with 1,000 speakers, and Central Yupik, with a grand total of 10,000 speakers.

In monographs summarizing the current status of languages, one encounters the same types of phrases monotonously repeated. "Ubykh [that Turkish language with 80 consonants] . . . the last fully competent speaker, Tevfik Esen, of Haci Osman, died in Istanbul 10/92. A century ago there were 50,000 speakers in the Caucasus valleys east of the Black Sea." "Cupeño [an Indian language of southern California] . . . nine speakers out of a total population of 150 . . . all over 50 years old . . . nearly extinct." "Yamana [an Indian language formerly spoken in southern Chile and Argentina] . . . three women speakers [in Chile], who are married to Spanish men and raised their children as Spanish speakers . . . extinct in Argentina."

The degree of language endangerment varies around the world. The continent in most desperate straits linguistically is Aboriginal Australia, where originally about 250 languages were spoken, all with under 5,000 speakers. Today, half of those Australian languages are already extinct; most of the survivors have under 100 speakers; fewer than 20 are still being passed on to children; and at most a few are likely still to be spoken by the end of the 21st century. Nearly as desperate is the plight of the native languages of the Americas. Of the hundreds of former Native American languages of North America, one-third are already extinct, another third have only a few old speakers, and only two (Navajo and Yupik Eskimo) are still being used for broadcast on local radio stations—a sure sign of trouble in this world of mass communications. Among the thousand or so native languages originally spoken in Central and South America, the only one with a secure future is Guarani, which along with Spanish is the national language of Paraguay. The sole continent with hundreds of native languages not already in dire straits is Africa, where most surviving native languages have tens of thousands or even millions of speakers, and where populations of small sedentary farmers currently seem to being holding on to their languages.

How languages disappear

How do languages go extinct? Just as there are different ways of killing people—by a quick blow to the head, by slow strangulation, or by prolonged neglect—so too are there different ways of eradicating a language. The most direct way is to kill almost all of its speakers. That was how white Californians eliminated the language of the last "wild" Indian of the United States, a man named Ishi (Plate 29) belonging to the Yahi tribe of about 400 people, living near Mount Lassen. In a series of massacres between 1853 and 1870 after the California gold rush had brought hordes of European settlers into California, settlers killed most Yahi, leaving Ishi and his family, then Ishi alone, to survive in hiding until 1911. British colonists eliminated all the native languages of Tasmania in the early 1800s by killing or capturing most Tasmanians, motivated by a bounty of five pounds for each Tasmanian adult and two pounds for each child. Less violent means of death produce similar results. For example, there used to be thousands of Native Americans of the Mandan tribe on the Great Plains of the United States, but by 1992 the number of fluent Mandan speakers was reduced to six old people, especially as a result of cholera and smallpox epidemics between 1750 and 1837.

The next most direct way to eradicate a language is not to kill its speakers, but instead to forbid them to use their language, and to punish them if they are caught doing so. In case you wondered why most North American Indian languages are now extinct or moribund, just consider the policy practised until recently by the United States government regarding those languages. For several centuries we insisted that Indians could be "civilized" and taught English only by removing Indian children from the "barbarous" atmosphere of their parents' homes to English-language-only boarding schools, where use of Indian languages was absolutely forbidden and punished with physical abuse and humiliation. To justify that policy, J. D. C. Atkins, the U.S. commissioner for Indian affairs from 1885 to 1888, explained, "The instruction of Indians in the vernacular [that is, in an Indian language] is not only of no use to them, but is detrimental to the cause of their education and civilization, and it will not be permitted in any Indian school over which the Government has any control. . . . This [English] language, which is good enough for a white man and a black man, ought to be good enough for the red man. It is also believed that teaching an Indian youth in his own barbarous dialect is a positive detriment to him. The first step to be taken toward civilization, toward teaching the Indians the mischief and folly of continuing in their barbarous practices, is to teach them the English language."

After Japan annexed Okinawa in 1879, the Japanese government adopted a solution described as "one nation, one people, one language." That meant educating Okinawan children to speak Japanese and no longer letting them speak any of the dozen native Okinawan languages. Similarly, when Japan annexed Korea in 1910, it banned the Korean language from Korean schools in favor of Japanese. When Russia re-annexed the Baltic republics in 1939, it replaced the Estonian, Latvian, and Lithuanian languages in schools with Russian, but those Baltic languages continued to be spoken in homes and resumed their status as national languages when the republics regained independence in 1991. The sole surviving Celtic language on the European mainland is Breton, which is still the primary language of half a million French citizens. However, the French government's official policy is in effect to exclude the Breton language from primary and secondary schools, and Breton's use is declining.

But in most cases language loss proceeds by the more insidious process now under way at Rotokas. With political unification of an area formerly occupied by sedentary warring tribes come peace, mobility, and increasing intermarriage. Young people in search of economic opportunity abandon their native-speaking villages and move to urban centers, where speakers of their own tribal language are greatly outnumbered by people from other tribal backgrounds, and where people needing to communicate with each other have no option except to speak the majority language. Increasing numbers of couples from different language groups marry and must resort to using the majority language to speak to each other; hence they transmit the majority language to their children. Even if the children do also learn a parental language, they must use the majority language in schools. Those people remaining in their natal village learn the majority language for its access to prestige, power, commerce, and the outside world. Jobs, newspapers, radio, and television overwhelmingly use the majority language shared by most workers, consumers, advertisers, and subscribers.

The usual result is that minority young adults tend to become bilingual, and then their children become monolingual, in the majority language. Transmission of minority languages from parents to children breaks down for either or both of two reasons: parents want their children to learn the majority language, not the parents' tribal language, so that their children can thrive in school and in jobs; and children don't want to learn their parents' language and only want to learn the majority language, in order to understand television, schools, and their playmates. I have seen these processes happening in the United States to immigrant families from Poland, Korea, Ethiopia, Mexico, and many other countries, with the shared result that the children learn English and don't learn their parents' language. Eventually, minority languages are spoken only by older people, until the last of them dies. Long before that end is reached, the minority language has degenerated through loss of its grammatical complexities, loss of forgotten native words, and incorporation of foreign vocabulary and grammatical features.

Of the world's 7,000 languages, some are in much more danger than are others. Crucial in determining the degree of language endangerment is whether a language is still being transmitted at home from parents to children: when that transmission ceases, a language is doomed, even if 90 more years will pass before the last child still fluent in the language, and with him or her the language itself, dies. Among the factors making it likely that parent-to-child transmission will continue are: a large number of speakers of the language; a high proportion of the population speaking the language; government recognition of the language as an official national or provincial language; speakers' attitude towards their own language (pride or scorn); and the absence of many immigrants speaking other languages and swamping native languages (as happened with the Russian influx into Siberia, the Nepali influx into Sikkim, and the Indonesian influx into Indonesian New Guinea).

Presumably among the languages with the most secure futures are the official national languages of the world's sovereign states, which now number about 192. However, most states have officially adopted English, Spanish, Arabic, Portuguese, or French, leaving only about 70 states to opt for other languages. Even if one counts regional languages, such as the 22 specified in India's constitution, that yields at best a few hundred languages officially protected anywhere in the world. Alternatively, one might consider languages with over a million speakers as secure, regardless of their official status, but that definition also yields only 200 or so secure languages, many of which duplicate the list of official languages. Some small languages are safe because of governmental support, such as Faroese, spoken by the 50,000 inhabitants of Denmark's self-governing Faroe Islands, and Icelandic, spoken as the official language of 300,000 Icelanders. Conversely, some languages with over a million speakers but no or until recently limited state support are threatened, such as Nahuatl (over 1,400,000 speakers in Mexico) and Quechua (about 9,000,000 speakers in the Andes). But state support doesn't guarantee a language's safety, as illustrated by the fading of the Irish language and the rise in the English language in Ireland, despite strong Irish governmental support for Irish and the teaching of Irish as an official language in Irish schools. It's on these bases that linguists estimate that all except a few hundred of the world's current 7,000 languages will be extinct or moribund by the end of this century—if current trends continue.

Are minority languages harmful?

Those are the overwhelming facts of worldwide language extinction. But now let's ask, as do many or most people: so what? Is language loss really a bad thing? Isn't the existence of thousands of languages positively harmful, because they impede communication and promote strife? Perhaps we should actually *encourage* language loss. This view was expressed by a deluge of listener comments sent into the British Broadcasting Corporation after it broadcast a program trying to defend the value of disappearing languages. Here is a sample of the quotes:

"What an extraordinary amount of sentimental rubbish! The reason that languages died out was that they were the expression of moribund societies incapable of communicating the intellectual, cultural, and social dynamics required for sustained longevity and evolution."

"How ridiculous. The purpose of language is to communicate. If nobody speaks a language, it has no purpose. You might as well learn Klingon."

"The only people that 7,000 languages are useful to are linguists. Different languages separate people, whereas a common language unites. The fewer living languages, the better."

"Humanity needs to be united, that's how we go forwards, not in small-knit tribes unable to communicate with one another. What good is there in even having five languages? Document them by all means, learn what we can from them, but consign them to history where they belong. One world, one people, one common language, one common goal, perhaps then we can all just get along."

"7,000 languages is 6,990 too many if you ask me. Let them go."

There are two main reasons that people like those who wrote to the BBC give in order to justify getting rid of most of the world's languages. One objection can be summarized in the one-liner "We need a common language in order to communicate with each other." Yes, of course that's true; different people do need some common language in order to communicate with each other. But that doesn't require eliminating minority languages; it just requires that speakers of minority languages become bilingual themselves in a majority language. For example, Denmark is the seventh-richest country in the world, although virtually the only people who speak the Danish language are the 5,000,000 Danes. That's because almost all Danes also fluently speak English and some other European languages, which they use to do business. Danes are rich and happily Danish, *because* they speak Danish. If Danes want to go to the effort of becoming bilingual in Danish and English, that's their own business. Similarly, if Navajo Indians want to go to the effort of becoming bilingual in Navajo and English, that's their business. The Navajos aren't asking and don't even want other Americans to learn Navajo.

The other main reason that people such as those who wrote to the BBC give to justify getting rid of languages is the belief that multiple languages cause civil wars and ethnic strife, by encouraging people to view other peoples as different. The civil wars tearing apart so many countries today are determined by linguistic lines—so it is claimed. Whatever the value of multiple languages, getting rid of them may supposedly be the price we have to pay if we are to halt the killing around the globe. Wouldn't the world be a much more peaceful place if the Kurds would just switch to speaking Turkish or Arabic, if Sri Lanka's Tamils would consent to speak Sinhalese, and if Quebec's French and the U.S. Hispanics would just switch to English?

That seems like a strong argument. But its implicit assumption of a monolingual utopia is wrong: language differences aren't the most important cause of strife. Prejudiced people will seize on any difference to dislike others, including differences of religion, politics, ethnicity, and dress. The worst mass killings in Europe since the end of World War II involved Eastern Orthodox Serbs and Montenegrans (who later split from each other), Catholic Croats, and Muslim Bosnians in the former Yugoslavia slaughtering each other, even though all of them speak the same language, Serbo-Croat. The worst mass killings in Africa since the end of World War II were in Rwanda in 1994, when Hutu people killed nearly a million Tutsi and most of Rwanda's Twa people, all of them speaking the Rwanda language. The worst mass killings anywhere in the world since the end of World War II were in Cambodia, where Khmer-speaking Cambodians under their dictator Pol Pot killed about two million other Khmer-speaking Cambodians. The worst mass killings anywhere in the world, anytime in history, were in Russia under Stalin, when Russians killed tens of millions of people, most of whom also spoke Russian, over supposed political differences.

If you believe that minorities should give up their languages and adopt the majority language in order to promote peace, ask yourself whether you also believe that minorities should promote peace by giving up their religions, their ethnicities, and their political views. If you believe that freedom of religion, ethnicity, and political view but not of language is an inalienable human right, how would you explain your inconsistency to a Kurd or a French Canadian? Innumerable examples besides those of Stalin, Pol Pot, Rwanda, and the former Yugoslavia warn us that monolingualism is no safeguard of peace.

Given that people do differ in language, religion, ethnicity, and political view, the only alternative to tyranny or mass killing is for people to live together in mutual tolerance. That's not an idle hope. Despite all the past wars over religion, people of different religions do co-exist peacefully in the United States, Germany, Indonesia, and many other countries. Similarly, many countries that practise linguistic tolerance find that they can accommodate people of different languages in harmony: for example, 2 native languages in the Netherlands (Dutch and Frisian), 2 in New Zealand (English and Maori), 3 in Finland (Finnish, Swedish, and Lapp), 4 in Switzerland (German, French, Italian, and Romansh), 43 in Zambia, 85 in Ethiopia, 128 in Tanzania, and 286 in Cameroon. On a trip to Zambia when I visited a high school classroom, I recall one student asking me, "Which tribe in the United States do you belong to?" Then each student told me, with a smile, his or her tribal language. Seven languages were represented in that small classroom, and no one seemed ashamed, afraid, or intent on killing each other.

Why preserve languages?

All right, so there's nothing inevitably harmful or burdensome about preserving languages except the effort of bilingualism for the minority speakers themselves, and they can decide for themselves whether they're willing to put up with that effort. Are there any positive advantages of preserving linguistic diversity? Why shouldn't we just let the world converge on its five top languages of Mandarin, Spanish, English, Arabic, and Hindi? Or let's push that argument one step further, before my English-speaking readers enthusiastically answer, "Yes!" If you think that small languages should give way to big languages, a logical conclusion is that we should all adopt the world's biggest language, Mandarin, and let English die out. What's the use of preserving the English language? Among many answers, I'll mention three.

First, with two or more languages, we as individuals can be bilingual or multilingual. I discussed earlier in this chapter the evidence for cognitive advantages of bilingual individuals. Even if you're skeptical about bilingualism's reported protection against symptoms of Alzheimer's disease, everyone fluent in more than one language knows that knowledge of different languages enriches one's life, just as a large vocabulary in one's first language permits a richer life than does a small vocabulary. Different languages have different advantages, such that it's easier to express some things, or to feel in certain ways, in one language than in another. If the much-debated Sapir-Whorf hypothesis is correct, a language's structure molds the way in which that language's speakers think, with the result that one views the world and thinks differently when one switches languages. Hence language loss doesn't only curtail freedom of minorities; it also curtails the options of majorities.

Second, languages are the most complex product of the human mind, each differing in its sounds, structure, and pattern of thought. But a language itself isn't the only thing lost when a language goes extinct. Literature, culture, and much knowledge are encoded in languages: lose the language, and you lose much of the literature, culture, and knowledge. Different languages have different number systems, mnemonic devices, and systems of spatial orientation: for instance, it's easier to count in Welsh or Mandarin than in English. Traditional peoples have local-language names for hundreds of animal and plant species around them: those encyclopedias of ethnobiological information vanish when their languages vanish. While Shakespeare can be translated into Mandarin, we English-speakers would regard it as a loss to humanity if Hamlet's speech "To be or not to be, that is the question" were available only in Mandarin translation. Tribal peoples also have their own oral literatures, and losses of those literatures also represent losses to humanity.

But perhaps you're still thinking, "Enough of all this vague talk about linguistic freedom, unique cultural inheritance, and different options for thinking and expressing. Those are luxuries that rate low priority amid the crises of the modern world. Until we solve the world's desperate socio-economic problems, we can't waste our time on bagatelles like obscure Native American languages."

Then please think again about the socio-economic problems of the people speaking all those obscure Native American languages (and thousands of other obscure languages around the world). They are the poorest segment of American society. Their problems are not just narrow ones of jobs, but broad ones of cultural disintegration. Groups whose language and culture disintegrate tend to lose their pride and mutual self-support, and to descend into socio-economic problems. They've been told for so long that their language and everything else about their culture are worthless that they believe it. The resulting costs to national governments of welfare benefits, healthcare expenses, alcohol-related and drug-related problems, and drain on rather than contribution to the national economy are enormous. At the same time, other minorities with strong intact cultures and language retention—like some recent groups of immigrants to the U.S.—are already contributing strongly to the economy rather than taking from it. Among native minorities as well, those with intact cultures and languages tend to be stronger economically and to place fewer demands on social services. Cherokee Indians who complete Cherokee language school and remain bilingual in Cherokee and English are more likely to pursue their education, obtain jobs, and earn higher salaries than Cherokees who can't speak Cherokee. Aboriginal Australians who learn their traditional tribal language and culture are less prone to substance abuse than are culturally disconnected Aborigines.

Programs to reverse Native American cultural disintegration would be more effective and cheaper than welfare payments, for Native American minorities and for majority taxpayers alike. Such programs aim at long-term solutions; welfare payments don't. Similarly, those countries now racked by civil wars along linguistic lines would have found it cheaper to emulate countries (like Switzerland, Tanzania, and many others) based on partnerships between proud intact groups than to seek to crush minority languages and cultures.

Language as a focus of national identity can mean the difference between group survival and disappearance not only to minorities within a country but to whole nations as well. Consider the situation in Britain early in World War II, in May and June of 1940, when French resistance to the invading Nazi armies was collapsing, when Hitler had already occupied Austria and Czechoslovakia and Poland and Norway and Denmark and the Low Countries, when Italy and Japan and Russia had signed alliances or pacts with Hitler, and when the United States was still determined to remain neutral. Britain's prospects of prevailing against the impending German invasion appeared bleak. Voices within the British government argued that Britain should seek to make some deal with Hitler, rather than to attempt a hopeless resistance.

Winston Churchill responded in the House of Commons on May 13 and June 4, 1940, with the two most quoted and most effective 20th-century speeches in the English language. Among other things, he said, "I have nothing to offer but blood, toil, tears and sweat. . . . You ask, what is our policy? I will say. It is to wage war, by sea, land, and air, with all our might and with all the strength that God can give us: to wage war against a monstrous tyranny, never surpassed in the dark, lamentable catalog of human crime. . . . We shall not flag or fail. We shall go on to the end, we shall fight in France, we shall fight in the seas and ocean, we shall fight with growing confidence and growing strength in the air, we shall defend our island, whatever the cost may be, we shall fight on the beaches, we shall fight on the landing-grounds, we shall fight in the fields and in the streets, we shall fight in the hills; we shall never surrender."

We know now that Britain never did surrender, did not seek a settlement with Hitler, continued to fight, after a year gained Russia and then the United States as allies, and after five years defeated Hitler. But that outcome was not predestined. Suppose that the absorption of small European languages by large languages had reached the point in 1940 at which the British and all other Western Europeans had adopted Western Europe's largest language, namely, German. What would have happened in June 1940 if Churchill had been addressing the House of Commons in the German language, rather than in English?

My point is not that Churchill's words were untranslatable; they ring as powerful in German as in English. ("Anbieten kann ich nur Blut, Müh, Schweiss, und Träne. . . .") My point is instead that the English language is a proxy for everything that made the British keep fighting against seemingly hopeless odds. Speaking English means being heir to a thousand years of independent culture, history, increasing democracy, and island identity. It means being heir to Chaucer, Shakespeare, Tennyson, and other monuments of literature in the English language. It means having different political ideals from Germans and other continental Europeans. In June 1940, speaking English meant having something worth fighting and dying for. While no one can prove it, I doubt that Britain would have resisted Hitler in June 1940 if the British had already been speaking German. Preservation of one's linguistic identity is not a bagatelle. It keeps Danes rich and happy, and some native and immigrant minorities prosperous, and it kept Britain free.

How can we protect languages?

If you now at last agree that linguistic diversity isn't harmful and might even be good, what can be done to slow the present trend of dwindling linguistic diversity? Are we helpless in the face of the seemingly overwhelming forces tending to eradicate all but a few big languages from the modern world?

No, we're not helpless. First, professional linguists themselves could do a lot more than most of them are now doing. The great majority of linguists assign low priority to the study of vanishing languages. Only recently have more linguists been calling attention to our impending loss. It's ironic that so many linguists have remained uninvolved at a time when languages, the subject of their discipline, are disappearing. Governments and society could train and support more linguists to study and tape-record the last speakers of dying languages, so as to preserve the option that surviving members of the population can revive the language even after the last aged speaker dies—as happened with the Cornish language in Britain, and as may now be happening with the Eyak language in Alaska. A notable success story of language revival is the modern reestablishment of Hebrew as a vernacular language, now spoken by 5,000,000 people.

Second, governments can support minority languages by policies and by allotting money. Examples include the support that the Dutch government gives to the Frisian language (spoken by about 5% of the Netherlands' population), and that the New Zealand government gives to the Maori language (spoken by under 2% of New Zealand's population). After two centuries of opposing Native American languages, the U.S. government in 1990 passed an act to encourage their use, and then allocated a small amount of money (about $2,000,000 per year) to Native American language studies. As that number illustrates, though, governmental support for endangered languages has a long way to go. The money that the U.S. government spends to preserve endangered animal and plant species dwarfs its expenditures to preserve endangered languages, and the money spent on one bird species alone (the California condor) exceeds that spent on all of our 100-plus endangered Native American languages combined. As a passionate ornithologist, I'm all in favor of spending money for condors, and I wouldn't want to see money transferred from condor programs to Eyak language programs. Instead, I mention this comparison to illustrate what seems to me a gross inconsistency in our priorities. If we value endangered birds, why don't we assign at least as much value to endangered languages, whose importance one might think would be easier for us humans to understand?

Third, there's a lot that minority speakers themselves can do to promote their languages, as the Welsh, Quebec French, and various Native American groups have been doing recently with some success. They are the living custodians of their language—the people in by far the best position to pass the language on to their children and to other members of the group, and to lobby their government for support.

But such minority efforts will continue to face an uphill struggle if strongly opposed by the majority, as has happened all too often. Those of us majority-speakers and our governmental representatives who don't choose actively to promote minority languages can at least remain neutral and avoid crushing them. Our motives for doing so include ultimately selfish motives as well as the interests of minority groups themselves: to pass on a rich and strong world, rather than a drastically impoverished and chronically sapped world, to our children.

CHAPTER 11

Salt, Sugar, Fat, and Sloth

Non-communicable diseases ▪ Our salt intake ▪ Salt and blood pressure ▪ Causes of hypertension ▪ Dietary sources of salt ▪ Diabetes ▪ Types of diabetes ▪ Genes, environment, and diabetes ▪ Pima Indians and Nauru Islanders ▪ Diabetes in India ▪ Benefits of genes for diabetes ▪ Why is diabetes low in Europeans? ▪ The future of non-communicable diseases

Non-communicable diseases

When I began working in Papua New Guinea in 1964, the vast majority of New Guineans still lived largely traditional lifestyles in their villages, growing their own food and consuming a low-salt, low-sugar diet. The dietary staples in the Highlands were root crops (sweet potato, taro, and yams) providing about 90% of Highlanders' caloric intake, while the lowland staple was starch grains from the heart of sago palm trees. People with some cash bought small quantities of trade store foods as luxury items: crackers, tinned fish, and a little salt and sugar.

Among the many things that impressed me about New Guineans was their physical condition: lean, muscular, physically active, all of them resembling slim Western body-builders. When not carrying loads, they ran along steep mountain trails at a trot, and when carrying heavy loads they walked all day at my own unencumbered walking pace. I recall a small woman who appeared to weigh no more than 100 pounds, carrying a 70-pound rice bag resting on her back and suspended by a strap around her forehead, up boulder-strewn river beds and mountains. During those early years in New Guinea I never saw a single obese or even overweight New Guinean.

New Guinea hospital records, and medical examinations of New Guineans by physicians, confirmed this appearance of good health—at least in part. The non-communicable diseases that kill most First World citizens today—diabetes, hypertension, stroke, heart attacks, atherosclerosis, cardiovascular diseases in general, and cancers—were rare or unknown among traditional New Guineans living in rural areas. The absence of those diseases wasn't just because of a short average lifespan: they still didn't appear even among those New Guineans who did live into their 60s, 70s, and 80s. An early-1960s review of 2,000 admissions to the medical ward of the general hospital of Port Moresby (the capital and largest city) detected not a single case of coronary artery disease, and only four cases of hypertension, all four in patients of mixed racial origins rather than unmixed New Guineans.

But that's not to say that traditional New Guineans enjoyed a carefree health utopia: far from it. The lifespans of most of them were, and still are, shorter than in the West. The diseases that killed them, along with accidents and interpersonal violence, were ones that have by now been largely eliminated as causes of death in the First World: gastrointestinal infections producing diarrhea, respiratory infections, malaria, parasites, malnutrition, and secondary conditions preying on people weakened by those primary conditions. That is, we Westerners, despite having traded our set of traditional human illnesses for a new set of modern illnesses, enjoy on the average better health and longer lives.

Already in 1964, the new killers of First World citizens were beginning to make their appearance in New Guinea, among those populations that had had the longest contact with Europeans and had begun to adopt Western diets and lifestyles. Today, that Westernization of New Guinea diets, lifestyles, and health problems is in a phase of explosive growth. Tens of thousands, perhaps hundreds of thousands, of New Guineans now work as businesspeople, politicians, airline pilots, and computer programmers, obtain their food in supermarkets and restaurants, and get little exercise. In cities, towns, and Westernized environments one commonly sees overweight or obese New Guineans. One of the highest prevalences of diabetes in the world (estimated at 37%) is among the Wanigela people, who were the first New Guinea population to become extensively Westernized. Heart attacks are now reported among city-dwellers. Since 1998 I have been working in a New Guinea oil field whose employees eat all three daily meals in a buffet-style cafeteria where one helps oneself to food, and where each dining table has a salt-shaker and sugar-shaker. New Guineans who grew up in traditional village lifestyles with limited and unpredictable food availability react to these predictable daily food bonanzas by piling their plates as high as possible at every meal, and inverting the salt and sugar dispensers over their steaks and salads. Hence the oil company hired trained New Guinean health workers to educate staff on the importance of healthy eating. But even some of those health workers soon develop Western health problems.

These changes that I have been watching unfold in New Guinea are just one example of the wave of epidemics of non-communicable diseases (NCDs) associated with the Western lifestyle and now sweeping the world. Such diseases differ from infectious (communicable) and parasitic diseases, which are caused by an infectious agent (such as a bacterium or virus) or a parasite, and which are transmitted ("communicate" themselves) from person to person through spread of the agent. Many infectious diseases develop quickly in a person after infection by the agent, such that within a few weeks the victim is either dead or recovering. In contrast, all of the major NCDs (as well as parasitic diseases and some infectious diseases, such as AIDS and malaria and tuberculosis) develop slowly and persist for years or decades until they either reach a fatal end or are cured or halted, or until the victim dies of something else first. Major NCDs in the current wave include various cardiovascular diseases (heart attacks, strokes, and peripheral vascular diseases), the common form of diabetes, some forms of kidney disease, and some cancers such as stomach, breast, and lung cancers. The vast majority of you readers of this book—e.g., almost 90% of all Europeans and Americans and Japanese— will die of one of these NCDs, while the majority of people in low-income countries die of communicable diseases.

All of these NCDs are rare or absent among small-scale societies with traditional lifestyles. While the existence of some of these diseases is attested already in ancient texts, they became common in the West only within recent centuries. Their association with the current explosive spread of the modern Western lifestyle around the world becomes obvious from their epidemics among four types of population. In the cases of some countries that became rich recently and suddenly, and most of whose inhabitants now "enjoy" the Western lifestyle—Saudi Arabia and the other Arab oil-producing nations, plus several suddenly affluent island nations including Nauru and Mauritius—the entire national population is at risk. (For instance, of the world's eight countries with national diabetes prevalences above 15%, every one is either an Arab oil-producer or an affluent island nation.) Other epidemics are striking citizens of developing nations who emigrated to the First World, suddenly exchanged their formerly spartan lifestyle for a Western lifestyle, and are thereby developing NCD prevalences higher either than those of their countrymen who stayed home and continued their traditional lifestyle, or than those of long-term residents of their new host countries. (Examples include Chinese and Indians emigrating overseas [to Britain, the U.S., Mauritius, and other destinations more affluent than China or India], and Yemenite and Ethiopian Jews emigrating to Israel.) Urban epidemics are being recorded in many developing countries, such as Papua New Guinea, China, and numerous African nations, among people who migrate from rural areas to cities and thereby adopt a sedentary lifestyle and consume more store-bought food. Finally, still other epidemics involve specific non-European groups that have adopted a Western lifestyle without migrating, and that have thereby sadly become famous for some of the world's highest prevalences of diabetes and other NCDs. Often-cited textbook examples include the Pima Indians of the U.S., New Guinea's Wanigela people, and numerous groups of Aboriginal Australians.

These four sets of natural experiments illustrate how the adoption of a Western lifestyle, no matter what leads to it, by people previously with a traditional lifestyle results in NCD epidemics. What these natural experiments don't tell us, without further analysis, is which particular component or components of the Western lifestyle trigger the epidemic. That lifestyle includes many components occurring together: low physical activity, high calorie intake, weight gain or obesity, smoking, high alcohol consumption, and high salt consumption. Diet composition usually shifts to low intake of fiber and high intakes of simple sugars (especially fructose), saturated fats, and trans-unsaturated fats. Most or all of these changes happen simultaneously when a population Westernizes, and that makes it difficult to identify the relative importance of individual ones of these changes in causing an NCD epidemic. For a few diseases the evidence is clear: smoking is especially important as a cause of lung cancer, and salt intake is especially important as a cause of hypertension and stroke. But for the other diseases, including diabetes and several cardiovascular diseases, we still don't know which of these co-occurring risk factors are most relevant.

Our understanding of this field has been stimulated especially by the pioneering work of S. Boyd Eaton, Melvin Konner, and Marjorie Shostak. Those authors assembled information on our "Paleolithic diet"—i.e., the diet and lifestyle of our hunter-gatherer ancestors and of modern surviving hunter-gatherers—and on the differences between the principal diseases affecting our ancestors and modern Westernized populations. They reasoned that our non-communicable diseases of civilization arise from a mismatch between our bodies' genetic constitution, still largely adapted to our Paleolithic diet and lifestyle, and our current diet and lifestyle. They proposed tests of their hypothesis and offered recommendations about diet and lifestyle to reduce our exposure to our new diseases of civilization. References to their original articles and book will be found under the Further Readings for this chapter.

Non-communicable diseases associated with the Western lifestyle offer perhaps this book's most immediately practical example of the lessons that can be extracted from traditional lifestyles. By and large, traditional people don't develop the set of the NCDs that I've discussed, while by and large most Westernized people will die of these NCDs. Of course, I'm not suggesting that we adopt a traditional lifestyle wholesale, overthrow state governments, and resume killing each other, infanticide, religious wars, and periodic starvation. Instead, our goal is to identify and adopt those particular components of the traditional lifestyle that protect us against NCDs. While a full answer will have to wait for more research, it's a safe bet that the answer will include traditional low salt intake and won't include traditional lack of state government. Tens of millions of people around the world already consciously use our current understanding of risk factors in order to lead healthier lives. In the remainder of this chapter I shall discuss two NCD epidemics in more detail: the consequences of high salt intake and of diabetes.

Our salt intake

While there are many different chemicals falling into the category termed "salts" by chemists, to laypeople "salt" means sodium chloride. That's *the* salt that we crave, season our food with, consume too much of, and get sick from. Today, salt comes from a salt-shaker on every dining table and ultimately from a supermarket, is cheap, and is available in essentially unlimited quantities. Our bodies' main problem with salt is to get rid of it, which we do copiously in our urine and in our sweat. The average daily salt consumption around the world is about 9 to 12 grams, with a range mostly between 6 and 20 grams (higher in Asia than elsewhere).

Traditionally, though, salt didn't come from salt-shakers but had somehow to be extracted from the environment. Imagine what the world used to be like before salt-shakers became ubiquitous. Our main problem with salt then was to acquire it rather than to get rid of it. That's because most plants contain very little sodium, yet animals require sodium at high concentrations in all their extracellular fluids. As a result, while carnivores readily obtain their needed sodium by eating herbivores full of extracellular sodium, herbivores themselves face problems in obtaining that sodium. That's why the animals that you see coming to salt licks are deer and antelope, not lions and tigers. Human hunter-gatherers who consumed much meat, such as the Inuit and San, thus met their salt requirement readily, though even their total salt intake was only 1 or 2 grams per day because much of their prey's sodium-rich blood and other extracellular fluids became lost in the course of butchering and cooking. Among traditional hunter-gatherers and farmers consuming a diet high in plant food and with limited meat, those living on the seacoast or near inland salt deposits also have easy access to salt. For instance, average daily salt consumption is around 10 grams among the Lau people of the Solomon Islands, who live on the coast and use salt water for cooking, and also among Iran's Qashqa'i nomadic herders, whose homeland has natural salt deposits on the surface.

However, for dozens of other traditional hunter-gatherers and farmers whose daily salt intake has been calculated, it falls below 3 grams. The lowest recorded value is for Brazil's Yanomamo Indians, whose staple food is low-sodium bananas, and who excrete on the average only 50 milligrams of salt daily: about 1/200 of the salt excretion of the typical American. A single Big Mac hamburger analyzed by *Consumer Reports* contained 1.5 grams (1,500 milligrams) of salt, representing one month's salt intake for a Yanomamo, while one can of chicken noodle soup (containing 2.8 grams of salt) represents nearly two months of Yanomamo salt consumption. A possible record was set by a Chinese-American restaurant near my home in Los Angeles. Its double pan-fried noodles combo dish was reportedly analyzed as containing one year and three days' worth of Yanomamo salt intake: 18.4 grams.

Hence traditional peoples crave salt and go to great lengths to obtain it. (We, too, crave salt: just try eating nothing but fresh, unprocessed, un-salted food for one day, and then see how wonderful salt tastes when you finally sprinkle some on your food.) New Guinea Eastern Highlanders with whom I have worked, and whose diet consists up to 90% of low-sodium sweet potatoes, told me of the efforts to which they used to go to make salt a few decades ago, before Europeans brought it as trade goods. They gathered leaves of certain plant species, burned them, scraped up the ash, percolated water through it to dissolve the solids, and finally evaporated the water to obtain small amounts of bitter salt. The Dugum Dani people of the Western New Guinea Highlands made salt from the only two natural brine pools in their valley, by plunging a spongy piece of banana trunk into a pool to soak up brine, removing the piece and drying it in the sun, burning it to ash, and then sprinkling water on the ash and kneading the moist mass into cakes to be consumed or traded. After all that traditional effort to obtain small quantities of impure bitter-tasting salt, it's no wonder that New Guineans eating in Western-style cafeterias can't resist grabbing the salt-shaker on the dining table and letting the stream of pure salt run out onto their steaks and salads at every meal.

With the rise of state governments, salt became widely available and pro-duced on an industrial scale (as it still is today) from salt-water drying pans, salt mines, or surface deposits. To its use as a seasoning was added its use, reportedly discovered in China around 5,000 years ago, to preserve food for storage over the winter. Salt cod and salt herring became fixtures of the Eu-ropean diet, and salt became the most traded and most taxed commodity in the world. Roman soldiers were paid in salt, so that our word "salary" for pay is derived not from the Latin root for "money" or "coins" but from the Latin root for "salt" (*sal*). Wars were fought over salt; revolutions broke out over salt taxes; and Mahatma Gandhi rallied Indians against the perceived injustice of British colonial rule by walking for one month to the ocean, violating British laws by illegally making salt for himself on the beach from the freely available salt water, and refusing to pay the British salt tax.

As a result of the relatively recent adoption of a high-salt diet by our still largely traditional bodies adapted to a low-salt diet, high salt intake is a risk factor for almost all of our modern non-communicable diseases. Many of these damaging effects of salt are mediated by its role in raising blood pressure, which I'll discuss below. High blood pressure (alias hypertension) is among the major risk factors for cardiovascular diseases in general, and for strokes, congestive heart disease, coronary artery disease, and myocardial infarcts in particular, as well as for Type-2 diabetes and kidney disease. Salt intake also has unhealthy effects independent of its role in raising blood pressure, by thickening and stiffening our arteries, increasing platelet aggregation, and increasing the mass of the heart's left ventricle, all of which contribute to the risk of cardiovascular diseases. Still other effects of salt intake independent of blood pressure are on the risks of stroke and stomach cancer. Finally, salt intake contributes indirectly but significantly to obesity (in turn a further risk factor for many non-communicable diseases) by increasing our thirst, which many people satisfy in part by consuming sugary high-calorie soft drinks.

Salt and blood pressure

Let's now pause for a quick crash course on blood pressure and hypertension, to help you understand what those numbers mean when your doctor inflates a rubber cuff about your arm, listens, deflates the cuff, and finally pronounces, "Your blood pressure is 120 over 80." Blood pressure is expressed in units of millimeters of mercury: the height to which your blood pressure would force up a column of mercury in case, God forbid, your artery were suddenly connected to a vertical mercury column. Naturally, your blood pressure changes throughout each heart stroke cycle: it rises as the heart squeezes, and it falls as the heart relaxes. Hence your physician measures a first number and then a second number (e.g., 120 and 80 millimeters of mercury), referring respectively to the peak pressure at each heartbeat (called systolic pressure) and to the minimum pressure between beats (termed diastolic pressure). Blood pressure varies somewhat with your position, activity, and anxiety level, so the measurement is usually made while you are resting flat on your back and supposedly calm. Under those conditions, 120 over 80 is an average reading for Americans. There is no magic cut-off between normal blood pressure and high blood pressure. Instead, the higher your blood pressure, the more likely you are to die of a heart attack, a stroke, kidney failure, or a ruptured aorta. Usually, a pressure reading higher than 140 over 90 is arbitrarily defined as constituting hypertension, but some people with lower readings will die of a stroke at age 50, while others with higher readings will die of a car accident in otherwise good health at age 90.

In the short run, your blood pressure increases with your anxiety level and with vigorous exercise. In the long run, though, it increases with other factors, especially with salt intake (for reasons discussed below) and (in us Westernized moderns but not in traditional peoples) with age. The relationship between salt intake and blood pressure was noted more than 2,000 years ago in the Chinese medical text *Huangdi neijing suwen*, which says, "Therefore if large amounts of salt are taken, the pulse will stiffen and harden." In recent experiments on captive chimpanzees, our closest animal relatives, their blood pressure while consuming a Purina Monkey Chow diet providing 6 to 12 grams of salt per day (like most modern humans eating a Western diet) was a pleasingly healthy 120 over 50, but it increased with age (also like modern humans on a Western diet). After a year and seven months on a high-salt diet of up to about 25 grams per day, the chimps' blood pressure rose to about 155 over 60, qualifying them to be called hypertensive by human standards, at least as judged by their systolic blood pressure.

For us humans it's clear that salt intake does influence blood pressure, at least at the opposite extremes of very low and very high salt intake. The international INTERSALT project of the 1980s used a uniform methodology to measure salt intake and blood pressure in 52 populations around the world. The population that I already mentioned as having the world's lowest recorded salt intake, Brazil's Yanomamo Indians, also had the world's lowest average blood pressure, an astonishingly low 96 over 61. The two populations with the next two lowest salt intakes, Brazil's Xingu Indians and Papua New Guinea Highlanders of the Asaro Valley, had the next two lowest blood pressures (100 over 62, and 108 over 63). These three populations, and several dozen other populations around the world with traditional lifestyles and low salt intakes, showed no increase in blood pressure with age, in contrast to the rise with age in Americans and all other Westernized populations.

At the opposite extreme, doctors regard Japan as the "land of apoplexy" because of the high frequency of fatal strokes (Japan's leading cause of death, five times more frequent than in the United States), linked to high blood pressure and notoriously salty food. Within Japan these factors reach their extremes in northern Japan's Akita Prefecture, famous for its tasty rice, which Akita farmers flavor with salt, wash down with salty miso soup, and alternate with salt pickles between meals. Of 300 Akita adults studied, not one consumed less than 5 grams of salt daily (three months of consumption for a Yanomamo Indian), the average Akita consumption was 27 grams, and the most salt-loving individual consumed an incredible 61 grams—enough to devour the contents of the usual 26-ounce supermarket salt container in a mere 12 days. That record-breaking Akita man consumed daily as much salt as an average Yanomamo Indian in three years and three months. The *average* blood pressure in Akita by age 50 was 151 over 93, making hypertension the norm. Not surprisingly, Akita's frequency of death by stroke was more than double even the Japanese average, and in some Akita villages 99% of the population died before 70.

The evidence is thus striking that extreme variations in salt intake have big effects on blood pressure: very low salt intake results in very low blood pressure, and very high salt intake results in very high blood pressure. However, most of us will never follow a diet as extreme as that of a Yanomamo Indian or an Akita farmer. Instead, we would like to know whether more modest variations in salt intake, within the middle of the range of world salt intakes, have at least some modest effects on blood pressure. For several reasons, it really isn't surprising that there is still some controversy about effects of variation within this middle range. The middle range encompasses only a narrow spread of salt intake: for instance, 48 of the 52 populations in the INTERSALT study (all populations except the Yanomamo and the three other low-salt outliers) had mean salt intakes falling between 6 and 14 grams per day. Individual variation in salt intake and blood pressure within most populations is large and tends to obscure average differences between populations. Salt intake itself is notoriously difficult to measure consistently unless one confines people in a hospital metabolic ward for a week and measures salt levels in all of their foods consumed and urine produced. That's completely impossible to do for Ya-nomamo Indians in the jungle, as well as for most of us city-dwellers wanting to lead normal lives outside metabolic wards. Instead, salt intake is commonly estimated from 24-hour urine collections, but those values are subject to huge variation from day to day, depending on whether one happens to eat a Big Mac or a can of chicken noodle soup on some par-ticular day.

Despite those causes of uncertainty, many natural experiments as well as manipulative experiments indicate to me that variations of salt intake within the normal range do affect blood pressure. Regional variation, mi-gration, and individual variation provide natural experiments. Salt intake is higher for coastal people than for interior people in Newfoundland and in the Solomon Islands, and it's higher for rural Nigerians living near a salt lake than for nearby rural Nigerians not living near a salt lake; in each case the higher-salt population has higher average blood pressure. When rural Kenyans or Chinese move to cities, their salt intake often rises, and so does their blood pressure. Salt intake in Japan nearly doubles from south to north to reach its maximum in the already-mentioned Akita Pre-fecture in the north, and that salt trend is paralleled by a trend in hyper-tension and in deaths from stroke. Among individual Japanese in a single city (Takayama), hypertension and stroke deaths increase with salt intake.

As for manipulative experiments, Americans on a (mildly) low-salt diet for 30 days, New Guineans on a (mildly) high-salt diet for 10 days, and Chinese on a (mildly) low-salt or high-salt diet for 7 days all experienced a rise or fall in blood pressure paralleling the experimental rise or fall in salt intake. Epidemiologists in a suburb of the Dutch city of The Hague, with the cooperation of the mothers of 476 newborn infants, randomly assigned the infants (most of them breast-fed) for six months to either of two diets of food supplements differing by a factor of 2.6 in salt content.

The blood pressure of the slightly high-salt babies increased progressively above the blood pressure of the slightly low-salt babies over the course of the six months, when the experimental intervention ended and the babies proceeded to eat whatever they wanted for the next 15 years. Interestingly, the effects of those six months of salt intake in infancy proved to be permanent: as teen-agers, the former slightly high-salt babies still had blood pressures above those of the slightly low-salt babies (perhaps because they had become permanently conditioned to choose salty food). Finally, in at least four countries notorious for high average levels of salt consumption and resulting stroke deaths—China, Finland, Japan, and Portugal—government public health campaigns that lasted years or decades achieved local or national reductions in blood pressure and in stroke mortality. For instance, a 20-year campaign in Finland to reduce salt intake succeeded in lowering average blood pressure, and thereby cut 75% or 80% off of deaths from stroke and coronary heart disease and added 5 or 6 years to Finnish life expectancies.

Causes of hypertension

For us to be able to deal with the problem of high blood pressure, we have to understand what else besides high salt intake can cause it, and why high salt intake can cause it in some individuals but not in others. Why is it that some of us have much higher blood pressure than do others of us? In 5% of hypertensive patients there proves to be a clearly identifiable single cause, such as hormonal imbalance or use of oral contraceptives. In 95% of patients, though, there is no such obvious cause. The clinical euphemism for our ignorance in such cases is "essential hypertension."

We can assess the role of genetic factors in essential hypertension by comparing how closely blood pressure agrees between closer or more distant relatives. Among people living in the same household, identical twins, who share all of their genes, have quite similar blood pressure; the similarity is lower but still significant for fraternal twins, ordinary siblings, or a parent and biological child, who share about half of their genes. The similarity is still lower for adopted siblings or a parent and adopted child, who have no direct genetic connection but share the same household environment. (For those of you familiar with statistics and correlation coefficients, the correlation coefficient for blood pressure is 0.63 between identical twins, 0.25 between fraternal twins or parent and biological child, and 0.05 between adopted siblings or parent and adopted child. A coefficient of 1.00 between identical twins would mean that blood pressure is almost completely determined by genes, and that nothing you do [after being conceived] has any effect on your blood pressure.) Evidently, our genes do have a big effect on our blood pressure, but environmental factors also play a role, because identical twins have very similar but not identical blood pressures.

To place these results in perspective, let's contrast hypertension with a simple genetic disease like Tay-Sachs disease. Tay-Sachs disease is due to a defect in a single gene; every Tay-Sachs patient has a defect in that same gene. Everybody in whom that gene is defective is certain to die of Tay-Sachs disease, regardless of the victim's lifestyle or environment. In contrast, hypertension usually involves many different genes, each of which individually has a small effect on blood pressure. Hence different hypertensive patients are likely to owe their condition to different gene combinations. Furthermore, whether someone genetically predisposed to hypertension actually develops symptoms depends a lot on lifestyle. Thus, hypertension is not one of those uncommon, homogeneous, and intellectually elegant diseases that geneticists prefer to study. Instead, like diabetes and ulcers, hypertension is a shared set of symptoms produced by heterogeneous causes, all involving an interaction between environmental agents and a susceptible genetic background.

Many environmental or lifestyle factors contributing to the risk of hypertension have been identified by studies that compare hypertension's frequency in groups of people living under different conditions. It turns out that, besides salt intake, other significant risk factors include obesity, exercise, high intake of alcohol or saturated fats, and low calcium intake. The proof of this approach is that hypertensive patients who modify their lifestyles so as to minimize these putative risk factors often succeed in reducing their blood pressure. We've all heard the familiar mantra of our doctor: reduce salt intake and stress, reduce intake of cholesterol and saturated fats and alcohol, lose weight, cut out smoking, and exercise regularly.

So, how does the link between salt and blood pressure work? That is, by what physiological mechanisms does increased salt intake lead to a rise in blood pressure, in many but not all people? Much of the explanation involves an expansion of the body's extracellular fluid volume. For normal people, if we increase our salt intake, the extra salt is excreted by our kidneys into our urine. But in individuals whose kidney salt excretion mechanisms are impaired, excretion can't keep pace with increased salt intake. The resulting excess of retained salt in those people triggers a sensation of thirst and makes them drink water, which leads to an increase in blood volume. In response, the heart pumps more, and blood pressure rises, causing the kidney to filter and excrete more salt and water under that increased pressure. The result is a new steady state, in which salt and water excretion again equals intake, but more salt and water are stored in the body and blood pressure is raised.

But why does a rise in blood pressure with increased salt intake show itself in some people but not in most people? After all, most people manage to retain a "normal" blood pressure despite consuming over 6 grams of salt per day. (At least Western physicians consider their blood pressure normal, although a Yanomamo physician wouldn't.) Hence high salt intake by itself doesn't automatically lead to hypertension in everybody; it happens in only some individuals. What's different about them?

Physicians apply a name to such individuals in whom blood pressure responds to a change in salt intake: they're termed "salt-sensitive." Relatively twice as many hypertensive individuals as normotensive individuals (people with normal blood pressure) turn out to be salt-sensitive. Nevertheless, most deaths due to elevated blood pressure are not among hypertensives, defined as people having greatly elevated blood pressure (140 over 90), but among normotensive individuals with only moderately elevated blood pressure—because normotensive people far outnumber hypertensives, and the greater individual risk of death in hypertensives isn't by a sufficiently large factor to offset the larger factor by which normotensives outnumber hypertensives. As for the specific physiological difference between hypertensive and normotensive people, there is much evidence that the primary problem of hypertensive people lies somewhere in their kidneys. If one transplants a kidney from a normotensive rat to a hypertensive rat as an experiment, or from a normotensive human kidney donor to a seriously ill hypertensive human in order to help the hypertensive person, the recipient's blood pressure falls. Conversely, if one transplants a kidney from a hypertensive rat to a normotensive rat, the latter's blood pressure rises.

Other evidence pointing to a hypertensive person's kidneys as the site of origin of the hypertension is that most of the many human genes known to affect blood pressure turn out to code for proteins involved in kidney sodium processing. (Remember that salt is sodium chloride.) Our kidneys actually excrete sodium in two stages: first, a filter called the glomerulus at the beginning of each kidney tubule filters blood plasma (containing salt) into the tubule; and second, most of that filtered sodium is then re-absorbed back into the blood by the rest of the tubule beyond the glomerulus; the filtered sodium that isn't re-absorbed ends up excreted into the urine. Changes in either of those two steps can lead to high blood pressure: older people tend towards high blood pressure because they have lower glomerular filtration, and hypertensives tend to it because they have more tubular re-absorption of sodium. The result in either case—less sodium filtration, or more sodium re-absorption—is more sodium and water retention and higher blood pressure.

Physicians commonly refer to the postulated high tubular sodium re-absorption of hypertensive people as a "defect": for example, physicians say, "Kidneys of hypertensives have a genetic defect in excreting sodium." As an evolutionary biologist, though, I hear warning bells going off inside me whenever a seemingly harmful trait that occurs frequently in a long-established and large human population is dismissed as a "defect." Given enough generations, genes that greatly impede survival are very unlikely to spread, unless their net effect is somehow to increase survival and reproductive success. Human medicine has furnished the best example of seemingly defective genes being propelled to high frequency by counter-balancing benefits. For example, sickle-cell hemoglobin is a mutant gene that tends to cause anemia, which is undoubtedly harmful. But the gene also offers some protection against malaria, and so the gene's net effect in malarious areas of Africa and the Mediterranean is beneficial. Thus, to understand why untreated hypertensives are prone to die today as a result of their kidneys' retaining salt, we need to ask under what conditions people might have benefited from kidneys good at retaining salt.

The answer is simple. Under the conditions of low salt availability ex-perienced by most humans throughout most of human history until the recent rise of salt-shakers, those of us with efficient salt-retaining kidneys were better able to survive our inevitable episodes of salt loss from sweat-ing or from an attack of diarrhea. Those kidneys became a detriment only when salt became routinely available, leading to excessive salt retention and hypertension with its fatal consequences. That's why blood pressure and the prevalence of hypertension have shot up recently in so many pop-ulations around the world, now that they have made the transition from traditional lifestyles with limited salt availability to being patrons of su-permarkets. Note the evolutionary irony: those of us whose ancestors best coped with salt-deficiency problems on Africa's savannahs tens of thou-sands of years ago are now the ones at highest risk of dying from salt-excess problems today on the streets of Los Angeles.

Dietary sources of salt

If by now you're convinced that it would be healthy for you to decrease your salt intake, how can you go about it? I used to think that I had already done it, and that my own salt habits were virtuous, because I never, ever, sprinkle salt on my food. While I've never measured my salt intake or output, I naively assumed it to be low. Alas, I now realize that, if I did measure it, I would find it to be far above Yanomamo levels, and not so far below the levels of Americans who use salt-shakers.

The reason for this sad realization has to do with the sources from which we actually ingest our dietary salt. In North America and Europe only about 12% of our salt intake is added in the home and with our knowledge, either by whoever is cooking or by the individual consumer at the table. It's only that 12% that I virtuously eliminated. The next 12% is salt naturally present in the food when it's fresh. Unfortunately, the re-maining 75% of our salt intake is "hidden": it comes already added by others to food that we buy, either processed food or else restaurant food to which the manufacturer or the restaurant cook respectively added the salt. As a result, Americans and Europeans (including me) have no idea how high is their daily salt intake unless they subject themselves to 24-hour urine collections. Abstaining from the use of salt-shakers doesn't suffice to lower drastically your salt intake: you also have to be informed about selecting the foods that you buy, and the restaurants in which you eat.

Processed foods contain quantities of salt impressively greater than the quantities in the corresponding unprocessed foods. For instance, compared to fresh unsalted steamed salmon, tinned salmon contains 5 times more salt per pound, and store-bought smoked salmon contains 12 times more. That quintessential fast-food meal of one take-away cheeseburger and fried potatoes contains about 3 grams of salt (one-third of a day's total average salt intake for an American), 13 times the salt content of an otherwise similar home-made unsalted steak and fried potatoes. Some other processed foods with especially high salt content are canned corned beef, processed cheese, and roast peanuts. Surprisingly to me, the biggest source of dietary salt in the U.S. and UK is cereal products—bread, other baked goods, and breakfast cereals—which we usually don't think of as being salty.

Why do manufacturers of processed foods add so much salt? One reason is that it's a nearly costless way to make cheap unpalatable foods edible. Another reason is that increasing the salt content of meat increases the weight of water bound in meat, so the final product weight can cheaply be increased 20% by bound water. In effect, the manufacturer provides less meat itself and still gets the same price for a "pound" of meat, which actually now consists of only 83% original meat plus 17% bound water. Yet another reason is that salt is a major determinant of thirst: the more salt you consume, the more fluid you drink, but much of what Americans or Europeans drink is soft drinks and bottled waters, some of them sold by the same companies selling you the salty snacks and processed foods that made you thirsty. Finally, the public has become addicted to salt and now prefers salted to unsalted foods.

A different picture for the breakdown of the sources of consumed salt emerges in East and South Asia and most of the developing world, where most ingested salt doesn't come from processed or restaurant foods but from salt added in the consumer's own house. For instance, in China 72% of ingested salt is added during cooking or at the table, and another 8% is in salty soy sauce. In Japan the main sources of ingested salt are soy sauce (20%), salty miso soup (10%), salted vegetables and fruits (10%), fresh and salted fish (10%), and salt added in restaurants, in fast-food outlets, and at home (10%). That's why salt intake in many Asian countries exceeds 12 grams per day. In developing countries, salt in sauces, seasonings, and pickled foods contributes along with salt added during cooking.

The high national health costs that hypertension, stroke, and other salt-related diseases inflict in the form of medical and hospital expenses and lost work lives have now motivated some governments to mount long-lasting national campaigns to help their citizens decrease their salt intake. But the governments quickly realized that they couldn't achieve that goal without enlisting the cooperation of the food industry to reduce the amounts of salt added by the industry to processed foods. The reductions have been gradual ones of just 10% or 20% less salt added to foods every year or two—a reduction too small for the public to notice. The UK, Japan, Finland, and Portugal have operated such campaigns for between two and four decades, resulting in the decreases in salt intake and consequent reductions in national medical costs and improvements in national health statistics that I already mentioned.

Are we citizens of industrial nations thus helpless pawns in the hands of food manufacturers, and is there little that we can do to lower our salt intake and blood pressure except to pray for an effective government anti-salt campaign? Actually, there is a big step that you can take besides avoiding use of salt-shakers: you can eat a healthy diet high in fresh foods and low in processed foods—specifically, a diet high in vegetables, fruits, fiber, complex carbohydrates, low-dairy products including cheeses, whole grains, poultry, fish (yes, you can eat fatty fish), vegetable oils, and nuts, but low in red meat, sweets, sugar-containing beverages, butter, cream, cholesterol, and saturated fats. In controlled experiments on volunteers, such a diet, termed a DASH diet—Dietary Approaches to Stop Hypertension—markedly lowers blood pressure.

Perhaps you're already thinking: "There's no way that I'll subject myself to a tasteless low-fat diet and destroy my pleasure in food, just in order to live 10 more years! I'd rather enjoy 70 years filled with great food and wine than 80 years of tasteless low-salt crackers and water." In fact, the DASH diet is modeled on the so-called Mediterranean diet, with a luscious fat content of 38%, getting its name from the fact that that's what Italians, Spaniards, Greeks, and many French people actually eat traditionally. (That fat of the DASH and Mediterranean diets is high in so-called mono-unsaturated fat, the type of fat that is good for us.) Those people aren't eating crackers and water: they're enjoying the greatest cuisines of Western civilization. Italians, who spend hours every day consuming their glorious pastas, breads, cheeses, olive oils, and other triumphs of Italian kitchens and farms, are still on the average among the slimmest people in the Western world. At the same time, we Americans, whose diet is anything but Mediterranean, have on the average the biggest waistlines in the Western world. One-third of adult Americans are obese, and another one-third of us are "merely" overweight, but we don't even have the consolation of knowing that it's the price we pay for the pleasures of Italian cuisine. You, too, can enjoy great food *and* be healthy.

Diabetes

Western diets that are high in sugar and in sugar-yielding carbohydrates are to diabetes as salt is to hypertension. When my twin sons were still too young to have learned healthy eating habits, taking them to a supermarket meant for my wife and me traversing a gauntlet of sweet dangers. Among breakfast foods, my kids were tempted by the choice between Apple Cinnamon Cheerios and Fruit Loops, respectively 85% and 89% carbohydrate according to their manufacturers, with about half of that carbohydrate in the form of sugar. Boxes picturing the famous turtles with Ninja powers seduced children to ask for Teenage Mutant Ninja Turtles Cheese Pasta Dinner, 81% carbohydrate. Snack choices included Fruit Bears (92% carbohydrate, no protein) and Teddy Graham's Bearwich chocolate cookies with vanilla cream (71% carbohydrate); both listed corn syrup, as well as sugar, among their ingredients.

All of these foods contained little or no fiber. Compared with the diet to which our evolutionary history adapted us, they differed in their much higher content of sugar and other carbohydrates (71% to 95% instead of about 15% to 55%) and much lower protein and fiber content. I mention these particular brands, not because they are unusual, but precisely because their content was typical of what was available. Around the year 1700 sugar intake was only about 4 pounds per year per person in England and the U.S. (then still a colony), but it is over 150 pounds per year per person today. One-quarter of the modern U.S. population eats over 200 pounds of sugar per year. A study of U.S. eighth-graders showed that 40% of their diet consisted of sugar and sugar-yielding carbohydrates. With foods like the ones I just mentioned lurking in supermarkets to tempt kids and their parents, it's no wonder that consequences of diabetes, the commonest disease of carbohydrate metabolism, will be the cause of death for many readers of this book. It's also no wonder that we readers suffer from tooth decay and cavities, which are very rare in the !Kung. While living in the 1970s in Scotland, where consumption of pastries and sweets was prodigious, I was told that some Scottish people had already as teen-agers lost most of their teeth due to tooth decay.

The ultimate cause of the many types of damage that diabetes wreaks on our bodies is high blood concentrations of the sugar glucose. They cause the spilling-over of glucose into the urine: a manifestation from which stems the disease's full name, diabetes mellitus, meaning "running-through of honey." Diabetes isn't infectious or rapidly fatal, so it doesn't command press headlines, as does AIDS. Nevertheless, the world epidemic of diabetes today far eclipses the AIDS epidemic in its toll of death and suffering. Diabetes disables its victims slowly and reduces their quality of life. Because all cells in our body become exposed to sugar from the bloodstream, diabetes can affect almost any organ system. Among its secondary consequences, it is the leading cause of adult blindness in the U.S.; the second leading cause of non-traumatic foot amputations; the cause of one-third of our cases of kidney failure; a major risk factor for stroke, heart attacks, peripheral vascular disease, and nerve degeneration; and the cause of over $100 billion of American health costs annually (15% of our costs due to all diseases combined). To quote Wilfrid Oakley, "Man may be the captain of his fate, but he is also the victim of his blood sugar."

As of the year 2010, the number of diabetics in the world was estimated at around 300 million. This value may be an underestimate, because there were likely to be other undiagnosed cases, especially in medically under-surveyed countries of the developing world. The growth rate in the number of diabetics is about 2.2% per year, or nearly twice the growth rate of the world's adult population: i.e., the percentage of the population that is diabetic is increasing. If nothing else changes in the world except that the world's population continues to grow, to age, and to move to cities (associated with a more sedentary lifestyle and hence increased prevalence of diabetes), then the number of cases predicted for the year 2030 is around 500 million, which would make diabetes one of the world's commonest diseases and biggest public health problems. But the prognosis is even worse than that, because other risk factors for diabetes (especially affluence and rural obesity) are also increasing, so that the number of cases in 2030 will probably be even higher. The current explosion in diabetes' prevalence is occurring especially in the Third World, where the epidemic is still in its early stages in India and China, the world's two most populous countries. Formerly considered a disease mainly of rich Europeans and North Americans, diabetes passed two milestones by the year 2010: more than half of the world's diabetics are now Asians, and the two countries with the largest number of diabetics are now India and China.

Types of diabetes

What normally happens when we consume some glucose (or other glucose-containing carbohydrates)? As the sugar is absorbed from our intestine, its concentration in our blood rises, signaling the pancreas to release the hormone insulin. That hormone in turn signals the liver to decrease glucose production, and signals muscle and fat cells to take up the glucose (thereby halting the rise in blood glucose concentration) and to store it as glycogen or as fat, to be used for energy between meals. Other nutrients, such as amino acids, also trigger the release of insulin, and insulin has effects on food components other than sugar (such as preventing the breakdown of fat).

Many different things can go wrong in that normal course of events, and so the term "diabetes mellitus" covers a wide variety of underlying problems linked by shared symptoms arising from high levels of blood sugar. That diversity can be crudely partitioned into two groups of diseases: so-called Type-2 or non-insulin-dependent diabetes mellitus (also known as "adult-onset diabetes"), and the much less common Type-1 or insulin-dependent diabetes mellitus (also known as "juvenile-onset diabetes"). The latter is an autoimmune disease in which a person's antibodies destroy the person's own pancreatic cells that secrete insulin. Type-1 diabetics tend to be thin, to produce no insulin, and to require multiple daily injections of insulin. Many of them carry certain genes (certain so-called HLA alleles) that code for elements of the immune system. Type-2 diabetes instead involves increased resistance of body cells to the person's own insulin, so that cells fail to take up glucose at normal rates. As long as the pancreas can respond by releasing more insulin, the cells' resistance can be overcome, and blood glucose remains within a normal range. But eventually the pancreas becomes exhausted, it may no longer be able to produce enough insulin to overcome that resistance, blood glucose levels rise, and the patient develops diabetes. Type-2 diabetes patients tend to be obese. In early stages of the disease they can often control their symptoms by dieting, exercising, and losing weight, without requiring tablets or insulin injections.

However, distinguishing Type-2 and Type-1 diabetes can be difficult, because Type-2 diabetes is now increasingly appearing already in teen-agers, while Type-1 diabetes may not first appear until in adulthood. Even Type-2 diabetes (as defined by insulin resistance) is associated with many different genes and manifests itself by varied symptoms. All of my subsequent discussion in this chapter will concern the much more common (about 10 times commoner) Type-2 diabetes, which I shall henceforth refer to simply as "diabetes."

Genes, environment, and diabetes

More than 2,000 years ago, Hindu physicians noting cases of "honey urine" commented that such cases "passed from generation to generation in the seed" and also were influenced by "injudicious diet." Physicians today have rediscovered those deadly insights, which we now rephrase by saying that diabetes involves both genetic and environmental factors, and possibly also intra-uterine factors affecting the fetus during pregnancy. Evidence for a role of genes includes the 10-times-higher risk of getting diabetes if you have a diabetic first-degree relative (a parent or a sibling) than if you don't. But diabetes, like hypertension, is not one of those simple genetic diseases (as is sickle-cell anemia) in which a mutation in the same gene is responsible for the disease in every patient. Instead, dozens and dozens of different genetic susceptibility factors for diabetes have been identified, many of them united only by their common feature that a mutation in any of those genes may result in high blood-glucose levels due to insulin resistance. (I mention again that these comments apply to Type-2 diabetes; Type-1 diabetes involves its own separate set of genetic susceptibility factors.)

In addition to those genetic factors in diabetes, diabetes also depends upon environmental and lifestyle factors. Even if you are genetically pre-disposed to diabetes, you won't necessarily get the disease, as would be the case if you carried a pair of genes for muscular dystrophy or Tay-Sachs disease. The risk of developing diabetes increases with age, and with hav-ing diabetic first-degree relatives, and with being born of a diabetic mother, which you yourself can't do anything about. But other risk factors that predict diabetes are factors under our control, including especially being overweight, not exercising, eating a high-calorie diet, and consum-ing much sugar and fat. Most diabetics (I emphasize again, most Type-2 diabetics) can reduce their symptoms by reducing those risk factors. For example, the prevalence of diabetes is 5 to 10 times higher in obese people than in those of normal weight, so that diabetes patients can often regain health by dieting, exercising, and losing weight, and those same measures can protect people predisposed to diabetes against getting the disease.

Many types of natural experiments, including ones that I mentioned at the beginning of this chapter as demonstrating the relation between the Western lifestyle and non-communicable diseases in general, specifically illustrate the role of environmental factors in diabetes. The worldwide rise in those factors underlies the current worldwide diabetes epidemic. One such type of natural experiment involves the rise and fall of diabetes prev-alences accompanying the rise and fall of Western lifestyle and affluence in the same population. In Japan, graphs against time of diabetes preva-lence and economic indicators are parallel, down to details of year-to-year wiggles. That's because people eat more, hence they risk developing more diabetes symptoms, when they have more money. Diabetes and its symp-toms decline or disappear in populations under starvation conditions, such as French diabetes patients under the severe food rationing imposed during the 1870–1871 siege of Paris. Groups of Aboriginal Australians who temporarily abandoned their acquired sedentary Western lifestyle and resumed their traditional vigorous foraging reversed their symptoms of diabetes; one such group lost an average of 18 pounds of body weight within seven weeks. (Remember that obesity is one of the leading risk factors for diabetes.) Decreases in diabetes symptoms and in waist circumference were also noted for Swedes who for three months abandoned their very un-Mediterranean Swedish diet (over 70% of calories from sugar, margarine, dairy products, alcohol, oil, and cereals) and adopted instead a Mediterranean diet typical of slim Italians. Swedes who adopted a "Paleolithic diet" designed to resemble that of hunter-gatherers became even healthier and developed even slimmer waists.

Another natural experiment is provided by the sky-high explosions of diabetes among groups that emigrated and thereby gave up a vigorous Spartan lifestyle to adopt sedentary high-calorie low-exercise living based on abundant supermarket food. A dramatic example involved the Yemenite Jews who were airlifted to Israel by Operation Magic Carpet in 1949 and 1950, and were thereby plunged abruptly into the 20th century from formerly medieval conditions. Although Yemenite Jews were almost free of diabetes upon reaching Israel, 13% of them then became diabetic within two decades. Other migrants who sought opportunity and instead found diabetes included Ethiopian Jews moving to Israel, Mexicans and Japanese moving to the U.S., Polynesians moving to New Zealand, Chinese moving to Mauritius and Singapore, and Asian Indians moving to Mauritius, Singapore, Fiji, South Africa, the U.S., and Britain.

Developing countries that have recently been growing more affluent and Westernized have correspondingly been growing more diabetic. In first place stand the eight Arab oil-producers and newly affluent island nations that now lead the world in national diabetes prevalences (all of them above 15%). All Latin American and Caribbean countries now have prevalences above 5%. All East and South Asian countries have prevalences above 4% except for five of the poorest countries, where prevalences remain as low as 1.6%. The high prevalences of the more rapidly developing countries are a recent phenomenon: India's prevalence was still below 1% as recently as 1959 but is now 8%. Conversely, most sub-Saharan African countries are still poor and still have prevalences below 5%.

Those national averages conceal large internal differences that constitute further natural experiments. Around the world, urbanization results in less exercise and more supermarket food, obesity, and diabetes. Individual urban populations that thereby achieved notably high diabetes prevalences include the already mentioned Wanigela people of Papua New Guinea's capital city (37% prevalence) and several groups of urban Aboriginal Australians (up to 33%). Both of those cases are all the more striking because diabetes was unknown among New Guineans and Australians under traditional conditions.

Thus, the Western lifestyle somehow increases the risk that those enjoying it will become diabetic. But the Western lifestyle consists of many interlinked components: which components contribute most to the risk of diabetes? While it isn't easy to tease apart the effects of correlated influences, it appears that the three strongest risk factors are obesity and sedentary lifestyle (which you can do something about) and family history of diabetes (which you can't do anything about). Other risk factors that you can't control are either high or low birth weight. While diet composition surely acts at least in part by its relation to obesity, it also seems to have some independent influence: among people matched for obesity, those consuming a Mediterranean diet appear to be at lower risk than those with high intakes of sugar, saturated fatty acids, cholesterol, and triglycerides. Not exercising may create risks mainly through predisposing towards obesity, while smoking, inflammation, and high alcohol consumption appear to be independent risk factors. In short, Type-2 diabetes originates with genetic factors and possibly intra-uterine factors, which may become unmasked later in life by lifestyle factors resulting in disease symptoms.

Pima Indians and Nauru Islanders

These proofs of an environmental role in diabetes are illustrated by the tragedies of the two peoples with the highest rates of diabetes in the world: Pima Indians and Nauru Islanders. To consider the Pimas first, they survived for more than 2,000 years in the deserts of southern Arizona, using agricultural methods based on elaborate irrigation systems, supplemented by hunting and gathering. Because rainfall in the desert varies greatly from year to year, crops failed about one year in every five, forcing the Pimas then to subsist entirely on wild foods, especially wild jackrabbits and mesquite beans. Many of their preferred wild plants were high in fiber, low in fat, and released glucose only slowly, thereby constituting an ideal antidiabetic diet. After this long history of periodic but brief bouts of starvation, the Pimas experienced a more prolonged bout of starvation in the late 19th century, when white settlers diverted the headwaters of the rivers on which the Pimas depended for irrigation water. The result was crop failures and widespread starvation. Today the Pimas eat store-bought food. Observers who visited the Pimas in the early 1900s reported obesity to be rare and diabetes almost non-existent. Since the 1960s, obesity has become widespread among the Pimas, some of whom now weigh more than 300 pounds. Half of them exceed the U.S. 90th percentile for weight in relation to height. Pima women consume about 3,160 calories per day (50% over the U.S. average), 40% of which is fat. Associated with this obesity, Pimas have achieved notoriety in the diabetes literature by now having the highest frequency of diabetes in the world. Half of all Pimas over age 35, and 70% of those at ages 55 to 64, are diabetic, leading to tragically high occurrences of blindness, limb amputations, and kidney failure.

My second example is Nauru Island, a small remote tropical Pacific island colonized by Micronesians in prehistoric times. Nauru was annexed by Germany in 1888, was occupied by Australia in 1914, and eventually achieved independence in 1968 as the world's smallest republic. However, Nauru also has a less welcome distinction as the grimly instructive site of a rarely documented phenomenon: an epidemic of a genetic disease. Our familiar epidemics of infectious diseases flare up when transmission of the infectious agent increases, and then wane when the number of susceptible potential victims falls, due both to acquired immunity of the survivors and to differential mortality of those who are genetically susceptible. An epidemic of a genetic disease flares up instead because of a rise in environmental risk factors, and then wanes when the number of susceptible potential victims falls (but only because of the preferential deaths of those who are genetically more susceptible, not because of acquired immunity; one doesn't acquire immunity to diabetes).

The traditional lifestyle of Nauruans was based on agriculture and fishing and involved frequent episodes of starvation because of droughts and the island's poor soils. Early European visitors nevertheless noted that Nauruans were plump, and that they admired big fat people and put girls on a diet to fatten them and so make them more attractive in their eyes. In 1906 it was discovered that most of Nauru underlying those poor soils consists of rock with the world's highest concentration of phosphate, an essential ingredient of fertilizer. In 1922 the mining company extracting the rock finally began to pay royalties to the islanders. As a result of this new wealth, average sugar consumption by Nauruans reached a pound per day in 1927, and laborers were imported because Nauruans disliked working as miners.

During the Second World War Nauru was occupied by Japanese military forces, who imposed forced labor, reduced food rations to half a pound of pumpkin per day, and then deported most of the population to Truk, where half of them died of starvation. When the survivors returned to Nauru after the war, they regained their phosphate royalties, abandoned agriculture almost completely, and resumed shopping in supermarkets, heaping their shopping carts with big bags of sugar and eating double their recommended calorie intake. They became sedentary and came to rely on motor vehicles to travel around their little island (averaging one and a half miles in radius). Following independence in 1968, per-capita annual phosphate royalties rose to $23,000, making Nauruans among the world's richest people. Today they are the most obese Pacific Island population, and the one with the highest average blood pressure. Their average body weight is 50% greater than that of white Australians of the same height.

Although colonial European physicians on Nauru knew how to recognize diabetes and diagnosed it there in non-Nauruan laborers, the first case in a Nauruan was not noted until 1925. The second case was recorded in 1934. After 1954, however, the disease's prevalence rose steeply, and it became the commonest cause of non-accidental death. One-third of all Nauruans over the age of 20, two-thirds of those over age 55, and 70% of those few who survive to the age of 70 are diabetics. Within the past decade the disease's prevalence has begun to fall, not because of mitigation of environmental risk factors (obesity and the sedentary lifestyle are as common as ever), but presumably because those who are genetically most susceptible have died. If this interpretation should prove correct, then

Nauru would provide the most rapid case known to me of natural selection in a human population: an occurrence of detectable population-wide selection within less than 40 years.

Diabetes in India

Table 11.1 summarizes for comparison some prevalences of diabetes around the world. It's obvious that there are big differences among countries in their national average prevalences, ranging from low values of 1.6% in Mongolia and Rwanda up to high values of 19% in the United Arab Emirates and 31% in Nauru. But Table 11.1 also illustrates that these national averages conceal equally big differences within any given country related to differences in lifestyle: at least in developing countries, wealthy or Westernized or urban populations tend to have much higher prevalences than do poor or traditional or rural populations.

India provides excellent examples of those subnational differences. (For this information I am grateful to Professor V. Mohan, of the Madras Diabetes Research Foundation.) The average prevalence in India as of the year 2010 was 8%. But there was little diabetes in India until just a few decades ago. Surveys in 1938 and 1959, in large cities (Calcutta and Mumbai) that are today strongholds of diabetes, yielded prevalences of only 1% or less. Only in the 1980s did those numbers start to rise, first slowly and now explosively, to the point where India today harbors more diabetics (over 40,000,000) than any other nation. The reasons are essentially the same as those behind the diabetes epidemic around the world: urbanization, rise in standard of living, the spread of calorie-rich sweet and fatty fast foods cheaply available in cities to rich and poor people alike, and increased sedentariness associated with replacement of manual labor by service jobs, and with video games and television and computers that keep children (and adults) seated lethargically watching screens for hours every day. Although the specific role of TV has not been quantified in India, a study in Australia found that each hour per day spent watching TV is associated with an 18% increase in cardiovascular mortality (much of it related to diabetes), even after controlling for other risk factors such as waist circumference, smoking, alcohol intake, and diet. But those factors

Table 11.1. Prevalences of Type-2 diabetes around the world

POPULATION	PERCENTAGE PREVALENCES
European and Middle Eastern "Whites"	
41 Western European countries	6 (range, 2–10)
4 overseas Western European countries (Australia, Canada, New Zealand, U.S.)	8 (range, 5–10)
1 very poor Arab country (Yemen)	3
2 poor Arab countries (Jordan, Syria)	10
6 wealthy Arab countries	16 (range, 13–19)
Yemenite Jews, traditional	~0
Yemenite Jews, Westernized	13
Africans	
rural Tanzania	1
Rwanda	2
urban South Africa	8
U.S. African-Americans	13
Asian Indians	
urban India, 1938–1959	~1
rural India today	0.7
urban Singapore	17
urban Mauritius	17
urban Kerala	20
urban Fiji	22
Chinese	
rural China	~0
urban Hong Kong	9
urban Singapore	10
urban Taiwan	12
urban Mauritius	13

Table 11.1. *(continued)*

POPULATION	PERCENTAGE PREVALENCES
Pacific Islanders	
Nauru, 1952	0
Nauru, 2002	41
Nauru, 2010	31
Papua New Guinea, traditional	~0
Papua New Guinea, urban Wanigela	37
Aboriginal Australians	
traditional	~0
Westernized	25–35
Native Americans	
Chile Mapuche	1
U.S. Pima	50

The numbers in the right-hand column are prevalences of diabetes in percent: i.e., the percent of the population suffering from Type-2 diabetes. These values are so-called age-standardized prevalences, which have the following meaning. Because Type-2 prevalence in a given population increases with age, it would be misleading to compare raw values of prevalence between two populations that differ in their age distributions: the raw values would be expected to differ merely as a result of the different age distributions (prevalence would be higher in the older population), even if prevalences at a given age were identical between the two populations. Hence one measures the prevalence in a population as a function of age, then calculates what the prevalence would be for that whole population if it had a certain standardized age distribution.

Note the higher prevalences in wealthy, Westernized, or urban populations than in poor, traditional, or rural populations of the same people. Note also that those lifestyle differences give rise to contrasting low-prevalence and high-prevalence (over 12%) populations in every human group examined except Western Europeans, among whom there is no high-prevalence population by world standards, for reasons to be discussed. The table also illustrates the rise and subsequent fall of prevalence on Nauru Island, caused by rapid Westernization and then by the operation of natural selection against victims of diabetes.

notoriously increase with TV watching time, so the true figure must be even larger than that 18% estimate.

Buried within that national average prevalence of 8% is a wide range of outcomes for different groups of Indians. At the low extreme, prevalence is only 0.7% for non-obese, physically active, rural Indians. It reaches 11% for obese, sedentary, urban Indians and peaks at 20% in the Ernakulam district of southwest India's Kerala state, one of the most urbanized states. An even higher value is the world's second-highest national prevalence of diabetes, 24%, on the Indian Ocean island of Mauritius, where a predominantly Indian immigrant community has been approaching Western living standards faster than any population within India itself.

Among the lifestyle factors predictive of diabetes in India, some are also familiar as predictors in the West, while other factors turn Western expectations upside down. Just as in the West, diabetes in India is associated with obesity, high blood pressure, and sedentariness. But European and American diabetologists will be astonished to learn that diabetes' prevalence is higher among affluent, educated, urban Indians than among poor, uneducated, rural people: exactly the opposite of trends in the West, although similar to trends noted in other developing countries including China, Bangladesh, and Malaysia. For instance, Indian diabetes patients are more likely to have received graduate and higher education, and are less likely to be illiterate, than non-diabetics. In 2004 the prevalence of diabetes averaged 16% in urban India and only 3% in rural India; that's the reverse of Western trends. The likely explanation for these paradoxes invokes two respects in which the Western lifestyle has spread further through the population and been practised for more years in the West than in India. First, Western societies are much wealthier than Indian society, so poor rural people are much better able to afford fast foods inclining their consumers towards diabetes in the West than in India. Second, educated Westerners with access to fast foods and sedentary jobs have by now often heard that fast foods are unhealthy and that one should exercise, whereas that advice has not yet made wide inroads among educated Indians. Nearly 25% of Indian city-dwellers (the subpopulation most at risk) haven't even heard of diabetes.

In India as in the West, diabetes is due ultimately to chronically high blood glucose levels, and some of the clinical consequences are similar. But in other respects—whether because lifestyle factors or people's genes differ between India and the West—diabetes in India differs from the disease as we know it in the West. While Westerners think of Type-2 diabetes as an adult-onset disease appearing especially over the age of 50, Indian diabetics exhibit symptoms at an age one or two decades younger than do Europeans, and that age of onset in India (as in many other populations as well) has been shifting towards ever-younger people even within the last decade. Already among Indians in their late teens, "adult-onset" (Type-2 or non-insulin-dependent) diabetes manifests itself more often than does "juvenile-onset" (Type-1 or insulin-dependent) diabetes. While obesity is a risk factor for diabetes both in India and in the West, diabetes appears at a lower threshold value of obesity in India and in other Asian countries. Symptoms also differ between Indian and Western diabetes patients: Indians are less likely to develop blindness and kidney disease, but are much more likely to suffer coronary artery disease at a relatively young age.

Although poor Indians are currently at lower risk than are affluent Indians, the rapid spread of fast food exposes even urban slum-dwellers in India's capital city of New Delhi to the risk of diabetes. Dr. S. Sandeep, Mr. A. Ganesan, and Professor Mohan of the Madras Diabetes Research Foundation summarized the current situation as follows: "This suggests that diabetes [in India] is no longer a disease of the affluent or a rich man's disease. It is becoming a problem even among the middle income and poorer sections of the society. Studies have shown that poor diabetic subjects are more prone to complications as they have less access to quality healthcare."

Benefits of genes for diabetes

The evidence for a strong genetic component to diabetes poses an evolutionary puzzle. Why is such a debilitating disease so common among so many human populations, when one might have expected the disease to disappear gradually as those people genetically susceptible to it were removed by natural selection and didn't produce children carrying their genes?

Two explanations applicable to some other genetic diseases—recurrent mutations and lack of selective consequences—can quickly be eliminated in the case of diabetes. First, if prevalences of diabetes were as low as those of muscular dystrophy (about 1 in 10,000), the genes' prevalence could be explained as nothing more than the product of recurring mutations: that is, babies with a new mutation being born at the same rate as older bearers of such mutations die of the disease. However, no mutation occurs so frequently as to appear anew in 3% to 50% of all babies, the actual frequency range for diabetes in Westernized societies.

Second, geneticists regularly respond to the evolutionary puzzle by claiming that diabetes kills only older individuals whose child-bearing or child-rearing years are behind them, so the deaths of old diabetics supposedly impose no selective disadvantage on diabetes-predisposing genes. Despite its popularity, this claim is wrong for two obvious reasons. While Type-2 diabetes does appear mainly after age 50 in Europeans, in Nauruans and Indians and other non-Europeans it affects people of reproductive age in their 20s and 30s, especially pregnant women, whose fetuses and newborn babies are also at increased risk. For instance, in Japan today more children suffer from Type-2 than Type-1 diabetes, despite the latter's name of juvenile-onset diabetes. Moreover (as discussed in Chapter 6), in traditional human societies, unlike modern First World societies, no old person is truly "post-reproductive" and selectively unimportant, because grandparents contribute crucially to the food supply, social status, and survival of their children and grandchildren.

We must therefore instead assume that the genes now predisposing to diabetes were actually favored by natural selection before our sudden shift to a Westernized lifestyle. In fact, such genes must have been favored and preserved independently dozens of times by natural selection, because there are dozens of different identified genetic disorders resulting in (Type-2) diabetes. What good did diabetes-linked genes formerly do for us, and why do they get us into trouble now?

Recall that the net effect of the hormone insulin is to permit us to store as fat the food that we ingest at meals, and to spare us the breakdown of our already accumulated fat reserves. Thirty years ago, these facts inspired the geneticist James Neel to speculate that diabetes stems from a "thrifty genotype" making its bearers especially efficient at storing dietary glucose as fat. For example, perhaps some of us have an especially hair-triggered release of insulin in rapid response to a small rise in blood glucose concentration. That genetically determined quick release would enable those of us with such a gene to sequester dietary glucose as fat, without the blood concentration of glucose rising high enough for it to spill over into our urine. At occasional times of food abundance, bearers of such genes would utilize food more efficiently, deposit fat, and gain weight rapidly, thereby becoming better able to survive a subsequent famine. Such genes would be advantageous under the conditions of unpredictably alternating feast and famine that characterized the traditional human lifestyle (Plate 26), but they would lead to obesity and diabetes in the modern world, when the same individuals stop exercising, begin foraging for food only in supermarkets, and consume high-calorie meals day in and day out (Plate 27). Today, when many of us regularly ingest high-sugar meals and rarely exercise, a thrifty gene is a blueprint for disaster. We thereby become fat; we never experience famines that burn up the fat; our pancreas releases insulin constantly until the pancreas loses its ability to keep up, or until our muscle and fat cells become resistant; and we end up with diabetes. Following Arthur Koestler, Paul Zimmet refers to the spread of this diabetes-promoting First World lifestyle to the Third World as "coca-colonization."

So accustomed are we in the First World to predictable amounts of food at predictable times each day that we find it hard to imagine the often-unpredictable fluctuations between frequent food shortages and infrequent gluts that constituted the pattern of life for almost all people throughout human evolution until recently, and that remain so in many parts of the world today. I've often encountered such fluctuations during my fieldwork among New Guineans still subsisting by farming and hunting. For example, in one memorable incident I hired a dozen men to carry heavy equipment all day over a steep trail up to a mountain campsite. We arrived at the camp just before sunset, expecting to meet there another group of porters carrying food, and instead found that they had not arrived because of a misunderstanding. Faced with hungry, exhausted men and no food, I expected to be lynched. Instead, my carriers just laughed and said, "Orait, i nogat kaikai, i samting nating, yumi slip nating, enap yumi kaikai tumora" ("OK, so there's no food, it's no big deal, we'll just sleep on empty stomachs tonight and wait until tomorrow to eat"). Conversely, on other occasions at which pigs are slaughtered, my New Guinea friends have a gluttonous feast lasting several days, when food consumption shocks even me (formerly rated by my friends as a bottomless pit) and some people become seriously ill from overeating.

Table 11.2. Examples of gluttony when food is abundantly available

Daniel Everett (*Don't Sleep, There Are Snakes,* pages 76–77). "They [the Piraha Indians of South America] enjoy eating. Whenever there is food available in the village, they eat it all. . . . [But] missing a meal or two, or even going without eating for a day, is taken in stride. I have seen people dance for three days with only brief breaks. . . . Pirahas [visiting] in the city for the first time are always surprised by Western eating habits, especially the custom of three meals a day. For their first meal outside of the village, most Pirahas eat greedily—large quantities of proteins and starch. For the second meal they eat the same. By the third meal they begin to show frustration. They look puzzled. Often they ask, 'Are we eating again?' Their own practice of eating food when it is available until it is gone now conflicts with the circumstances in which food is always available and never gone. Often after a visit of three to six weeks, a Piraha [originally weighing between 100 and 125 pounds] will return as much as 30 pounds overweight to the village, rolls of fat on their belly and thighs."

Allan Holmberg (*Nomads of the Long Bow,* page 89). "The quantities of food eaten on occasion [by the Siriono Indians of Bolivia] are formidable. It is not uncommon for four people to eat a peccary of 60 pounds at a single sitting. When meat is abundant, a man may consume as much as 30 pounds within 24 hours. On one occasion, when I was present, two men ate six spider monkeys, weighing from 10 to 15 pounds apiece, in a single day, and complained of being hungry that night."

Lidio Cipriani (*The Andaman Islanders,* page 54). "Cleaning themselves, to the Onges [of the Andaman Islands in the Indian Ocean], means painting themselves to ward off evil and to remove, so they said, the smell of pig fat after the colossal orgies which follow a particularly good hunt, when even they find the stench too much. These orgies, which give them appalling indigestion for days, are followed by an apparently instinctive variation of their diet to raw or cooked vegetable foods. On three occasions from 1952 to 1954 I was present at one of the solemn pork and honey orgies. The Onges ate almost until they burst, and then, hardly able to move, cleaned up by a grand painting session."

Ditto, page 117. "As the tide goes down, the shoals [of fish called pilchards] are caught in the reefs stretching out to sea all around the island and the Onges leave everything to man-handle the canoes from pool to pool and fill them to overflowing. The water is almost saturated with fish, and the Onges go on and on until they have nothing more they can use to hold the catch. Nowhere else in the world have I seen anything like this wholesale slaughter. The pilchards of the Andamans are rather larger than usual, some weighing as much as half a kilogram or more. . . . Men, women and children work feverishly, plunging their hands into the heaving mass of fish so that they reek of it for days. . . . Everyone cooks and eats at the same time until (temporarily) unable to eat anymore, when the rest of the haul is laid on improvised racks with fires of green wood making smoke underneath. When, a few days later, all is gone, fishing begins again. And so life goes on for weeks, until the shoals have passed the islands."

These anecdotes illustrate how people accommodate to the pendulum of feast and famine that swung often but irregularly through our evolutionary history. In Chapter 8 I summarized the reasons for the frequency of famine under traditional living conditions: food shortages associated with day-to-day variation in hunting success, short bouts of inclement weather, predictable seasonal variation in food abundance through the year, and unpredictable year-to-year variation in weather; in many societies, little or no ability to accumulate and store surplus food; and lack of state governments or other means to organize and integrate food storage, transport, and exchanges over large areas. Conversely, **Table 11.2** collects some anecdotes of gluttony around the world at times when food becomes available in abundance to traditional societies.

Under these traditional conditions of starve-and-gorge existence, those individuals with a thrifty genotype would be at an advantage, because they could store more fat in surplus times, burn fewer calories in spartan times, and hence better survive starvation. To most humans until recently, our modern Western fear of obesity and our diet clinics would have seemed ludicrous, as the exact reverse of traditional good sense. The genes that today predispose us to diabetes may formerly have helped us to survive famine. Similarly, our "taste" for sweet or fatty foods, like our taste for salt, predisposes us to diabetes and hypertension now that those tastes can be satisfied so easily, but formerly guided us to seek valuable rare nutrients. Note again, just as we saw for hypertension, the evolutionary irony. Those of us whose ancestors best survived starvation on Africa's savannahs tens of thousands of years ago are now the ones at highest risk of dying from diabetes linked to food abundance.

Thus, the starve-and-gorge lifestyle traditionally shared by all human populations resulted in natural selection of genes for a thrifty genotype that served us well under those starve-and-gorge conditions, but that has then caused virtually all populations to end up with a propensity for diabetes under modern Western conditions of unremitting food abundance. But why, by this reasoning, are Pima Indians and Nauruans unusual in their world-record diabetes prevalences? I think that's because they were subjected in the recent past to world-record strengths of selection for a thrifty genotype. The Pimas started out sharing with other Native

Americans their exposure to periodic starvation. They then experienced a further prolonged bout of starvation and selection in the late 19th century, when white settlers ruined their crops by cutting off their sources of irrigation water. Those Pimas who survived were individuals who were genetically even better adapted than other Native Americans to survive starvation by storing fat whenever food had become available. As for Nauruans, they suffered two extreme bouts of natural selection for thrifty genes, followed by an extreme bout of coca-colonization. First, like other Pacific Islanders, but unlike the inhabitants of continental regions, their population was founded by people who undertook inter-island canoe voyages lasting several weeks. In numerous attested examples of such lengthy voyages, many or most of the canoe occupants died of starvation, and only those who were originally the fattest survived. That is why Pacific Islanders in general tend to be heavy people. Second, the Nauruans were then set apart even from most other Pacific Islanders by their extreme starvation and mortality during the Second World War, leaving the population presumably even more enriched in diabetes susceptibility genes. After the war, their newfound wealth based on phosphate royalties, their superabundant food, and their diminished need for physical activity led to exceptional obesity.

Three lines of human evidence and two animal models support the plausibility of Neel's thrifty-gene hypothesis. Non-diabetic Nauruans, Pima Indians, African Americans, and Aboriginal Australians have postprandial levels of plasma insulin (in response to an oral glucose load) several times those of Europeans. New Guinea Highlanders, Aboriginal Australians, Maasai tribespeople of Kenya, and other peoples with traditional lifestyles have blood glucose levels far below those of white Americans. Given ample food, diabetes-prone populations of Pacific Islanders, Native Americans, and Aboriginal Australians do exhibit more propensity to obesity than do Europeans: first they gain weight, then they develop diabetes. As for animal models, laboratory rats carrying genes predisposing them to diabetes and obesity survive starvation better than do normal rats, illustrating the advantage of those genes under occasional conditions of famine. The Israeli sand rat, which is adapted to a desert environment with frequent scarcities of food, develops high insulin levels, insulin resistance, obesity, and diabetes when maintained in the laboratory on a "Westernized rat diet" with abundant food. But those symptoms reverse when the sand rat's food is restricted. Hence diabetes-prone laboratory rats and Israeli sand rats serve as models both of the benefits of thrifty genes and of hair-triggered insulin release under "traditional rat conditions" of starve-and-gorge, and of the costs of those genes under "supermarket rat conditions."

Why is diabetes low in Europeans?

Diabetologists used to point to Pimas and Nauruans as the glaring exceptions of high diabetes prevalence, standing out from a world in which the relatively low diabetes prevalence of Europeans was taken as the norm. But the information that has become available in recent decades shows that, instead, Europeans are the exception in their low prevalence, contrasting with the high prevalence reached by Westernized populations of everyone else. Pimas and Nauruans are "merely" the highest of that normal high prevalence, already approached closely by some Aboriginal Australians and New Guinean groups. For every well-studied large non-European population grouping, we now know of some Westernized subgroup with a prevalence above 11%, usually above 15%: Native Americans, North Africans, sub-Saharan Black Africans, Middle Easterners, Indians, East Asians, New Guineans, Aboriginal Australians, Micronesians, and Polynesians. Compared to that norm, Europeans, and overseas Europeans in Australia, Canada, New Zealand, and the U.S., are unique among the modern world's populations in their relatively low prevalence. All 41 national European values for the prevalence of diabetes (Table 11.1, first row) fall between 2% and 10%, with a mean value of only 6%.

That's astonishing when one reflects that Europeans in Europe itself and overseas are the world's richest and best-fed people, and the originators of the Western lifestyle. We refer to our indolent, obese, supermarket way of life as Western precisely because it arose first among Europeans and white Americans and is only now spreading to other peoples. How can we account for this paradox? Why don't Europeans now have the highest, rather than the lowest, prevalence of diabetes?

Several experts in the study of diabetes have suggested to me informally that perhaps Europeans traditionally had little exposure to famine, so that they would have undergone little selection for a thrifty genotype. Actually, though, history provides abundant documentation of famines that caused widespread severe mortality in medieval and Renaissance Europe and earlier. Those repeated famines should have selected for thrifty genes in Europe, just as everywhere else. Instead, a more promising hypothesis is based on Europe's recent food history since the Renaissance. The periodic widespread and prolonged famines that used to rack Europe, like the rest of the world, disappeared between about 1650 and 1900 at different times in different parts of Europe, beginning in the late 1600s in Britain and the Netherlands, and continuing into the late 1800s in southern France and southern Italy. With one famous exception, Europe's famines were ended by a combination of four factors: increasingly efficient state intervention that rapidly redistributed surplus grain to famine areas; increasingly efficient food transport by land and especially by sea; increasingly diversified European agriculture after Columbus's voyage of AD 1492, thanks to European voyagers bringing back many New World crops (such as potatoes and corn); and, finally, Europe's reliance not on irrigation agriculture (as in many populous areas of the world outside Europe) but instead on rain agriculture, which reduced the risk of a crop failure too widespread to be solved by food transport within Europe.

The famous exception to the end of Europe's famines was of course the Irish potato famine of the 1840s. Actually, that was the exception that proved the rule, by illustrating what happened even in Europe when the first three above-mentioned factors ending famines elsewhere in Europe didn't operate. The Irish potato famine was due to a disease of a single strain of potato in an agricultural economy that was unusual in Europe in its reliance on that single crop. The famine occurred on an island (Ireland) governed by an ethnically different state centered on another island (Britain) and notorious for the inefficiency or lack of motivation of its response to the Irish famine.

These facts of Europe's food history lead me to offer the following speculation. Several centuries before the advent of modern medicine, Europeans, like modern Nauruans, may have undergone an epidemic of diabetes that resulted from the new reliability of adequate food supplies, and that eliminated most diabetes-prone bearers of the thrifty genotype, leaving Europe with its low prevalence of diabetes today. Those gene-bearers may have been undergoing elimination in Europe for centuries, as a result of many infants of diabetic mothers dying at birth, diabetic adults dying younger than other adults, and children and grandchildren of those diabetic adults dying of neglect or reduced material support. However, there would have been big differences between that postulated cryptic earlier European epidemic and the well-documented modern epidemics among Nauruans and so many other peoples today. In the modern epidemics, abundant and continually reliable food arrived suddenly—within a decade for Nauruans, and within just a month for Yemenite Jews. The results were sharply peaked surges in diabetes's prevalence to 20%–50% that have been occurring right under the eyes of modern diabetologists. Those increases will probably wane quickly (as already observed among Nauruans), as individuals with a thrifty genotype become eliminated by natural selection within a mere generation or two. In contrast, Europe's food abundance increased gradually over the course of several centuries. The result would have been an imperceptibly slow rise in diabetes prevalence in Europe, between the 1400s and the 1700s, long before there were any diabetologists to take note. In effect, Pimas, Nauruans, Wanigelas, educated urban Indians, and citizens of wealthy oil-producing Arab nations are telescoping into a single generation the lifestyle changes and consequent rise and fall of diabetes that unfolded over the course of many centuries in Europe.

A possible victim of this cryptic epidemic of diabetes that I postulate in Europe was the composer Johann Sebastian Bach (born in 1685, died in 1750). While Bach's medical history is too poorly documented to permit certainty as to the cause of his death, the corpulence of his face and hands in the sole authenticated portrait of him (Plate 28), the accounts of deteriorating vision in his later years, and the obvious deterioration of his handwriting possibly secondary to his failing vision and/or nerve damage are consistent with a diagnosis of diabetes. The disease certainly occurred in Germany during Bach's lifetime, being known there as *honigsüsse Harnruhr* ("honey-sweet urine disease").

The future of non-communicable diseases

In this chapter I've discussed just two among the many currently exploding non-communicable diseases (NCDs) linked to the Western lifestyle:

hypertension and its consequences, and Type-2 diabetes. Other major NCDs that I haven't had space to discuss, but that S. Boyd Eaton, Melvin Konner, and Marjorie Shostak do discuss, include coronary artery disease and other heart diseases, arteriosclerosis, peripheral vascular diseases, many kidney diseases, gout, and many cancers including lung, stomach, breast, and prostate cancer. Within the Western lifestyle I've discussed only some risk factors—especially salt, sugar, high calorie intake, obesity, and sedentariness. Other important risk factors that I have mentioned only briefly include smoking, high alcohol consumption, cholesterol, triglycerides, saturated fats, and trans fats.

We've seen that NCDs are overwhelmingly the leading causes of death in Westernized societies, to which most readers of this book belong. Nor is it the case that you'll have a wonderful carefree healthy life until you suddenly drop dead of an NCD at age 78 to 81 (the average lifespan in long-lived Western societies): NCDs are also major causes of declining health and decreased quality of life for years or decades before they eventually kill you. But the same NCDs are virtually non-existent in traditional societies. What clearer proof could there be that we have much to learn, of life-and-death value, from traditional societies? However, what they have to teach us is not a simple matter of just "live traditionally." There are many aspects of traditional life that we emphatically don't want to emulate, such as cycles of violence, frequent risk of starvation, and short lifespans resulting from infectious diseases. We need to figure out which specific components of traditional lifestyles are the ones protecting those living them against NCDs. Some of those desirable components are already obvious (e.g., exercise repeatedly, reduce your sugar intake), while others are not obvious and are still being debated (e.g., optimal levels of dietary fat).

The current epidemic of NCDs will get much worse before it gets better. Sadly, it has already reached its peak in Pimas and Nauruans. Of special concern now are populous countries with rapidly rising standards of living. The epidemic may be closest to reaching its peak in wealthy Arab oil countries, further short of its peak in North Africa, and under way but still due to become much worse in China and India. Other populous countries in which the epidemic is well launched include Bangladesh, Brazil, Egypt, Indonesia, Iran, Mexico, Pakistan, the Philippines, Russia,

South Africa, and Turkey. Countries with lower populations in which the epidemic is also under way include all countries of Latin America and Southeast Asia. It is just beginning among the not-quite 1 billion people of sub-Saharan Africa. When one contemplates those prospects, it's easy to become depressed.

But we're not inevitably the losers in our struggles with NCDs. We ourselves are the only ones who created our new lifestyles, so it's completely in our power to change them. Some help will come from molecular biological research, aimed at linking particular risks to particular genes, and hence at identifying for each of us the particular dangers to which our particular genes predispose us. However, society as a whole doesn't have to wait for such research, or for a magic pill, or for the invention of low-calorie potato chips. It's already clear which changes will minimize many (though not all) risks for most of us. Those changes include: not smoking; exercising regularly; limiting our intake of total calories, alcohol, salt and salty foods, sugar and sugared soft drinks, saturated and trans fats, processed foods, butter, cream, and red meat; and increasing our intake of fiber, fruits and vegetables, calcium, and complex carbohydrates. Another simple change is to eat more slowly. Paradoxically, the faster you wolf down your food, the more you end up eating and hence gaining weight, because eating rapidly doesn't allow enough time for release of hormones that inhibit appetite. Italians are slim not only because of their diet composition but also because they linger talking over their meals. All of those changes could spare billions of people around the world the fates that have already befallen the Pimas and the Nauruans.

This advice is so banally familiar that it's embarrassing to repeat it. But it's worth repeating the truth: we already know enough to warrant our being hopeful, not depressed. Repetition merely re-emphasizes that hypertension, the sweet death of diabetes, and other leading 20th-century killers kill us only with our own permission.

At Another Airport

From the jungle to the 405 ▪ Advantages of the modern world ▪
Advantages of the traditional world ▪ What can we learn?

From the jungle to the 405

At the end of an expedition of several months to New Guinea, mostly
spent with New Guineans at campsites in the jungle, my emotional transition back to the modern industrial world doesn't begin at Papua New
Guinea's Port Moresby airport, with which I began this book's Prologue.
That's because, on the long plane flight from New Guinea back to Los
Angeles, I use the time to transcribe my field notes, relive daily events of
my months in the jungle, and remain mentally in New Guinea. Instead,
the emotional transition begins in the baggage claim area of Los Angeles
airport, and it continues with the reunion with my family waiting outside
baggage claim, the drive home along the 405 Freeway, and my confronta-
tion with piles of accumulated mail and e-mails on my desk. Shifting from
New Guinea's traditional world to Los Angeles pummels me with a conflicting mixture of feelings. What are some of them?

First and foremost are the joy and relief of being back with my wife and
children. The U.S. is my home, my country. I was born and grew up here.
Americans include friends whom I've known for 60 or 70 years, and who
share and understand my life history, my culture, and many of my interests. I'll always speak English better than any other language. I'll always
understand Americans better than I understand New Guineans. The U.S.
has big advantages as a base to live. I can expect to have enough food, to

enjoy physical comfort and security, and to live almost twice as long as the average traditional New Guinean. It's much easier to satisfy my love of Western music, and to pursue my career as an author and university geographer, in the U.S. than in New Guinea. All of those are reasons why I choose to live in the U.S. Much as I love New Guinea and New Guineans, I've never considered moving there.

A different emotion hits me when I exit the Los Angeles airport onto the 405 Freeway. The landscape around me on the freeway consists entirely of an asphalt road grid, buildings, and motor vehicles. The sound environment is traffic noise. Sometimes but not always, the Santa Monica Mountains, rising 10 miles north of the airport, are visible as a blur through the smog. The contrast with New Guinea's pure clear air, the variegated green shades of its dense jungle, and the excitement of its hundreds of bird songs could not be starker. Reflexively, I turn down the volume knobs on my senses and my emotional state, knowing that they will stay turned down for most of the time during the following year until my next New Guinea trip. Of course one can't generalize about differences between the traditional world and the industrial world just by contrasting New Guinea jungle with the 405 Freeway. The advantage of beauty and of emotional opening-up would be reversed if I were instead returning from months in Port Moresby itself (one of the world's most dangerous cities) to our summer home in Montana's gorgeous Bitterroot Valley, under the snow-capped forested peaks of North America's Continental Divide. Nevertheless, there are compelling reasons why I choose Los Angeles as my base, and why I choose New Guinea jungle and the Bitterroot Valley just for trips. But LA's advantages come at a heavy price.

Returning to urban life in the U.S. means returning to time pressures, schedules, and stress. Just the thought of it raises my pulse rate and my blood pressure. In New Guinea jungle there is no time pressure, no schedule. If it's not raining, I walk out of camp each day before dawn to listen to the last night bird songs and the first morning bird songs—but if it's raining, I sit in camp, waiting for the rain to stop; who knows when that will be. A New Guinean from the nearest village may have promised me yesterday that he'll visit camp "tomorrow" to teach me bird names in his local language: but he doesn't have a wristwatch and can't tell me when he'll come, and perhaps he'll come another day instead. In Los Angeles, though, life is heavily scheduled. My pocket diary tells me what I shall be doing at what hour on what day, with many entries months or a year or more off in the future. E-mails and phone calls flood in all day every day, and have to be constantly re-prioritized into piles or numbered lists for responding.

Back in Los Angeles, I gradually shed the health precautions that I adopted as reflexes in New Guinea. I no longer press my lips tightly shut while showering, lest I inadvertently contract dysentery by licking a few drops of infected water off my lips. I no longer have to be so scrupulous about frequently washing my hands, nor about keeping an eye on how the plates and spoons in camp are washed or on who touched them. I no longer have to monitor each scratch on my skin, lest it develop into a tropical ulcer. I stop taking my weekly anti-malaria pills and constantly carrying vials of three types of antibiotics. (No, all those precautions are not paranoid: there are serious consequences to omitting any of them.) I no longer have to wonder whether a twinge in my abdomen might mean appendicitis, at a jungle location from which I couldn't get to a hospital in time.

Returning to Los Angeles from New Guinea jungle carries for me big changes in my social environment: much less constant, direct, and intense interactions with people. During my waking hours in New Guinea jungle, I'm almost constantly within a few feet of New Guineans and ready to talk with them, whether we are sitting in camp or out on a trail looking for birds. When we talk, we have each other's full attention; none of us is distracted by texting or checking e-mail on a cell phone. Camp conversations tend to switch back and forth between several languages, depending on who is in camp at the moment, and I have to know at least the bird names in each of those languages even if I can't speak the language. In contrast, in Westernized society, we spend far less time in direct face-to-face conversation with other people. It's estimated that the average American instead spends eight hours per day in front of a screen (of a computer, TV, or hand-held device). Out of the time that we do spend interacting with other people, most of that interaction is indirect: by e-mail, phone, text-messaging, or (decreasingly) letters. By far most of my interactions in the U.S. are monolingual in English: I count myself lucky if I get to converse in any other language for a few hours a week. Of course, those differences don't mean that I constantly cherish New Guinea's direct, intense, omnipresent, full-attention, multilingual social environment: New Guineans can be frustrating as well as delightful, just as can Americans.

After 50 years of commuting between the U.S. and New Guinea, I've worked out my compromises and found my peace. Physically, I spend about 93% of my time in the U.S. and occasionally in other industrial countries, and about 7% of my time in New Guinea. Emotionally, I still spend much of my time and thoughts in New Guinea, even when I am physically in the U.S. New Guinea's intensity would be hard to shake off even if I wanted to do so, which I don't. Being in New Guinea is like seeing the world briefly in vivid colors, when by comparison the world elsewhere is gray.

Advantages of the modern world

Because most of the remainder of this chapter will be about features of traditional life from which we in the modern world can usefully learn, let's begin by reminding ourselves of an obvious conclusion. Traditional life should not be romanticized: the modern world does offer huge advantages. It's not the case that citizens of Westernized societies are fleeing in droves from steel tools, health, material comfort, and state-imposed peace, and are trying to return to an idyllic hunter-gatherer lifestyle. Instead, the overwhelming direction of change is that hunter-gatherers and small-scale farmers who know their traditional lifestyle, but who also witness a Westernized lifestyle, are seeking to enter the modern world. Their reasons are compelling, and include such modern amenities as material goods that make life easier and more comfortable; opportunities for formal education and jobs; good health, effective medicines, doctors, and hospitals; personal security, less violence, and less danger from other people and from the environment; food security; much longer lives; and a much lower frequency of experiencing the deaths of one's children (e.g., about two-thirds of traditional Fayu children died in childhood). Naturally, it is not true that every traditional village that modernizes, and every villager who moves to a city, succeed in obtaining these hoped-for advantages. But some do, and most villagers can see that other people enjoy these advantages, and many villagers aspire to them.

For example, Aka Pygmy women interviewed by Bonnie Hewlett mentioned the following reasons for abandoning their traditional hunter-gatherer lifestyle in the forest to settle down as village farmers: material goods such as salt, pepper, palm oil, pots and pans, machetes, beds, and lanterns; good clothes and shoes; a healthier life; the opportunity to send one's children to school; that it is easier to obtain plant food from fields than to gather it in the forest; and that it is easier and safer and faster to hunt animals with a gun than to make nets and extract kicking, biting, and slashing animals trapped in nets. Ache Indians interviewed by Kim Hill and A. Magdalena Hurtado named their motives for giving up life in the forest and moving to reservation settlements: to acquire a shotgun, a radio, and new clothes; to keep themselves and their children well fed and healthy; to live longer; and to have many children survive to become adults. Western material goods that my New Guinea friends value include, most notably, matches, steel axes, clothes, a soft bed, and an umbrella. (To understand the value of an umbrella, remember that rainfall in New Guinea ranges up to 500 inches per year or higher). New Guineans also value non-material benefits such as medical care, schooling for children, and the end of tribal warfare. Ishi, the Yahi Indian of Northern California who gave up his hunter-gatherer lifestyle around the age of 50 to spend his last years in San Francisco, initially admired matches and glue above all other European inventions, and with time also grew fond of houses, furniture, flush toilets, running water, electric lights, gas stoves, and railroad trains. Sabine Kuegler's sister Judith, upon moving for a year from her family home in the New Guinea jungle to Germany, was astonished by all the different brands of chocolate bars available in a German supermarket.

These are among the many obvious and concrete advantages of the Western lifestyle mentioned by people who have grown up among the insecurities, dangers, and discomforts of traditional societies. Other, subtler advantages are mentioned by educated New Guinea friends whose survival needs were already being met in their New Guinea village, and who admire other things about life in the United States. They cite access to information, access to a broad diversity of people, and more rights for women in the U.S. than in New Guinea. One New Guinea friend surprised me by telling me that what she most likes about life in the U.S. is its "anonymity." She explained that anonymity means to her the freedom to step away from the social bonds that make life in New Guinea emotionally full, but also confining. To my friend, anonymity includes the freedom to be alone, to walk alone, to have privacy, to express oneself, to debate openly, to hold unconventional views, to be more immune to peer pressures, and not to have one's every action scrutinized and discussed. It means the freedom to sit in a café on a crowded street and read a newspaper in peace, without being besieged by acquaintances asking for help with their problems. It means the freedom of Americans to advance themselves as individuals, with much less obligation to share their earnings with all their relatives than in New Guinea.

Advantages of the traditional world

Now, let's hear the other side of the story. What do people who have lived both in traditional societies and in WEIRD societies value about the former and find missing in the latter?

The most frequent and important observations involve life-long social bonds. Loneliness is not a problem in traditional societies. People spend their lives in or near the place where they were born, and they remain surrounded by relatives and childhood companions. In the smaller traditional societies (tribes and bands of just a few hundred people or fewer), no one is a stranger. While either girls or boys (in most traditional societies, girls) move from their natal group upon getting married, the move is usually over a sufficiently small distance that one can regularly visit one's blood relatives.

In contrast, the risk of loneliness is a chronic problem in populous industrial societies. The expression "feeling alone in a crowded room" isn't just a literary phrase: it's a basic reality for many Americans and Europeans living in large cities, and working among people whom they barely know. People in Western societies frequently move long distances, their children and friends also independently move long distances, and so one is likely to end up far from one's closest relatives and childhood friends. Most people that one encounters are strangers and will remain strangers. Children routinely leave their parents' house and set up their own household on marrying or becoming economically independent. As one American friend who spends much time in Africa summed it up, "Life in Africa is materially poor and socially/emotionally rich, while U.S. life is materially rich and socially/emotionally poor." Other frequent observations are the greater time pressures, scheduling constraints, stress levels, and competitiveness in Western societies than in traditional societies. I emphasize once again that there are respects in which features of the traditional world persist in many parts of modern industrial societies, such as rural areas, where everyone knows everyone else and most people spend their lives near their birthplace.

To put a personal face on these generalizations, I'll quote some poignant observations by children of American businesspeople or missionaries who grew up in New Guinea, the Philippines, or Kenya and then moved to the United States as teen-agers and told me about their experiences:

"American boys are macho, talk macho, and beat up other kids. Nice kids don't do well in the U.S."

"After growing up with kids in New Guinea, the first thing that struck me as different about the U.S. was that kids go into their houses, close the doors, play video games, and leave their houses again to go to school. In New Guinea, we kids were constantly out of doors, playing with each other."

"African children are with people all of the time. We kids were indoors only to sleep. We could go into any house, knowing that we were welcome there. But American children are often not with other children. Nowadays, with the availability of video games, the problem of staying in your house by yourself is even worse in the U.S. than it was when I was growing up and there was only TV and no video games."

"Out in the Philippines, children call all adults 'aunt' and 'uncle.' We're in and out of any house in the village. When it's dinnertime, we eat in whoever's house we happen to be in at that time, with other children."

"American children are less sociable than New Guinea children. In New Guinea, I'm used to smiling and saying hello to anyone that I pass, and to starting a conversation. But American children walk past each other or walk past strangers, don't start a conversation, and don't say hello. When I smile and say hello, then they respond, but they don't initiate it themselves."

"In the U.S., people have to be entertained, and they don't know how to entertain themselves."

"In Africa, if you need something, you make it for yourself, and as a result you know how it is put together and how it works. In the U.S., if you need something, you go buy it, and you don't know how it is put together."

"American children have less creativity than New Guinea children, because everything is pre-packaged for them [Plates 17, 18]. In New Guinea, if you see an airplane and you want to have a model airplane, you make a model airplane yourself out of wood or out of sticks. You then play games with the airplane, making it swoop and making noises. My brother and I imitated the flight of an airplane in detail with our home-made airplanes. But American children just get their packaged toy airplanes and don't imitate its flight in detail."

"In Africa you share things. For example, while I was in school, I acquired a red inner tube of a rubber tire. Rubber was valuable to make slingshots. For a long time, I shared pieces of my valuable red inner tube with other kids for them to make slingshots. But in the U.S., if you acquire something valuable, you keep it for yourself and you don't share it. In addition, nobody in the U.S. would know what to do with an inner tube."

"The biggest adjustment I had to make on moving from New Guinea to the U.S. was my lack of freedom. Children have much more freedom in New Guinea. In the U.S. I was not allowed to climb trees. I was always climbing trees in New Guinea; I still like to climb trees. When my brother and I came back to California and moved into our house there, one of the first things we did was to climb a tree and build a tree house; other families thought that was weird. The U.S. has so many rules and regulations, because of fear of being sued, that kids give up on the opportunity for personal exploration. A pool has to be fenced so that it's not an 'attractive nuisance.' Most New Guineans don't have pools, but even the rivers that we frequented didn't have signs saying 'Jump at your own risk,' because it's obvious. Why would I jump unless I'm prepared for the consequences? Responsibility in the U.S. has been taken from the person acting and has been placed on the owner of the land or the builder of the house. Most Americans want to blame someone other than themselves as much as possible. In New Guinea I was able to grow up, play creatively, and explore the outdoors and nature freely, with the obligatory element of risk, however well managed, that is absent from the average risk-averse American child-hood. I had the richest upbringing possible, an upbringing inconceivable for Americans."

"A frustration here in the U.S. is the constant pressure to be working. If you're sitting around enjoying a cup of coffee in the afternoon, you should feel guilty because it's a wasted opportunity to be making money. But if you are one of those people that are making money instead of enjoy-ing a cup of coffee, you don't save that extra money you made, you just live a more expensive life so that you have to keep working more and more. The U.S. has lost its ability (for the most part) to find the balance between work and play or relaxation. In New Guinea, shops close down in the middle of the day and re-open in the late afternoon. That is extremely un-American."

"I was shocked at the lack of moral compass of my peers in the U.S. In a society as pluralistic as America, there can be little basis for standing on what you believe is true and right. In New Guinea, certainly truth is cul-turally interpreted and applied, but it *is* acknowledged as existing and being knowable."

"Kids here in the U.S., and perhaps Americans in general, are obsessed with goods. Upon our last return to California, we were impressed with the latest fads or 'must-haves,' in this case large flat-screen plasma TVs. What will it be six months from now?"

"Everyone in the U.S. is in their own tight box. The African young people I knew were intensely interested in what went on in other parts of the world and were geographically literate. One of our pastimes was to quiz each other on the location of various countries, the names of world leaders, and of sports heroes. Of course they knew the names of Kenya's national soccer champs and long-distance runners, but they were equally familiar with American, British, German, and Brazilian superstars. They had heard of the Lone Ranger, Wilt Chamberlain, and Muhammad Ali and were constantly asking me what life was like in the U.S. When I first arrived in the U.S., I expected to be asked about life in Africa but soon came to realize that very few people had much interest in anything other than what directly affected them on a day-to-day basis. Lifestyles, customs, and events elsewhere in the world were of minor interest, and I learned to stop talking about Africa. Many people in the U.S. have acquired a great many things, but they remain paupers so far as their knowledge and understanding of the rest of the world is concerned. They seem to be comfortably enclosed within their walls of carefully constructed, selective ignorance."

What can we learn?

The world of yesterday shaped our genes, culture, and behavior for most of the history of behaviorally modern *Homo sapiens,* who arose between 60,000 and 100,000 years ago. As deduced from the archaeological record, changes in lifestyle and in technology unfolded extremely slowly until they began to accelerate with the earliest origins of agriculture around 11,000 years ago in the Fertile Crescent. The oldest state governments arose, again in the Fertile Crescent, only around 5,400 years ago. That means that the ancestors of all of us alive today were still living in yesterday's world until 11,000 years ago, and that the ancestors of many of us were still doing so much more recently. Direct contact with the outside world began only within recent generations in the most populous areas of New Guinea, and direct outside contact and state government still haven't arrived for a few remaining groups in New Guinea and Amazonia.

Of course, much of yesterday's world is still with us today, even in the most densely populated areas of modern industrial societies. Life in sparsely populated rural areas of the Western world still preserves many aspects of traditional societies. Nevertheless, there are big differences between the traditional world and our modern WEIRD (Western, educated, industrial, rich, and democratic) societies. Traditional peoples have been unconsciously executing thousands of experiments on how to operate a human society. We can't repeat all those experiments intentionally under controlled conditions in order to see what happens. But we can still learn from what actually did happen.

Some of what yesterday's world teaches us is to be grateful for our modern societies, and not to bad-mouth them across the board. Almost all of us would say good riddance to chronic warfare, infanticide, and abandoning the elderly. We understand why small-scale societies often have to do those cruel things, or get trapped into doing them. Fortunately, though, with state governments we're not necessarily trapped in war cycles, and with sedentary lifestyles and food surpluses we're not forced to practise infanticide and abandonment of the elderly. We would also say good riddance to the strangling of widows, and to other cruelties that certain traditional societies practise as cultural idiosyncrasies, although nothing about their environment or subsistence forces them to do it.

But there are other features of yesterday's world that, instead of horrifying us, are likely to appeal to many readers of this book. Some of those features—such as not sprinkling salt on our food at the dinner table–are ones that we can easily incorporate into our individual lives, regardless of whether our whole society around us also adopts them. Other features that we admire will be harder for us to adopt individually if the society around us doesn't also change: it's hard to raise our children like New Guinea children when all other children around them are being raised like modern American children. Still other decisions to adopt features of traditional societies require action by our society as a whole. Realizing that adopting admired features of yesterday's world thus requires a mixture of individual decisions and societal decisions, what are some of the things that we can do?

Diet and eating habits are an area in which there is a lot that we can do as individuals to help ourselves. Think again about the startling fact that virtually no traditional New Guineans die of stroke, diabetes, or heart attacks. That doesn't mean that you have to resume tribal warfare and adopt a diet consisting 90% of sweet potatoes if you, too, want to avoid dying of those diseases. Instead, you can enjoy some of the world' greatest cooking and live peacefully *and* avoid those diseases, by incorporating three enjoyable habits into your life: exercising; eating slowly and talking with friends while you eat, instead of gulping down your food by yourself; and selecting healthy foods like fresh fruits, vegetables, low-fat meat, fish, nuts, and cereals, while avoiding foods whose labels show that they're high in salt, trans fats, and simple sugars. This is also an area where society (i.e., voters, government, and food manufacturers) can make things easier for us, by adopting healthier standards for processed foods, as Finland and other countries have been doing.

Another thing that we can do individually or as couples, without waiting for society as a whole to change, is to raise our children bilingually or multilingually, like so many children in traditional societies. Many Americans could have done so but refrained, because they were told that hearing two languages would confuse children. We now know that, far from confusing children, it brings life-long benefits to their thinking, as well as enriching their lives. Many American couples know more than one language: each parent could speak a different language to their children and raise them as "crib bilinguals." Immigrant couples could speak their native language to their children, instead of preventing their children from hearing the parents' native language: the children will quickly pick up English from other children anyway. I say to all of us (myself included) who have struggled to learn languages in school or as adults, spending thousands of hours studying grammar books and memorizing vocabulary and listening to language tapes, and nevertheless ending up speaking with an accent and without fluency: you could have spared yourself all that effort, and ended up speaking fluently and without an accent, if your parents had raised you bilingually. We should think of this when we are figuring out how to raise our children and grandchildren.

Besides multilingualism, child-rearing by traditional societies offers many other model options from which we can choose. All prospective parents should ask themselves which of the following options make sense for them: a period of on-demand nursing insofar as it's practical, late weaning, maintaining physical contact between the infant and some adult, co-sleeping (get a firm mattress or a crib in your bedroom, and discuss it with your pediatrician!), transporting infants vertically and facing forwards, much allo-parenting, responding quickly to a child's crying, avoiding physical punishment, giving your child freedom to explore (appropriately monitored!), multi-age playgroups (valuable for both the younger and the older children), and helping your kids learn to entertain themselves rather than stifling them with manufactured "educational toys" and video games and other pre-packaged entertainment. You may find individual adoption of some of these measures difficult if your neighborhood or local society as a whole doesn't change: when all of the kids on the block have video games and only your house doesn't, you may find your children wanting to spend all their time in other kids' homes. But it's worth thinking seriously about these choices: the independence, security, and social maturity of children in traditional societies impress all visitors who have come to know them.

Still another thing that we can do individually is to assess realistically the dangers inherent in our lifestyles, and to adopt New Guinea–style constructive paranoia selectively. My New Guinea friends figured out not to sleep underneath dead trees in the jungle, and to pay attention to seemingly innocent-looking broken sticks in the ground—even though the odds are that they could sleep for dozens of nights under a dead tree and ignore dozens of seemingly innocuous sticks without getting into trouble. But they know that, if they adopt those incautious practices hundreds of times, the odds will eventually catch up with them. For most of us Westerners, life's major hazards aren't dead trees or sticks in the ground, but they also aren't terrorists, nuclear reactors, plane crashes, and the other spectacular but realistically insignificant hazards that we obsess about. Instead, accident statistics show that most of us should be constructively paranoid about cars (driven by ourselves or by other people), alcohol (consumed by ourselves or by other people), and (especially as we get older) stepladders and slipping in showers. For each of us, there are some other risks that we should also be thinking about, depending on our particular individual lifestyle.

Our religion (or lack of religion) is yet another choice that we make as individuals. Many of us go through difficult periods of life when we re-assess our religious beliefs. At such times, it's worth remembering that our choice of religion is a broader and more complex matter than just adopting metaphysical beliefs that we've decided are true, or rejecting beliefs that we've decided are false. As I write these lines, I'm reflecting on the different choices made by three friends whom I've known for decades: one, a life-long Unitarian for whom her church has been a central focus of her life; the second, a life-long Jew for whom his religion and his wrestling with his relationship to Israel have been a core of his identity; and the third, a German friend raised a Catholic, living in an overwhelmingly Catholic area of Germany, who recently astonished me by converting at age 40 to Protestantism. In all three cases, my friends' decisions to maintain or to change their religion have depended on roles of religion other than as a source of beliefs. Those various roles have waxed and waned at different times for my friends through their lifetimes, just as they have waxed and waned in different historical periods for societies over the millennia. The roles include the search for satisfying explanations of ultimate questions about the physical world; dealing with anxiety and stressful situations; making sense of the death of a loved one, of the prospect of one's own death, and of other painful events; justifying one's moral principles of behavior, and one's obedience or disobedience to authority; and identifying oneself as a member of a group whose ideals one shares. For those of us going through a period of religious turmoil, perhaps it might help clarify our thinking to remember that religion has meant different things to different societies, and to be honest with ourselves about what religion does or might mean specifically to us.

Turning now to admired features of traditional societies whose implementation requires both individual action and societal action, I already mentioned one example: reduction of dietary salt intake, a goal towards which we can make some progress as individuals, but which requires actions by governments and food manufacturers if we are also to reduce our cryptic salt intake in processed foods. We can similarly reduce our individual risk of diabetes by exercise and appropriate diets, but governments can also contribute in ways such as public awareness campaigns and regulating sales of fattening foods in public school cafeterias. As for how society (and not just bilingual parents of infants) can foster multilingualism and combat language extinction, some governments (e.g., Switzerland's) work hard to preserve their language diversity; other governments (e.g., that of the U.S.) only recently stopped working hard to eradicate their nation's diversity of native languages; and still other governments (e.g., the French in the region of Brittany) continue to oppose retention of a native language.

The status of the elderly also depends on both individual and societal decisions. Increasing numbers of older people make themselves valuable in new ways, ease the lives of their working adult children, and enrich the lives of their grandchildren and of themselves, by providing high-quality one-on-one child care to their grandchildren. Those of us who are parents between the ages of 30 and 60 may be starting to wonder what quality of life we shall enjoy, and how our children will treat us, when we reach old age. We should remember that our children are now watching how we care for our own elderly parents: when it comes our own time to be receiving rather than giving care, our children will remember and be influenced by our example. Society can enrich the lives of the elderly as a group, and can enrich society itself, by not requiring retirement at some arbitrary age for people able and eager to continue working. Mandatory retirement policies have been falling by the wayside in the United States in recent decades, have not led to incapable older people clinging to jobs as initially feared, and have instead retained the services of the most experienced members of our society. But far too many European institutions still require employees at the peak of their productivity to retire, just because they have reached some arbitrary age in the absurdly low range of 60 to 65 years.

In contrast to eating slowly and providing crib bilingualism, which we can do independently ourselves while waiting for changes in society as a whole, combining the advantages of traditional justice with the advantages of state justice will mostly require societal decisions. Two mechanisms that I discussed are restorative justice and mediation. Neither is a panacea, both appear useful under some circumstances but not other circumstances, and both require policy decisions by our court systems. If you see possible value in these options, your role as an individual is to join movements promoting these mechanisms in courts; you can't adopt them by yourself. But you may be able to utilize by yourself the New Guinea emphasis on informal mediation, emotional clearance, and reestablishment of relationships (or of non-relationships) in disputes the next time that you find yourself in a private dispute where tempers are rising.

The societies to which most readers of this book belong represent a narrow slice of human cultural diversity. Societies from that slice achieved world dominance not because of a general superiority, but for specific reasons: their technological, political, and military advantages derived from their early origins of agriculture, due in turn to their productive local wild domesticable plant and animal species. Despite those particular advantages, modern industrial societies didn't also develop superior approaches to raising children, treating the elderly, settling disputes, avoiding non-communicable diseases, and other societal problems. Thousands of traditional societies developed a wide array of different approaches to those problems. My own outlook on life has been transformed and enriched by my years among one set of traditional societies, that of New Guinea. I hope that you readers as individuals, and our modern society as a whole, will similarly find much to enjoy and adopt from the huge range of traditional human experience.

Acknowledgments

I acknowledge with pleasure my debts to many colleagues and friends for their help with this book. I owe special thanks to eight friends who critiqued the entire manuscript and poured time and effort into suggestions for improving it: my wife Marie Cohen, Timothy Earle, Paul Ehrlich, Alan Grinnell, Barry Hewlett, Melvin Konner, Michael Shermer, and Meg Taylor. Those same thanks and more are due to my editors Wendy Wolf at Viking Penguin (New York) and Stefan McGrath at Penguin Group (London), and to my agent John Brockman, who not only read the whole manuscript but also helped in innumerable ways at every stage from the book's conception through all stages of its production.

Michelle Fisher-Casey typed and retyped the whole manuscript, many times. Boratha Yeang tracked down sources. Ruth Mandel tracked down photographs, and Matt Zebrowski prepared the maps.

I presented much of the material of this book to my classes of undergraduates at the University of California at Los Angeles, where I teach in the Geography Department. Those students constantly confronted me with fresh and stimulating outlooks. The department's faculty members and staff have provided me with a constantly supportive environment. At a workshop that James Robinson and I co-organized at Harvard University, participants brainstormed about many topics of this book.

Earlier versions of some paragraphs or material of several chapters appeared as articles in *Natural History* magazine, *Discover* magazine, *Nature* magazine, the *New York Review of Books*, and *The New Yorker*.

Over the last half-century, thousands of New Guineans, Indonesians, and Solomon Islanders shared with me their insights, life stories, and world views, and lived with me the experiences that I relate in this book. My debt to them for enriching my life is enormous. I have dedicated this book to one such friend, Meg Taylor (Dame Meg Taylor), who was born in New Guinea's Wahgi Valley and grew up in the Highlands of Papua New Guinea. Her mother was Yerima Manamp Masi of the Baiman Tsenglap clan, while her father was the Australian patrol officer James Taylor, leader of the famous Bena-to-Hagen patrol in 1933 and the 1938–1939 Hagen-to-Sepik patrol. After studying law at the University of Papua New Guinea and Melbourne University (Australia), Meg became private secretary to the first Chief Minister and then Prime Minister of Papua New Guinea, Sir Michael Somare, as the country transitioned from self-government to independence in 1975. She practised law in Papua New Guinea, served as a member of the Law Reform Commission, and pursued further studies in law at Harvard as a Fulbright Scholar. Meg was Ambassador of Papua New Guinea to the United States, Mexico, and Canada from 1989 to 1994. She has served on the boards of international conservation and research organizations; Papua New Guinea companies in the natural resources, financial, and agricultural sectors; and companies listed on the Australian Securities Exchange. In 1999 Meg was appointed to the post of Vice President Compliance Advisor/Ombudsman of the World Bank Group. Meg is the mother of her daughter Taimil, and aunt to many young family members in the Highlands. She will return home upon completion of her current World Bank assignment in Washington, D.C.

Many friends and colleagues generously helped me in connection with individual chapters, by sending me articles and references, telling me of their experiences and conclusions, talking through ideas, and criticizing my chapter draft. They include: Gregory Anderson, Stephen Beckerman, Ellen Bialystok, David Bishop, Daniel Carper, Elizabeth Cashdan, Barbara Dean, Daniel Dennett, Joel Deutsch, Michael Goran, Mark Grady, K. David Harrison, Kristen Hawkes, Karl Heider, Dan Henry, Bonnie Hewlett, William Irons, Francine Kaufman, Neal Kaufman, Laurel Kearns, Philip Klemmer, Russell Korobkin, Ágnes Kovács, Michael Krauss, Sabine Kuegler, David Laitin, Francesca Leardini, Steven LeBlanc, Graham Mac-Gregor, Robert McKinley, Angella Meierzag, Kenneth Mesplay, Richard Mills, Viswanatha Mohan, Elizabeth Nabel, Gary Nabel, Claire Panosian, Joseph Peckham, Lloyd Peckham, Dale Price, David Price, Samuel Price, Lynda Resnick, Jerome Rotter, Roger Sant, Richard Shweder, Charles Taylor, Minna Taylor, Eugene Volokh, Douglas White, Polly Wiessner, David Sloan Wilson, Lana Wilson, Bruce Winterhalder, Richard Wrangham, and Paul Zimmet.

Support for these studies was generously provided by the National Geographic Society, Conservation International, Skip and Heather Brittenham, Lynda and Stewart Resnick, the Summit Foundation, and the Eve and Harvey Masonek and Samuel F. Heyman and Eve Gruber Heyman 1981 Trust Undergraduate Research Scholars Fund.

To all these people and organizations, I express my heartfelt thanks.

Further Readings

These suggestions of some selected references are for those interested in reading further. Rather than listing extensive bibliographies, I have favored citing recent publications that do provide extensive bibliographies of the earlier literature. In addition, I cite some key earlier books and articles that I think may be of particular interest to readers, or that I specifically quote in my text. A journal title (in italics) is followed by the volume number, followed after a colon by the first and last page numbers, and then by the year of publication in parentheses. Because this book is aimed at a wide audience, I have not footnoted individual statements in the text, and the references instead are designed to supplement individual topics and whole chapters. To reduce this book's cost, I print here only the references of most general relevance: those to the whole book, and those to the Prologue. The remaining references, to Chapters 1–11 and to the Epilogue, are posted online on a freely available Web site (http://www.jared diamondbooks.com).

References applicable to this whole book

I provide here three sets of references or comments: references to a few books especially useful for the purposes of this volume, because they provide explicitly comparative information on many societies; explanation of references to the names of individuals whom I met; and references for 39 traditional societies around the world from which I have frequently drawn examples in my book.

General comparative references. An excellent comparative study of human societies around the world especially appropriate to readers of my book is Allen Johnson and Timothy Earle, *The Evolution of Human Societies: From Foraging Group to Agrarian*

State, 2nd ed. (Stanford: Stanford University Press, 2000). This volume compares many aspects of human societies at different levels of organization, summarizes case studies of 19 specific societies, provides many references to the literature on each of those societies, and uses a more finely divided classification of societies than my four-fold classification into bands, tribes, chiefdoms, and states. An equally excellent comparative account of Aboriginal Australian societies is Ian Keen, *Aboriginal Economy and Society: Australia at the Threshold of Colonisation* (South Melbourne: Oxford University Press, 2004). As do Johnson and Earle for the world, Keen provides seven case studies sampling the range of geography, environment, and social organization of Native Australians. Three books that specifically survey hunter-gatherer societies around the world are Richard Lee and Irven DeVore, eds., *Man the Hunter* (Chicago: Aldine, 1968); Frances Dahlberg, ed., *Woman the Gatherer* (New Haven: Yale University Press, 1981); and Richard Lee and Richard Daly, eds., *The Cambridge Encyclopedia of Hunters and Gatherers* (Cambridge: Cambridge University Press, 1999). A valuable cross-cultural survey often consulted by cultural anthropologists is a project of the Cross-Cultural Cumulative Coding Center established at the University of Pittsburgh under the direction of George Murdock. For hundreds of pre-industrial societies around the world, it coded over a thousand cultural variables. Tabulations of its data include George Murdock, *Ethnographic Atlas* (Pittsburgh: University of Pittsburgh Press, 1967); Herbert Barry III and Alice Schlegel, *Cross-Cultural Samples and Codes* (Pittsburgh: University of Pittsburgh Press, 1980); and the Web sites http://www.yale.edu/hraf, http://ehrafworldcultures.yale.edu, and http://ehrafarchaeology.yale.edu.

Names of individual New Guineans. My text includes numerous anecdotes of conversations or events that transpired while I was bird-watching or chatting with individual New Guinea friends. While an anecdote by itself doesn't establish anything, it can be a useful way to illustrate, and to put a human face on, a general point. It is standard practice among journalists to provide the true names, identifying details, and localities of individuals mentioned, so that others may contact and further question the individual and thereby obtain new knowledge. That was also formerly the practice among anthropologists, and it was my practice in the past.

However, anthropologists now appreciate that their informants may be vulnerable and may suffer harm if their behavior and views become known. Cultural misunderstandings can easily arise, for example when a New Guinea villager is contacted out of the blue by a stranger with whom the New Guinean does not have an on-going relationship, and whose motives and explanations are unclear, and who may mislead or exploit the New Guinean. Hence it is now anthropological and sociological practice to change (fictionalize) or conceal the names of study locations and informants. In any ethnographic research one is now expected to avoid revealing details that would make it possible to trace a specific source for social data. As one anthropologist friend explained it to me, "The idea behind this practice is to protect informants from others who may want to find them or harm them for a variety of reasons." The code of ethics of the American Anthropological Association now states, "Anthropological researchers have primary ethical obligations to the people . . . with whom they work. Those obligations can supersede the goal of seeking new knowledge." For these reasons, throughout this book I have followed current anthropological practice, and I have consistently removed or changed names and identifying details when I recount stories or events in the lives of my New Guinea friends.

Frequently cited studies. For the reasons explained in the Prologue, I have repeatedly cited studies of a sample of 39 traditional societies around the world, so that readers can gain a sense of how different aspects of a particular society fit together. I group together here some references for accounts of these societies, rather than providing references one by one under the chapter in which I first mention that particular society. The 39 societies include 10 from New Guinea and neighboring islands, 7 from Australia, 5 each from Eurasia and Africa and South America, and 7 from North America.

New Guinea. Dani: books by Johan Broekhuijse, Karl Heider, Robert Gardner, and Peter Matthiessen, with details given under the Further Readings for Chapter 3. Daribi: Roy Wagner, *The Curse of Souw: Principles of Daribi Clan Definition and Alliance in New Guinea* (Chicago: University of Chicago Press, 1967) and *Habu: The Innovation of Meaning in Daribi Religion* (Chicago: University of Chicago Press, 1972). Enga: Polly Wiessner and Akii Tumu, *Historical Vines: Enga Networks of Exchange, Ritual, and Warfare in Papua New Guinea* (Washington, DC: Smithsonian Institution Press, 1998); plus references in Johnson and Earle (2000: see above), especially to the books and papers of Mervyn Meggitt. Fayu: Sabine Kuegler, *Dschungelkind* (München: Droemer, 2005). My quotations from that book are drawn from that German edition; its slightly shortened English translation appeared as Sabine Kuegler, *Child of the Jungle* (New York: Warner Books, 2005). Two other books by Kuegler that discuss the Fayu are Sabine Kuegler, *Ruf des Dschungels* (München: Droemer, 2006) and Sabine Kuegler, *Jägerin und Gejagte* (München: Droemer, 2009). Fore: Ronald Berndt, *Excess and Restraint: Social Control Among a New Guinea Mountain People* (Chicago: University of Chicago Press, 1962). Hinihon: Angella Meinerzag, *Being Mande: Personhood, Land, and Naming System Among the Hinihon in the Adelbert Range/Papua New Guinea* (Ph.D. dissertation, University of Heidelberg, 2007). Kaulong: Jane Goodale (not to be confused with the primatologist Jane Goodall), *To Sing with Pigs Is Human: the Concept of Person in Papua New Guinea* (Seattle: University of Washington Press, 1995). Mailu Island: Bronislaw Malinowski, *Natives of Mailu* (Adelaide: Royal Society of South Australia, 1915). Trobriand Islands: see bibliography by Johnson and Earle (2000, above). Tsembaga Maring: Roy Rappaport, *Pigs for the Ancestors: Ritual in the Ecology of a New Guinea People*, 2nd ed. (Long Grove, IL: Waveland Press, 1984); plus bibliography by Johnson and Earle (2000, above).

Australia. Ian Keen (2004, above) gives bibliographies for seven societies: the Ngarinyin of the Northwest, the Yolngu of Arnhem Land, the Sandbeach of Cape York, the Yuwaaliyaay of interior New South Wales, the Kunai of the southeast, the Pitjantjatjara of the Western Desert, and the Wiil and Minong of the Southwest.

Eurasia. Agta of the Philippines: Thomas Headland, *Why Foragers Do Not Become Farmers: A Historical Study of a Changing Ecosystem and Its Effect on a Negrito Hunter-Gatherer Group in the Philippines* (Ph.D. dissertation, University of Hawaii, 1986); John Early and Thomas Headland, *Population Dynamics of a Philippine Rain Forest People: The San Ildefonso Agta* (Gainesville: University Press of Florida, 1998). Ainu of Japan: Hitoshi Watanabe, *The Ainu Ecosystem: Environment and Group Structure* (Seattle: University of Washington Press, 1973). Andaman Islanders of the Bay of Bengal: A. R. Radcliffe-Brown, *The Andaman Islanders* (Glencoe, IL: Free Press, 1948); Lidio Cipriani, *The Andaman Islanders* (New York: Praeger, 1966). Kirghiz of Afghanistan and Nganasan of Siberia: see bibliography by Johnson and Earle (2000, above).

Africa. Hadza of Tanzania: Frank Marlowe, *The Hadza: Hunter-Gatherers of Tanzania* (Berkeley: University of California Press, 2010); Kristen Hawkes, James O'Connell, and Nicholas Blurton Jones, "Hadza children's foraging: juvenile dependency, social arrangements and mobility among hunter-gatherers," *Current Anthropology* 36: 688–700 (1995), "Hadza women's time allocation, offspring provisioning and the evolution of post-menopausal lifespans," *Current Anthropology* 38: 551–577 (1997), and "Hunting and nuclear families: some lessons from the Hadza about men's work," *Current Anthropology* 42: 681–709 (2001). !Kung of southwestern Africa: Nancy Howell, *Demography of the Dobe !Kung,* 2nd ed. (New York: Aldine de Gruiter, 2000) and *Life Histories of the !Kung: Food, Fatness, and Well-being over the Life-span* (Berkeley: University of California Press, 2010); Richard Lee, *The !Kung San: Men, Women, and Work in a Foraging Society* (Cambridge: Cambridge University Press, 1979); Lorna Marshall, *The !Kung of Nyae Nyae* (Cambridge, MA: Harvard University Press, 1976); Marjorie Shostak, *Nisa: The Life and Words of a !Kung Woman* (Cambridge, MA: Harvard University Press, 1981); Elizabeth Marshall Thomas, *The Harmless People,* rev. ed. (New York: Vintage Books, 1989). Nuer of the Sudan: E. E. Evans-Pritchard, *The Nuer of the Sudan: A Description of the Modes of Livelihood and Political Institutions of a Nilotic People* (Oxford: Oxford University Press, 1940). Pygmies of Central Africa (consisting actually of at least 15 ethnolinguistic groups of African forest foragers): Colin Turnbull, *The Forest People* (New York: Touchstone, 1962), for the Mbuti group; Luigi Luca Cavalli-Sforza, ed., *African Pygmies* (Orlando: Academic Press, 1986); Barry Hewlett, *Intimate Fathers: The Nature and Context of Aka Pygmy Paternal Infant Care* (Ann Arbor: University of Michigan Press, 1991) and Bonnie Hewlett, *Listen, Here Is a Story: Ethnographic Life Narratives from Aka and Ngandu Women of the Congo Basin* (New York: Oxford University Press, 2012), for the Aka group; and Barry Hewlett and Jason Fancher, "Central Africa hunter-gatherer research traditions," in Vicki Cummings et al., eds., *Oxford Handbook of the Archaeology and Anthropology of Hunter-Gatherers* (Oxford: Oxford University Press, in press), for an annotated bibliography. Turkana of Kenya: see bibliography by Johnson and Earle (2000, above).

North America. Calusa of Florida: Randolph Widmer, *The Evolution of the Calusa: A Nonagricultural Chiefdom on the Southwest Florida Coast* (Tuscaloosa: University of Alabama Press, 1988). Chumash of the California mainland: Lynn Gamble, *The Chumash World at European Contact: Power, Trade, and Feasting among Complex Hunter-Gatherers* (Berkeley: University of California Press, 2008). Island Chumash of California: Douglas Kennett, *The Island Chumash: Behavioral Ecology of a Maritime Society* (Berkeley: University of California Press, 2005). Iñupiat of northwest Alaska: Ernest Burch Jr., *The World System of the Iñupiaq Eskimos: Alliance and Conflict* (Lincoln: University of Nebraska Press, 2005). Alaska North Slope Inuit, Great Basin Shoshone, and Northwest Coast Indians: see bibliographies by Johnson and Earle (2000, above).

South America. Ache of Paraguay: Kim Hill and A. Magdalena Hurtado, *Ache Life History: The Ecology and Demography of a Foraging People* (New York: Aldine de Gruyter, 1996). Machiguenga of Peru: see bibliography by Johnson and Earle (2000, above). Piraha of Brazil: Daniel Everett, *Don't Sleep, There Are Snakes: Life and Language in the Amazonian Jungle* (New York: Pantagon, 2008). Siriono of Bolivia: Allan Holmberg, *Nomads of the Long Bow: The Siriono of Eastern Bolivia* (Garden City, NY: Natural History Press, 1969). Yanomamo of Brazil and Venezuela: Napoleon Chagnon, *Yanomamo,* 5th ed. (New York: Wadsworth, 1997); and bibliography by Johnson and Earle (2000, above).

References applicable to the Prologue: At the Airport

Gavin Souter, *New Guinea: The Last Unknown* (Sydney: Angus and Robertson, 1964) provides a good account of the early exploration of New Guinea, in a book ending a dozen years before Papua New Guinea became independent. My online references for Chapter 1 give citations for books describing and illustrating first contacts between Australians and New Guinea Highlanders.

As for why Western, educated, industrialized, rich, and democratic societies are WEIRD by the standards of more traditional societies over the rest of the world, Joseph Henrich, Steven Heine, and Ara Norenzayan explain the reasons briefly in "Most people are not WEIRD," *Nature* 466: 29 (2010), and at more length in "The Weirdest people in the world?," *Behavioral and Brain Sciences* 33: 61–135 (2010).

Chapter 14 of my book *Guns, Germs, and Steel* (New York: Norton, 1997) discusses the evolution of societies from bands to states according to the classification used in my present book, while Johnson and Earle (2000, cited above) discuss those transitions in more detail and with a more finely divided classification of societies. Classic accounts of the classification of human societies include two books by Elman Service: *Primitive Social Organization* (New York: Random House, 1962) and *Origins of the State and Civilization* (New York: Norton, 1975).

Some classic books of anthropology that provide examples of the different approaches mentioned in my text to explain differences among human societies are as follows: John Bodley, *The Power of Scale: A Global History Approach* (London: Sharpe, 2003); Timothy Earle, *Bronze Age Economics: The Beginnings of Political Economies* (Boulder, CO: Westview, 2002); Timothy Earle, ed., *Chiefdoms: Power, Economy, and Ideology* (Cambridge: Cambridge University Press, 1991); Marvin Harris, *Cultural Materialism: The Struggle for a Science of Culture* (New York: Random House, 1979); Marshall Sahlins, *Culture and Practical Reason* (Chicago: University of Chicago Press, 1976); Clifford Geertz, *The Interpretation of Cultures* (New York: Basic Books, 1973); Michel Foucault, *The Archaeology of Knowledge* (New York: Pantheon Books, 1972); Marshall Sahlins, *Stone Age Economics* (Chicago: Aldine, 1972); Marvin Harris, *The Rise of Anthropological Theory: A History of Theories of Culture* (New York: Crowell, 1968); Claude Leví-Strauss, *Structural Anthropology* (New York: Doubleday, 1963); Julian Steward, *Theory of Culture Change* (Urbana: University of Illinois Press, 1955); Alfred Kroeber, *The Nature of Culture* (Chicago: University of Chicago Press, 1952).

Kim Hill et al., "Co-residence patterns in hunter-gatherer societies show unique human social structure," *Science* 331: 1286–1289 (2011) analyze the patterns of who is actually related to whom in 32 present-day foraging bands.

The quotation on page 477, about the difficulties of interpreting field observations of modern traditional societies, comes from page 15 of Ian Keen's 2004 book cited above.

Pioneering studies of methodologically rigorous oral history are two books by Jan Vansina: *Oral Tradition: a Study in Historical Methodology* (London: Routledge and Kegan Paul, 1965) and *Oral Tradition as History* (London: James Currey, 1985). For readers interested in exploring some fascinating aspects of societal variation that I do not discuss, thereby earning myself the gratitude of readers for reducing the length of this already long book, one suggestion is Richard Nisbett, *The Geography of Thought: How Asians and Westerners Think Differently . . . and Why* (New York: Free Press, 2003). On his page 43 Nisbett briefly discusses cognitive differences between hunter-gatherers, traditional farming peoples, and industrial peoples. Joseph Henrich et al., eds., *Foundations of Human Sociality: Economic Experiments and Ethnographic Evidence from Fifteen Small-Scale Societies* (Oxford: Oxford University Press, 2004) discuss differences among traditional and industrial societies in their sense of fairness, reciprocity, and pursuit of self-interest.

For a detailed case study illustrating the difficulties of transferring one society's practices and lessons to another society, see Elizabeth Watson, *Living Terraces in Ethiopia: Konso Landscape, Culture, and Development* (Woodbridge, UK: James Currey, 2009).

Sources of knowledge about traditional societies

On pages 23–24 I briefly summarized our four sources of information, blurring into each other and each with its own advantages and disadvantages, about traditional societies. For readers (especially scholars) interested in learning more about these various sources, I now provide a more extended discussion.

The most obvious method, and the source of most of the information in this book, is to send trained social or biological scientists to visit or live among a traditional people, and to carry out a study focusing on some specific topic. The scientists variously identify themselves as practitioners of different disciplines, including anthropologists, biologists, economists, ethnographers, geneticists, historians, linguists, physicians, political scientists, psychologists, and sociologists. The authors publish their results as scientific articles or books, often frame their study at the outset in terms of some particular question or hypothesis to be tested, and often (especially nowadays) gather quantitative data to be presented in tables of numbers. As applied to traditional human societies, this is the scientific approach that has evolved over centuries as the best approach for obtaining reliable knowledge of the real world, whether it's the world of human societies, or else the worlds of bacteria, molecules, rocks, or galaxies.

Two main types of difficulty have arisen in applying this approach to the study of traditional human societies. Naturally, these difficulties do not invalidate such studies; they merely need to be borne in mind in interpreting the conclusions, and they explain why we resort to other sources of information as well. The Australian anthropologist Ian Keen introduced his book on Aboriginal Australian societies by summarizing these difficulties as follows: "The main issues of interpretation arising from the work of professionally trained anthropologists are that they are late in colonial/post-colonial trajectories, and particular paradigms strongly shape (and limit) their interpretations. However, within their fields of interest these works tend to be the most thorough and systematic."

Keen's warning about studies late in colonial/post-colonial trajectories refers to a dilemma inherent in cultural anthropology, analogous to the Heisenberg Uncertainty Principle in physics. That principle states, in effect, that any physical measurement inevitably perturbs the system being studied and thereby introduces uncertainty into what the true value would have been if the system had not been perturbed. (Specifically in particle physics, the principle states that it's impossible to measure simultaneously the exact values of both a particle's position and its velocity.) To appreciate the corresponding dilemma in cultural anthropology, recall that modern anthropological studies of Aboriginal Australia began in the 20th century, and ethnographic accounts began in the 19th century before the rise of modern professional anthropology. However, Europeans had already landed in Australia in 1616 and founded their first settlement in 1788, while Macassans (Indonesian fishermen) had regularly been visiting northern Australia for many centuries before European arrival, and unidentified Austronesian people from Indonesia somehow introduced dogs (dingoes) and possibly other life forms and technologies into Australia several thousand years ago.

Modern studies of Aboriginal Australians have thus been of societies radically changed from their pre-European or pre-Macassan condition, because most of the population had already been killed by European-introduced and perhaps also Macassan-introduced diseases, conquered and subjected to the control of

Euro-Australian state government, prevented from exercising traditional fire man-agement (i.e., burning) of their landscape, driven off their prime lands targeted for European settlement, and deprived of part of their subsistence base by the impacts on native animals and plants of European-introduced cats, foxes, sheep, and cattle and Austronesian-introduced dingoes. Similarly, while the !Kung of the Kalahari Desert are often taken as models of hunter-gatherers, the detailed studies of the !Kung that began in the 1960s, and that I cite frequently in this book, have been of people who had already given up their traditional bone arrow-points for metal points, had stopped raiding each other, had recently been trading with and encroached on by Bantu herders, and must somehow have been influenced by other Bantu herders who reached southern Africa almost 2,000 years ago.

More generally, all 20th-century studies of hunter-gatherers have been of socie-ties in actual or potential contact with food producers (farmers and/or herders). Un-til around 11,000 years ago, however, all human societies were hunter-gatherers, so that hunter-gatherers were in contact only with other hunter-gatherers. Only in a few parts of the world, such as Australia, the Arctic, and western North America, did even the first non-scientist Western explorers encounter hunter-gatherers still living in a world of hunter-gatherers. These facts have provoked heated arguments about the relevance of modern studies to past societies: are modern hunter-gatherers too different from past hunter-gatherers to have any relevance to understanding them? That view is surely too extreme: as anthropologist Melvin Konner has expressed it, if today one could take a group of Westerners and dump them naked and without tools in isolation somewhere in the African savannah, within two generations either they would all be dead or else they would have independently re-invented many observed features of hunter-gatherer societies. But at minimum, one must recognize that mod-ern traditional peoples are not frozen models of the distant past.

As for Ian Keen's other warning, within any science at any particular time there are preferred research areas for systematic study and funding, and other areas that remain neglected. For instance, until recently few anthropologists carried out stud-ies focusing specifically on childhood or old age among traditional peoples. Field observers are discouraged from going out on scientific "fishing trips" and recording everything that they notice; they are expected to produce books and articles on some specific subject. At a given time there are also certain interpretations and phenomena that tend to be preferred, and others that are considered unpalatable. For example, there has been vigorous controversy over whether or not the famous anthropologist Margaret Mead skewed her descriptions of Pacific Islander sexual behavior to fit preconceptions held by a then-current school of anthropology; and there are still strong views that traditional peoples aren't warlike, or that if they are warlike it's an artifact of European contact, or that if they really are warlike one shouldn't describe their wars because it's politically harmful to do so.

A second source of knowledge about traditional societies seeks to peel back some recent changes in modern traditional societies, by interviewing living non-literate people about their orally transmitted histories, and by reconstructing in that way

their history over several generations. Naturally, this method poses its own problems, and its practitioners have gained much experience of techniques (pioneered
especially by Jan Vansina) to cross-check and ensure the reliability of the information elicited.

For example, the American anthropologist Polly Wiessner and the Enga artist
Akii Tumu collaborated to study the oral history of the Enga people, the largest language group in the Highlands of Papua New Guinea. While written history began
for the Enga only with the arrival of literate Europeans in the 1930s, the Enga are
exceptional among New Guineans in keeping track of historical events through a
body of historical traditions (termed *atone pii*) that they recognize as distinct from
myths (termed *tindi pii*), and that go back 8 to 10 generations (250 to 400 years).
Between 1985 and 1998 Wiessner and Tumu interviewed elders in 110 Enga tribes.
They tested the correctness of the interview responses by looking for consistency
between accounts given by different clans, and by different tribes; by examining
whether accounts of wars and migrations given by descendants of participants on
opposite sides of the war or migration, and given by neighboring groups, agreed; and
by checking whether information offered about one sphere of life (e.g., ceremonial
pig exchanges) corresponded to information offered about different spheres of life
(e.g., land use and agricultural production). They also checked the oral accounts
against two independently datable events that affected all Highland groups of Papua
New Guinea, including the Enga: a massive volcanic eruption of nearby Long Island
in the 17th century, which deposited a layer of chemically identifiable ash (tephra) all
over the Eastern Highlands, and about which the Enga and other Highlanders have
an oral tradition of a "time of darkness," when ash darkened the sun for several days;
and the arrival of the sweet potato, which transformed Highlands agriculture and
societies between 250 and 400 years ago. By these cross-checking and cross-dating
methods, Wiessner and Tumu were able to reconstruct detailed histories of tribe
dispersals, population growth, population size, environmental conditions, agricultural subsistence, crops cultivated, trade, leadership, social organization, wars, migrations, and the development of ceremonies and cults over the last eight Enga
generations, long before European arrival in the New Guinea Highlands.

This method of oral reconstruction is applicable to only some traditional peoples,
perhaps just a minority of them, because many or most peoples do not retain detailed
oral knowledge going back more than a few generations. That depends on factors
such as their social organization, their degree of insistence on first-hand experience,
who tells stories, the context of telling stories, and the degree of participation by
listeners in story-telling. For example, the missionary linguist Daniel Everett found
that Brazil's Piraha Indians refused to discuss anything that they had not seen with
their own eyes, and hence were scornful of Everett's efforts to tell them about the life
of Jesus: "Did you see him yourself? If not, how can you believe it?" Similarly, the
many studies carried out among !Kung people from the 1960s onwards have failed to
recover detailed information concerning events or conditions of !Kung life more
than a few generations ago. On the other hand, among the Enga, historical stories are

recounted in the men's house, listeners comment on and correct mistakes in the stories, and powerful individuals are not permitted to distort history in order to advance their own interests.

A third approach to learning about traditional societies shares the goals of oral reconstruction, insofar as it seeks to view the societies before they were visited by modern scientists. While scientists have been among the first outsiders to contact some traditional peoples—such as the "discovery" of the Baliem Valley Dani by the Third Archbold Expedition from the American Museum of Natural History in 1938—more often scientists have been preceded by government patrols, traders, missionary linguists, or explorers. That was obviously true for the vast majority of traditional societies of the New World, Africa, Australia, and the Pacific islands, because they were "discovered" by Europeans from AD 1492 until the early 20th century, before modern anthropology had coalesced as a discipline doing fieldwork. Even the recent first contacts of New Guinea and Amazonian tribes from the 1930s until today have usually not been made by scientists, because of the resources required and the dangers involved. By the time scientists arrive, the tribal culture has already begun to change as a result of contacts.

But we may still learn a lot from the anecdotal descriptions left by those first scientifically untrained visitors. The obvious disadvantage is that their accounts are less systematic, less quantitative, and less informed by rigorous method and the existing body of knowledge about other tribes. A compensating obvious advantage is that the resulting information refers to a tribal society less modified than when encountered later by scientists. A less obvious advantage is that the unsystematic and unscientific nature of those first observations can actually be a strength. Untrained visitors often describe broadly whatever strikes them, and thereby may discuss facets of a society that would be ignored by a scientist sent out with research support to study some particular phenomenon.

An example is a remarkable book (*Dschungelkind*) about Indonesian New Guinea's Fayu people, written by a German woman called Sabine Kuegler. During my first visit to Indonesian New Guinea in 1979, my helicopter pilot told me of a terrifying visit that he had recently made to a just-discovered group of Fayu nomads on behalf of a missionary couple, Klaus and Doris Kuegler. At the invitation of the Fayu, the Kueglers then brought their three young children to live among the Fayu and were the first outsiders that most Fayu saw. The Kueglers' middle daughter, Sabine, thus grew up among the Fayu from ages 7 to 17, at a time when there were still no outsiders there other than the Kuegler family. On moving to Europe to pursue a European education and to become a European, Sabine published in 2005 a book about her experiences and observations.

Sabine's book lacks data tables, tests of rival hypotheses, and summaries of the current state of some subfield of anthropology. Instead, readers of her book will gain a vivid sense of Fayu life just after first contact, including arrows whizzing through the air, dangers, accidents, and deaths. Because Sabine's playmates were Fayu children and she grew up partly as a Fayu herself, her book approximates an autobiography of a Fayu, but one endowed with a dual perspective as a Fayu and a Westerner. Sabine was thus able to notice Fayu characteristics—such as their sense of time, physical difficulties of Fayu life, and the psychology of being a Fayu—that a Fayu would take for granted and not bother to mention. Equally moving is Sabine's account of returning to Europe, and of seeing European society through her partly Fayu eyes, which let her notice features of European life (e.g., issues of dealing with strangers, or the dangers of crossing a road) that a European would take for granted. Perhaps, some day, a scientist will visit the Fayu and will describe some aspect of their society. But, by then, the Fayu will be drastically different people from those encountered by the Kueglers in 1979. No scientist will be able to repeat Sabine's experience, and to describe what it was like to grow up with and to think and feel as a nearly traditional Fayu.

The remaining method for learning about traditional societies, and the sole source of information about past societies without writing and not in contact with literate observers, is archaeology, whose advantages and disadvantages are the opposites of those associated with modern observers. By excavating and radiocarbon-dating a site, archaeologists can reconstruct a culture up to tens of thousands of years before it was contacted and changed by the modern world. Thus, concerns about perturbing effects of modern contact and of the resident sociologist disappear completely. That's a huge advantage. The corresponding disadvantage is that fine detail, such as daily events and people's names, motives, and words, is lost. Archaeologists also face the disadvantage of more uncertainty and more required effort in extracting social conclusions from their physical manifestations preserved in archaeological deposits. For instance, archaeologists attempt to deduce individual inequality in social status and wealth indirectly from differences in the buried grave goods and sizes of tombs in cemeteries excavated laboriously over the course of several field seasons. A modern ethnographer might observe such inequalities directly in one day of fieldwork—but the results would apply to a society changed to an uncertain degree by modern contact.

Thus, our four methods for understanding traditional societies differ in their strengths and weaknesses. We can have increased confidence in conclusions if all four methods can be applied and yield similar results. For example, we have information about tribal wars from modern scientific observations (e.g., Jan Broekhuijse and Karl Heider's detailed accounts of Dani warfare described in Chapter 3), from oral reconstructions (such as those by Polly Wiessner and Akii Tumu), from anecdotal accounts (such as Sabine Kuegler's among the Fayu), and from archaeological evidence (such as excavated battle armor and skulls split by axes). When these four approaches disagree in their conclusions, we have to figure out why: perhaps the society changed with time or under contact.

Index

Note: Plate numbers refer to insert illustrations. Plates 1–28 appear between pages 148 and 149; plates 29–47 appear between pages 308 and 309.

Illustration Credits